Europe without Borders

Europe without Borders

A HISTORY

**ISAAC
STANLEY-BECKER**

PRINCETON UNIVERSITY PRESS
PRINCETON & OXFORD

Published by Princeton University Press
41 William Street, Princeton, New Jersey 08540
99 Banbury Road, Oxford OX2 6JX

press.princeton.edu

Library of Congress Cataloging-in-Publication Data

Names: Stanley-Becker, Isaac, 1993– author.
Title: Europe without borders : a history / Isaac Stanley-Becker.
Description: Princeton ; Oxford : Princeton University Press, [2025] |
    Includes bibliographical references and index.
Identifiers: LCCN 2024012589 (print) | LCCN 2024012590 (ebook) |
    ISBN 9780691261768 (hardback) | ISBN 9780691261744 (ebook)
Subjects: LCSH: Schengen Agreement (1985 June 14) | Freedom of movement—
    Europe—History. | Admission of nonimmigrants—Europe—History. | Noncitizens—
    Civil rights—Europe. | Border security—Europe—History. | Europe—Emigration
    and immigration. | Europe—Economic integration. | Europe—Boundaries—History. |
    BISAC: SOCIAL SCIENCE / Emigration & Immigration | HISTORY / Europe / General
Classification: LCC JV7590 .S728 2025 (print) | LCC JV7590 (ebook) | DDC 325.409—
    dc23/eng/20240809
LC record available at https://lccn.loc.gov/2024012589
LC ebook record available at https://lccn.loc.gov/2024012590

British Library Cataloging-in-Publication Data is available

Editorial: Priya Nelson and Emma Wagh
Production Editorial: Kathleen Cioffi
Text and Jacket Design: Heather Hansen
Production: Danielle Amatucci
Publicity: Kate Hensley and Carmen Jimenez
Copyeditor: Lachlan Brooks

Jacket image: Philipp / Adobe Stock

This book has been composed in Miller with Gotham

Printed in the United States of America

10 9 8 7 6 5 4 3 2 1

For my parents

CONTENTS

ILLUSTRATIONS

Figures

Maps

Europe without Borders

Introduction

THE GUARANTEE OF free movement in Europe derives its name from a pastoral village in Luxembourg where vineyards cover the rolling hillsides and the remains of a castle dating from the medieval era still stand. The village, Schengen, lies on the banks of the Moselle River, at the tri-point border where France and Germany touch Luxembourg—a place of apt symbolism for the abolition of borders among European countries.[1] There, as the twentieth century drew to a close, the signing of a multilateral treaty affirmed a commitment to create a cosmopolitan European territory, an area where people and goods would be free to move across national frontiers without hindrance, a Europe without borders.

Schengen was the name Europeans gave to this territory of free movement. So unusual was its creation that the European Commission sought to clarify, in a factsheet explaining the value of the "Free Movement of People," that Schengen was not a new member of the European Union but a place that had been founded as "an area of document-free circulation." What the factsheet did not delineate were the limits of free movement—how undocumented foreigners were barred from circulating freely in Schengen. But it gave notice that a transnational system of surveillance operated to track "suspect persons" in this borderless area.[2]

Acclaimed as a symbol of a united Europe, the Schengen treaty signed in 1985 brought together five countries—France, West Germany, Luxembourg, Belgium, and the Netherlands—in an intergovernmental agreement to dismantle their internal borders. The treaty set forth the guarantee of free movement, promoting economic and social union by lifting barriers against the flow of goods and people across the frontiers of Schengen. The preamble of the treaty declared that the "ever closer union of the peoples of the Member States of the European Communities should find its expression in the freedom to cross internal borders for all nationals of the Member States and in the free movement of goods and services."[3] At once, the Schengen treaty extended the principles of free market exchange to the border crossing of people and restricted the free movement of persons to Europeans. The critical word was "nationals."

So closely is Schengen tied to a triumphal account of European union that the birth pangs of the project of free movement have been all but obscured. Formed at the twilight of the Cold War, Schengen appeared to embody the values of liberal internationalism, the promise of a European community of nations where people, goods, capital, and information all would circulate freely.[4] The "spirit of Schengen" entered the language of international politics.[5] The states that brokered the treaty proposed Schengen as a geopolitical model of European freedom, a barrier "against all totalitarianisms."[6] Schengen is now so interwoven into the fabric of European law that it requires an endeavor of historical recovery to understand the perplexities of the guarantee of free movement of persons at the time of its emergence.[7]

This book is the first to undertake that task; it explores the genesis of Schengen's free movement guarantee and the conflict over its boundaries. It traces how the free movement of persons developed as a concept linked to the market but distinct from economic life, a concept that expressed aspirations for European citizens' rights but that took on new meaning against the backdrop of decolonization and the burgeoning human rights discourse of the postwar era.[8] The account moves from the negotiating table at European summits to the judge's dais in courts of law to the street protests of undocumented immigrants who laid claim to the right of free movement reserved for nationals within the Schengen area. In exploring origins, this book is not an account of Schengen once the treaty came fully into force, in 1995, and thereafter became joined to European Union law, as the dismantling of borders deepened the dilemmas posed by the bloc's eastward expansion. Nor is this book about the refugee crisis sweeping Europe in the twenty-first century. Such topics have been ably examined by others: journalists, economists, and political scientists.[9] Yet to tell the story of a cosmopolitan right of free movement casts new light on Schengen's significance in the making of the European Union.[10] No less, it reveals how Schengen became a site of conflict over the guarantee of free movement. It recasts understanding of migration and globalization, as well as of citizenship and human rights.[11]

Indisputably, Schengen opened a new chapter in the globalization of economic exchange by eliminating border controls within Europe. It advanced the achievement of a single market for goods, capital, labor, and services inaugurated by the Rome Treaty of 1957, which founded the European Economic Community that formed the basis of the European Union.[12] It expressed the aspirations of ascendant neoliberalism in removing barriers to the operation of the free market.[13] At the same time, Schengen made concrete a political ideal of democratic civic solidarity among the continent's peoples that France's president, François Mitterrand, christened "Citizens' Europe."[14] West Germany's chancellor, Helmut Kohl, welcomed the "ever closer union of European peoples" that became enshrined in the Schengen treaty.[15]

But Schengen's crucial innovation was to classify the bearers of transnational freedom of movement simply as persons—not as economic actors. That shift, I argue, marked a turning point in the European development of free movement, giving a humanist cast to a market paradigm. The shift would amplify a form of personal liberty entailing the "power of locomotion," in the classic statement of Sir William Blackstone on fundamental rights, "of changing situation, or moving one's person to whatsoever place one's own inclination may direct."[16] Such liberty would also prompt new forms of state surveillance, heightening conflict over the right of border crossing. For undocumented migrants, free movement lay at the heart of the search for recognition. In the words of a leader of that search, Madjiguène Cissé, a Senegalese woman who sought to live in Paris, every person possessed the right "to travel, to migrate, to circulate, to receive and be received."[17]

Under the Schengen treaty, all "the peoples" who counted as nationals of European Community states became free to traverse the internal borders of the Schengen area. This capaciousness differed from the terms of the Rome Treaty, which predicated unchecked border crossing on economic activity pursued within a common market, allowing free movement only for lucrative purposes, such as employment—and only to economic actors, such as "workers."[18] It also differed from the 1948 Universal Declaration of Human Rights, which safeguarded movement within the territory of a single nation, along with the right to leave and return to one's country, provisions echoed by a 1963 protocol to the European Convention on Human Rights.[19] Conceptually and geographically, therefore, Schengen transformed the principle of free movement, extending it from the arena of the market and the area of the nation to the transnational space of Citizens' Europe. That shift in meaning gave deeper legitimacy to economic integration by lodging the utility of the internal market within the flourishing of a cosmopolitan European community.[20]

By no means, however, did Schengen envision unrestricted free movement. The treaty's guarantees were at once expansive and exclusionary: expansive in applying to people, but exclusionary in including only European nationals. The shift from a purely economic to a humanist paradigm of free movement was restricted by citizenship. The liberty of moving one's person inside a Europe without borders would depend on belonging to a European state.[21] From the outset, the vision of cross-border free movement was hedged by alarm about foreign migrants; the exclusionary logic appeared in Schengen's earliest blueprints, as the treatymakers laid the ground rules for detecting non-Europeans and compiled lists of countries posing immigration risks, whose peoples they termed "undesirables."[22] Thus was launched a security regime aimed at fortifying Schengen's external borders, blocking illegal immigration, and tracking the movement of foreign nationals. Implementing free movement gave rise to new modes of surveillance—a computerized Schengen information system used to issue alerts on people and goods—that augmented the power of member states and intergovernmental agencies to prevent the border crossing of migrants classified as "aliens."[23] With this surveillance system, Schengen also provided a model for the European community, spurring the development of a transnational policing infrastructure, including the European Union Agency for Law Enforcement Cooperation, known as Europol, and the European Border and Coast Guard Agency, known as Frontex.[24]

As Schengen widened the ambit of free movement, then, it gave new force to the exclusion of nonnationals of European countries. The treaty required the Schengen states to harmonize immigration restrictions and act jointly to police the common territory and adopt rules distinguishing between Europeans and non-Europeans.[25] And as the status of foreign migrants grew more precarious, such measures became a catalyst for the uprising of Europe's undocumented denizens who called themselves *sans-papiers*—"without papers." As the Schengen treaty took effect, the sans-papiers movement arose in France, and spread across Europe, shaped by colonialism's afterlives and formed by refugees, asylum-seekers, exiles, and workers of all kinds deemed alien—immigrants from countries mostly in West Africa and the Maghreb.[26] The sans-papiers refused to be categorized as an alien presence within the Schengen area, claiming free movement as a human right—a right attached neither to citizenship nor to the market. The sans-papiers mobilization also forms part of Schengen's history, a countermovement to the nationalism that would intensify with the rise of the Great Replacement narrative—*Le Grand Remplacement*—that conjured fears of immigrants of color overrunning the European community.[27]

The plan for Schengen came into being slowly, developing over the course of more than a decade: from a European Council meeting in Fontainebleau in 1984, which set the stage for the drafting of the Schengen treaty a year later; to the adoption in 1990 of a convention implementing the treaty, which took full effect in 1995; to the signing of the Treaty of Amsterdam in 1997, which incorporated Schengen into European Union law, entering into force two years later. In 1999, the European Parliament termed Schengen an "experimental garden" for all of Europe.[28]

Yet the Schengen area has never been coextensive with the European Union or with its forerunner, the European Community.[29] Borders came down first among the five countries that framed the treaty. Today, the area includes twenty-five of the twenty-seven European Union members, encompassing more than 400 million people and twenty-nine European nations, extending from Portugal and Spain to Romania, Poland, and Finland—across a territory that was divided by the Iron Curtain at the time of Schengen's founding.[30] According to the European Parliament, Schengen was the "key milestone in establishing an internal market with free movement of persons."[31]

Schengen, however, has drawn less attention from historians than have other landmarks of European economic and political integration, from the founding of the European Coal and Steel Community in 1952 to the accession of former Eastern Bloc states to the European Union, starting in 2004.[32] The making of Schengen receives only glancing mention in leading scholarship on the European Union, with stress on the economic dividends to member states.[33] Nor is the origin of Schengen's fraught guarantee of free movement explored in depth in pathbreaking studies that trace the long roots of European border rules, illustrate the significance of national security in European planning, probe the challenges of multiculturalism, examine the uncertainties of democracy, and place migration at the center of Europe's history since the Second World War.[34] Summarily, the limit of the guarantee is captured in *Postwar*, Tony Judt's grand synthesis, "The Schengen Treaty was a boon for the citizens of participating states, who now moved unhindered across open borders between sovereign states," Judt wrote. "But residents of countries outside the Schengen club were obliged to queue—quite literally—for admission."[35] What remains unexamined is how that limit became defined—how arguments over state sovereignty and national security and individual rights pervaded the prolonged work of treatymaking—and how Schengen's pairing of freedom and exclusion became contested.

For the most part, the study of Schengen has focused not on origins but on the operation of the treaty, and has been the province of political scientists, sociologists, geographers, criminologists, and international relations theorists.[36] Attention to the consequences of opening borders has led to influential yet disparate conclusions—chief among them that Schengen represents a mainstay of internationalism, an instrument of capital accumulation in Europe's internal market, a cornerstone of a repressive "fortress Europe," and an impetus for *Sicherheitshysterie*, or "security hysteria."[37] But

Schengen makes no appearance in leading works on economic globalization that address the outcomes of European integration.[38]

The inception of free movement in Schengen's creation is
therefore one of the great unstudied projects in postwar European
history.[39] My aim in exploring that project is to reveal the cruel
anomalies of human movement in a world where capital and commodities travel globally with far less restraint and where national
citizenship is an enduring precondition for the exercise of fundamental rights.[40] This Schengen story sets the development of the
treaty, a complex administrative instrument, against the backdrop
of global events—the fall of the Berlin Wall, an increase in migration flows across the Mediterranean world, intensifying fear of
international terrorism, cycles of economic recession and recovery, and the legacies of anti-colonialism. All shaped the terms of
free movement. Revolutionary change in Europe in 1989 became a
turning point in Schengen's emergence, opening new frontiers for
migration across Europe. The waning of the Cold War meant that
the guarantee of free movement would apply in a world of newly
permeable borders. How the tearing down of the Berlin Wall figured in Schengen's creation has been an untold story.

This book is made possible by the opening of government
archives that hold the history of Schengen's creation. Diplomatic
memoranda, confidential annexes, draft agreements, meeting
notes, and private correspondence disclose the treatymaking: the
long, often rancorous debate over the terms of free movement,
as well as the negotiation of issues of sovereignty, transnational-
ism, and the rule of law. Because of regulations barring access to
many diplomatic records for thirty years, much of this paperwork,
archived at the Council of the European Union and the European
Commission as well as at state agencies, has not previously been
examined. Evidence of the experience of the sans-papiers is harder
to discover. But litigation in European courts and newspaper
accounts of street protests and memoirs written by sans-papiers
leaders offer a vantage point on the conflict over the principles of
freedom and exclusion inscribed in the Schengen treaty.

Many of the actors in this account were Schengen's architects—
foreign ministers, heads of state, and local administrators, with

a prominent role played by officials from France and West Germany, the historic adversaries that led the treatymaking. Others were influential Euroskeptics—legislators, philosophers, historians, lawyers, and journalists. Some made a living by moving goods across Europe's internal market—truckers and shippers. And others were foreigners seeking to exercise free movement in the Schengen area—among them spokespersons for the sans-papiers, migrants who challenged the boundaries of citizenship and criticized European integration as a neocolonial enterprise. All became brokers of ideas that crossed borders.

To study Schengen is to take seriously the notion that it was, as the treatymakers said, "a laboratory." But what sort of laboratory? In the words of a Dutch state secretary for foreign affairs, Pieter Dankert, it was a laboratory "for the enterprise 'free movement of persons.'"[41] To Schengen's exponents, the corps of diplomats and their legislative supporters, the dismantling of internal borders would transform a continent devastated by world war into an area of liberty, democratic pluralism, and Pan-European peace.[42] That cosmopolitanism remained joined to the world of the market. As this book seeks to show, the laboratory of free movement always was meant to promote trade, giving moral legitimacy to the development of an unfettered European single market. But only nationals of Citizens' Europe were to cross borders as freely as capital and goods. As this book seeks also to show, Schengen was a laboratory of free movement always meant to join Euro-nationalist rules of exclusion with neoliberal principles of market freedom. And from that laboratory emerged both a transnational security apparatus protecting Schengen's boundaries and the unrest of undocumented migrants claiming free movement as a human right.

1

A Market Paradigm
of Free Movement

A PALACE ONCE home to the French monarchy was a strange setting for a Socialist statesman's proposal for the creation of "Citizens' Europe." But at the Château de Fontainebleau, in June 1984, French president François Mitterrand announced a project for the renewal of the European Community, one promising to deepen civic bonds and enhance everyday life. It would guarantee the free movement of persons crossing Europe's borders. A year later, this guarantee would be inscribed in the Schengen treaty.

"Voilà," proclaimed Mitterrand at Fontainebleau, at the close of a European Council meeting held at the palace. In a word, he marked the Council's agreement to bring a new social dimension to European economic integration, to establish on the pillars of the common market a Citizens' Europe. This would "give the political structures of the Community a new impetus," bringing into being "a living, active Europe." Among the innovations would be a common European passport enabling free movement across the continent.[1] The Council's conclusions anticipated the abolition of barriers "for people crossing intra-Community frontiers." A committee of diplomats would develop the project.[2]

The conception of Citizens' Europe drew on principles defined at earlier moments of European planning, reaching back to the founding document of the European Economic Community, the

Treaty of Rome. Adopted in 1957, the Rome Treaty formed a cornerstone of postwar regeneration, laying the foundation for a common market in which labor, goods, and capital all would circulate freely, advancing European economic integration amid Cold War rivalry.[3] The Rome Treaty's antecedents, in turn, reached back to European cosmopolitanism emergent in the interwar years, and, long before that, to meditations on peace offered by luminaries of Romanticism and philosophers of the Enlightenment. At Fontainebleau in 1984, however, the planning reflected the press of recent events—new dynamics of globalization but also the stalled progress of European integration caused by the worldwide economic turmoil of the prior decade, the result of the breakdown of the Bretton Woods monetary system and the jolts of the oil crisis.[4] As European nations confronted prolonged economic recession alongside the aftershocks of decolonization, the commitments made at Fontainebleau joined the creation of Citizens' Europe to the flourishing of a single market for commodity exchange. The purpose was to benefit "the everyday life of the citizen," stated the Commission of the European Communities.[5] At the heart of that project lay the guarantee of transnational free moment, a guarantee indebted to ascendant principles of neoliberalism and to cosmopolitan ideals of human rights.

The expansive aspirations expressed at Fontainebleau, however, ran contrary to the currents of European Community jurisprudence.[6] In February 1985, the European Court of Justice handed down a decision in *Gravier v. City of Liège* that addressed the right of free movement and the authority of European Community institutions to guarantee that right.[7] The case concerned the study of cartoon art—a dispute about an enrollment fee imposed on a French national, Françoise Gravier, attending art school in Belgium. She claimed that the fee was discriminatory, levied only on nonnationals, inhibiting her right to traverse borders. The court struck down the fee, recognizing her claim. Yet it set forth a market paradigm of free movement. According to the court, the right to circulate within the European Community belonged only to economic agents—not to all citizens of member nations.[8] *Gravier* contradicted the vision of a Citizens' Europe in which free movement would constitute a fundamental right of European belonging, untethered from market pursuits. The ruling came down from the court just as negotiations were unfolding over the proposals of the European Council, and in the midst of the treatymaking that would create Schengen as the territorial embodiment of Citizens' Europe.

At issue in *Gravier* was the meaning of the principle of free movement introduced in the Treaty of Rome. In forming the European Economic Community and providing for a common European market, the treaty defined free movement as part of economic life. The freedom to cross borders within the European Community depended on economic activity—on engaging in gainful work or other commercial pursuits. The treaty vested the European Community with authority to guarantee the unobstructed border crossing of goods, capital, and persons, specifying "freedom of movement for workers."[9] The decision in *Gravier* made explicit the boundaries of that guarantee, restricting it to economic agents, narrowly interpreting the right of free movement to entail economic activity yet broadly interpreting economic activity to include all kinds of pursuits, not least art education. Thus *Gravier* gave legal force to the association of free movement with a sprawling European marketplace.

It was this market paradigm of free movement that Citizens' Europe was meant to reach beyond. Both the Fontainebleau summit and the *Gravier* case set the stage for the intergovernmental negotiations that would lead to the sweeping guarantee of free movement in the Schengen treaty. This juxtaposition of events—the expansive planning announced at Fontainebleau and the restrictive ruling delivered in *Gravier*—has gone unnoticed in stories of European union. But it gave impetus to Schengen's innovations. Precisely because of the limits on free movement under European Community law, Europhile statespersons embarked on treatymaking outside Community institutions. Citizens' Europe would remain aspirational, never enshrined in Community law.[10] Nonetheless, it proved generative of a program of European union in which the guarantee of free movement would be premised not solely on the logic of the marketplace.

———————————

The planning for Citizens' Europe arose from a meeting of the European Council preoccupied with the condition of the Community's finances. The prime ministers and presidents who convened at the Fontainebleau Palace in June 1984 devoted much of their discussion to resolving budgetary imbalances. The Community was then composed of ten member states: Belgium, Denmark, France, Greece, Ireland, Italy, Luxembourg, the Netherlands, West Germany, and the United Kingdom. Their leaders undertook to address value-added taxes, reconcile industrial and agricultural agreements, and correct inequities between the relative prosperity of each state and its financial obligations.[11] But they also pledged to adopt new measures for reviving European cooperation, for promoting not only economic integration and commercial activity but also civic bonds and a transnational form of patriotic identity. From that pledge emerged a blueprint for Citizens' Europe.[12]

The conclusions laid down at Fontainebleau dedicated an entire section to envisioning the framework for Citizens' Europe and justifying its creation. A Citizens' Europe would fortify unity across the continent as well the global standing of the European Community. The conclusions declared: "The European Council considers it essential that the Community should respond to the expectations of the people of Europe by adopting measures to strengthen and promote its identity and its image both for its citizens and for the rest of the world." As an advisory body, the Council had hortatory authority but no formal legislative power.[13]

Nonetheless, the Fontainebleau conclusions enumerated measures that would constitute Citizens' Europe. There would be symbolic devices for conjuring European identity, heraldic instruments such as a flag and an anthem, European sports teams, and volunteer youth committees supporting "development projects in the Third World."[14] There would also be "a single document for the movement of goods." And, binding together Europe's citizens, there would be measures promoting unobstructed border crossing: a European passport and the "abolition of all police and customs formalities for people crossing intra-Community frontiers."[15] A meeting about money yielded a call for the free movement of people—not simply workers.

In a partnership symbolizing postwar reconciliation, France and West Germany acted as the principal advocates for Citizens' Europe. François Mitterrand, a onetime Vichy official who joined the Resistance and then ascended in France's Socialist

Party, allied with the West German chancellor, Helmut Kohl, of the Christian Democratic Union, who had removed burned bodies from the ashes as a conscripted Hitler Youth member.[16] On the eve of the Fontainebleau meeting, Mitterrand, who was then the European Council's president, appeared before the European Parliament at Strasbourg, where he acclaimed "the European idea," recalling how it was "inherited from the war" and served to "bring together peoples whom force and bloodshed had divided." Now, he said, the continent's leaders must be faithful to the pact that "binds the European countries together . . . the Treaty of Rome" while also "carrying us beyond this Treaty," renovating "international geopolitics."[17] Not only global affairs but domestic politics shaped his aims, particularly countering the rise of the nationalist, anti-immigrant National Front party.[18] Mitterrand celebrated cosmpolitan values: "There is a field in which Europe stands . . . instinctively, namely human rights" in opposition to "terrorism and oppression . . . everywhere in the world."[19] Kohl was more explicit in setting European unity against a Cold War backdrop, arguing that the ideological battle against communism required both completing the common market and burnishing it with civic legitimacy. "The Soviet Union will only get along with the construction of Europe to the extent that we make it a reality," he said in an address in Aachen, a town nestled on the border with Belgium and the Netherlands. "It would be a mistake to believe that we can create and maintain in this world a common economic space without ever daring to take the step towards political unity."[20] In concert, Mitterand and Kohl proposed a European idea extending beyond the economistic principles of the Rome Treaty.

Those aspirations found a platform at Fontainebleau. The Council gave authority to an ad hoc committee, composed of representatives from Community nations, to study elements of Citizens' Europe and to make proposals. It also set a schedule for this work. The Fontainebleau conclusions called for the creation of a European passport available to member-state citizens by January 1, 1985. Furthermore, by the summer of 1985, measures were to be taken to achieve both the single document for the movement of goods and the abolition of all police barriers and customs rules for people crossing intra-Community frontiers.[21] Thus the guarantee of the

FIGURE 1.1. In an iconic image, François Mitterrand of France and Helmut Kohl of West Germany clasped hands at Verdun, in 1984. The partnership between the onetime adversaries drove the Schengen treatymaking. Credit: Francolon / Simon / GAMMA RAPHO

free movement of persons was to be instituted swiftly, within a year of the Fontainebleau endorsement of Citizens' Europe.

Yet the notion of Citizens' Europe—resting on an expansive right of free movement—had been developing for years. Its conception was the work of statespersons who sought to give a humanist cast, and a political foundation, to the economic model of European union. Their vision returned to a capacious idea of European cosmopolitanism that had gained currency in the interwar period, and reemerged after the Second World War, only to be displaced by the economism of the Rome Treaty.

The first formal statement of a Citizens' Europe came from the Belgian prime minister, Leo Tindemans, who sought, in 1975, to define the term European Union. That name would not be given to the European Community until the Maastricht Treaty of 1992, which remade an economic community into a political union, giving birth to the European Union. But years earlier, the European Council gave Tindemans the task of formulating the terms of union.

FIGURE 1.2. Leo Tindemans, the Belgian prime minister shown here in 1977 announcing the formation of a new government in Brussels, prepared a report in 1975 defining the term "European Union." The report, in proposing a "Citizens' Europe," foreshadowed the Fontainebleau summit of 1984 and the Schengen treaty. Credit: Keystone-France / GAMMA RAPHO

He knew the necessity of free movement, having fled Belgium when the Nazis invaded, and he later studied government with another Nazi refugee, Henry Kissinger, at Harvard. Rather than adhering to his professor's realpolitik, Tindemans stressed the significance of popular legitimacy.[22] This was evident in his *Report on European Union* for the Council. "We must listen to our people" to prevent a "return to selfish national attitudes," he argued. "What do the Europeans want?" he asked. "What do they expect from a united Europe?" Replying to his own query, he proposed a "citizen's Europe." By that, he meant a social bond, recognizing that the "construction of Europe is not just a form of collaboration between States" but a "*rapprochement* of peoples who wish to go forward together." In his view, deepening disaffection, caused by the end of postwar economic expansion, demanded a new idea of European union.[23]

Tindemans's conception of Citizens' Europe had two main elements, fusing the individual and the social: "Protection of rights" and "External signs of our solidarity." Globalization had rendered the nation an insufficient guardian of "fundamental freedoms," he wrote. Citizens' Europe offered an answer—transnational enforcement of rights via direct appeal to the European Court of Justice. Such a system would reassert, at the European level, "that element of protection and control of our society which is progressively slipping from the grasp of State authority due to the . . . internationalization of social life." It would not rely simply on juridical institutions, however. Instead, Tindemans argued, Citizens' Europe would encompass a new, common experience of European life. That would arrive through a passport union enabling free movement, including cross-border access to necessities such as health care. "When Europeans can move about within the Union, can communicate among themselves . . . without national frontiers adding to the problems of distance," he anticipated, "European Union will become for them a discernible reality." Anything less was "technocratic Europe."[24]

The aspiration to make political union a reality for the people of Europe had a venerable lineage. It traced back to Enlightenment ideals of a cosmopolitan community that took root in the eighteenth century and flourished in the peace movement that followed the Napoleonic Wars. And it revived ambitions, advanced after the First World War, for programs of European political integration—a Pan-Europe or a United States of Europe—programs vanquished by a very different kind of Pan-European regime: the Third Reich. Justifications for European union in the interwar years ranged widely, from promoting interstate peace to protecting the continent's colonial possessions, from fortifying the free market to constraining the forces of capital through transnational institutions.[25] However, such ambitions shared a certainty that Europe's past pointed ineluctably toward a cosmopolitan future. As Spain's philosopher-statesman Ortega y Gasset wrote in 1926, "the unity of Europe as a society is not an ideal but a fact of a very ancient everyday life."[26]

Fundamental to the planning for Pan-European peace was the theory of a "pacific federation"—a cosmopolitanism conceived by the philosopher Immanual Kant at the end of the eighteenth century that found fervent advocates in the century that followed.[27] Kant envisioned a "great political body of the future," not a single European superstate but a federation enhancing the freedom of its members. As an antidote to war, this body would reflect the virtues of a "universal *cosmopolitan existence*," Kant argued.[28] The peace movement of the nineteenth century, which emerged after the downfall of Napoleon's imperial ambitions, embraced Kant's vision of federation. Cosmpolitanism had no more eloquent exponent than Victor Hugo, the literary artist-cum-statesman, who gave iconic expression to the poetics of Romanticism and the politics of French republicanism. At the Paris Peace Congress, in 1849, he foresaw Europe's nations "blended into a superior unity"—a "United States of Europe"—in advocating universal accord and free movement: "The cessation of international animosities, the effacing of frontiers on the map, and of the prejudices of the heart." Soon, he said, the battlefield would become "the market open to commerce" and people would "traverse the earth, as the gods of Homer did the sky." And democracy would reign; from the ballot box would issue "an assembly which shall be as it were the soul of all; a supreme and popular council."[29] Always, the prophecy of democratic federation stood in opposition to militaristic Pan-Europeanism. In a message to the 1875 Peace Conference, after the Franco-Prussian War and the founding of Imperial Germany, Hugo contrasted two worlds: "To make Germany is to construct an empire, that is, night; to make Europe is to give birth to democracy, that is, light." But principles of democratic universalism also vindicated European colonialism— to advance "civilization." In Hugo's words, "God offers Africa to Europe. Take it."[30]

The following century, European cosmopolitanism remained inseparable from colonial objectives, with visions of a continental demos linked to Africa's exploitation. In the interwar years, the most sweeping of these programs—the International Pan-European Movement, or simply Paneuropa—came from Richard Coudenhove-Kalergi, a philosopher-politician of Austrian and Japanese descent. He launched his movement in 1923 with a manifesto addressed simply to "Europeans!" It proposed forging multinational bonds by "dismantling" frontiers and creating a "defensive alliance" and "customs union," bordered by Russia, the Atlantic, and the Mediterranean. Only European political integration could avert both military conflict and economic subjugation, argued Coudenhove-Kalergi, warning against "Russian hegemony" and "American capital." He envisioned an independent European bloc, within the League of Nations, that would "save Europe." And it would include "the colonies of the European states."[31]

The program of Paneuropa laid claim to canonical cosmopolitan theory. Coudenhove-Kalergi's manifesto spoke of what "Kant imagined," and echoed Victor Hugo in seeking to realize a "United States of Europe."[32] A fuller account of the project came in his book *Pan-Europa*, which began with a bleak report on European life after the First World War: "Misery, unrest, discontent, hatred, and fear." He described a Europe made irrelevant by the global power of Britain, the United States, and the Soviet Union: "From the center of the world Europe has moved to its periphery." Drawing on concepts of core and periphery central to imperial theory, he called for European union as a shield against a Russian world empire: "Unification will take place either voluntarily by the formation of a pan-European Federation, or else forcibly by a Russian conquest."[33] A Pan-European movement would entail "political and economic consolidation of all the states from Poland to Portugal into a federal union." Coudenhove-Kalergi acclaimed federation as "salvation."[34]

Likewise, Pan-Europeanism laid stress on democratic principles. This point was paramount, as Coudenhove-Kalergi sought to raise support for European union across the Western world. In a statement delivered to the American Foreign Policy Association in 1925, he exalted American democracy—"the great example you gave to the world"—while arguing on behalf of the "union of all democracies of the European continent." Further, he claimed that European union must first and foremost be political in nature, not economic: "If Pan-Europe is not constituted politically, we shall very soon have another war in Europe."[35] And political union, as he had postulated in *Pan-Europa*, meant the creation of a borderless space to avert territorial warfare among European neighbors. "There is but one radical way to a permanent and just solution of the European frontier question, and that is: not the alteration, but the abolition, of those frontiers."[36] Among his proposals were symbols and instruments of political unity—a European flag, a European anthem, a common passport—provisions echoed in the Fontainebleau planning for Citizens' Europe.[37]

Fundamental also to the Paneuropa program was affirming colonial ties to Africa, which Coudenhove-Kalergi considered Europe's "nearest neighbor." But a neighbor of a different sort. In 1929, Coudenhove-Kalergi wrote of Africa as "Europe's plantation." In an expansive treatment of the frontier question, recognizing no continental boundaries, he enthused about economic opportunities south of the Mediterranean: "Africa could provide Europe with raw materials for its industry, food for its population, settlement area for its overpopulation, labor for its unemployed, and markets for its products."[38] Africa would allow Europe to become one. From the vantage point of democratic cosmopolitanism, Africa again appeared on offer for Europe's taking.

Over time, the Paneuropa project won certain notable endorsements; it was welcomed by French prime ministers Aristide Briand and Léon Blum, as well as by Konrad Adenauer, the president of the State Council of Prussia and later the first chancellor of the Federal Republic of Germany. And it drew support from figures in science and the arts, not least Sigmund Freud and Thomas Mann.[39] But others kept a distance. Albert Einstein, in a letter to Coudenhove-Kalergi in 1932, criticized the movement as a cult of personality. "The Pan-European movement is entirely linked to your name." He also objected to the "decidedly hostile stance against today's Russia." Signing up to Pan-Europe, Einstein wrote, "would mean taking sides, which is definitely not what I want."[40]

By then, however, Paneuropa was languishing in the community of European nations. Aristide Briand had raised the prospect of a

FIGURE 1.3. Richard Coudenhove-Kalergi, the Austrian Japanese politician and founder of the International Pan-European Movement, opens the inaugural session of the Pan-European Congress in Vienna on May 18, 1934. Credit: Keystone France / GAMMA RAPHO

"federal link" at the League of Nations Assembly in September 1929 and had distributed a memo on the matter a year later. But the response of European governments was muted, and the League referred the proposal to a committee, where it stalled as the Great Depression and the rise of the Nazis commanded attention.[41]

Other variants of European cosmopolitanism fared no better in the interwar years. Social-democratic parties embraced federalism for diverse reasons, with some opposing economic nationalism as an obstacle to free trade but others seeking political union to constrain the forces of Anglo-American capital that appeared to threaten not only European ways of life but also political sovereignty on the continent.[42] At a 1925 congress in Heidelberg, Germany's Social Democrats adopted a new party program calling for a United States of Europe. At a Brussels conference the following year, the Labor and Socialist International proposed a European customs union. With the onset of Europe's Great Depression, labor parties and trade unionists across the continent renounced protectionism, advocating federation.[43] But it was the Heidelberg Program that paired the aim of European union with a dual critique of capitalist political economy and colonial exploitation. "As its influence increases, finance capital uses state power to dominate foreign territories as markets, sources of raw materials and sites for capital investments," the program declared. The necessity was "to overcome the capitalist system and to protect humanity from warlike destruction." Therefore, social-democratic cosmopolitanism sought "the United States of Europe in order to achieve solidarity of interests between the peoples of all continents."[44] But the ascent of fascist Pan-Europeanism made a cruel mockery of that ideal.

Nazi repression fell with brutal force on the Paneuropa project. The Third Reich banned the movement, incinerating Coudenhove-Kalergi's book at a public burning. Hitler abhorred the Austrian-Japanese spokesman of European unity, condemning him, in *Mein Kampf*, as an *Allerweltsbastard*, or "cosmopolitan bastard."[45] After the annexation of Austria in the Anschluss of 1938, Coudenhove-Kalergi escaped to the United States, where he wrote *The Crusade for Pan-Europe*. Part memoir, part history, part pacifist call to arms, it told of "a life, a dream, and a fight"—a life devoted to "internationalism, in the face of an era of frantic nationalism; a dream of the United States of Europe, and its fight against the rising tide of Hitlerism." As the continent became a battlefield, Coudenhove-Kalergi argued for resurrecting Pan-European cosmopolitanism: "A United States of Europe is right."[46]

Indeed, the exigencies of war intensified calls for European unification. Before the bloodshed ended, new measures had advanced economic integration, carrying a promise of greater political unity. A principal architect of the wartime efforts was Paul-Henri Spaak, a Socialist who served as Belgium's foreign minister and sought to develop a program of European cooperation. In 1944, he helped found the Benelux Customs Union, unifying his country with Luxembourg and the Netherlands in a free-trade treaty signed by the three governments-in-exile in London. A letter from Spaak to his staff explained the more far-reaching aims of the trade alliance, advising that the customs union was "designed to foster economic

FIGURE 1.4. Paul-Henri Spaak, shown on the left in 1952 during demonstrations calling for a federal Europe, was a Belgian politician and influential Europeanist who helped form the Benelux Customs Union during the war and served as the first president of the European Coal and Steel Community. His 1956 report, proposing a common market and other forms of multinational cooperation, laid the groundwork for the Treaty of Rome. Credit: Keystone-France / GAMMA RAPHO

recovery and to create the conditions for a more permanent union at a later date."[47]

Grander ambitions with roots in the interwar era were also revived, as mass death on the continent breathed new life into European cosmopolitanism. By 1946, disparate national movements had joined together in the Union of European Federalists, which defined free movement as a fundamental aim. Notably, first among the guarantees demanded in a "Message to Europeans"—resolutions drawn up by the Swiss federalist Denis de Rougement and endorsed by hundreds of delegates at the 1948 Congress of Europe in The Hague—was "free movement of persons, ideas and goods" in a united Europe. Next was a call for a charter of human rights.[48] Proposals emerged anew for creating a transnational system of democratic governance. It was Coudenhove-Kalergi, having returned from his American exile to settle in France, who composed a "Memorandum on the Organization of a Parliament for Europe." The premise was that Pan-Europeanism would spawn a politics of federalism, promoting "the cause of European Union."[49] The program of federalist internationalism claimed moral authority as an heir to wartime Resistance, although as preparation for postwar reform, it initally yielded few results. And while support came from across the political spectrum, partisans of a neoliberal world order—at the time forming an international organization of their own, the Mont Pelerin Society—were prominent in federalist ranks, favoring interstate federation to achieve a global free market. That led sectors of the labor movement to view the landmark Congress of Europe as an anti-communist enterprise.[50]

Other early blueprints for a postwar federal Europe had a radical inheritance. One, a manifesto calling for a socialist federation, was drafted on an island in the Tyrrhenian Sea where political prisoners were held captive. Altiero Spinelli, a disciple of the Marxist thinker Antonio Gramsci, was imprisoned for opposing Italy's fascist government and confined on the island of Ventotene during the war.[51] In 1941, he worked covertly with fellow inmate Ernesto Rossi to write *For a Free and United Europe: A Draft Manifesto*.[52] The document, which would come to be known simply as the *Ventotene Manifesto*, advocated an end to national sovereignty—"the abolition of the division of Europe into national, sovereign states"— and the creation of a cosmopolitan federation founded on social democratic principles. It argued that such a transformation would occur naturally, dialectically, as the devastations of world war ultimately revealed the common humanity of the European people, a humanity that would overcome the antagonisms of nationalism. "The collapse of the majority of the states of the continent . . . has already placed the destinies of the European populations on

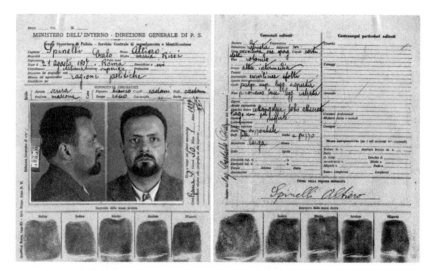

FIGURE 1.5. Altiero Spinelli was arrested by Italian authorities in 1927 for writing critically of the fascist government and interned during the war on the island of Ventotene, where he wrote the manifesto calling *For a Free and United Europe*, known as the *Ventotene Manifesto*. Credit: Latina national archive, from "La mia solitaria fierezza" by Mario Leone (Atlantide Editore)

common ground," declared the manifesto, foreseeing a united Europe that would arise from a "revolutionary crisis . . . in solid, state structures."[53] Scribbled on cigarette papers, smuggled to Rome, and secretly printed, the *Ventotene Manifesto* circulated within the Italian Resistance, becoming the program of the Movimento Federalista Europeo, a federalist movement founded clandestinely in Milan in 1943. Among the founders was Spinelli, newly freed from his island captivity. Yet the movement soon turned away from *Ventotene*'s revolutionary calls for abolishing nation-states, instead advocating a superstate that would oversee trade, national borders, military affairs, and the supervision of European colonies.[54]

After the war, an uneasy dialogue developed between the cosmopolitanisms of political union and market freedom as models of Pan-Europeanism. Consider the diverging approaches to forming a European community taken by Spinelli, the theorist of the federal state who would become a leading figure in the Union of European Federalists, and Spaak, the theorist of the common market who

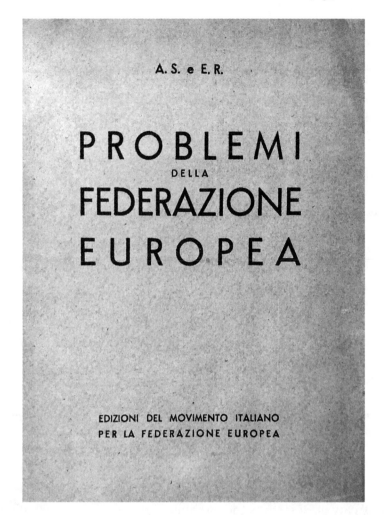

FIGURE 1.6. The cover of the book *Problemi della federazione europea* (Problems of the European Federation), featuring the initials of its authors, Altiero Spinelli and Ernesto Rossi. This edition, published in Rome in 1944, included the *Ventotene Manifesto*, as well as two new essays written by Spinelli, addressing such themes as the United States of Europe, Marxist politics, and federalist politics. Credit: Fondazione Pietro Nenni

had served as the first president of the European Coal and Steel Community. Viewing European union as a basis for world peace and the "diffusion of civility," Spinelli worked for the creation of a European Constituent Assembly, a federal democratic sovereign, "a political authority controlling foreign, financial, and economic policy."[55] Meanwhile, Spaak also sought a Europe "of a supranational character." His aim was merging the Coal and Steel Community, founded in 1952, with a plan for a European Defense Community, introduced the same year, to form a European Political Community based on economic interdependence, as presaged by the Benelux Customs Union.[56] But that project was stillborn by 1954, stopped by the defeat of the defense plan, with France fearing German rearmament and refusing loss of national sovereignty and colonial prerogatives.[57] Spaak scaled back his ambitions, becoming centrally preoccupied with overseeing Coal and Steel planning for economic union, proposing not a federal state but rather the "fusion of markets."[58] This drew a warning from Spinelli in an open letter declaring the primacy of the political and decrying the shibboleths of classical liberalism: "The market is not a 'natural' institution."[59]

Thus the long history of pacifist Pan-Europeanism pointed to the creation of a common market and a cosmopolitan state, a legacy imprinted in the postwar vision of abolishing national borders within a Citizens' Europe. Again, consider the viewpoints of the Benelux Customs Union's architect and the *Ventotene Manifesto*'s author. A common market, as Spaak wrote, would "affect all economic activities"; a federal state, as Spinelli wrote, would "say, 'We, the people of Europe'"—contrasting theories of union that would govern the meanings of free movement.[60]

———————————

The Treaty of Rome was the instrument that emerged when plans for a supranational European political body ran aground in the years just after the war. The treaty institutionalized economic alliance—the fusion of markets within the European community— by providing for the establishment of a common market. Yet the drive to make the people of Europe more central to the project of integration persisted, to reach beyond a purely economic model of union. That meant attaching the guarantee of free movement to a demos, not simply a market.

A report adoped by the Coal and Steel Community—the *Brussels Report on the General Common Market* (1956)—undergirded the Rome Treaty. It was drafted by Spaak, who led an intergovernmental committee appointed by the Coal and Steel member states: Belgium, France, Italy, Luxembourg, the Netherlands, and West Germany. Known eponymously as the Spaak Report, it proposed an expansive customs union, operating as a common market where goods, capital, and labor would circulate freely, along with cooperation in the energy, telecommunications, and transport sectors. The report arose from resolutions put forth at the 1955 Coal and Steel conference in Messina, Italy, which called for promoting a united Europe, starting "in the economic field," by forming "a common European market" that would allow free trade across national borders, ensuring the "full play of competition" and allowing the "introduction of freedom of movement for workers." According to the resolutions, the common market would not require political federation but rest instead on policy "harmonization" and "appropriate institutional means."[61]

As mandated by the Messina Conference, the Spaak Report set out a design for a common market encompassing the entire economic activity of the European community—"in the name of greater productivity." It envisioned the conditions of freedom opened by "the prospects of a real common market," as economic exchange crossed borders without restraint in a regime of "liberalization," through the "free circulation of goods" and the "free circulation of labor" and the "free movement of capital." And rights would be protected, rights economic in nature, as trade barriers disappeared, fostering the resurgence of Western European commerce. Notably, capital's free movement would yield "the unrestricted right of nationals of member States to obtain, to transfer, and to use capital within the Community anywhere in the common market." Among the essential rights yoked to capital's free movement would be entrepreneurship and ownership, "the right to create new enterprises, to acquire shares in existing enterprises," promoting the flow of wealth-producing activity across borders.[62]

Such was the framework proposed for economic union. It was a framework that drew on long-established liberal doctrines of free trade. But it also reflected emergent ideas, coalescing into neoliberalism, about the role of intergovernmental institutions in safeguarding market freedom, particularly the cross-border pursuit of wealth. "The establishment of economic union . . . the abolition of economic barriers," as Friedrich Hayek theorized of interstate federalism, "would do away with the impediments as to the movement of men, goods, and capital between the states. . . . The material benefits that would spring from the creation of so large an economic area can hardly be overestimated," including the "advantages derived from the possession of colonies." Writing in 1939, after the Anschluss, Hayek viewed securing peace as a main purpose of federation, but he held that economic union must be the basis for any form of political union. Moreover, federation would bring "less government," he claimed, for the power of nations to interfere with market freedoms would be restricted, while agreement among nations would be hard to attain, leading to "no legislation," rather than "state legislation." Paradoxically, federalism would have only a "negative power."[63]

Sovereignty, then, would lie in the market. In a program of "international liberalism," wrote Hayek, the prevailing power would be "the impersonal forces of the market." Accordingly, union would constitute "one single market," so that "goods, men, and money can move freely over the interstate frontiers." In sum, the value of the new liberalism would depend on "free movements" across a vast territory without internal borders.[64]

The Treaty of Rome codified the principles of international liberalism, defining the common market as the axis of European economic life. Adopted by the Coal and Steel countries in 1957, the treaty founded the European Economic Community and provided for cooperation under the guidelines of the Spaak Report. It declared an intent to develop international trade, set up a customs union, and remove the barriers dividing Europe. The foremost task was "establishing a common market." But more than a trading bloc concerned the treatymakers in Rome. Their work culminated in a set of rules that formed Europe's legal foundation and prepared for the achievement of a common market reaping the rewards of unfettered global capitalism.[65]

The Rome Treaty articulated humanist ideals loftier than its practical mandates on economic union. Nowhere was this contrast clearer than in the guarantee of free movement. The treaty proclaimed a broad guarantee—"the abolition, as between Member States, of obstacles to freedom of movement for persons, services and capital"—as a fundamental principle of "an ever-closer union among the European peoples." Yet the inventory of advantages served by free movement as a principle of union was strictly economic in nature, products of a common market that was supposed to afford closer ties among member countries. The treaty listed a multitude of aims: "A harmonious development of economic activities, a continuous and balanced expansion, an increased stability, an accelerated raising of the standard of living," along with "balanced trade and fair competition," "a common commercial policy," and "abolition of restrictions on international trade." At the same time, it stated the Community's purpose "to ensure the economic and social progress of their countries" as well as "improvement of the living and working conditions of their peoples." Economic unity would "strengthen peace and liberty," and the common market would "favor the harmonization of social systems."[66]

Always, the social good figured as a byproduct of improved economic life. The Rome Treaty made this evident in the section on the "Free Movement of Persons, Services and Capital," which treated persons only as laborers, protecting the freedom of workers alone to cross borders. "Freedom of movement for workers shall be secured within the Community," the treaty declared. Labor's free movement would parallel that of goods in the customs union and "the movements of capital liberalized." Where the treaty used rights language and dealt with social entitlements, it offered an economic framework. Addressing the "field of social security . . . to provide freedom of movement for workers," it provided that "migrant workers and their dependants" would have a "right to benefits" and a social fund would be formed to increase "employment opportunities for workers in the common market" and their "geographical and occupational mobility." Likewise, it recognized the freedom of establishment, meaning the "right to take up and pursue activities as self-employed persons and to set up . . . companies or firms." That included entrepreneurship and management of companies, wealth-producing pursuits by economic agents. Concerning association and collective bargaining, the treaty spoke of a workplace "right."[67]

The principle of free movement thus underwrote the common market paradigm. Nevertheless, the Rome Treaty did not locate all individual rights in economic exchange alone. A provision on equal treatment made no mention of commercial activity in requiring member countries to collaborate in ensuring all Community nationals the "protection of persons and the enjoyment and protection of rights under the same conditions as those accorded by each State to its own nationals."[68] That guarantee implied that economic integration required not just market freedoms but fundamental human protections. And it suggested that individual rights were the mechanism for turning privileges attached to national citizenship into universal guarantees.

Never understood as giving force to a maximalist Pan-European vision, the Treaty of Rome did not count political union as an aim. It did not speak of federalism—nor of democracy. Yet the treaty's affirmation of a closer union among the European people became a lodestar of more humanist notions of intergovernmental cooperation. It would inspire enduring efforts to place Europe's people at the center of unity projects. It underlay Leo Tindemans's conceptualization of Citizens' Europe, in his 1975 *Report on European Union* to the European Council. But it also influenced less grand planning, guiding the efforts of the continent's leaders to explore how a passport union might complement the common market in enabling the free movement of persons and the goods they carried.

A decade before Fontainebleau, a Paris meeting of the European Council called for devising a uniform travel document that would expedite border crossing within the European Community. The proposal emerged just as the use of new internal passports began in the Soviet Union, the world's largest country, covering a sixth of the Earth's land surface.[69] It also coincided with the efforts of member states to restrict the entry of non-European workers as national economies contracted, measures that nonetheless failed to curb the influx of foreigners arriving illegally or as asylum seekers.[70] Which raised the question of whether citizens of Community states would acquire "special rights" of mobility in a passport union.[71]

The European Commission endorsed that idea in a report on the "establishment of a Passport Union at the Community level."[72] Issued in the summer of 1975, as Tindemans was drafting his study of European union, the Commission report found that unrestricted travel would imply a zone of common citizenship, demarcated by the possession of individual rights. It explicitly likened the transit of people to the traffic in goods, with the common market an analogy for a European space of document-free circulation. "Passport Union . . . calls to mind . . . the concept of Customs Union," it noted. "Establishing a Passport Union would provide arrangements in respect of persons similar to those provided by a Customs Union in respect of goods." Bluntly, the Commission report transposed the logic of commodity exchange to the movement of Europeans, equating merchandise with people.[73]

At the very moment, then, that Tindemans coined the term Citizens' Europe to conceptualize a European union transcending economic life, the European Commission conceived of a passport union as a kind of market arena. The ethos of each came to echo in a *Draft Treaty Establishing the European Union* presented to Community countries a decade later. The draft won passage in the European Parliament in 1984 but went unratified by states protective of their sovereignty, just as the idea of a supranational European Political Community had been spurned after the war.[74] Still, it held potent symbolic force, and its fusion of civic and economic values would in turn echo in the Fontainebleau conclusions on Citizens' Europe later that year. The draft treaty declared a regenerative political purpose—"reviving the democratic unification of Europe" and guaranteeing fundamental rights to "citizens of the Union." It called for the "free movement of persons and ideas, together with the improvement of international commercial and monetary relations."[75] In a union founded on democratic cosmopolitanism, the free movement of people would not depend on economic activity.

The *Draft Treaty*'s author was Altiero Spinelli, whose *Ventotene Manifesto* remained a source of inspiration for the European federalist project. The onetime anti-fascist political prisoner had become an Italian member of the European Parliament, where he continued to press for federal constitutionalism as a framework for further unification. The *Draft Treaty* reflected his thinking, four decades in the making, on the prospect of supranational politics and human freedom. At the time of the Rome Treaty's adoption, Spinelli had written of the "mockery of the Common Market," arguing for the primacy of political union, holding that the common

FIGURE 1.7. Altiero Spinelli, who drafted a manifesto calling for a federated Europe while interred on the Italian island of Ventotene during the Second World War, as a member of the European Parliament in 1984. Credit: Communautés européennes.

market must be founded on "a permanent political will" with rule-making power.[76] That vision found expression in the *Draft Treaty*, which outlined a fully federal Europe that would direct coopera-tive trade and foreign policies, enforced by supranational rules. It linked social needs in the European community with liberal economic internationalism: "A humane and harmonious development of society" and "economic development of its peoples with a free internal market." It restated the Rome Treaty in seeking "ever closer union"—but in different terms. For the Spinelli draft defined union as a work of democratic humanism, not simply a common market, affirming European identity as rooted in "the principles of pluralist democracy, respect for human rights and the rule of law."[77]

The *Draft Treaty* foresaw a citizens' Europe—"citizens of the Union." It promised to translate member-state citizenship into transnational citizenship, with national belonging as the premise of a new European demos. "Citizens of the Member States shall *ipso facto* be citizens of the Union," the *Draft Treaty* declared. "Citizenship of the Union shall be dependent upon citizenship of a Member State."[78] It said nothing of a "Passport Union." But it projected the creation of a cosmopolitan space of free movement across borders—an area where "the free movement of persons and goods . . . implies in particular the abolition of personal checks at internal frontiers"—without presupposing an equivalence of people and goods.[79]

The *Draft Treaty* was the most immediate antecedent of the Fontainebleau conclusions. In February 1984, the European Parliament approved the draft, but it was not taken up for consideration by Community countries resistant to ceding political authority to supranational institutions.[80] In June 1984, however, the European Council ratified its spirit by announcing the advent of Citizens' Europe at Fontainebleau. The statements were terse, without rhetorical flourish. The conclusions did not include an elaborate defense of the democratic thrust of Citizens' Europe, nor a discussion of shared sovereignty, nor an explanation of how abolishing internal frontiers to enable the free movement of people and goods would affect security measures. But in a press conference at Fontainebleau, Mitterrand spoke capaciously about Citizens' Europe, which would touch everything from border checkpoints to university diplomas, from customs rules to common environmental regulations to a European passport. Asked about terrorism across open borders, he hastened to reply with assurances that "the free passage of frontiers . . . would still be the object of police surveillance. Not all is allowed." And he explained that an ad hoc committee would begin work, "so that the people's Europe, the Citizens' Europe can be set in motion."[81]

By the autumn, the European Council's ad hoc committee had set to work. In September 1984, the European Commission put its imprimatur on the Fontainebleau conclusions, approving the planning for the full free movement of people and goods in Citizens' Europe. A communication from the Commission titled *A Citizens' Europe: Implementing the conclusions of the Fontainebleau European Council* confirmed the schedule set by the Council: a European passport, the abolition of internal border controls—"the free passage across the Community's internal frontiers of Community citizens"—all within a year's time.[82]

The European Commission thus echoed the Fontainebleau Council, laying stress on European longing for free movement and popular support for closer union. It noted that border controls were considered "very annoying by citizens" but also recognized the "legitimate interests of internal security." Likewise, it noted a "fundamental consensus of European public opinion on the need for a Citizens' Europe . . . which will have real effects on the everyday life of Europeans."[83] At Fontainebleau, however, the project of creating Citizens' Europe had already begun to evoke criticism from Euroskeptics, as reflected in journalistic accounts of the Council meeting. Some wondered at the notion of a "nation-less European citizen."[84] Others doubted the practicality of diverting attention away from the European Community's budget crisis, of starting "a great political project in a period of economic recession."[85] A more lyrical objection likened Citizens' Europe to surrealist poetry, reciting words from "Inventory," a poem by Jacques Prévert that lists random objects and images. "A few flowers" and "one raccoon . . . another raccoon . . . five or six raccoons"—this was the incoherent ambition of Citizen's Europe, observed *Le Matin*, a Paris newspaper, "despite the absence of a raccoon."[86]

———————————

It fell to the ad hoc committee appointed by the Fontainebleau Council to turn aspirational conclusions into tangible measures—to develop the proposals for free movement and cosmopolitan political identity into procedures that would make Citizens' Europe a boon to everyday life. Its work culminated in a pair of reports to the European Council focusing on the transit of people and traffic in goods, the abolition of internal border checks, and the cultivation of European identity through devices of symbolic value. Its proposals were as specific as using a green decal, featuring a white E, on the windshields of vehicles to enable unobstructed border crossing by Community travelers, and as broad as deepening understanding of European cultural heritage. All of this followed from the directives on Citizens' Europe issued by the European Council and European Commission.[87] But the ad hoc committee ventured into new territory—an area unforeseen at Fontainebleau—by connecting free movement to the problem of residence, a problem that raised the stakes of including noneconomic actors within the guarantee of free movement. Which was to add yet another raccoon to Citizens' Europe's inventory. "It is indeed a very complex program on which work has to continue without delay," the committee said. And adding to the urgency was a new mandate from the European Commission, calling for the completion of the internal market by 1992 to create a "Europe without borders"—*Europe sans frontières*.[88]

The committee was composed of representatives from Community states and the European Commission. Among them were historians, economists, lawyers, and diplomats. The group's formal title was the Ad Hoc Committee on Citizens' Europe.[89] Its chairman was Pietro Adonnino, an Italian member of the European Parliament. He was a lawyer, a professor at the Royal Naval Technical Institute in Naples, and president of the International Fiscal Association.[90] Like Altiero Spinelli, he sat in the European Parliament. Otherwise, the two men were very different. Spinelli was a Eurocommunist and dissident; Adonnino was a Christian Democrat and a technocrat. Yet Adonnino introduced the first ad hoc report by stating that the "Committee intends to stress the political role it has to play."[91]

In light of the political dimensions of its work, the ad hoc committee held discussions with members of the European Parliament, seeking "constant contact . . . with the elected representatives of the European citizens."[92] Its stated aim was proposing "tangible advantages" to Community citizens, eliminating rules that "cause irritation," and "making the Community more credible in the eyes of its citizens."[93] The committee described how the idea of Europe had emerged from the ashes of war, achieved by "the work of those who experienced the horrors and destruction of war." Citizens' Europe, free movement—the postwar work would continue so "that future generations will understand and appreciate one another across borders," and through that recognition come to "realize the benefits to be derived from closer cooperation and solidarity."[94]

The ad hoc committee's first report, of March 1985, began with the priority of free movement, as set by the Fontainebleau conclusions: "Freedom of movement for Community citizens" and "freedom of movement of goods," both forms of "frontier traffic."[95] It outlined immediate, practical steps for lifting border controls and simplifying travel, such as displaying the green decal marked with the E to signal compliance with customs rules—easily observed as vehicles passed across borders at reduced speed. At airports and seaports also, controls at points of departure would be removed for Community citizens.[96] No longer would travelers be caught up in a tangle of red tape and border formalities, with a uniform European passport further allowing the "freedom of movement of citizens and of their personal goods within the Community."[97] The flow of goods would likewise be expedited by removing restrictions on transport services and reducing their costs, as well as by simplifying policies governing border trade, such as harmonizing fiscal rules. "Achieving a European Community in which goods and money can be freely moved," the report stated, would produce "the advantages not just of a common market without tariff barriers but of a smooth-running single market in which the full benefits of lower costs of transport and travel . . . can be realized for the benefit of the Community citizen." Particularly, the report noted, a "free transport market" would fulfill the terms of the Rome Treaty.[98]

Planning Citizens' Europe appeared all the more urgent because of a new timetable for completing the internal market introduced by the European Commission, the report explained. The common market's growth had proceeded since the Rome Treaty, launched with a customs union, but, in a program newly submitted to the European Parliament on March 12, 1985, the Commission proposed that a fully unified internal market at last be achieved by 1992.[99] As the ad hoc committee was preparing its report, the Commission's president, Jacques Delors, of France, appealed to the Parliament to adopt that schedule. He called for a "barrier-free economic area," for abolishing without delay the "barriers to free movement of goods and persons." Yet he also looked beyond market precepts. He affirmed the Fontainebleau aim to create Citizens' Europe, premised on the "fundamental principle that people should be able to move freely across borders." In a vow of civic intent, especially striking for a former finance minister, he argued for a need "to transcend the 'economism' which has stamped European integration," and to make union "an intrinsic part of national life, meaning not only the political culture of each country but also the political and social struggles that make up the fabric of society."[100] Supporting this program, the ad hoc committee termed its work a "necessary corollary." The overarching purpose was forming "a Europe without borders."[101]

Where the ad hoc report departed from—or rather surpassed— the Fontainebleau plan was in advising that free movement in Citizens' Europe include a right of residence. The committee reasoned that moving freely across borders also meant a right to stay in any member country of the European Community. Nothing had been said about residence in the Fontainebleau conclusions on the free movement of people. But the ad hoc committee inserted a new principle, declaring in the March 1985 report to the European Council: "The Committee is convinced that the right of a citizen of a Member State of the Community to reside in any other Member State of his free choice is an essential element of the right to freedom of movement."[102] A residence right would expand the scope of free movement far beyond the Rome Treaty's guarantees, to encompass not only all European people rather than simply economic actors, but also attachment to a place rather than simply the act of circulating across borders like goods in a market. The problem was the prospect of a residence right claimed by a nonmarket actor.

That problem set in relief the breadth of a guarantee of free movement that transcended economism. The ad hoc committee acknowledged the complexity of a residence right that linked the freedom to cross borders with a right to stay anywhere within the European Community. It pointed to the economic costs of a noneconomic guarantee of free movement that would include the choice to live in any member state: "Citizens wanting to reside in a country other than their own should not become an unreasonable burden on the public purse in the host country."[103] The concern about nonnationals becoming public charges was as old as doctrines of settlement that excluded foreigners from poor relief.[104] It signaled the significance of nationality even in a cosmopolitan Citizens' Europe.

No less, the problem of residence brought home the inequivalence of people and goods, as paired subjects of free movement, while also reflecting the perplexities posed by noneconomic agents crossing the frontiers of a political community founded on a common market. As goods circulated, they were exchanged for value, used, or consumed. Workers, too, added value, wherever they went. But people not counting as economic agents—uninvolved in market activity—threatened to burden the public purse, using up resources rather than producing value. The risks carried by the free border crossing of people and goods were incommensurate, which the ad hoc committee recognized in proposing that a right of residence rest on proof of sufficient wealth to subsist without depending on public assistance: "By allowing that any person wishing to make use of the right of residence can be made to prove that they have sufficient resources at the level of social assistance in the host country and of adequate provisions in case of illness."[105] Inadvertently, a residence right would renew an economic model of free movement, based not on work but on wealth ownership. Instead of exploring that outcome, the committee left the problem for the European Council to resolve, calling for a "political decision of principle on a general right of residence for all citizens of the Community."[106]

The ad hoc committee's final report of June 1985 concentrated on measures of more symbolic value and political significance designed to strengthen European identity and add cultural legitimacy to the achievement of the internal market. In broad terms, it discussed the need for initiatives that would create a common European worldview: addressing the role of museums and the media; proposing a Euro-lottery, foot races through European countries, and a European academy of science, technology, and art; and explaining that fluency in multiple Community languages would deepen a sense of shared cultural heritage. Enhancing "the

Community's image in the minds of its people" would promote "support for the progress of Europe," the ad hoc report stated.[107] It recommended codifying and simplifying Community law, and harmonizing divergent national rules, as well as introducing uniform electoral procedures for the European Parliament and requiring all Community states to give equal protection to the rights of free speech and assembly of all Community citizens. "It is crucial for the Community's image that its law be implemented in the Member States without discrimination," the report declared.[108] The proposals gave salience also to education, emphasizing "student mobility" and university cooperation "beyond borders," along with foreign language training and a "Europe Exchange" program.[109]

At length, the ad hoc report explored how heraldic devices, iconography, and ceremonial practices would inspire European solidarity. It advocated using a flag at both national and international events, proclaiming the Community's existence to the public. For an emblem, it recommended a blue rectangle, emblazoned with a circle of twelve gold stars, surrounding a gold letter E. As an anthem at ceremonial events, it proposed "Ode to Joy," from Beethoven's Ninth Symphony, as music "representative of the European idea."[110] In closing, the report advised that border signs at internal frontiers should share a common European design—without obsolete, restrictive markings—to manifest "progress made towards a genuine single market and the unity of the European Community."[111] Free movement, too, would be endowed with symbols of a Europe without borders.

The European Council swiftly approved the reports of the Ad Hoc Committee on Citizens' Europe, agreeing to the first set of plans at a Brussels meeting in March 1985 and the final set in Milan in June 1985. The Brussels conclusions said little besides calling for member states and the European Commission to implement the measures while asking ministers to reach decisions on unresolved questions.[112] Again, in Milan, the conclusions were brief, pressing forward the work of implementation.[113] The Milan meeting also saw the Council embrace the Commission's program on economic integration, formally submitted as a white paper on completing the internal market.[114] Detailing some three hundred proposals for "building an expanding market and a flexible market," the white paper provided for removing physical, technical, and fiscal barriers on trade flows as well as ensuring that the free movement of people would not be "restricted to the workforce"—all to be completed by 1992.[115] Against the backdrop of the white-paper timetable, the European Council urged progress toward the creation of Citizens' Europe.[116]

The Council's summary approval of the planning for Citizens' Europe masked underlying divisions, however. Delays occurred in carrying out the proposals, and questions of a political nature went undecided. Certain ideas were realized expeditiously, such as the unfurling of a Community banner outside the seat of the European Commission in Brussels. Others exposed rifts within the European Community; not even the first steps toward free movement took effect across the member states, such as use of a European passport.[117] Soon after the Fontainebleau meeting in 1984, the European Commission warned of "a situation in which the political initiaves founder," stalling the removal of frontier barriers.[118] Mere piecemeal reform would give "the European citizen the impression of an unfinished or even non-existent Community," the Commission observed.[119] A year later, the European Council expressed concern at the delay, directing member states and Community institutions to proceed with decision-making.[120] But national delegations hesitated, refusing to end systematic passport checks as well as insisting on security measures and common immigration rules to balance the abolition of checkpoints.[121] The disagreements revealed deeper uncertainties. Minutes from a meeting of Helmut Kohl and François Mitterrand at Konstanz recorded how Germany was caught between transatlantic ties and France's vision of an independent Europe. Meanwhile, the fear in Paris was that the Fontainebleau aspirations would produce only trivial results.[122] Accounts of "Disunited Europe" appeared in newspapers, describing the absence of Community consensus on political cooperation.[123]

In particular, division arose over the ambit of free movement— how a right designed to transcend the economic parameters of the Rome Treaty would be claimed in practice. The uncertainties became the centerpiece of a September 1985 meeting on Citizens' Europe convened by the Committee of Permanent Representatives, a body of emissaries from Community states that prepares the agenda for European lawmaking.[124] The nub of the problem was the guarantee of free movement to nonmarket actors. And whether the guarantee would not simply reach beyond workers—to all Europeans—but go further still to grant a right of residence. If so, how would nations avert "severe pressure on public expenditure" if the claimants of a residency right of free movement were uninvolved in economic activity, such as students, or pensioners?[125] On that question, the decision-making struck an impasse. A memo on the meeting, prepared by a European Commission official, advised that a "political decision of principle" had yet to "clear away the problems."[126]

A further roadblock came in a legal judgment rendered by the European Court of Justice, which constrained the power of Community institutions under the Rome Treaty to act in spheres unrelated to economic life and confined the treaty's grant of free movement to commercial pursuits. The ruling in *Gravier v. City of Liège* disrupted the planning for Citizens' Europe. The architects of the internal market considered the judgment a "major problem" for plans to guarantee free movement to noneconomic actors.[127]

Françoise Gravier was a Frenchwoman who hoped to become a cartoon artist. In 1982, she traveled to Liège, a city in Belgium that lies along the Meuse River, near both Germany and the Netherlands. She began a program of art study at the Académie Royale des Beaux-Arts. The Liège academy had been founded in the eighteenth century, in a former convent, and later came to occupy a grand Renaissance Revival building in the city center. By the late twentieth century, it offered training in spatial, visual, and fine arts: drawing, painting, illustration, engraving, sculpture. Gravier chose the field of comic strips.[128]

Her program was a four-year course of art education. At the Académie Royale, that program was free of charge—for Belgians. For foreigners, however, there was a tuition fee, called a *minerval*, of 24,622 Belgian Francs for the academic year 1982–1983. "All foreign students must be aware that such education is not free of charge," the academy stated.[129] Under Belgian law, institutions of higher education funded by the state, such as the Académie Royale, had authority to impose an enrollment fee on foreign students to defray costs. Yet there were exemptions: for foreigners with a Belgian parent, or a parent gainfully residing in Belgium, and for foreigners from Luxembourg.[130] When Gravier sought an exemption from the *minerval*, the Académie Royale refused and denied her enrollment, finding that she did not qualify for a waiver under Belgian law. Consequently, the city of Liège revoked her residence permit.[131]

Court filings reveal little about Françoise Gravier, only that she was a citizen of France, the daughter of French parents, unmarried, and that she aspired to be a cartoon artist. But long after the litigation ended, reflecting on her case, she described her path from a childhood in Aix-en-Provence to the art academy in Liège to the European Court of Justice. She had always been interested in art; her father, a painter, took her to museums. After finishing her *baccalauréat* in 1981, she pursued drawing, settling in Paris. It was a romance that took her to Liège, where she enrolled at the Académie Royale.[132]

But Gravier had a keen sense of her rights, notably her right to equality of treatment under the law—and, especially, her right to free movement. The burden posed by the *minerval* was "enormous," she recalled. "I was completely stunned." Contacts in the Belgian labor movement connected her to a lawyer seeking a test case to challenge discriminatory national rules before a European court. "You're really the case I need," she remembered her lawyer saying. At that point, her aim was simply to stay in Liège, keep studying cartoon art, and avoid the *minerval*. She hardly perceived that the outcome of her case would hold meaning for other students, for the sovereignty of Belgium, or for European jurisprudence. She recalled, "I didn't say to myself, 'I'm going to attack the Belgian state.'"[133]

Gravier brought her case before the President of the Tribunal de Première Instance in Liège, challenging a fee levied only on foreigners, claiming that she should be free of a *minerval* not required of Belgian students, and not be denied the liberty to stay in Liège. That burden, she argued, violated the Rome Treaty, constituting discrimination on the basis of nationality and infringing on her freedom of movement to pursue art education.[134]

Because the dispute involved interpreting the Rome Treaty, the Belgian tribunal sent the case to the European Court of Justice.[135] The referral came with mention of a precedent, *Forcheri v. Belgian State*, where the Court of Justice found that the question of imposing a special educational fee on nonnationals fell "within the scope of the Treaty."[136] But the facts of *Forcheri* differed from those of *Gravier*, for the plaintiff in *Forcheri*, an Italian woman studying social work in Brussels, was married to a European official working in Belgium, and the court gave deference to Community law that recognized family bonds as an aspect of "the mobility of workers . . . in particular as regards the worker's right to be joined by his family and . . . integration of that family into the host country."[137] But Gravier was not the wife of a worker in Liège. No rules protecting family bonds figured in her case. Her claims for equality of treatment rested on her individual rights under the Rome Treaty.[138]

Gravier v. City of Liège thus reached the European high court—the case understood as posing a problem for Citizens' Europe. The litigation over the *minerval* concerned fundamental tenets of Community law. At issue were not simply the wrongs of discrimination due to nationality and of restraints on free movement, both of which contravened common market principles, but also the authority of the European Community, within the scope of the Rome Treaty, to guarantee the free circulation of its citizens. The plaintiff was Gravier, the aspiring cartoonist; the defendant was the city of Liège. The city was joined by the nation of Belgium, which required payment of the *minerval*, and the Communauté Française, which oversaw art education in the region. Because of the conflict's international significance, the European Commission intervened in the case, as did Denmark and the United Kingdom, as parties interested in the judicial interpretation of free movement under the Rome Treaty. The Commission joined Gravier, while Denmark and the United Kingdom supported Liège, the Communauté Française, and Belgium.[139]

The questions before the European Court of Justice were twofold: Was the *minerval* discriminatory on the basis of nationality? And was the study of cartoon art an economic activity entailing a right of free movement protected by the Rome Treaty? In other words, did the *minerval* pose a barrier to border crossing, thereby obstructing the mobility of persons essential to free exchange in a common market? In challenging the Académie Royale's fee, Gravier invoked two parts of the Rome Treaty: the ban on "any discrimination on grounds of nationality" found in the opening principles and the protection of the "Free Movement of Persons, Services and Capital" in Title III.[140] Her claims before the Belgian tribunal stressed services as an axis of free movement in the field of education.[141] But the arguments before the European Court of Justice broadened to turn on the mobility of labor, the liberty to set up undertakings, the nature of lucrative enterprise, and the pursuit of "vocational training . . . contributing to the harmonious development both of the national economies and of the common market."[142] How would profit making—*le but lucratif*—be construed?[143]

The law of free movement pervaded the case, therefore, in tandem with the problem of defining what constituted economic activity. The crux of Gravier's argument was that studying cartoon art was a profit-making, economic pursuit—education being indispensable to common market exchange, part of the freedom guaranteed to someone who "goes to another state"—and thus the *minorval* denied the equality of treatment owed to foreign students. "In all matters relating to the free movement of persons," she claimed, "it is the activity that one performs or that one wishes to perform that provides the right to stay."[144] By her lights, art education constituted economic activity that fell within the scope of the Rome Treaty.[145]

The matter of work was paramount: Gravier's situation with respect to employment, remuneration, and other conditions of labor, regarding which the treaty expressly stipulated that "freedom of movement shall entail the abolition of any discrimination based on nationality."[146] But this was no straightforward matter; Gravier acknowledged her identity as a student. She was "not a qualified employee or self-employed person or service provider," but a traveler "for the sole purpose of studying," she told the court.[147] The court's advocate general, responsible for delivering an advisory opinion, explained how the plaintiff's identity posed an original question: "The position is different if the would-be student is already a migrant worker or one of his dependents."[148] But she was simply a student.

Did simply being a student mean being uninvolved in economic activity? Not necessarily, Gravier argued. And certainly not if the study was of cartoon art. Although not a worker, she claimed that her activity was vital to the economic aspirations of the European Community, and that the *minerval* restricted the free circulation of students across borders that represented an "indispensable condition for achieving the free movement of wage workers."[149] Her brief to the court reviewed the development of Community law under the Rome Treaty, showing how it connected the free movement of labor with educational exchange and echoing the treaty's language in claiming that the linkage contributed to "a closer union between the peoples of Europe . . . to the movement of people in the Community."[150]

By Gravier's reasoning, education was steeped in the values of the market. No longer was knowledge an end in itself, but necessarily driven by a profit-making motive, *le but lucratif*, her brief claimed. "Nowadays, there are hardly any students who study for pleasure or for pure knowledge. Everyone aims to improve their professional training and obtain a profitable asset on the job market." Even artistic studies were designed to enable gainful work, "freelance or waged," Gravier argued. "The study of comic strips undoubtedly constitutes vocational training."[151] At the Académie Royale, she would be training to participate in the market.

By no means, then, did Gravier's claim to free movement transcend the economism that stamped the rights protected in the Treaty of Rome. In seeking to become a cartoon artist, in crossing the border from France to Belgium to study at the Académie Royale, she presented herself as a traveler pursuing human capital formation. Asked by the court to consider a clause of the treaty that expressly excluded "non-profit-making" from the domain of free movement, she replied that the clause had no bearing on her case, as her study was "economic activity," reiterating her right to be "a beneficiary of the Treaty. . . . And more particularly of . . . free movement."[152] Her aim was vocational training, not art without profit-making. In sum, her complaint against discrimination due to nationality found justification in the rules of the market.

As the Court of Justice deliberated, it heard from all the parties to the case on whether studying cartoon art counted as economic activity. It was just days after the Fontainebleau summit, in July 1984, as it happened, that the court had sent out a letter requesting commentary on a specific point of treaty interpretation: "The relevance . . . of the notion of 'companies which do not pursue a profit-making goal' . . . in particular with regard to companies operating in the field of education."[153] Did it matter that the Académie Royale, a state-sponsored Belgium school, was not a profit-making firm? Gravier said no, precisely because her own study was vocational training, economic in nature. The European Commission joined that view, replying that "the notion of 'non-profit making companies' is not relevant." Indeed, the Commission equated her art study with merchandise, arguing that her schooling fell within the treaty's scope, "just as with regard to the free movement of goods."[154] The city of Liège argued to the contrary; as Belgium explained on the city's behalf, the country's education system "presents an absence of the notion of profit or a lucrative goal."[155]

The defense of Liège rested on the claim that Gravier's studies were too distant from commerce to implicate the Rome Treaty's antidiscrimination doctrine. The argument relied also on the principle of national sovereignty, especially regarding education. Belgium claimed that the treaty covered only free movement oriented toward market exchange, and that it could not be construed to prevent member countries from allowing special privileges to their own citizens in providing education. The treaty's rules "only govern the free movement of persons in the course of their economic activities," Belgium argued, further asserting that national regulations held sway in education, with each country having "special responsibilities" toward its own nationals, and that the *minerval* was not a profit-making measure, supporting instead a system of public education finance that fell outside "the framework of community-defined economic activities."[156] Denmark likewise maintained that the Académie Royale had no profit motive, and that a service offered by "a person who does not work with a profit is not covered by the Treaty's rules," meaning that the free movement guarantee did not apply to Gravier's study of cartoon art.[157]

The fullest defense of national autonomy came from the United Kingdom, which argued that nonprofit schools subsidized by the state did not belong to the world of the market. Such schools were not acquisitive entities, not aimed at "carrying on a business"; their fees were designed to fund the pursuit of knowledge, not to finance "profit making concerns."[158] And such schools were creatures of the nation-state—"an expression of national educational and social policy"—for the benefit of the nation's citizens, and funded by the public, "out of the nation's taxes."[159] Their purpose was not "transaction of an essentially economic character," not producing wealth or participating in the arena of exchange value, but rather "advancing knowledge and learning."[160] The British argument admitted differences in schooling, noting "the term 'studies' is wide and uncertain" and ventures such as language training "run for profit."[161] But it touted its own national university system as the very exemplar of education advancing pure knowledge, remote from "the acquisition of gain."[162] It contested readings of Community law that would flood its schools with a tide of foreign students and burden the public purse, the prospect that "any citizen of a Member State could travel to another Member State for the sole purpose of pursuing a course of study and has an entitlement to any kind of subsidy from the host State on the same terms as the citizens of the host State."[163] Defending Belgian's *minerval* as a lawful act of state authority, it objected to expansive interpretations of both free movement and economic activity.

Conversely, the most explicit affirmation of art study as a market activity came from the European Commission. On Gravier's behalf, the Commission argued that education aimed at the acquisition of profit, possessing exchange value, which made intangible knowledge production a commodity tradable on the market. "Education is a product of intellectual activity and . . . constitutes a product which can be valued in money and is subject to commercial transactions," the Commission reasoned.[164] The most common subjects of foreign study—medicine, economics, and languages—carried market value, it pointed out, adding that a student who "goes to another member state" for job training would enter into a myriad of market transactions and make use of many products, from transport to entertainment. Such a student represented a key factor in an integrated marketplace, with a "right to professional formation." Though not a migrant worker, she could rightfully invoke "principles of free movement and the equality of workers within the Community."[165]

The European Commission therefore argued that the *minerval* stood as a discriminatory barrier against the mobility allowed by the Rome Treaty. It asked the court to recognize that "the right to free movement should not be understood in a narrow sense," drawing a blunt analogy between art study and the traffic in goods: "In fact, it is a question of assuring the free movement and exchange of economic activities in the same way that other provisions ensure the free movement and exchange of goods."[166] By that reasoning, the purpose of Gravier's border crossing evidently figured as profit-making.

———————

A decision in *Gravier v. City of Liège* came down from the European Court of Justice in February 1985. For about a year, the litigation had unfolded alongside the planning for Citizens' Europe, from the conclusions at Fontainebleau to the work of the ad hoc committee appointed by the European Council. As the European Commission was proposing ways to implement the Fontainebleau conclusions, it was intervening in the cartoon art case. And from the outset, the court recognized the case to be about the ambit of rights across borders. That was how Thijmen Koopmans, the Dutch member of the court serving as the so-called rapporteur in the case, summarized the pleadings: a Frenchwoman's claim to the freedoms of Belgian students, as "a right of nationals of other member States" and the city of Liège's denial of her "right to stay" once she refused to pay the *minerval*—the question being whether foreigners stood "on a footing of equality" with nationals as required by the Treaty of Rome.[167]

The European Court, composed of members from each Community country, meted out supranational justice. The court emerged from the founding of the Coal and Steel Community in 1952, and, with the adoption of the Rome Treaty, gained formal status in 1958 as an institution of the European Communities, seated in Luxembourg.[168] It was a "many-headed Hydra," said the Scottish jurist Alexander Mackenzie Stuart, who presided over the court that decided *Gravier*.[169] But the court's rulings did not include dissenting views. Accordingly, the judgment in the cartoon art case was unanimous in finding that the *minerval* violated the nondiscrimination guarantee of the Rome Treaty.

The *Gravier* decision was terse, fewer than a dozen pages. In short order, the court bought the economic argument of the plaintiff. It held that the study of cartoon art fell within the scope of the treaty, finding the *minerval* to be discriminatory on the grounds of nationality and courses on cartoon art to qualify as vocational training—an economic activity entailing a right of free movement. "Access to vocational training is in particular likely to promote free movement of persons throughout the Community," the court stated. Such liberties promoted trade, "contributing to the harmonious development both of the national economies and of the common market."[170]

The court did not dwell on the value of cartoon art or consider the relevance of stick-figure drawing to the free movement of workers. It did not cite *Tintin*, a comic that rose from the pages of a conservative Catholic newspaper in Belgium, *Le Vingtième Siècle*, to fame in the global marketplace.[171] Rather, it concluded matter-of-factly that the "term 'vocational training' includes courses in strip cartoon art." Of the *minerval*, the court declared, "Such unequal treatment based on nationality must be regarded as discrimination." Imposing a fee only on foreigners violated the Rome Treaty, insofar as the inequality abridged exchange within the marketplace of the Community, "whose objectives include *inter alia* the free movement of persons."[172]

In reaching that judgment, the court explored not only rules in the Rome Treaty on free movement, vocational training, and equality of treatment but also more recent doctrine created by the Council of Ministers.[173] It noted principles on mobility—"freedom of choice of occupation, place of training and place of work"—principles calling for "programs of visits" and stating that "effective common vocational training policy will help to bring about the freedom of movement for workers." And it cited the Council's findings on the value of "basic and advanced training" and the need for common measures among Community countries allowing all people to attain "technical knowledge and skill" and acquire the "highest possible level of training."[174]

The court drew particularly on Community guidelines that approached the acquisition of knowledge and skills from the vantage point of needs both macroeconomic and more personal, as it took account of the value of training as a factor recognized in European law. It invoked considerations of "the constantly changing needs of the economy" as well as of the good of training "to enable the individual to develop his personality and to take up a career."[175] The court made no mention of non-profit-making ventures in endorsing the notion that improvement of human capital added to the progress of the common market by developing the individual personality.

The court's emphasis on individual personality seemed resonant with postwar human rights principles. A language of personality did not apply to individuals in the Rome Treaty, appearing only in endowing commercial firms and the European Community with legal personality.[176] But it infused human rights charters, in what international lawyers called a "personalized" theory of rights recognition. In the 1948 Universal Declaration of Human Rights, the development of individual personality serves as a reason for the worldwide protection of human rights. Article 22 states, "Everyone, as a member of society . . . is entitled to the realization . . . of the economic, social and cultural rights indispensable for his dignity and the free development of his personality." Article 26 provides that "Education shall be directed to the full development of the human personality" in order to promote "respect for human rights and fundamental freedoms," and "understanding, tolerance and friendship among all nations, racial or religious groups," and the "maintenance of peace." Article 29 establishes that "Everyone has duties to the community in which alone the free and full development of his personality is possible," defining social obligation as a corollary of the right to develop one's personality. The European Human Rights Convention and the national legal traditions of European states also recognized the fulfillment of individual personality as an aspect of human dignity and freedom.[177]

In *Gravier*, however, the dignitary principles of the development of individual personality were absent. The court spoke of economic life, not human rights. In pairing the changing needs of the economy with the capacity for personal development, it attached the value of education to the development of the common market. It did not connect training that would develop the individual personality with the advancement of principles of understanding, tolerance, and friendship among nations. The decision reasoned in terms of free trade and cross-border exchange. Its language was economic, not humanist.

The decision was anything but rhetorical; the spare text expressed neither a view on European integration nor a philosophy of jurisprudence. The thought of the judges can be glimpsed, however, in lectures they delivered and papers they published in the years before the *Gravier* ruling. There, they explored the mandate of the European Court of Justice and the relationship between the common market and European law, doctrine that informed the judgment in *Gravier*.

The Scottish lawyer Alexander Mackenzie Stuart, who presided over the *Gravier* court, once said that his life had been forever shaped by his time in West Germany after the war. He had served in the Royal Engineers, which took him from his home in Aberdeen to the Ruhr region to rebuild bridges. Seeing the ruins of the Ruhr affected him deeply.[178] Less personally, he spoke of world war, and how European integration stood as a shield against its recurrence. In his Hamlyn Lectures, delivered in 1977 on European Community law, he said, "It must never be forgotten that the creation of the first of the Communities, the Coal and Steel Community, by eliminating some of the most enduring international tensions of that epoch, played a vital part in averting the danger of a third world conflagration." And in a world still divided between "democratic societies" and "collectivist forces," the purpose of the European Community— "maintaining a stable economy and improving the quality of life"— was as vital as ever. The role of the Court of Justice was sustaining the cosmopolitan rule of law created by the Community: "A new legal order."[179]

Mackenzie Stuart's Hamlyn Lectures, presented at the Institute of Advanced Legal Studies in London, offered his most extensive commentary on the court's work. He advised against taking "too Copernican a view" of the court, as if its seat in Luxembourg were the center of the universe. Nevertheless, he observed the power of its decisions: "It seems to me that the impact of Community law on daily life is increasingly evident." The effect could be felt across themes addressed in the Rome Treaty, from the removal of trade barriers to the encouragement of labor mobility and adoption of common economic policies. Mackenzie Stuart likened the treaty to an incoming tide, flowing everywhere, enlarging the sphere of Community authority and extending the sweep of the court's supranational jurisdiction, making the rule of law "more fundamental."[180]

European integration had inaugurated a new legal order, Mackenzie Stuart explained. In that legal order, cosmopolitan justice rested on a common market foundation. It differed from international law resting on universal human rights principles, for the European Community was "essentially a system of international integration in selected sectors of the economy"—a system that imposed "a legal superstructure upon these essentially economic provisions." Mackenzie Stuart spelled out the economism stamped on Community law: It was the law of "the Europe of the Customs Union"; of "economic co-ordination and control"; of the "operation of the Common Market." It was the law of the Rome Treaty's "market mechanism."[181] The Court of Justice, then, was a neutral arbiter but also an instrument of economic integration.

In this new legal order, founded on the market mechanism, the novelty further lay in the fusion of the supremacy of Community law with the protection of individual rights. What was diminished was the power of the nation-state. The cosmopolitanism of the common market became a font of individual rights. Mackenzie Stuart explained this as the "primacy of Community law" and the "direct effect" on rights claims, principles that together enabled the Community legal order to preempt national rules and guarantee rights enforceable in national courts, such that "Community law can in appropriate circumstances create rights in favour of individuals which national courts must protect."[182] Those principles found classic expression in *Van Gend en Loos*, a 1963 case in which the Court of Justice declared that "the Community constitutes a new legal order . . . for the benefit of which the States have limited their sovereign rights."[183] This was the "dialectic of the Treaty of Rome," Mackenzie Stuart observed. It was the sovereignty of supranational Community law that afforded citizens new power to assert individual rights against nation-states.[184]

But what sort of rights? The landmark case, *Van Gend en Loos*, concerned a Dutch import tax on formaldehyde, and Mackenzie Stuart provided a catalog of similar rights claims, justiciable under Community law, which all involved economic activity, from tariffs, subsidies, and patents to currency exchange rates, from the trade in butter, barley, and ewes' milk cheese to the free movement of workers. All had to do with the free movement of goods, capital, and persons. But by persons, Mackenzie Stuart meant only workers—and their right to mobility—citing the claims of "the worthy worker who finds obstacles in his path," such as a migrant worker deported across "the nearest available frontier" by a Community nation seeking to "curtail his freedom of movement." Mackenzie Stuart expressed his unease about proposals to broaden the Community's framework beyond the market. Even as he denied that his legal commentary was intended as "a political tract"—"Personal conviction," he said, "is a chancy fuel for the judicial engine"—he aired skepticism about "further integration," specifically responding to Tindemans's report on European union as he argued for setting legal limits on supranational power in keeping with free market doctrine. "The foundation of the existing Treaty is the market mechanism," Mackenzie Stuart said, "and if today it is felt that the market mechanism alone is not enough, equally it cannot be eliminated without changing the whole basis of the European Communities."[185]

For Mackenzie Stuart, then, the market made for the bedrock not simply of integration but of collective European life. His court's task was creating "ascertainable rights" within the frame of "a common economic policy," joining the guarantee of free trade with the restraint on national sovereignty and the vindication of the individual rights of economic actors. A legal order upholding Europe's common market rested on "personal right."[186]

The judges who sat with Mackenzie Stuart on the European Court shared his judicial philosophy and his view of the free market. One was Ulrich Everling, a West German jurist who had once served in his nation's Federal Ministry for Economic Affairs. He advanced a watchman role for the court in protecting unfettered trade: "Securing the Common Market by applying the prohibition of discrimination . . . and by protecting persons affected by unlawful acts." Writing in an American law journal, he explained the common market as the lifeblood of European aspirations: "Running like a red thread through the whole of the Court's case law is the idea that this core of the Community must remain sacrosanct." Like Mackenzie Stuart, he associated the sanctity of the free market with the "protection of individual rights," explaining that plaintiffs' claims gave rise to the court's "creations."[187] By this reasoning, everyday Europeans asserting their rights to participate in economic life were the authors of the Community's constitutional development.[188]

Also illustrative was the thought of the Dutch judge Thijmen Koopmans, the rapporteur in the *Gravier* case. A venerated jurist and an authority on comparative and constitutional law, he had taught at Leiden University and served in the legal department of the Council of Ministers and on the Supreme Court of the Netherlands. His approach to jurisprudence transcended borders—between private and public law, and between European and national law.[189] In a 1985 working paper for the European University Institute, appearing a month before the *Gravier* decision, he explained his conception of the relationship between market freedom and individual freedom, explicitly equating economic liberties with human rights. He wrote in response to the *Draft Treaty Establishing the European Union,* the Spinelli text approved by the European Parliament, which proposed to amplify the supranational authority of the European Community. Koopmans was skeptical of the project, of grafting principles of citizenship and civic bonds onto economic integration, just as Mackenzie Stuart had been of Tindemans's report. No political revision of the Community's identity would alter its foundation in "fundamental market freedoms," Koopmans wrote. His paper was titled "The Judicial System Envisaged in the Draft Treaty," and he examined technical issues of jurisdiction and judicial review in great detail. But he also explored the guarantee of fundamental rights, arguing that the guarantee was already incorporated into free market doctrine and that hewing to market doctrine itself would "strengthen the 'Europe of the Citizen.'"[190]

The premise of this argument was that free trade meant "rights and freedoms" founded on rules of equality and unfettered exchange across borders. "These market freedoms are individual freedoms derived from the concept of a common market. They have something in common with human rights," Koopmans wrote. "It may be true that classical human rights . . . find their basis in the freedom and dignity of the individual person; but some typical market freedoms, like the right to move freely or not to be discriminated against, are not far removed from this same sphere of thought."[191] In other words, market freedoms were the analogue of human rights, asserted by Europeans pursuing economic activity and upheld by the Court of Justice.

The decision in *Gravier* reflected the free market thinking of the judges who decided that the Belgian *minerval* violated the right of a Frenchwoman not to be discriminated against and to move freely. Their judgment presupposed that she was a worker in the making. It was not rooted in classical human rights, with a basis in individual freedom and dignity, but rather in the market freedoms derived from the concept of a common market that gave workers a right to cross borders with a profit-making motive. The decision emphasized "working life." The court took a broad view of the market mechanism, reasoning that cartoon art study would produce Gravier as a worker, that training at the Académie Royale counted as "preparation . . . for work." It recognized that she was not a migrant worker, but nonetheless incorporated her education into common market practice, invoking individual personality in the context of economic self-determination—the right to develop oneself by participating in the market. "'Vocational training' includes courses in strip cartoon art," the court held. "Any form of education which prepares for a qualification for a particular profession, trade or employment . . . is vocational training."[192] Accordingly, the court struck down the *minerval* as a burden on cosmopolitan market freedoms, advancing the primacy of Community law and the principle of direct effect on individual rights by using judicial power to limit Belgium's national sovereignty and uphold a Frenchwoman's right of free movement as an economic actor. She came under the Rome Treaty's protections not by virtue of her human dignity but on account of being a future worker.[193]

In *Gravier*, the Court of Justice reinforced the doctrine of nondiscrimination central to European jurisprudence as a facet of economic liberty. The decision expanded the realm of the market into an area not obviously touched by commercial pursuits. It endorsed the rights of all persons to pursue gainful activity of their own choosing, a path toward a profit-making venture that might lie across national borders. At the same time, the court reinforced a restrictive interpretation of European law under the Rome Treaty, binding supranational Community authority to transnational commerce, and tying the free movement of persons to the "mobility of labor."[194] In protecting the art student's rights, the court upheld uninterrupted commerce as the essence of European union.[195]

The decision lifted the *minerval*'s burden on Gravier. By then, she recalled, she had begun to glimpse the meaning of her case for the pursuit of education across the European Community. With greater hindsight, she came to see how the ruling was narrowly rooted in the economic logic of training for work—"and only on that," she said, "not because I will move freely . . . without being limited by money."[196]

At the Fontainebleau Palace, the European Council set forth a program for European integration that would turn a customs union into Citizens' Europe. It would deepen civic bonds and benefit everyday life, creating social interdependence and contributing to European renewal by supplementing the economic exchange of the common market. It would be developed by the institutions of the European Community. The European Commission provided for implementing the plan, elaborating on the Fontainebleau conclusions, and the Ad Hoc Committee on Citizens' Europe worked with the European Parliament in drafting measures to lay a new foundation for forming an ever-closer union among the European peoples, the aim first promulgated by the Treaty of Rome. At the heart of the project lay the free movement of persons—not only economic actors, but all persons who were citizens of Europe.

But *Gravier v. City of Liège* enshrined a market paradigm of free movement, offering an interpretation of European law that ran contrary to the aspirations of Citizens' Europe. The ruling in the case opened new vistas of economic life, by defining cartoon art study as economic activity, and it hastened the advent of the Erasmus Programme, a system of educational exchange that sent thousands of students across Europe's borders.[197] But *Gravier* did not amplify the meaning of freedom guaranteed by the Rome Treaty; it delivered justice that rested on a market foundation, expanding the concept of economic activity—but not of free movement—and tethering the cosmopolitan authority of the European Community to the development of the common market. The mandate that flowed from the treaty's principles, as the rapporteur Koopmans bluntly wrote of European planning, was "to promote a harmonious development of economic activities," not to attain "a common harmonious development of society."[198] So, too, as a legal adviser to the European Commission, Georges Kremlis, would later recall of the court's view of the art student's rights, "Rome was not a treaty oriented around personal freedoms, such as the free movement of people."[199] A noneconomic defense of free movement did not exist in Community law, which is why the judgment in *Gravier* presented a problem for the realization of Citizens' Europe.

Together, the Fontainebleau conclusions and the *Gravier* judgment gave impetus to the intergovernmental negotiations that would lead to the expansive guarantee of free movement in the Schengen treaty. Neither the planning of the European Council nor the ruling of the European Court of Justice required action by nation-states, but both spurred the treatymaking of France, West Germany, Belgium, Luxembourg, and the Netherlands. Although Citizens' Europe never became formally codified, Fontainebleau remained a touchstone of aspirations for social integration and free movement that would sweep beyond involvement in the common market. But *Gravier* laid bare the limits of Community authority to guarantee the free movement of persons unconnected to economic activity. Due to those boundaries, Schengen's creation occurred outside the framework of Community institutions, as Europhile statespersons condemned barriers at internal frontiers as the "most visible symbolic expression of the non-existence of Europe." It was to give concrete embodiment to a borderless Europe that treatymaking began at Schengen.[200]

2

A Treaty Signed on the Moselle River

THE ABOLITION OF borders across an expanse of Western Europe began with a voyage on the Moselle River. From its source, two thousand feet above sea level in the Vosges Mountains of France, the river twists and turns north into Luxembourg and across Germany, branching into tributaries that extend into Belgium. Hundreds of miles downstream, it flows into the Rhine at Koblenz. The Moselle first appeared in the historical record in the writings of Tacitus, who chronicled, in the *Histories*, the Roman upheavals of 69 CE. The river formed part of the natural environment shaping combat configurations at a time when much of the European continent fell under the authority of a single sovereign. By the First World War, it demarcated the boundaries of nation-states. Winding through verdant hills, the Moselle River has traced the course of Europe's transition from a domain of empire to a warring continent to a transnational community.[1]

Nowhere is the riparian symbolism more evident than in the Moselle Valley, where the river borders three countries: France, Germany, and Luxembourg. Near the tri-point border lies the village of Schengen. On June 14, 1985, diplomats met there to approve the treaty on free movement that would come to be known as the Schengen accord; the parties to the treaty were France, West Germany, and the Benelux states of Belgium, Luxembourg, and the

Netherlands.[2] As the site of the treaty's proclamation, Schengen embodied both the natural unity of European nations and the vision of free movement across borders.[3]

The ceremonial signing of the Schengen accord occurred aboard a riverboat on the Moselle. The midday sun beat down on the deck of the *Princesse Marie-Astrid* as the treatymakers gathered inside at a conference table: Robert Goebbels, Luxembourg's state secretary for foreign affairs; Catherine Lalumière, France's state secretary for European affairs; Waldemar Schreckenberger, state secretary to the West German chancellor; Paul de Keersmaeker, Belgium's state secretary for European affairs; and Willem Frederik van Eekelen, Dutch state secretary for foreign affairs.[4] A joint press release traced their work to the 1984 declaration at Fontainebleau seeking "Community belonging and . . . solidarity."[5]

The aspirations of the Schengen treaty were set forth just before the signing. A statement delivered by Goebbels, Luxembourg's representative, acclaimed the project. "With deep satisfaction," he began, "I am able to welcome you today to Schengen," a *Dräi-Länner-Eck*, "three-country corner," that symbolized the aim of unity. He explained that the agreement to dismantle internal borders, reached through less than a year of intergovernmental diplomacy, would further Pan-Europeanism. "Together we have been able to take a step forward on the path traced by the Treaties of Rome . . . in the matter of the movement of people, goods, capital and services," he affirmed, "bringing us closer to what is fitting to call the 'Europe of Citizens.'"[6] Schengen thus advanced the development of a common market under the Rome Treaty and the creation of a cosmopolitan Citizens' Europe by enabling the free movement of Europeans across a territory without internal frontiers.

The Schengen accord marked the advent of a new principle of freedom of movement. Schengen allowed persons to move freely across borders—not workers, the category used in the Treaty of Rome and construed by the European Court of Justice in *Gravier*. The freedom of European Community nationals to circulate throughout the Schengen area would no longer depend on market activity, on pursuing a profit-making venture. People would be bearers of that freedom, not economic actors.[7] A fundamental right of persons to free movement inside a nation-state existed by virtue

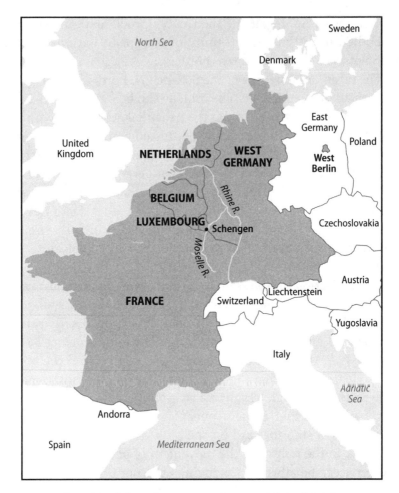

MAP 1. The original five Schengen member countries, with Schengen shown at the tripoint border among Luxembourg, France, and West Germany.

of international human rights covenants: the 1948 Universal Declaration of Human Rights and a 1963 protocol to the European Convention on Human Rights. But Schengen amplified the idea of free movement, extending it beyond the needs of the market as well as the borders of the nation, by allowing all persons who were nationals of European Community countries to move freely across a new transnational domain that would form a basis for Citizens' Europe.[8]

Under the treaty, however, freedom of movement would scarcely be uncircumscribed. Schengen would overcome a market paradigm of free movement but not distinctions based on nationality. For the opening of internal borders presupposed the exclusion of foreigners: fortifying the external borders of the Schengen area, enforcing restrictive immigration rules, and policing unauthorized migrants, as carried out by member states. Within Schengen, the free movement of persons across frontiers was meant for the people of Western Europe—and hedged by security measures requiring the assertion of national authority. To member states fell the power of defining the terms of national belonging that set the limits of the transnational Schengen community. At the signing ceremony, a pledge to combat "illegal immigration" sustained the affirmation that Schengen would benefit nationals of a Citizens' Europe by expanding freedom of movement.[9]

The event at Schengen went unnoticed by much of the European press. A state bulletin of the Grand Duchy of Luxembourg recorded Goebbels's words.[10] But an account in France's *Le Figaro* was virtually alone in finding significance in the signing of the treaty: "A more than symbolic step towards the unification of Europe."[11] Goebbels later recalled the pragmatism of the moment, the workaday diplomacy that produced the accord, saying simply: "We did our job as junior ministers."[12] The French signatory, Catherine Lalumière, said that it was only afterward, when the treaty finally entered into force a decade later, that Schengen "became a symbol of liberty."[13]

Although the treatymaking was not made public, the reams of paperwork it produced recorded Schengen's creation. Organized into working groups—immigration, police, transport, and customs—diplomats devised the terms of the accord, deliberating on the freedom of individuals and the mechanisms of the market, as well as on labor, migration, national security, and European union. They left evidence of their ideas in draft agreements, diplomatic memoranda, and confidential annexes—evidence that reflects how five countries of the European Community came to agree, in advance of Community institutions, to create a space without internal borders and allow free movement across the frontiers of sovereign nations.

The treatymaking gave free movement a meaning that transcended the logic of the market and yet served the purpose of market integration.[14] The Schengen accord bore the imprint of earlier intergovernmental pacts, which laid a foundation for unchecked border crossing. And it responded to outcry at border crossings, as Europeans called for free movement across the continent, agitation that emerged against the backdrop of the still-inchoate progress of the European Community toward union under the provisions of the Rome Treaty. By the time of the treaty signing on the Moselle River, the authors of the accord had come to think of Schengen as "a laboratory for the free movement of persons" that would develop both the common market and Citizens' Europe.[15]

About a decade after the signing of the Schengen treaty, a member of France's negotiating group, a police commissioner named Vendelin Hreblay, described the work of creating a territory of free movement in a world shaped by the Cold War. "The iron curtain was still a palpable reality and the 'wall of shame' still cut Berlin and Germany in two," he wrote. "To speak at that time of freedom of movement . . . was a veritable profession of faith. Translating these ideas into concrete reality could evoke fear, skepticism, but also hope." This portrait of the moment opened his treatise on Schengen: *La Libre circulation des personnes* (The free movement of people).[16]

The Schengen treaty expressed two primary aims: realizing the ideal of union among the people of Europe as declared at Fontainebleau, and augmenting the free movement of people and goods required by the Treaty of Rome. As the police commissioner wrote, it was understood that "first and most important . . . from which everything flows, is the free movement of persons." Free movement was the basis for establishing Schengen as "a common space" encompassing a vast part of Western Europe, and the opening of borders had "a symbolic meaning . . . of belonging to a new entity." But free movement did not mean an absence of state authority, for the Schengen countries would maintain "total mastery" of their own territory and jointly enforce controls at external borders.

Schengen's creation illustrated an essential principle: "Liberty and security are an inseparable pair."[17]

Schengen drew not only on the Rome Treaty's principles, but on other precedents for European integration. The signing ceremony paid tribute to the Fontainebleau conclusions as a warrant for abolishing barriers against people and goods crossing the frontiers of the European Community.[18] Yet even before Fontainebleau, a letter from France's president, François Mitterrand, to West Germany's chancellor, Helmut Kohl, had proposed a "political perspective" in pursuing European union and establishing "freedom of movement of persons, goods and services."[19] From that proposal emerged the Fontainebleau principles, giving rise to the idea of Citizens' Europe—and, in turn, Schengen as a domain of free movement. The preamble to the Schengen accord gave recognition to Fontainebleau as well as to the Rome Treaty. As precursors, the accord also cited the Benelux Economic Union and a pact made in Saarbrücken, West Germany, in July 1984.[20] As Goebbels said, all were "sources of inspiration and encouragement for us."[21]

The Benelux Economic Union was Schengen's earliest precursor. Founded in The Hague in 1958, Benelux allowed nationals of the three member states—Belgium, Luxembourg, and the Netherlands—free movement throughout the common area. It developed from the wartime Benelux Customs Union, formed by the governments-in-exile in 1944. A subsequent trilateral agreement, in 1960, fully eliminated internal checks while maintaining controls at external frontiers.[22]

The treaty of the Benelux states defined "economic progress" as the primary purpose of their union but did not restrict free movement to economic actors. Unlike the Rome Treaty, Benelux allowed broad freedoms of transit and residence—"freedom of movement, sojourn and settlement"—to nationals of the Benelux states. From that liberty followed equal legal treatment throughout the Benelux territory, the guarantee of "civil rights" and "individual rights and interests" along with freedom in trade and employment, social security benefits, and capital transactions. Although a commercial union, Benelux protected noneconomic rights while promoting cross-border market exchange.[23]

Just as significant as the Benelux small-state model in Schengen's origins was a bilateral pact between West Germany and France, the Saarbrücken agreement of 1984, which removed controls at their common border. A memo that circulated in West Germany's foreign office in June 1985—"Unterzeichnung des Abkommens" (Signing the agreement)—explained that Schengen was "analogous . . . to the Franco-German accord."[24] Signed in the West German city of Saarbrücken, next to the French border, the bilateral agreement emerged amid labor uprisings mounted at border crossings, which would also become a reference point in the multilateral diplomacy on Schengen.

Plans for Franco-German cooperation were already underway when long-distance truck drivers blockaded border crossings across Western Europe, protesting customs checks that delayed their passage. Sometimes the wait at the borders lasted as long as twenty hours.[25] "Try to imagine: no internet, no cell phones, no toilets," recalled Guy Van Hyfte, a Belgian truck driver who had transported refrigerators and other merchandise across the European continent. "Parking lots—two, three, four hundred big lorries, everybody together. Sometimes at night, you have to be careful what's happening. Doors have to be locked at all times."[26]

The unrest fueled calls for abolishing controls at the frontier between the historic adversaries, as their leaders together envisioned a Citizens' Europe unified in freedom against the Soviet Bloc. For a week in February 1984, the truckers' barricades halted the movement of goods and people from the English Channel to the Austrian Alps, making all too visible how border checks stood as barriers to the common market. One epicenter of the rebellion was the Mont Blanc Tunnel between France and Italy; others were the Paris-Lyons roadway and the Brenner Pass between Austria and Italy.[27] "The collective outburst of anger was directed at the dilly-dallying of customs officers . . . and the arrogance of the authorities. A powerful minority showed the state its fist," *Der Spiegel* reported, quoting a truckers' leader: "'We must be like wolves'" (*Wir müssen wie Wölfe sein*) "'who do not retreat, defend the pack and spread fear.'"[28]

The uprising made headlines across the globe, from Mumbai to New York. It was said to be "an apt metaphor"—a "traffic jam" that

FIGURE 2.1. Truck drivers block the departure of ferries in Calais in France—
part of extensive strikes by drivers to protest burdensome custom checks in 1984.
Credit: Patrick Aventurier / GAMMA RAPHO

symbolized the "political and economic paralysis of the old continent."[29] It became known as the "blockade of the 10,000 trucks," a
siege that extended for many miles, on roads covered with ice and
snow. The images "frightened the citizens of Europe . . . reminiscent of natural disasters." It was said to reveal "the failure of the
European Community's free market dreams." Freight perished in
the cold—livestock, milk, and millions of eggs. Factories stilled,
owing to a diminishing supply of parts. Fuel went undelivered. Ski-
ers could not get to the Alps.[30]

The blockade took place as unemployment rose across Europe,
cutting off trade, paralyzing much of the continent, intensifying
opposition to border controls that impeded the flow of goods and
transit of people. *Der Spiegel* reckoned that the chaos on the roads
was "*eines nationalen Happenings,*" like a surrealist political perfor-
mance, a "happening."[31] The revolt ended as governments pledged
to streamline customs checks and alter regulations of the trucking industry while troops used cranes to break up the blockade.[32]
Reports previously commissioned by the European Parliament on

the state of the internal market had quantified the costs of customs rules, estimating that the total price of "Non-Europe"—the failure to remove internal border restrictions—was 50 billion ECU (European Currency Unit), with about 12 billion lost on crossing borders, or between 5 and 10 percent of the value of the goods traded in the market.[33] But the burden of the complex rules and long waits fell most heavily on the truck drivers who made a living by crossing Europe's borders.[34]

In the blockade's aftermath, pressure on European officials mounted. As *Der Spiegel* observed from Hamburg, "The government in Paris had fallen into distress."[35] The pressure spurred the Franco-German initiative, connecting border rules to broader forms of cooperation. At a meeting of European diplomats in Strasbourg in May 1984, France's foreign minister, Roland Dumas, warned of barriers to free movement that "have been unbearable" and the outcry against the border crisis from a public that had been "traumatized." On France's behalf, he issued a "vow to advance the European social space."[36]

For Saarbrücken's framers, therefore, enabling border crossing belonged to a program joining social and economic integration. The accord arose from direct cooperation between France and West Germany, rather than within the framework of European Community political institutions. Impatient with progress toward European union, Mitterrand and Kohl shared a conviction that transnational policymaking was consistent with national authority, particularly when conducted through intergovernmental cooperation.[37] In a speech to the Bundestag in March 1984, Kohl had put forward a "European idea" that would be based on "Franco-German friendship"—"We will urge that first talks be held this year"—and would embrace more than common market exchange. "Financial effort and political commitment must be seen together," he said. "Any meaningful investment in Europe is always a down payment on the free future of the Germans."[38] At a meeting in May 1984 in Rambouillet, a commune near Paris, Kohl and Mitterrand set a July deadline for a bilateral lifting of border controls, saying little about the new procedures for free movement other than foreseeing different rules for nationals of European Community member states and foreign travelers. At a press conference, Mitterrand extolled the "spirit of restraint and sensitivity" that marked the Franco-German partnership, as he honored the fortieth anniversary of France's liberation from Nazi occupation. Meanwhile, transport ministers from West Germany and the Benelux states were meeting in Neustadt an der Aisch, near Nuremberg, to streamline trade. A month later, Mitterrand and Kohl met again, on the sidelines of the Fontainebleau Council, where they directed their foreign ministers to finalize a pact on free movement. The plan was to "be made known to the public opinion of the two countries," at the request of the West German embassy in France.[39] As *Bild*, a Berlin tabloid, reported: *Keine Grenzkontrollen*—"no border controls."[40]

The Saarbrücken agreement, approved on July 13, 1984, paired the immediate easing of checks at the border between France and West Germany with a longer-term goal of transferring controls to their external borders with other countries. The preamble declared the principle of free movement for nationals of the European Community: "To strengthen the solidarity between the two peoples by removing obstacles to free movement at the frontier between the two countries," France and West Germany would promote the European Community's aim of "ever closer union . . . expressed in the fact that all nationals of these States can cross the internal borders unhindered." The agreement provided for a simple visual check of vehicles crossing the border at reduced speed, so long as Community nationals affixed a green decal to their windshields to indicate compliance with police and customs requirements. It also pledged to combat illegal immigration and illicit trafficking. But the essential purpose was "ensuring the free movement of people and goods."[41]

Saarbrücken introduced the first steps toward abolishing controls on the movement of all nationals of the European Community, differing markedly from its antecedents—from Benelux, which applied only to nationals of the three member states, and from the Rome Treaty, which applied only to economic actors within the Community. Under Saarbrücken, the freedom of unhindered border crossing did not depend on market activity; and it encompassed all Community nationals. The breadth of free movement allowed by the bilateral accord signaled a bid for broader participation by member states of the European Community. Signed a month after the commitment

FIGURE 2.2. A green decal, marked with the letter E for Europe, was affixed to windshields to facilitate border crossings under the Saarbrücken Agreement of 1984 and the Schengen Agreement of 1985. Credit: Politisches Archiv des Auswärtigen Amts

to Citizens' Europe made at Fontainebleau, Saarbrücken anticipated progress toward European union spurred by free movement across the internal borders of Community nations.[42]

Under Saarbrücken, however, opening up free movement across the border between France and West Germany entailed sealing off this common space to non-Europeans. While expansively including all Community nationals, the agreement drew a strict distinction between foreigners and European citizens. A year before Saarbrücken's signing, a Bonn report described how police officials of the two nations had begun considering closer cooperation to promote "the passage of . . . citizens," balanced by efforts to "cut back the number of foreigners." A West German official stressed the need to surveil "all 'conspicuous' travelers," and the value of using a "coordinated information system for the exchange of data, in particular for those unwanted foreigners from third countries."[43] So, too, police trade unionists, who supported Saarbrücken, stressed the need for international security cooperation.[44] The question, then, was how to avert the entry of foreign migrants while abolishing borders. A letter from Mitterrand's chief of staff, Jean-Louis Bianco, to Kohl's chief of staff, Waldemar Schreckenberger, stated that Saarbrücken would rely on existing rules: "For nationals of non-EC countries, the currently practiced border controls will be maintained."[45] But the accord also required greater bilateral coordination of police procedures, harmonizing laws on illegal immigration, customs fraud, and irregular movements of capital. The two countries were to align their visa requirements for foreign migrants.[46]

In the autumn, as the dismantling of border controls between France and West Germany began, Kohl and Mitterand met in the town of Bad Kreuznach, where they delivered a statement on the progress of free movement. It was in Bad Kreuznach, which lies northeast of Saarbrücken, that the postwar reconciliation between France and West Germany had deepened, when Charles de Gaulle and Konrad Adenauer met there in 1958 and affirmed their countries' adherence to the Treaty of Rome.[47] Now Mitterrand and Kohl reviewed Saarbrücken's achievements, saying that the agreement allowed border crossing with no waiting time and would advance European union by "lifting obstacles to the free movement of persons, so that all nationals of member states can cross borders unhindered."[48]

As Saarbrücken became a model for a space without internal frontiers, protests developed against the everyday inconveniences of crossing borders elsewhere in the European Community, and public support grew for a fuller guarantee of free movement. Preparing for a common market seemed perverse when barriers blocked commonplace travel. Memories remain vivid of that moment. Even the equipment on a car could obstruct border crossing—"border police wanted my father to dismantle the fog lights," remembered a former official of the European Commission, describing the ordeal of family trips from Brussels to Bonn.[49] A former spokesperson on European affairs for West Germany's Social Democrats recalled participating in demonstrations seeking free movement. In Aachen, near Germany's border with Belgium and the Netherlands, "We demanded, 'Border controls finally come down.'"[50]

Meanwhile, the problem of reconciling free movement with the exclusion of non-Europeans grew more profound as the Saarbrücken accord became fused with the Benelux system. In December 1984, the Benelux states proposed to France and West Germany that the five countries join together to enable the flow of people and goods across their common borders. The proposal drew on the Fontainebleau concept of a Citizens' Europe while also citing advantages for the common market in "minimizing border stoppage time," addressing both social and economic union. It called for measures ranging from simple visual surveillance of vehicles to the full harmonization of migration and customs laws.[51] Amid the documents dealing with the opening of borders, a particularly revelatory paper on the Benelux proposal circulated in France's foreign ministry. Bluntly, it assessed the difficulty of enforcing rules based on national identity across an expanse of five countries: "We must be aware that if we take the path of abolishing checks at the border for Community nationals only, it will be very difficult to distinguish between them and nationals of third countries."[52]

The difficulty, then, was detection, so as to discern between Europeans and foreigners. The French paper—titled "Objectives of the Agreement of 13 July"—explored the consequences of amplifying Saarbrücken under the Benelux proposal by allowing absolutely unhindered border crossing within a common territory: "The logical conclusion is that to completely abolish internal controls for Community nationals implies that the same thing should be done for the others." In delineating the contours of the problem, France warned against diminishing state authority to block illegal migration, against a dismantling of borders that would fail to recognize "national provisions." An answer to the problem, expressed in confidential paperwork, lay in pairing liberty with security, free movement with surveillance: "The solution of privileging community travelers by freeing them from any obligation of control is only practical if there is an unstoppable means of identifying them for sure." Among the findings was that a green decal on a windshield would hardly suffice to hinder the circulation of foreign migrants.[53]

It was a problem, therefore, of the unintended consequences of a sweeping guarantee of the free movement of persons. Once the frontiers between countries ceased to serve as sites of control, the distinction between foreign migrants and nationals of the European Community would become illegible in practice. Undetected, non-Europeans would move across internal borders as freely as Europeans.

In Brussels, on February 27, 1985, diplomats from France, West Germany, and the Benelux countries met to begin negotiating a treaty on free movement across a space that would become Schengen. At the meeting's end, the treatymakers declared the inception of their work in a communiqué to the press: politics, persons, trade all were at stake. "Today, the political will of five countries has become evident"; the treaty would establish "the gradual abolition of border checks on the movement of persons and goods," and procedures against "illicit trafficking" and "illegal immigration" to pair freedom with security.[54]

The diplomats who met in Brussels became the primary negotiators, and most would sign the treaty in June.[55] All were state secretaries or high-level aides, principally responsible for foreign affairs, who had entered politics at the local level, their sympathies ranging from social democratic to center-right. They convened in a series of meetings across Europe, in the capitals of the countries that would become the Schengen states.

All of the main negotiators were lawyers, except for Robert Goebbels of Luxembourg. He was a journalist who became president of a Young Socialists' league, a city councilman, a member of the national parliament, and then Luxembourg's state secretary for foreign affairs and international trade.[56] France's representative, Catherine Lalumière, had taught public law at the Pantheon-Sorbonne before entering local politics in the Gironde region as a member of the Radical Party of the Left, which was a governing partner of the Socialists. She became a state secretary for foreign affairs in 1984, responsible for the Europe portfolio.[57] Waldemar Schreckenberger, of West Germany, had been a law professor at the University of Mainz before holding government positions in the state of Rhineland-Palatinate, where he allied with the Christian Democratic Union and rose to be a justice minister, and then Kohl's chief of staff, responsible for European policy.[58] Belgium's negotiator, Paul de Keersmaeker, had left his family's brewery business to serve as mayor of the village of Kobbegem, and then in Belgium's parliament, representing the center-right Christian People's Party. He became a member of the European Parliament, and then the Belgian state secretary for European affairs and agriculture.[59] For the Netherlands, the delegate was Virginie Korte-van Hemel, the state secretary for justice, who had served in the Dutch parliament as a member of the center-right Christian Democratic Appeal.[60] Later, it was Willem Frederik van Eekelen, who had worked in the Dutch foreign civil service before becoming a member of the Dutch parliament, representing the center-right People's Party for Freedom and Democracy, and then the Dutch state secretary for foreign affairs.[61]

The treatymaking unfolded at a far remove from the everyday experience of border crossing. But the work was influenced by the truck drivers' blockade, which had led to a preliminary set of negotiations that formed a prologue to the work on Schengen. A commercial pact between West Germany and the Benelux Union, made at Neustadt an der Aisch in May of 1984, provided for "simplification" of controls on trade across their common border.[62] Meanwhile, Benelux dignitaries observed the development of the Saarbrücken accord, addressing border cooperation in diplomatic meetings with representatives from both France and West Germany.[63] When a Benelux proposal on lifting border controls came to France and West Germany in December 1984, their foreign ministries circulated procedures for negotiating a complex fusion of the existing Saarbrücken and Benelux agreements, each with its own technical provisions.[64] In a separate bit of diplomacy, delegates from France and West Germany met in Bonn to settle on a common posture to adopt when the treatymaking began in Brussels.[65]

The December Benelux proposal sought closer economic union, declaring an aim "to achieve within the European framework a relaxation of the formalities on the cross-border traffic of persons and goods."[66] Together, West Germany, France and the Benelux countries defined a process for the project: political and technical. The first part would be setting forth *un accord politique global*—"a comprehensive political agreement." That declaration was to be made immediately to establish "the political importance of the border operation." The second part would be determining the technical rules of implementation—"la mise en oeuvre de l'accord politique global." Those would take longer to resolve, given the anticipation of "divergent positions."[67]

The purpose of the Brussels meeting in February was to begin drafting a statement of political intent on free movement, "a political declaration by the governments."[68] The treatymakers laid claim to the principles of Fontainebleau and the Treaty of Rome, defining the social and economic aims of opening their common borders as inseparable: "A contribution to 'Citizens' Europe' and to the construction of an internal European market."[69] They agreed to a summer approval of the political accord, setting up a committee structure for their work. A central negotiating group would deal with matters of broad concern, and four working groups would address specific areas: the movement of persons, trade, transportation, and security and police.[70] The Benelux countries pressed for swiftly offering "tangible results"; France stressed the problem of illegal immigration.[71]

The press communiqué from Brussels presented an origin story, telling the public how the Fontainebleau conclusions led to the Saarbrücken agreement and, in turn, to the overture of the Benelux countries to France and West Germany. It gave no place to the truckers' blockade a year earlier, or to other public agitation for free movement. Rather, it declared that the flow of people and goods across open borders would foster European identity by making "nationals of member states aware of belonging to the Community."[72]

The intergovernmental treatymaking proceeded independently of European Community institutions, yet it resonated with the aims established by the European Council. By March 1985, the Ad Hoc Committee on Citizens' Europe formed at Fontainebleau had issued a report finding that free movement would be valuable to both Community citizens and the completion of the common market.[73] In the European Parliament, a pro-trade faction, the Kangaroo Group, demanded the lifting of cumbersome border controls, noting the lessons of the truckers' protest. "Constructing the Mont Blanc Tunnel meant getting through 15 km of rock," the group reminded the parliament, calling for unhindered passage through border crossings: "Making the Internal Market work."[74]

During the drafting of the treaty, negotiators confronted differences in national conceptions of the logic of free movement—and the priority assigned to the transit of goods and people in creating a cosmopolitan space without internal borders. The differences held significance for matters of security and sovereignty as well. The Fontainebleau principles on Citizens' Europe called for dual measures on free movement within a year—using a "single document" for exchanging goods in the common market and removing all border checks for people crossing intra-community frontiers. The Benelux states gave "equal importance to the three parts: movement of persons, transportation, and movement of goods." As Goebbels said, this would advance the "internal European market" and "Citizens' Europe."[75] But France and West Germany together sought greater attention to the mobility of people, allowing their unhindered passage but also stopping illegal migration. It was travelers—persons—that most concerned France: *La circulation des voyageurs*. On opening borders, as Lalumière said, "It is a question in the first place of controls regarding the movement of travelers."[76] That was also the main concern of West Germany, as Schreckenberger laid stress on "reducing . . . in particular before the summer holidays . . . the controls on the movement of travelers." Moreover, regarding the differences in approach, he claimed the Benelux interest was in trade while the Saarbrücken agreement was as concerned with crime as with commerce: "If the Benelux memorandum attaches relatively greater importance to the circulation of goods, the Franco-German accord, on the other hand, puts emphasis on problems of police and security." Opening internal borders would require a "battle against crime."[77]

For West Germany and France, the effect of free movement on rules for immigration and asylum was paramount from the outset of the treatymaking. A telegram from Bonn to Paris reflected unease about unhindered border crossing in the space of five countries. Sent just before the Brussels meeting in February, the telegram addressed "Asylum Seekers in West Germany," describing an influx of migrants—five thousand in January alone, principally Tamils, from Sri Lanka—and called for stricter asylum rules that would block their entry and transit across Europe.[78] It said asylum seekers were roaming through West Berlin and traveling to France. "In Berlin, the refugees buy train tickets for Paris, by which they obtain a transit visa while crossing the border." It cited reports in the press, from the *Frankfurter Allgemeine Zeitung* to the *Quotidien Économique*, noting the public outcry against the migrants: "This influx raises serious concerns in public opinion."[79]

The interest of West Germany and France in pairing free movement with security measures also underlay a paper marked "confidential" that was prepared for the Brussels meeting. The paper juxtaposed Franco-German proposals, page by page, with the Benelux aims. There was agreement on many measures, from using green decals on windshields to transferring sanitary controls on plants, animals, and persons from common borders to the interior of countries to avoid traffic jams. But the juxtaposition also revealed contrasting priorities.[80] The Benelux proposals provided in the long term for police cooperation against "illegals" and other forms of crime. But the Franco-German paper advised that the countries harmonize practices immediately to protect "their territories vis-à-vis migratory flows," warning of the "consequences of removing border controls for matters of immigration." It also proposed systematic data exchange to prevent the illegal entry and residence of foreign migrants as well as trade in contraband goods.[81] On matters of sovereignty, the differences were still more marked. The Benelux idea of a unitary policy on immigration contrasted with the Franco-German plan simply to harmonize national laws enforced by the member states. Nor would France and West Germany agree to supranational authority over external borders.[82]

As the treatymaking continued, the working groups examined a web of complicated measures in seeking to surmount national differences. A French paper prepared for a March meeting in Paris cataloged the subjects, from harmonizing taxes on market exchange and regulating the transit of firearms to providing for the expulsion of illegal immigrants and cooperation on policing and information exchange. Among the proposals was creating a list of countries that posed "a migratory flow problem"—countries whose nationals would be classified as "undesirables."[83]

In April meetings in Brussels and Bonn, points of concern included the meaning of the phrases "short term" and "long term" as used in a draft of the treaty and the legal status of the "political declaration" as it would affect state autonomy. There was also debate on whether a review within the cabinet of each state would be required prior to the signing of the treaty.[84] Ongoing revisions of the text clarified the technical meaning of terms such as common borders and cross-border traffic.[85] In May, a telegram from West Germany to the foreign ministries of its partner countries noted that agreement had been reached on many issues, including capital controls, tax exemptions, and consultation before entering into agreements with nonmember countries.[86] One of the sticking points, between the Netherlands and West Germany, was on permits for the transit of commercial goods, a standoff ended by leaving the approval of licenses to bilateral agreements.[87] The Dutch prime minister, Ruud Lubbers, wrote to Helmet Kohl pledging to sign the accord, saying that benefits for commercial truckers as well as everyday travelers would come from a "Europe without borders."[88]

Protection of national sovereignty prevailed except in a single area of dispute—democratic consent. Because Dutch law made intergovernmental agreements subject to legislative approval, The Hague had proposed that the treaty either come before national parliaments for ratification or proceed simply as a statement of political principles rather than as an international legal commitment. The other countries objected to enabling a single national parliament to block the agreement, arguing that veto power could not be ceded to legislatures of member countries.[89] Ultimately, it was France that offered a compromise providing that the treaty would apply provisionally after its signing but take full effect after ratification of a later implementing convention. The concession satisfied the Dutch, based on their view that the accord would not reach the law of nations but would be "politically binding on the governments."[90] In France, however, the effect appeared different; as a French diplomat observed to Luxembourg's ambassador in Paris, France made no distinction between the law of the nation and the obligations of intergovernmental agreements: "Take the example of Saarbrücken: it is an agreement between governments; but it commits the state." Nonetheless, the argument over

FIGURE 2.3. The village of Schengen lies on the banks of the Moselle River, at the tripoint border where France, Germany, and Luxembourg meet. As the location of the signing ceremony for the agreement abolishing border controls and enabling free movement, it embodied the natural integration of Western European nations. Credit: Gilles Bassignac / GAMMA RAPHO

sovereignty seemed rather abstruse to some, although "an exquisite legal discussion."[91]

With a signing date set for June 14, the treatymaking concluded. The timing complied with the Fontainebleau principles, as well as with commitments made by the central negotiating group in Brussels. All that remained was the signing ceremony, which would occur a week before the summer solstice. A memorandum from Waldemar Schreckenberger about the ceremony circulated in West Germany's foreign office in early June. He returned to the question of international law, explaining that the treaty would necessarily acquire greater force than would a political declaration. "We need the binding effect under international law because many specialized agencies of the federal government and the states are involved in the implementation of the agreement," he wrote, adding that only the Dutch were uncertain on this point.[92] Furthermore, the political part of the accord would begin to apply immediately, "undoubtedly on June 15." His plan was to drive from Germany into France, stopping in Strasbourg, and from there to Luxembourg, to take part in the signing *am Dreiländereck*—at Schengen's triangle border.[93]

The Schengen treaty was signed on the afternoon of Friday, June 14, 1985. The occupation of Paris had begun on that day, in 1940, as the Germans entered the city; now the treaty was to open borders and expand the space of free movement as an embodiment of a Citizens' Europe envisioned by the wartime adversaries. The diplomats of the central negotiating group met aboard the riverboat to sign a bound copy of the agreement.

At the signing ceremony, the treatymakers took satisfaction in the work they had done in less than a year's time. Robert Goebbels marveled that the accord had emerged so soon after the start of the negotiating process in February: "In less than four months it was possible to do useful work and achieve the agreement that we are going to sign."[94] But the treaty signing did not seem a remarkable moment. "It was not an extraordinary event. It wasn't a revolution. . . . There were obstacles to the principle of free movement, so it reduced the obstacles," as Catherine Lalumière later recalled. "We thought we had made life easier for people. Schengen said, 'At the borders, pass, pass, pass—we won't bother you. In principle, you can pass; and we presume that you're honest.'"[95]

Schengen was meant to be about everyday life, about crossing borders freely. Only in hindsight, as Goebbels would later say, did the ceremony's consequences become evident. "It changed everything. . . . It's because of this text that we have now the free movement of people within Schengen."[96]

The text of the Schengen treaty was anything but revolutionary. Its title was prosaic—*Agreement between the Governments of the States of the Benelux Economic Union, the Federal Republic of Germany and the French Republic on the Gradual Abolition of Checks at Their Common Borders*—and in a brief six pages the treaty enumerated thirty-three technical measures providing for cross-border free movement of persons and goods. The declaration of a general political agreement appeared in the preamble, with a few phrases of intent:

FIGURE 2.4. Schengen treatymakers, including France's Catherine Lalumière (center) and Luxembourg's Robert Goebbels (left of Lalumière), met aboard the *Princesse Marie-Astrid* on the Moselle River in June 1985 to sign the Schengen Agreement. Credit: Jean Weyrich / Photothèque de la Ville de Luxembourg

> AWARE that the ever closer union of the peoples of the Member States of the European Communities should find its expression in the freedom to cross internal borders for all nationals of the Member States and in the free movement of goods and services;
> ANXIOUS to strengthen the solidarity between their peoples by removing the obstacles to free movement at the common borders between the States of the Benelux Economic Union, the Federal Republic of Germany and the French Republic . . .

The treaty announced the guarantee of free movement across the borderless interior of Schengen not as a transformative act of statecraft but rather as a fulfillment of founding promises made by the European Communities.[97]

The treaty stated the compromise made on ratification, that the accord was signed without reservations, and the measures would apply provisionally from the day after signing, with ratification to follow. It gave deference to the role of parliaments of the Schengen countries in reconciling the obligations created by the treaty with national constitutions. It did not establish any Schengen governing institutions, providing merely for meetings at regular intervals of authorities from the Schengen countries, as a corollary of the cooperation among their police and customs officials.[98]

The treaty anticipated the complete abolition of border checks at the common frontiers of the member states and the transfer of controls to the perimeter of the Schengen area. That was a long-term goal. First, checks would be simplified, as the states expanded cooperation; then, through a longer process of harmonizing regulations, internal border controls would be eliminated altogether. The measures would take effect in stages, certain changes applying a day after the treaty's signing, on June 15; others before January 1, 1986; and still others within a year. Long-term measures would be installed by January 1, 1990.[99]

Use of a technique for "simple visual surveillance" for private vehicles at common border crossings would start immediately, on June 15, enabling the unimpeded flow of traffic as a "general rule." The green decal on the windshield the decal having a diameter of at least eight centimeters—would signal compliance with border rules for people and goods, the goods as allowed by duty-free arrangements. If needed, random checks would ensure greater control; the stricter surveillance would occur off the main road so as not to interfere with the passage of other vehicles.[100]

Provisions on the transit of goods supported the workings of the internal market, developing economic integration. For example, measures concerning the "cross-border carriage of goods by road" detailed new procedures: allowing visual checks and simplifying license rules for commercial road transport; reducing stopping times, particularly for shipping merchandise by railroad; harmonizing value-added taxes; increasing the duty-free allowance on goods and trucking fuel; and waiving controls on the weights and dimensions of commercial vehicles and on driving and rest periods.[101] A long-term measure on the movement of goods would transfer all checks from common borders to external borders or to within the territories of the Schengen countries.[102]

Other rules merged market and social principles, setting up an equivalence between goods and people as subjects of free movement across borders. The treaty required the Schengen countries to guarantee equal treatment of nationals of member states carrying goods across common borders, fusing antidiscrimination doctrine with free-market provisions in banning "restrictions on entry to the Member States of goods possession of which is not prohibited for their nationals."[103]

The pairing of goods and persons also appeared in parallel provisions on information sharing designed to protect security. A provision on using a single customs document required collecting information and tracking the cross-border transit of goods via "a systematic, automatic exchange of the necessary data." People were to be tracked similarly, under rules on using data exchange to prevent "the unauthorized entry and residence of persons" and other illicit traffic, such as "smuggling." The treaty required a unified system of data exchange on goods and people to be incorporated into the methods of simplified visual surveillance at common borders.[104]

In the treaty's technical measures lay a grant of free movement profoundly different from the guarantees of other transnational charters. Governing a great expanse of Western Europe, the treaty recognized movement across Schengen's cosmopolitan space as a freedom that transcended economic life. Schengen applied to "persons"—sometimes considered as travelers or passengers.[105] The word "worker" does not appear in the treaty; nor does work or work life or economic activity—or market. Schengen thus differed from the Treaty of Rome, which predicated the border crossing of persons in the European Community on gainful pursuits, on being economic actors in the common market, on being workers.[106] Schengen reached beyond Saarbrücken also, extending a bilateral pact into a multinational treaty.

Likewise, the Schengen treaty amplified the grant of free movement in human rights covenants, transforming a right protected within a single nation-state into a freedom allowed across a transnational territory. "Everyone has the right to freedom of movement and residence within the borders of each State," affirmed the Universal Declaration of Human Rights, adopted in 1948.[107] The

FIGURE 2.5. Catherine Lalumière, France's main Schengen negotiator, shown in 1981, when she was minister of consumer affairs, with French president François Mitterrand. Credit. Keystone-France / GAMMA RAPHO

European Convention on Human Rights restated that entitlement in a 1963 protocol providing, "Everyone lawfully within the territory of a State shall, within that territory, have the right to liberty of movement."[108] Schengen extended the principle of free movement beyond the terrain of the nation and the operation of the market into a vast cosmopolitan space.

The treaty did not use rights language, yet in opening borders, in lifting physical barriers, it allowed unprecedented liberties. The preamble spoke of "ensuring the free movement of persons."[109] That did not count as a revolution in rights; nevertheless, by simply saying, in Lalumière's words, "at the borders, pass, pass, pass. . . . In principle, you can pass," the treaty remade the doctrine of free movement. It enshrined the crossing of national borders not simply as a need of the market but as a freedom of everyday life.[110]

The free movement of people described in the Schengen treaty was indeed of the most everyday kind. For example, on the most basic easing of the flow of traffic at border crossings with use of the green decal—which was to begin immediately—the treaty declared matter-of-factly, in Article 2: "With regard to the movement of persons, from June 15, 1985, the police and customs authorities shall as a general rule carry out simple visual surveillance of private vehicles crossing the common border at reduced speed, without requiring such vehicles to stop." Some measures for the long term were highly technical, as in Article 17, which linked free movement and lifting checks at common borders with harmonizing "administrative provisions concerning the prohibitions and restrictions on which the checks are based." Others aimed simply at making tourism easier, as in Article 19, which provided for harmonizing regulations on "the registration of travelers in hotels."[111] But none provided for a cross-border right of residence envisioned by the ad hoc committee developing plans for Citizens' Europe after Fontainebleau.[112]

Certainly, many of Schengen's measures on the free movement of persons carried economic value, expressing market principles; but none limited unchecked border crossing to sellers of labor or other economic actors. Clearly, an internal market would be advanced by enabling travelers to cross borders easily while carrying goods, and to stay in hotels, and shop for duty-free merchandise. Indeed, the treaty's preamble affirmed the triad of liberties sought by the European Community since the Treaty of Rome: "The free movement of persons, goods and services."[113] But none of Schengen's provisions restricted free movement across common borders to lucrative pursuits. Rather, the treaty allowed people free movement without an explicit market value.

Schengen thus constituted a cosmopolitan European social space as well as a forum for market exchange. By removing barriers to free movement at common borders, the treaty declared the aim of the Schengen countries "to strengthen the solidarity between their peoples."[114] While contributing to economic union, Schengen laid the ground for a Citizens' Europe where the vision of social solidarity assumed freedom of movement.

By definition, the treaty afforded free movement only to nationals of the European Community. While broadly recognizing persons as free to cross Schengen's internal borders, the treaty narrowly defined persons as "nationals"—however, nationals not only of the

Schengen countries, but all nationals of all European Community countries, a category of nationality expressing an emergent concept of transnational citizenship, which would later become codified in the founding of the European Union. The Schengen treaty's preamble declared that freedom to cross internal borders belonged to "the peoples of the Member States of the European Communities . . . all nationals of the Member States."[115] In Schengen, the grant of free movement attached strictly to European Community nationality.

The Schengen treaty made explicit that free movement depended on excluding "aliens," on blocking their border crossing—across the internal and external frontiers of the Schengen area. The green decal could not be used by foreigners; as the treaty's Article 3 expressly provided: "Nationals of the Member States of the European Communities wishing to cross the common border in a motor vehicle may affix to the windscreen a green disc. . . . This disc shall indicate that they have complied with border police rules." Likewise, only European nationals would be protected by nondiscrimination rules on carrying goods across the Schengen area. The Schengen states were to harmonize rules on entry and visas and "the law on aliens."[116] The measures on illegal migration were just as explicit, barring "unauthorized entry." The treaty warned of the risks of lifting barriers at common borders, "the adverse consequences in the field of immigration and security." It stressed the need to harmonize rules for the "protection of the entire territory of the five States against illegal immigration."[117] In distinguishing between nationals and foreigners, the treaty expressly addressed the status of Berlin, a most perilous place of European border crossing, stating: "This Agreement shall also apply to Berlin."[118]

To stop the flow of foreign migrants into and across Schengen, the treaty required pairing security with freedom. As barriers came down at interior borders, allowing European nationals to pass unhindered, controls would be transferred to Schengen's outer borders and police cooperation would heighten surveillance. Concerning "the movement of persons . . . to abolish checks at common borders," the treaty's Article 17 required the Schengen states "to take complementary measures to safeguard internal security and prevent illegal immigration by nationals of States that are not members of the European Communities." The complementary security measures entailed joint policing and cooperating on extradition and exchanging information to combat crime. The only right named in the treaty—the only use of the word—applied to cross-border police activity: "Introducing a right of hot pursuit for police officers."[119] Illegal migration would be punished by unfree movement.

On the day of the Schengen signing ceremony, the treatymakers said nothing of a set of annexes appended to the accord. The annexes were composed of lists of countries seen as posing immigration risks to the European community—countries whose nationals were classified as "undesirables."[120] The lists were not inscribed in the treaty but kept confidential; treatymakers had created them during their meetings. A protocol sent out just before the signing ceremony—marked "Draft confidential agreement" and dated June 4, 1985—assured the secrecy of the undesirable country lists: "The parties have agreed in confidence on the following provisions to clarify and complete the agreement concluded among them on June 14, 1985, in Schengen."[121] West Germany had requested that the lists remain secret. Soon, when the treatymakers set to work to devise a convention implementing the Schengen accord, the lists would figure in the "fight against illegal immigration."[122]

The country lists reflected the polarities of the world in which Schengen was created; in 1985, the undesirable countries ranged from East Germany and Poland to Algeria, Yemen, Haiti, South Africa, and China.[123] Many were former colonies, indicating colonialism's influence on Schengen's security apparatus. Over time, during the drafting of the Schengen implementing convention, the country lists would grow to include more than a hundred undesirable places. Most were in Africa and Asia, and all were classified as producers of undesirable migrants.[124] On the day of the signing ceremony, the country lists secretly annexed to the treaty defined the limits of free movement in Schengen.

A day after the Schengen treaty signing on the Moselle River, checkpoints began to come down at border crossings inside the common space. The green decal process began operating, allowing simple surveillance of vehicles crossing Schengen's internal frontiers. The checkpoints left standing were grouped at certain crossings, such as Aachen / Bildchen, between West Germany and Belgium; Brûly / Gré d'Hossus, between France and Belgium; and Remich / Nennig, between Luxembourg and West Germany.[125] The advent of free movement drew some public recognition. Brief news clips about Schengen appeared in West Germany's *Süddeutsche Zeitung* and Belgium's *Le Soir*.[126] On June 15, 1985, a Dutch newspaper, *Nieuwsblad van het Noorden*, reported: "Today marks the start of easing border control."[127]

Schengen did make everyday life easier, bringing change that was not dramatic but palpable nonetheless. The differences were perceptible, even if the intergovernmental diplomacy was not. That was the memory of Françoise Gravier. "People were freer," she recalled. Their right to cross borders was no longer tied to work, as checkpoints began to disappear within the Schengen area, only months after the European Court of Justice handed down a ruling in her case, holding that the Treaty of Rome guaranteed free movement only in pursuit of economic activity. "I didn't follow Schengen closely. Not at all," Gravier remembered. "But I know it was easier to move around."[128]

There was a greater sense of feeling "like a European," simply from the experience of traveling through the Schengen countries. Like Gravier, others recalled a new ease of movement, how "the motorway became more open. You passed the customs buildings— they were still right there—but no one had to stop anymore."[129] For truck drivers, whose blockade the year before had helped propel the removal of checkpoints, the treaty meant the end of weekends spent marooned at border crossings, waiting in line to complete paperwork. It did away with the need to keep chocolates and beer stashed in their trucks, to entice customs officers to sign off on their transit more quickly.[130] "What was my experience of Schengen?" mused the Belgian long-haul driver Guy Van Hyfte. "That I was able to drive my truck." As he swept his hand forward, he whistled, recalling the swift passage across borders. "That was the advance of Schengen."[131]

Until the signing of the treaty, Schengen was a village unremarkable but for the beauty of the landscape. Goethe had visited Schengen

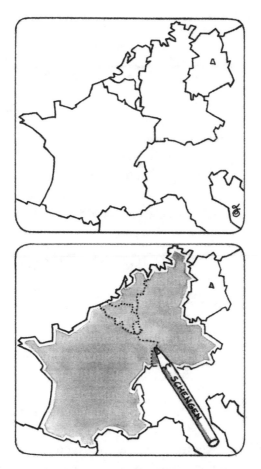

FIGURE 2.6. A 2024 drawing by Françoise Gravier, the plaintiff in *Gravier v. City of Liège*, shows how Schengen transformed the map of Europe, originally among the five countries that framed the accord. Credit: Françoise Gravier

when he was writing on perceptions of nature; Victor Hugo once drew a picture of the tower of the medieval castle that still stands near the riverbank.[132] After the Second World War, the village was renowned for its wine-making. It had never been a theater of high politics.

But in bequeathing its name to the treaty on free movement, Schengen became a landmark of European integration. Free movement across national borders became a right of European people only with the founding of the European Union, under the Maastricht

FIGURE 2.7. Victor Hugo's 1871 sketch of the tower of the medieval castle that still stands near the riverbank in Schengen. Public domain

Treaty, which provided: "Every citizen of the Union shall have the right to move and reside freely within the territory of the Member States."[133] But Schengen's creation provided an example. "The first progress of modern democracies was to abolish those internal frontiers," as a police commissioner-cum-treatymaker wrote. "The progress of the Schengen Accord is to abolish these same barriers among several countries."[134]

Schengen transcended the market paradigm of free movement, as well as the territorial limit of free movement within a nation-state. But as a laboratory of free movement, Schengen paired liberty with security—and with exclusion. It embodied the principles of Citizens' Europe, extending free movement not just to economic actors but to persons traveling across the interior frontiers of the expansive common space. But it limited that freedom to nationals of the European Community, excluding foreigners from the treaty's protections; Schengen was at once cosmopolitan and circumscribed by distinctions of nationality. And precisely because the treaty created a vast expanse of free movement, it required new techniques to safeguard security and compensate for abolishing borders inside the Schengen area. The aim of the treatymaking, as Waldemar Schreckenberger remembered the work done in 1985, was to form "a secure transnational space of free movement protected from cross-border criminality."[135]

Soon after the signing of the Schengen treaty, the everyday experience of free movement became the topic of a history lesson delivered to the Bundestag. Addressing the chamber in late June of 1985, West Germany's chancellor, Helmut Kohl, spoke of the accomplishments of the treatymaking. He placed Schengen within an account of postwar history as a path toward ending divisions among nations. He traced an arc of change, leading from the past, "the inferno of the Second World War"—to the present, "the opportunity to be free in Europe"—to the aspirations of the future, "to bring Europe closer to citizens in everyday life." As a harbinger of progress, the chancellor pointed to the "opening of borders our citizens have always demanded." The world of Citizens' Europe would be founded on "the permeability of borders."[136]

It would take Schengen's treatymakers until the end of the decade to draft the convention implementing free movement: to define the rules for abolishing internal borders and securing external borders and restricting border crossing by foreign migrants. By then, Europe had changed profoundly. The fall of the Berlin Wall meant that the Schengen treaty would apply in a world of newly permeable borders, raising the everyday stakes of free movement.

3

A Return to the
Moselle River

ON JUNE 19, 1990, European diplomats returned to the village of
Schengen to sign a treaty implementing the accord on free movement. Again, the treatymakers gathered aboard a boat on the Moselle
River for the signing ceremony. The 1985 accord was a brief charter
of intent; but the 1990 convention detailed a set of complex technical
measures designed to balance freedom and security, and it took half
a decade to negotiate. People and goods, borders, migration, visas,
crime, police cooperation, surveillance, and information exchange—
all were addressed in the implementing convention.[1] One subject
new to the convention was the treatment of asylum seekers in Schengen, a problem of free movement that blurred the boundary between
preventing illegal immigration and protecting human rights.[2] But
all of the convention's terms were recast by the prospect of German
reunification brought by the fall of the Berlin Wall.

The convention would not enter into force until ratified by the
national parliaments of the Schengen states. Nonetheless, the symbolism of the treaty signing, as a rite of European union, drew trib-
utes to free movement. The Dutch statesman Pieter Dankert, who
led the final work on the convention, acclaimed the opening of borders. "Schengen is here and I am happy," he said. "Forty years ago
who would have imagined that France, Germany, almost reunified,
and the Benelux would sign an accord here at Schengen." National

antagonisms had given way to "an accord that guarantees the abolition of borders." Dankert spoke of Schengen as an example for Europe, "a model, a laboratory . . . for the enterprise 'free movement of persons.'"[3]

But the ritual return to the Moselle River was preceded by years of conflict over the treatymaking that produced the implementing convention. The conflict emerged among the convention's authors, but also beyond their closed-door meetings, as critics raised concerns about national sovereignty, the status of foreign migrants in the Schengen area, and the secrecy of negotiations that lacked democratic safeguards. Particular difficulties had arisen, Dankert said, in reaching an "agreement on asylum procedures." And the treatymaking was disrupted by the fall of the Berlin Wall and the upheaval in Eastern Europe in the autumn of 1989, which made Schengen, "by including a future reunified Germany . . . also a historic agreement." It had been assumed that guaranteeing "free movement of people in the context of Schengen" would unfold swiftly, spurring the completion of the common market, but this became unfeasible, Dankert explained. "An agreement on the abolition of internal borders is a bit more complicated than was thought at the beginning."[4]

The impetus for drafting the implementing convention—defining the technical aspects of dismantling borders—was heightened by amendments to the Treaty of Rome introduced by the Single European Act of 1986. Under the act, the European Community set a deadline of January 1993 for completing a common market in which goods and people would move freely.[5] Simultaneously, the European Commission had affirmed Schengen as a laboratory that would establish "measures necessary for the liberalization of the circulation of passengers and goods."[6]

Again, as in 1985, the intergovernmental treatymaking was not made public.[7] Again, too, the authors of the implementing convention were diplomats—but also police commissioners, jurists, and economists. Their protracted negotiations, as well as inquiries made by human rights groups, became a forum for plainspoken arguments about the practical meaning of free movement.

The signing of the Schengen convention propelled globalization at the end of the twentieth century, underwriting the free flow of persons and goods in a cosmopolitan space, serving as a promissory note for Citizens' Europe and the single market. During the treatymaking, as world events intruded on the Schengen laboratory, the terms of the convention were shaped by both the lifting of the Iron Curtain and the surge of migrants coming into Schengen from Africa, Eastern Europe, and the Middle East. Provisions on German reunification were added to the convention's final drafts. But measures on asylum and visa rules were contested from the outset, reflecting the force of colonialism's afterlives in circumscribing free movement.[8] At the signing ceremony, as the treatymakers celebrated the abolition of borders, security forces restricted a demonstration mounted on the banks of the Moselle River by SOS-Racisme of Luxembourg, the Radical Socialist Party, and a Committee of Support for Political Prisoners of Western Europe. Schengen had become not only a landmark of European union but a site of human rights agitation.[9]

The path of the Schengen countries to the 1990 convention was thus more arduous than expressed by the acclamatory rhetoric of a Schengen laboratory. It was "a long march toward free movement," as a French treatymaker said.[10] The conflicting principles of freedom and exclusion were most explicit in the drafting of the convention's articles on asylum. With the fall of the Berlin Wall, which cast into question Schengen's eastern frontier, the conflict grew more acute. As a border symbolic of the Cold War world became permeable, the liberal principles of free movement and cosmopolitanism that animated Schengen appeared also to pose its deepest challenge.

In 1985, the Schengen treaty signing had drawn little notice worldwide, but news of the implementing convention flashed through Europe and across the Atlantic. *Le Monde* proclaimed a "Europe without borders."[11] The *Luxemburger Wort* hailed "the historic signing of the treaty."[12] American newspapers announced, "Welcome to Schengenland," and recorded the rhetoric at the signing ceremony: "Our agreement is a model . . . for the free movement of people."[13] But the accounts also noted the fault lines that had emerged over immigration, asylum, and fortification of Schengen's external borders.[14] As Belgium's *Le Soir* observed, Schengen evoked conflict over "human rights in . . . a high-risk area."[15]

More obscure, however, was the diplomacy that produced the convention, and the intergovernmental paperwork that went into its drafting. Again, working groups dealt with the movement of people and goods, security, customs, and transport, while newly addressing asylum and data exchange. On questions of sovereignty and security, ministries of justice and interior exerted influence equal to that of foreign ministries, as the treatymakers determined the rules of free movement. The gist of their work was pairing free-dom and security—reducing the risks of dismantling borders with compensatory measures enhancing surveillance and policing—and completing the convention before the deadline to achieve Europe's single market. As the Luxembourg delegate Robert Goebbels recalled, "We had to invent everything."[16]

The politics of the Schengen countries influenced the treatymak-ing, as did developments in European Community law and policy, which informed the drafting of the convention's provisions on border crossing and mutual assistance in security matters, all of which entailed reconciling supranational and national authority. Doctrine established by supplements to the Treaty of Rome, European Com-mission white papers on the single market, and decisions of the European Court of Justice guided the long course of negotiations. The treatymaking occurred outside the framework of Community institutions but alongside European planning for the free movement of goods and people within the single market.

During the negotiations, center or center-right parties held power throughout the Schengen area, except for in France, where François Mitterrand, a Socialist, held the presidency, while cohabi-tating with a neo-Gaullist prime minister, Jacques Chirac, and his conservative parliamentary majority from 1986 to 1988.[17] Domestic politics in France were unsettled by the rising electoral threat posed by the National Front, which had captured seats in the National Assembly by 1986. As anti-immigrant populism gained influence in France, guarantees of security and sovereignty took on still more significance in the Schengen negotiations.[18] In West Germany, as well, xenophobia was on the rise, with hostility aimed especially at migrant laborers and asylum seekers; far-right violence targeted *Wirtschaftsflüchtlinge,* or economic refugees.[19] Across the Schengen states, there was rising fear of international terrorism, leading to a counterterrorism summit held in Paris in 1987.[20]

France led the drafting of the Schengen convention, as the first nation to chair the central negotiating group after the approval of the 1985 treaty. At pivotal moments of treatymaking, as in 1989, it also chaired the critical working group on the movement of persons. West Germany remained a powerful partner, but as reunification absorbed Kohl's government, France was said to be instrumental to Schengen's "locomotive" effect on European integration, especially in taking on a dual presidency in 1989, of the Schengen group in the early part of the year and of the Council of Ministers in the latter.[21] States were sovereign in the Schengen laboratory, which gave no rulemaking authority to supranational European Community institutions but allowed observer status at negotiations to the European Commission.[22]

On the very day of the first Schengen treaty's signing, June 14, 1985, the European Commission called for swift action to achieve economic freedom under the Rome Treaty. That would require "abolition of obstacles to the free movement of persons." The directive came in a white paper on "completing the internal market," which criticized the persistence of barriers, "the setbacks and delays of the past." Without addressing Schengen's creation, the white paper advised unrestricted cross-border market exchange, explicitly equating the free movement of persons and merchandise: "What is true for goods, is also true for services and for people."[23]

Such an equivalence—between the exchange of goods and the circulation of human beings—had framed the Community's approach to free movement since the Rome Treaty's adoption. Although not approved, the 1975 proposal on the passport union had treated free movement as a corollary of a common market, "in respect of individuals similar to . . . a Customs Union in respect of goods."[24] A decade later, the white paper reiterated that citizens of the European Community must have freedom to "exercise their economic activities" across borders. Like Schengen, however, the white paper recognized the free movement of persons—not only economic actors—as a factor of a common market. "Measures to ensure the free movement of individuals must not be restricted to the workforce only," stated the white paper, explaining the costs of border controls that put a "burden on industry" and impeded the growth of a "broader and deeper Community."[25]

The white paper cited the Fontainebleau conclusions—the commitments made to both a Citizens' Europe and a common market—in affirming free movement as imperative to European political economy. It offered "a double reason for removing the physical barriers—an economic reason and a political reason." By this dual reasoning, Europe must become "more than a free trade area," for that would not use "economic resources to the maximum advantage," nor would a customs union alone "satisfy the aspirations of the people of Europe." It had become axiomatic that economic integration required political and social union, assuring the cross-border transit of people and merchandise and inspiring faith in the liberal project as Europe sought greater influence in a bipolar world.[26]

The white paper also ran parallel to Schengen principles in stressing the risks of free movement and the need for compensatory security measures. Crucially, it acknowledged the limits of the Community's supranational authority, noting that "protective measures" fell outside the scope of integration defined by the Rome Treaty. Accordingly, new security techniques—"means other than controls at the internal frontiers"—would fall within state sovereignty.[27]

As work began on the implementing convention, a trio of Schengen countries—West Germany, France, and the Netherlands—joined with Britain and Denmark in bringing a case to the European Court of Justice to defend the authority of nation-states over the movement of persons within their territory. The case, *Germany and Others v. Commission*, challenged a European Commission rule that required European Community nations to consult with each other, as well as with the Commission, when regulating immigration from non-Community countries. The Commission was the defendant, supported by the European Parliament. The litigation gave the court reason to delineate the boundaries of supranational and national sovereignty, and to decide whether jurisdiction over immigration, involving issues of both security and employment, belonged to Community institutions or to member states.[28]

The Commission rule concerned the movement, labor, and living conditions of non-Europeans. It required Community review of measures governing foreign workers and their families, with respect to "entry, residence and employment, including illegal entry, residence and employment," as well as "equal treatment in living and working conditions" and the "voluntary return of such persons to their countries of origin."[29] Such issues were also addressed in the Schengen treatymaking, and the aim of the Commission rule was "harmonization of national legislation on foreigners," a central aim of Schengen.[30]

But in *Germany v. Commission*, the plaintiff countries objected that regulating the movement of foreigners was a national prerogative. Their argument underscored a problem likewise critical in the negotiations over the implementing convention—that migration implicated security concerns at the heart of national sovereignty. The grievance of the plaintiffs was procedural, directed not at the aim of harmonization but at rulemaking by the Commission that trespassed on state power. As France argued, "policy on foreign nationals . . . involves questions of public security for which the Member States alone are responsible."[31] The plaintiff countries claimed sole authority to share or withhold information, a capacity that the Schengen states would eventually institutionalize through a transnational system of data exchange.[32]

In a 1987 decision, the European Court of Justice struck down the Commission rule because it reached beyond economic activity—beyond a market paradigm of movement. The court distinguished between the jurisdiction of European institutions and the authority of nations, defining the areas of governance belonging to each. Migrant work came within the supranational power of the European Community, while security fell exclusively within the authority of nations. Because immigration lay at the intersection of these distinct spheres of sovereignty, jurisdiction would vary by circumstance. Rulemaking on foreign migrants would lie within the framework of Community cooperation only when work was at stake, involving the "Community employment market."[33]

In *Germany v. Commission*, as in *Gravier v. City of Liège*, the court tied the Rome Treaty's grant of cosmopolitan power to market activity. The questions at stake were different: the scope of the

European Commission's power, rather than an art student's free movement. But both cases concerned the link between border crossing and the labor market. And, in both, the court defined the rights that attached to economic life—the rights of the European Community in *Germany v. Commission*, the rights of individuals in *Gravier*.[34] It rejected the claim that immigration regulation was noneconomic. But it was an overreach of Commission authority, the court found, to impose rules aimed at nonworkers, at "immigrant communities in general without distinction between migrant workers and other foreigners."[35] Outside of economic life, control over the movement of persons remained the prerogative of states.

The judgment both reiterated that work formed the basis of the European Community's power to govern migration and established that control of the noneconomic movement of persons belonged to states. The court expressly affirmed the authority of Community countries to govern migration "by adopting national rules or by negotiating international instruments"—a finding that may have been a tacit recognition of the ongoing Schengen treatymaking.[36] For the doctrine set forth in *Germany v. Commission* offered a legal foundation for the Schengen countries in claiming authority to negotiate an international instrument abolishing border controls and balancing security with free movement.

While the European Court of Justice was still weighing the rival claims to sovereignty in the case, the European Community sought to advance both economic and political unification through the Single European Act. Adopted by Community member states in 1986, and entering into force a year later, the act supplemented the Rome Treaty and hewed to the white paper's directives in setting a deadline of December 31, 1992, for completing the internal market, "an area without internal frontiers."[37] The European Commission explained that Schengen and the Single European Act had the "same goal," enabling the free movement of goods, people, capital, and services, with the Schengen treatymaking illustrating the "political credibility of the objective of abolishing controls at the internal borders."[38]

The Single Act's provisions did not directly invoke Schengen, yet the commitment to removing internal frontiers signaled that free movement, as in the Schengen area, would extend to all citizens, whether workers or not. The act endorsed "the European idea," pledging not only to complete the internal market but also to "improve the economic and social situation" and promote unity and "freedom, equality and social justice," and "principles of democracy and compliance with the law and with human rights." In amending the Rome Treaty, it anticipated a borderless regime where people would cross frontiers as freely as goods, their liberty no longer conditioned on economic activity. But the act also addressed security, seeking "co-operation on questions of European security."[39] It was a plan built on the principles of Schengen.

The Single Act paired the achievement of the internal market with enhanced Community authority. It accelerated Council of Ministers decision-making on the internal market by providing for majority approval rather than unanimity. At the same time, it protected national authority "to promote the free movement of persons" by cooperating outside Community institutions—implicitly, as in the Schengen treatymaking. A political declaration appended to the act applied explicitly to foreign migrants: their "entry, movement and residence."[40]

The Single Act emerged alongside Schengen's development at the intergovernmental level. A deregulatory, free-market agenda had been a European priority since the global recession of the 1970s, when West Germany began pressing for new proposals to reduce trade barriers. A decade later, that effort expanded when Mitterrand sought to shore up his domestic influence by embarking on a European turn. Together, then, France and West Germany sought European integration that would extend beyond the 1984 Saarbrücken Agreement. Notably, one of the diplomats guiding France's pursuit of the internal market was the Schengen treatymaker Catherine Lalumière. Perhaps it was no coincidence that the Commission published the white paper on the internal market on the day of the Schengen treaty's signing.[41]

The stakes of the work on the Schengen implementing convention became increasingly evident to European planners bound by the timetable set by the Single Act: completing the internal market by the end of 1992. A Commission memo expressed the significance assigned to Schengen for the internal market's achievement by warning, as the negotiations dragged on, that, "If the Schengen

5 . . . fail, this will be interpreted as the impossibility of arriving in 1992 at the suppression of controls on people in the Community and will thus have political consequences."[42] As Pierre de Boissieu, an official in France's foreign ministry, explained in a report interpreting the Single Act's effect on foreigners, the rules on border crossing remained to be determined. "Who is guaranteed the right of free movement?" asked de Boissieu, who would later become an architect of the Maastricht Treaty. "This question has only been asked recently about people; it has been asked for 30 years about goods, services and capital."[43] The delayed reckoning reflected the limits of the Rome Treaty's market paradigm, and therefore the absence of Community law guidance on rights of noneconomic free movement. Altering Community law would be a formidable task, requiring conditions satisfying each member country, as Lalumière noted at a meeting on the internal market.[44] Instead, Schengen would set the precedent for a novel body of rules governing the free movement of people and defining the bearers of that right.

The Single Act specified neither the significance of nationality nor the role of member states in realizing free movement. The act's free movement provisions spoke broadly of "persons"—not European nationals alone. That denoted, as de Boissieu wrote, "persons who are in the territory of the Community." In other words, abolishing internal border controls would make national distinctions inoperative, allowing the "free movement for all goods, services, capital and persons . . . whatever their nationality of origin." Put simply, "free movement is, unless otherwise decided, totally independent of nationality questions." That left member states with rulemaking authority to control free movement inside their borders.[45] As a model, Schengen would produce the norms for freedom and control, as well as for intergovernmental cooperation and national autonomy, in advancing the completion of the internal market.

When the Single Act came into force in 1987, drafts of the Schengen implementing convention had not yet been made public. But records of the negotiations stressed the reciprocal relationship between dismantling borders inside the Schengen area and achieving closer European union by the 1992 deadline. That was the gist of a French memorandum titled "A Step Towards a Citizens'

Europe: The Free Movement of Persons." It advised that Schengen was "very useful to Europe," an "active Laboratory that gave rise to innumerable meetings, developments, drafts." Yet reconciling supranationalism and state sovereignty created "difficult points," where free movement guarantees appeared in conflict with national security protections, encumbering a "long march . . . toward a Europe without borders."[46]

On June 14, 1988, the Schengen treatymakers marked the third anniversary of the signing of the Schengen accord by gathering in Remich, a village on the banks of the Moselle River, just north of Schengen. Without ceremony, they took stock of the progress made on the implementing convention. It was still unfinished, after three years of work, but a press communiqué promised that a draft would be done later that year, announcing that the text was far along, with much accomplished in the "fields of police and security as well as of the movement of people and goods."[47] The public communiqué contrasted with the secrecy of the negotiations.

Almost a year later, a French diplomat appeared before the European Commission to explain why a convention was not yet complete. "For the implementation of this free movement . . . the elaboration of a convention which, at the moment I am speaking to you, has reached a point where I cannot tell you that it is complete, but I can certainly assure you that it is almost complete," said Émile Cazimajou, France's inter-ministry coordinator for free movement, on behalf of the Schengen countries. The difficulty was finding agreement on security and safety—"so-called compensatory measures"—to pair with removing borders: "This explains why we lost a little time." But he vowed that like "pioneers . . . veritable trailblazers on virgin land," the treatymakers were not at "risk of losing ourselves in swamps from which we may never get out."[48]

From the outset, the treatymakers viewed Schengen as an area of risk—where free movement across common borders intruded on the security and sovereignty of nation-states. The work of allaying that risk dissolved the consensus achieved so rapidly in 1985. Devising measures to balance freedom and security, from reinforcing external borders to harmonizing national rules on the movement of people and goods, led to five years of intergovernmental disagreement. The conflict disrupted the schedule that had been set by the Schengen negotiating groups: a convention signing ceremony in 1988, followed by ratification in 1989, with the treaty entering fully into force by January 1, 1990.[49]

From the outset, too, Schengen's risks were associated with foreign migrants, especially from countries whose nationals were classified as undesirable. On the movement of persons, the 1985 accord had envisioned long-term "measures to safeguard internal security and prevent illegal immigration." It fell to drafters of the implementing convention to hedge the risks posed by foreign migrants who, once inside the Schengen area, could scarcely be distinguished from European travelers. "Neither has their nationality written on their face," as Cazimajou curtly told the French foreign ministry in 1988.[50] Nor was the difference between lawful asylum seekers and illegal migrants facially apparent.

That indeterminacy compelled new ways of controlling persons in Schengen's transnational area of freedom. Again, the treaty drafting dealt with the transit of goods, capital, services, and persons, but it was dominated by devising rules for external borders, asylum, and visas, as well as for data exchange through what became the Schengen Information System. The anxiety was about the border crossing of foreigners, such as the journey of a stateless Palestinian who voyaged as a stowaway from Morocco to France, where he worked as an itinerant laborer for some years, and then traveled by train to Belgium, where he worked briefly as a painter, and then took a train to the Netherlands, where he was denied asylum, and then went to West Germany, and later to Britain, where he was also refused asylum and sent back to the Netherlands. Finally, he left Europe, stowed away on a ship bound for Australia.[51] But his passage had been free across Schengen's borders.

Work on the implementing convention followed the procedures used for the 1985 accord. A central negotiating group again led the planning, which was parceled out to working groups. A group on the movement of persons dealt with borders, and a security group with harmonizing criminal codes, joint policing, and judicial assistance. Others managed goods, customs, and transport, addressing issues ranging from value-added taxes to use of the green decal on windshields. There was a taskforce on illegal immigration, and four subgroups, whose responsibilities included public health and public morality, focused on the transfer of controls to Schengen's external border. An editorial committee produced drafts of the convention.[52]

Always the work remained closed to public view, with access allowed only to observers from European Community institutions, and never to international human rights organizations. Even when aiming to harmonize national asylum rules, while adhering to the 1951 Geneva Convention on the Status of Refugees, the Schengen working groups did not involve the United Nations refugee office. But delegates from the Schengen countries—state secretaries and officials from justice, foreign affairs, and interior ministries—convened every six months, under a rotating presidency, to deliberate on the terms of the treatymaking. Their summits coincided with domestic initiatives, as each state directed police officials to increase the "monitoring of migratory flows."[53]

The secret lists of the undesirables occupied a central place in the treatymaking, as the work on the convention slowly unfolded. By the autumn of 1985, the governments of West Germany and France were deploying the lists as part of the effort of dismantling borders, as recorded in a memorandum titled "Strengthening Controls on Nationals of Sensitive Countries on the Matter of Irregular Migration." The Benelux states were advised to do the same in preparation for a meeting in Brussels later that year.[54] The lists specified the countries whose nationals would be subject to strict common visa rules to enter any Schengen state, guiding the harmonizing of disparate national visa requirements. The technicalities of visa rules, a seemingly banal topic, were critical to securing Schengen's external borders, and therefore to the provisions of the implementing convention, establishing not only the terms of entry but also the privileges of sojourn, residence, and access to employment and social benefits. By the end of 1985, the working group on the movement of persons had sent out a memo on "Issuance of Visas to Third-Country Nationals Posing Security Problems."[55]

Confidential communiqués proposed common measures for surveilling migrants from countries posing a "risk of illegal immigration." Proof would be required of legitimate travel, such as inspection of intimate ties as a barrier against marriages of convenience, or documentation of an intent to exit, such as a return ticket. And data was to be shared among the Schengen countries on yearly visa requests.[56] Particular scrutiny was aimed at migration from former French colonies in Africa, as treatymakers honed the implementing convention as an instrument of racial exclusion. A West German memorandum noted that a main reason for imposing a visa obligation on non-Europeans "was that illegal immigration to France is becoming so great in more and more former French colonies that France itself has to abolish visa freedom."[57]

An approach proposed by the Benelux states was a ranking of risk, classifying countries whose nationals were undesirable by the level of danger posed in the areas of illegal immigration and national security. A "major risk" would be a 1; a "moderate risk" a 2; and a "latent risk" a 3. A secret memo of November 1985, dealing with the lists of the undesirables, explained that the rankings would assist in compiling a "common list," bringing greater uniformity to national rules. Countries assigned a 1 in both categories—as major risks in security and illegal immigration—included Morocco and Tunisia, as well as Iran, Iraq, Poland, and Suriname. Others, such as Ethiopia and Afghanistan, received a 1 for illegal immigration but only a 3 for security. Still others, such as East Germany and Egypt, had a 1 for security, with the risk of illegal immigration still unranked. Countries whose nationals were undesirable spanned the globe, but nearly half were in Africa and the Middle East.[58]

But there was disagreement on which countries would be subject to which restrictions, as well as on the procedures for checking visa documents and refusing entry. By 1988, discrepancies in national visa rules threatened to derail the negotiations. A draft of the convention troubled the French interior minister, Pierre Joxe, who rejected language that would hold any Schengen state responsible for foreign migrants not subject to a visa requirement. "As long as the states party to the Schengen Agreement cannot agree on a common list of countries subject to the visa requirement," Joxe wrote, "France cannot consider easing the controls exercised on its common borders on foreigners outside the Community."[59] By 1989, migrants from all but four of the countries whose nationals were classified as undesirable had been placed under visa obligations for entry into the Schengen area. Of the remaining four—Yugoslavia, Colombia, Singapore, and Malaysia—Yugoslavia (ranked as a major risk for illegal immigration, and as a moderate risk for security) proved most controversial. That was because West Germany opposed subjecting its nationals living in Central and Eastern Europe to visa requirements.[60]

Still, there was no disagreement that free movement in Schengen would be a right guaranteed only to citizens of European Community member states—or, for a limited time, to foreigners allowed a visa to enter. Distinctions of nationality unaddressed in the Single Act took precedence in the Schengen planning, for dismantling borders always was meant to entail the exclusion of undesirable immigrants. So, too, there was fixed agreement on balancing security and freedom in opening internal borders. Consider the affirmations at a 1986 meeting of coordinators of free movement. "More freedom means more security," avowed West Germany's Waldemar Schreckenberger, viewing Schengen as a "European space." France's Bernard Bosson advocated restrictive asylum and visa rules for "reinforcing security." As Robert Goebbels declared, "Questions of security take priority."[61]

Yet the rifts over visas exposed deeper strains of conflict. A Bonn meeting of the central negotiating group in 1987 failed to reach consensus on security protections. Rules on East German nationals, controls at external borders, requirements that foreigners report their movements within Schengen—all were of "capital importance" yet presented "serious difficulties," wrote Émile Cazimajou.[62] At a summit of Schengen negotiators the year before, it had become apparent that France and West Germany no longer spoke with one voice. France dwelled on terrorism and "security problems"; West Germany on "large influxes of people seeking asylum," with its interior minister, Friedrich Zimmermann, warning that there was "no adequate instrument" to deal with the entry of refugees from Palestine, Iran, Ghana, Pakistan, and Bangladesh.[63]

The question of German nationality deepened the rifts, a question shaped by geopolitical conflict outside of Schengen's borders. West Germany proposed exemptions from common visa rules for East Germans who would disavow allegiance to the Soviet Bloc and "renounce their identity" in order to hold West German passports. But other delegations hesitated to recognize a transcendent German patrimony, with echoes of the expansionist concept of *Lebensraum*, or living space, while also hesitating to have "a public confrontation on such a delicate issue."[64]

The legacies of empire also sharpened conflict over the question of accession to the Schengen treaty, casting doubt on Schengen's capacity to withstand its own territorial expansion. As the negotiations dragged on, Italy submitted an accession bid in 1987, adding to the stakes of immigration restriction.[65] The central negotiating group welcomed Italy's overture—"an important contribution to the achievement of an internal European market"—but member states were wary of Italy's population of undocumented immigrants, by some counts totaling almost a million.[66] Thus Schengen's external border, at the mountainous, 320-mile frontier between France and Italy, became a focal point in the play of intergovernmental diplomacy preoccupied with blocking migratory flows from countries whose nationals were undesirable. In particular, France opposed admitting Italy, as a landing place in the route from the Maghreb countries to the heart of Europe, fearful of a tide of migrants from its former colonies crossing through the Schengen area.[67] Italy's accession was postponed, but it gained observer status at the negotiations after assenting to new visa obligations for countries from North Africa. Meanwhile, the treatymaking stalled over the risks of free movement.[68]

Slowly, Schengen took shape as a system of dualisms—of freedom and security, unity and exclusion, and cosmopolitan exchange and national autonomy. The principle of state sovereignty, upheld by the European Court of Justice, was repeatedly invoked by the Schengen countries in aiming to harmonize national codes on migration, asylum, trade, criminal justice, and privacy, which undergirded the opening of internal borders. Because there was no Schengen federal authority, "no supranational structure at the Schengen level," as the Benelux secretary general wrote to France's foreign ministry, it was "the signatories" that possessed full "political responsibility."[69]

Safeguards for national autonomy underlay many proposals for pairing freedom and security. For example, the working group on persons sought a common fund, with each state tithed, to cover

MAP 2. By the spring of 2024, Schengen had come to include twenty-five of the twenty-seven European Union members, encompassing more than 400 million people and twenty-nine European nations.

the costs of deporting unwanted migrants, but national authorities would retain control over decisions on the removals and carry out the deportations.[70] As a communiqué in France's interior ministry explained, "Each party undertook to exercise particularly vigilant control."[71] The point was that harmonized migration rules would depend on the will of each Schengen state.

But matters of sovereignty were not easily settled. For instance, minutes from a meeting of the working group on persons held at The Hague in January 1987 recorded conflict over the allocation of power over security at Schengen's perimeter. France and West Germany sought state authority, arguing that "control of external borders must remain within national jurisdiction." Conversely, the Benelux countries called for greater integration, drawing on their experience with union, proposing border control as "a common task with a view to the most uniform application of the conditions of entry of foreigners." A compromise preserved national control of external borders based on rules to be decided in concert.[72]

By the autumn of 1988, the working group on persons had drawn up a set of "indispensable conditions" for completing the removal of internal border controls. Chief among them were asylum, immigration regulation, and visa requirements, all of which involved disputed issues of sovereignty and security. By the end of the year, the conditions were still unresolved, and a draft of the convention still unfinished.[73] On both security and sovereignty, France's defense officials especially were unyielding, insisting on the authority to maintain controls on foreigners at all French borders until an effective security system was in place.[74] There was intense controversy over the obligation of foreigners to declare their entry into the Schengen territory: immediately, at the external border; or later, in the course of transit through the interior. When agreement could not be reached on the more restrictive procedure, a declaration at the external border, France rejected provisions to remove all internal controls, at least for a transition period, preserving barriers to free movement. The reason was "respect for . . . national legislation."[75]

Meanwhile, Schengen statespersons enthused about fulfilling a "moral contract" that would form lasting bonds of "symbolic value."[76] Such rhetoric, however, was tempered by pragmatic statements of the value that lay in abolishing borders and the limits required in a space of freedom. It was the accumulation of "economic benefits" that would outweigh the "disadvantages associated with the free movement of people," as the Dutch minister of justice explained at a conference on terrorism in Europe.[77] And it was axiomatic that European unification involved the power to exclude, as

France's interior minister assured his country's parliament, noting that measures would be taken to limit the circulation of foreigners as an unintended consequence of opening internal borders.[78] Free movement's benefits would be reserved for Europeans.

1989 was the year the Schengen convention was supposed to have been ratified; instead, the treatymakers contrived to explain why it was still unfinished. A report prepared for a meeting of the Council of Ministers titled *Free Moment of People in Europe* summed up the dilemmas that plagued the work: "We have to reconcile two contradictory imperatives," it began, explaining the need to protect "the security of a territory that's very exposed, especially by its multiple land borders, to illegal immigration, to terrorism," but also the need to prevent "conditions that undermine certain essential guarantees with respect, for example, to civil liberties, judicial procedure."[79] The central negotiating group admitted that a most basic rule was still unresolved—whether internal controls would be removed only at land borders, or also at seaports and airports.[80]

1989 was also the year the question of asylum in Schengen emerged from the closed doors of the treatymaking. The secrecy was lifted at a conference of the European Council on Refugees and Exiles, in the Dutch city of Zeist, where Pieter Dankert, a principal Schengen negotiator, delivered the opening address. He spoke hopefully of Schengen's significance in advancing the internal market and abolishing border controls, but bleakly of the right of refugees to move as freely as goods, capital, and European nationals. There was a "tightening of controls on aliens," an inhospitality to "refugees out of all parts of the world. . . . What is going on has less to do with the needs of a Europe free of internal borders than with the wish of most West European countries to stop the flood." Nor would Schengen offer new safeguards; for Dankert revealed that the convention's draft provisions left national refugee laws untouched, warning that state sovereignty in a borderless territory "cannot be in the best interest of asylum seekers."[81]

The refugee conference made public that Schengen would not bring unity to asylum rules within the European community or introduce less restrictive norms. All too clearly, the negotiators had found that refugee questions complicated both free movement and intergovernmental cooperation. "Asylum issues are very sensitive," as France's Cazimajou wrote to Delors, the European Commission president, soon after the conference, while averring that Schengen's provisions would adhere to humanitarian law.[82] Yet agreement on a common approach proved elusive, and a sense of crisis pervaded the negotiations, as thousands of asylum seekers entered the Schengen area. In West Germany and France, the increase was greatest; in 1989, some 150,000 refugees were projected to arrive in West Germany, and 50,000 in France, their ranks having doubled in just a few years' time.[83]

At least one point was undisputed: that the Schengen countries must prevent "refugees in orbit"—migrants circulating across the area lodging "multiple or fraudulent" asylum claims—and that the problem lay in free movement. The aim was to hold just one state responsible for each claim. But were asylum seekers entitled to move freely inside Schengen while waiting for a decision in their cases? On entering a Schengen country, should a refugee be at liberty to cross into others, like the Palestinian who stowed away from Morocco to France and then traveled through Belgium, the Netherlands, and West Germany? Should an asylum seeker have free movement across Schengen?[84]

The problem of asylum deepened the split between France and West Germany. And it set in relief the conflict over the scope of state sovereignty in controlling borders and the movement of persons. Inconsistences marked the approach of each of the most powerful of the Schengen countries. While seeking a privileged status for East Germans entering its territory, West Germany sought restraints on the mobility of asylum seekers from elsewhere in the world, in order to stop the "attraction effect." By contrast, France, while promoting immigration restrictions, sought wide latitude for asylum seekers once inside Schengen, in order to create parity: "In the name of the principle of free movement . . . the applicants could circulate on the territory of all states party to the Schengen Agreement." All of this was recorded in an April 1989 paper titled "Franco-German Relations and Questions Concerning the Right to Asylum" prepared for a meeting of European ministers.[85]

The growing distance between France and West Germany prolonged the treatymaking, bogging down the march toward a borderless Europe. It occurred against the landscape of a bipolar world, whose geopolitics influenced the work in the Schengen laboratory. By 1989, more than half of the asylum seekers in West Germany came from countries in Eastern Europe, making the ambit of free movement inseparable from the borders drawn by the Cold War.[86]

In November 1989, the fall of the Berlin Wall halted the work on the Schengen convention. Earlier that autumn, when a final text seemed almost complete, a signing ceremony had been set for December. But the revolutionary events sweeping across Eastern Europe, auguring German reunification, disrupted the treatymaking.[87] Never had the pressure of events fallen so powerfully on the effort of abolishing controls, as the dismantling of the Berlin Wall and the decline of the Cold War order recast the risks of free movement. For the Schengen countries, compensatory security appeared all the more essential, not only to fortify external borders but to control the flow of people across a newly porous continent, where barriers were suddenly collapsing. A new German question arose, as Schengen's perimeter shifted eastward.

The status of a divided Berlin had figured in the Schengen treaty of 1985, a year that saw the opening of paths toward détente between West and East, with the beginning of Russian *perestroika*.[88] But as the Schengen states declared free movement a basis of Citizens' Europe, the line dividing Germany remained fixed in place, symbolized by the wall that cleft Berlin. That meant part of the divided capital would belong to Schengen, even though West Berlin shared no borders with other Schengen countries. "This agreement shall also apply to Berlin," stated Article 29 of the 1985 treaty, which gave West Germany sole authority to alter that provision.[89]

In principle, the problem of Berlin had been settled; yet it reemerged—*Das Berlin-Problem*. The city operated as a valve of movement out of Eastern Europe, an entrepôt for "asylum tourism," as West German diplomats balefully explained in 1986. By then, a rise in asylum requests and visa overstays was said to be overwhelming the country, but consular officials warned that a crackdown on migrants would be impractical because of the volume of traffic moving between Berlin and West Germany. There were also legal hurdles, for West Germany's postwar Basic Law gave constitutional protection to the right of asylum.[90] The country's diplomatic corps viewed Schengen as a source of solutions for the Berlin problem, anticipating a harmonizing of refugee policy across Europe; the "project of dismantling borders," wrote Hanspeter Hellbeck, who had been an envoy in France before serving in East Germany, was at once the "asylum seeker question."[91]

Initially, Berlin was just a minor theme in the drafting of the implementing convention. At a 1987 meeting of ministers and state secretaries of the Schengen countries, held in Berlin to honor the city's 750th anniversary, the concern was not with the perplexities of free movement there; rather, the summit, led by Waldemar Schreckenberger, approved common controls at Schengen's external borders.[92] Within the working groups, recurring arguments on the status of German nationals in Eastern Europe led only to assurances that free movement guarantees would "apply to Berlin."[93] The Berlin border drew little attention.

In the autumn of 1989, that changed. As revolutionary unrest swept across Eastern Europe, thousands of East Germans escaped to Hungary, Austria, Poland, and Czechoslovakia, seeking asylum in West German embassies. Mass protests convulsed the German Democratic Republic, with more than a million East Germans taking control of the streets, and calling for democracy, civil liberties, and the freedom to travel.[94] With the fall of the Berlin Wall, on November 9, the city took on extraordinary significance, standing at Schengen's external frontier, its borders opened to the free movement of people from Eastern Europe. As the razing of the wall began, as many as three million East German people crossed into West Berlin and nearby towns.[95]

By early December, West Germany had proposed a declaration reaffirming that the Schengen treaty would cover Berlin. It sought approval from the Bonn Group, an influential circle of diplomats from France, Britain, the United States, and West Germany formed after the war to consult on the German question. A telegram of December 4, 1989, titled "Accord de Schengen: 'Question de Berlin,'" sent from Bonn to France's foreign ministry by the French ambassador, Serge Boidevaux, stated that the Berlin declaration would not alter the rights and responsibilities of France, Britain,

FIGURE 3.1. The uprisings that breached the Berlin Wall in the fall of 1989 delayed the Schengen treatymaking as diplomats reckoned with the prospect of German reunification and the expanded scope of free movement. Credit: Eric Bouvet / GAMMA RAPHO

and the United States with respect to the city. If the Bonn group approved, the Schengen convention could be signed on December 15. The Americans and British advised further consideration of the role of the allies in Berlin while agreeing that Schengen should proceed. Suddenly, the Berlin problem drew transatlantic attention to the Schengen treatymaking.[96]

Pressure to complete the Schengen convention came from the European Community. It was a moment of inflection, warned officials of the European Commission, in early December. "The importance and potential fragility of the Schengen Agreement are such that any delay in signing entails real risks," advised staff of the Commission. Postponing Schengen would thwart the internal market's completion, opening "a Pandora's box" that would upset the timetable of the Single European Act.[97]

Meanwhile, the scale of human movement, which breached the Berlin Wall, brought the treatymaking to a standstill. As the unrest deepened in Eastern Europe, so did the rupture between

West Germany and France. West Germany aimed to make a unilateral declaration that East Germany was not "a foreign country" in relation to West Germany, so that East Germans would not count as foreign nationals, and that all Germans entering West Germany would be exempt from visa rules and residency requirements across the Schengen area. As an annex to the convention, the declaration would not require the signature of the other Schengen states. But France dissented, viewing peremptory German reunification as "the problem."[98] The conflict was still unresolved when an invitation to the convention signing went out from Luxembourg on December 12. It would be held at the chapel of the Schengen castle, on December 15. After a brief press conference, the delegations would dine at Léa Linster, a Michelin-star restaurant in the nearby town of Frisange.[99]

But the German question resisted a quick settlement, and the convention's signing was postponed on the eve of the ceremony. It was West Germany that sought the delay, "an additional time of reflection."[100] At a meeting in Bonn, the central negotiating group agreed to the principle of one German nationality, as declared in the Basic Law of the Federal Republic. That meant all German people would come within the free movement guarantee, not only to enter West Germany but to cross the entire Schengen area without visas, provided that West Germany adhered to the convention's security regime.[101] But there was no agreement on the declaration that East Germany was not a foreign country with respect to West Germany. For that principle would extend the Schengen area across a border that ran from the Baltic Sea to Czechoslovakia, bringing about forty thousand square miles of Eastern European territory within the guarantee of free movement.[102]

Schengen's German question appeared fateful also because the implementing convention would become the first international treaty to govern the status of East Germany after the fall of the Berlin Wall.[103] As the European Community impatiently awaited the convention, on December 15, the day the signing was supposed to have occurred, the Schengen countries instead issued a "Common Declaration" of intent to resume negotiations. That work would address outstanding issues, from asylum to the transport of goods.[104] But according to a French telegram of December 18, sent to the foreign ministries of the Schengen countries as well as the governments of Italy, Spain, and Britain, the "failure of the negotiation" stemmed from "difficulties of German origin."[105]

The French telegram recounted the breakdown of the treaty-making, how the revolutions of 1989 transformed the work of guaranteeing free movement in a borderless Europe. As originally conceived, Schengen assumed a divided Germany, but the prospect of reunification would mean a renewal of an expansive German power on the continent, an outcome unforeseen by the other Schengen states. "The German difficulty had to do with sorting out the question of the relations between the FRG and the GDR in the climate created by the unexpected events in the Eastern European countries," wrote the telegram's author, Émile Cazimajou. Despite efforts at negotiation—"tête-à-tête between the heads of the German and French delegations"—the impasse could not be overcome. "Finally, in the night of December 13 to 14, Bonn took the initiative to break off the discussion."[106] At that point, the other Schengen foreign ministries rejected a West German request for a December 15 meeting in Luxembourg to hear a statement on the opening of the inter-German border. Just days earlier, the convention had seemed nearly complete, a prelude to achieving the internal market. But as 1989 ended, there was "a peripeteia"—a sudden change of circumstance—a "failure of Schengen."[107]

The irony of a treaty to dismantle borders faltering because of a wall's collapse was not lost on the European press. "Europe without borders stumbles in Schengen," reported Le Monde, and the obstacle was "paradoxically, freedom to come and go reclaimed in the East."[108] The migration of people across Eastern Europe's frontiers into West Germany directed attention to the unfinished treaty and the dual aims of removing internal controls and securing external borders. Already, by the summer of 1989, Schengen had drawn adverse commentary. A project meant as a "signal for the citizens of Europe," found the Deutsches Allgemeines Sonntagsblatt, was going "down the drain."[109] The criticism came from across the political spectrum: impatient European integrationists; refugee advocates calling for greater protection for asylum seekers; Euro-skeptic nationalists claiming that Schengen would attract too many immigrants. The negotiating groups took note of the opinion: "Detri-

mental to human rights," "repressive," "dangerous laxity." Such indict-
ments, wrote Cazimajou, filled the "press campaign . . . against the
Schengen Agreement."[110]

Berlin appeared as an example of Schengen's contradictions,
even before the wall fell.[111] The city was said to symbolize the impossibility of reconciling free movement with security, a place that if
made borderless would open Schengen to migrants from the Eastern Bloc and enforce surveillance abridging civil liberties. A piece
grimly titled "Big Brother Replaces the Customs Officer," which ran
in *Der Spiegel*, argued that the delay of "borderless Europe" laid
bare a "gap between political wishful thinking and practical reason,
between Euro-populism and the sense of the possible."[112] Tracking
the emancipatory "exodus from the GDR," *Der Spiegel* highlighted
the counter-logic of security in the Schengen countries: "The free
ride for free citizens has far-reaching consequences for . . . national
search methods."[113] In France, fears mounted that Schengen would
cause "serious dangers . . . immigration by Turkish workers . . . the
arrival of Germans from the east," as a Gaullist leader, Bernard-
Claude Savy, wrote in a piece distributed by the political club Avenir
et Liberté (Future and Freedom).[114] *Présent*, a Catholic paper with
close ties to France's National Front, greeted the fall of the Berlin Wall by attacking supranationalist "euphoria" and secret diplomacy by "obscure technocrats." The diatribe, titled "In the Fog of
the 'Schengen Territory,'" appeared alongside a polemic attributing
the "immigration-invasion" to a set of dangerous beliefs: "Socialist
ideology, globalist ideology, third-world ideology, the ideology of
so-called anti-racism, the soft ideology of totalitarian humanitari-
anisms . . . the religion of modern times, of our dechristianized and
secularized times." *Présent* warned, "We sail in full fog."[115]

Le Monde used a different atmospheric metaphor in depicting
Schengen's failings, describing the December postponement as a
"Thunderbolt on the Borders." It traced the events leading to the
collapse of negotiations on East Germany—the disagreements on
security and asylum measures, influenced by a "growing sensitivity
of the public . . . to non-European immigrants, particularly of Muslims, whether Turks, Iranians, Pakistanis or North Africans"—and
then the upheavals in Eastern Europe, the "iron curtain a museum
piece." Schengen presented an "irony of history . . . the arrival of

East Germans on the European scene delays the disappearance . . . of border controls"; it was a treaty struck by a "thunderbolt."[116] As one anonymous negotiator said, "Schengen may well go down in history as the city where Europe failed."[117]

But other treatymakers spoke openly of the German question's meaning for Schengen, how it raised uncertainty about European union, about free movement, about whether Schengen's eastern border would "pass on the Elbe or on the Oder," as Luxembourg's Robert Goebbels told the press. "The way things are going, it will be better to be a commodity or capital . . . than a person."[118] The difference between the border crossings of goods and people had become acutely apparent with the Berlin Wall in ruins. As Goebbels cryptically observed, commodities had value, unlike rights.

By the spring of 1990, the treatymaking had resumed, following the first—and only—free parliamentary elections in East Germany, which brought the Christian Democratic Union to power and advanced its program of reunification with the West.[119] A proposal from the West German delegation to the central negotiating group called for returning to a text of the convention drafted late in 1989, but with three essential amendments: inclusion of East Germany; waiver of visa requirements for Eastern Bloc countries undergoing democratic change; and greater protection for individual privacy in keeping with national law. "Recent developments have led the Federal Republic of Germany and the German Democratic Republic to consider unification," wrote Lutz Stavenhagen, a high-level adviser to Kohl, urging that a "unified Germany will remain incorporated in the European Community."[120]

Notably, the East Germany amendment would bring a country once classified as undesirable, its people ranked as a major risk to security, inside Schengen's expanse of free moment. The overture of West Germany anticipated support for reunification and the reform efforts taking hold in the countries of Eastern Europe. "Already today, during the transitional period, the GDR is not considered as a foreign state in relation to the Federal Republic of Germany. . . . German nationals may freely enter the Federal territory and move freely within the Schengen area," Stavenhagen wrote, adding that West Germany intended "soon to abolish visa requirements for Hungarian and Czechoslovak nationals."[121]

Again, however, France was troubled by the German question, taking a guarded approach to the prospect of reunification and East Germany's entry into Schengen. Its opposition to a resurgent German nationalism was a focus of a state visit at the Elysée Palace in Paris, in January 1990, when French president François Mitterrand met with British prime minister Margaret Thatcher. According to British diplomatic correspondence, marked "Secret and Personal," Mitterrand had recounted the December impasse on Schengen, saying that "Chancellor Kohl had telephoned him to complain that the French were dragging their feet and must sign the agreement. He had given the necessary instructions to the French Interior Minister, only to find the next day that the Germans were insisting on expanding the agreement automatically to include East Germany. The Germans could not be allowed to throw their weight around like this." Reportedly, Mitterrand spoke apprehensively of West Germany's aims, unsure if Europe was prepared for German expansionism, recalling the dangers of the past:

> The sudden prospect of reunification had delivered a sort of mental shock to the Germans. Its effect had been to turn them once again into the 'bad' Germans they used to be. They were behaving with a certain brutality and concentrating on reunification to the exclusion of everything else. . . . Of course the Germans had the right to self-determination. But they did not have the right to upset the political realities of Europe.

Aspersions on "bad Germans" aside, Mitterrand saw inevitability in West Germany's claims. "There was a logic to reunification," he allegedly said. "It would be stupid to say no to reunification. In reality there was no force in Europe which could stop it happening. None of us were going to declare war on Germany." For France, therefore, realism would mean East Germany's incorporation into Schengen.[122]

Nothing in West Germany's bid to resume negotiations betrayed the depth of the bilateral tensions with France, nor the opposition from other Schengen countries. On the contrary, it proposed that Schengen would illustrate—within an international European framework—the new status of Germany, on the verge of reunification. "Schengen plays a signal role in this context," Stavenhagen argued. "In the case of the unification of the two German states, it will apply equally to the present territory of the German Democratic Republic."[123]

By this reasoning, Schengen presented the answer to the German question, its guarantees of freedom and security offering a model for the European Community in recognizing German reunification. By April, the central negotiating group had agreed to sign the convention while still amending its provisions. In May, the terms of a compromise on Germany were still being refined, as were the rules for the movement of foreigners. Meanwhile, the United Nations High Commissioner for Refugees was made privy to a draft of the treaty. In early June, a briefing paper by the Churches Committee for Migrants in Europe, an ecumenical advocacy group, noted that the international refugee agency had declined to certify that Schengen complied with the Geneva Convention on asylum. By then, however, the treatymaking had ended.[124] The convention would be signed on June 19, 1990.

———————————————

On the eve of the return to the Moselle River for the signing of the Schengen convention, the removal began of the remains of the Berlin Wall.[125] Both events were laden with symbolism for European union. The razing of the last ruins of the wall honored the revolutionary claims to free movement; the return to the riparian border reaffirmed the emergence of a borderless Europe.

But the implementing convention never used the phrase "free movement of persons." A charter of rules and regulations, it offered no declaration of a political intent to achieve a closer union of the European people, unlike the 1985 Schengen treaty. Tersely, the convention's preamble stated an agreement to take further measures to remove internal controls—"to abolish checks at their common borders on the movement of persons and facilitate the transport and circulation of goods at those borders"—invoking the economic aims of the Treaty of Rome and the Single European Act: "That the internal market shall comprise an area without internal frontiers."[126] Of the convention's 142 articles, most set forth security measures limiting movement.

A settlement of the German question appeared at the end of the convention—as declarations anticipating reunification, which were adopted at the time of signing. West Germany had prevailed in most of its proposals, above all on East Germany. A joint declaration by all the Schengen countries assented to West Germany's unilateral declarations, recognizing that East Germany was "not a foreign country in relation to the Federal Republic of Germany" and that rules on border checks with foreign countries would not apply between the two German countries. The joint declaration also foresaw German reunification and Schengen's eastward extension: "After the unification of the two German States, the scope of the Convention shall under international law also extend to the current territory of the German Democratic Republic."[127] But visa rules would not be waived for German nationals in Eastern Europe, even when all German territory belonged to Schengen.

A guarantee of a right of Europeans to unchecked border crossing within Schengen did not appear in the convention; nor was it promised by the 1985 treaty. Yet the abolition of internal borders plainly carried a new grant of freedom to the people of Europe, envisioned in the 1985 affirmation that lifting controls would enable the "free movement of persons," meaning "nationals of the Member States of the European Communities"—a freedom that would help bring closer union, "solidarity between their peoples by removing obstacles to free movement."[128] The absence of such liberatory language in the convention reflected the weight given to security in implementing the abolition of border controls, the compensatory measures argued over during the long years of treatymaking.

The provisions of the convention dealt mainly with restricting border crossing. Key terms were defined—"border crossing point" and "aliens" and "asylum seeker" and "third state" and "border checks"—preliminary to articles enumerating rules on security cooperation, asylum, visas, and regulations for the transit of goods.[129] All were quite technical, unadorned by statements of ideological purpose.

The restrictions on movement began in the convention's first chapter, "Crossing Internal Borders," which allowed unchecked passage across Schengen's internal borders, including land borders, seaports for ferry connections, and airports for internal flights.

But the grant of mobility was qualified by a provision allowing the Schengen countries to reassert national checks at internal borders, for a limited time, as required by "public policy or national security." A related provision allowed national "exercise of police powers" regarding foreigners within the Schengen territory. Other provisions left intact national laws on identity papers: "the requirement to hold, carry and produce permits." All recognized the authority of the Schengen countries to restrict internal border crossing on grounds of security.[130]

Rights language rarely appeared in the convention, and never with respect to free movement, even of Europeans. Rather, it applied principally to national autonomy in matters of security. The convention affirmed state sovereignty, protecting the right of the Schengen countries to control foreign migrants within their borders, decide asylum cases, restrict the geographical scope of visas, police border crossings, and close their borders. It also upheld international norms in recognizing asylum rights and data privacy, but such rights did not guarantee free passage across the Schengen territory.[131]

Nor did the convention create a Schengen government or judiciary. Rather, its regulatory system for dismantling internal borders relied on harmonizing national law, assuring the power of the Schengen countries to control their external borders and regulate immigration. Therefore, the convention did not provide for adjudicating between the claims of states and persons; for example, in the case of an asylum seeker expelled from a Schengen state, redress would be sought in national courts or European tribunals. Schengen's only administrative body would be an executive committee, composed of members from each member country and responsible simply for guiding the implementation process. Nor did the convention include a clause sought by the European Commission recognizing the supremacy of Community law. Rather it fused intergovernmental cooperation with national sovereignty: "Uniform principles, within the scope of national powers and national law."[132]

In great detail, the convention defined the system of checks on cross-border movement at external borders—measures to block "aliens." The checks would apply not only to people but to the objects they carried and the vehicles in which they traveled: "All persons shall undergo at least one such check in order to establish their identities. . . . In order to detect and prevent threats to the national security and public policy. . . . Such checks shall always be carried out on aliens." Additional measures extended the restrictions on movement into Schengen's interior, providing for transborder cooperation in identifying and tracking suspects. To combat high crime—murder, rape, arson, human trafficking, breach of gun laws, aggravated robbery—the convention allowed police to cross Schengen's internal borders. "Aliens" would be traced through Schengen's information system; arrests and prosecution would be governed by national law.[133]

On visas, too, the convention struck a compromise between common principles and national law. A common visa would be used for short stays of fewer than three months, if foreigners met the common conditions to cross borders—a valid reason, proof of subsistence, and no record of security breaches—with expulsion required upon the visa's expiration. Exceptions to the common rules would be allowed only when compelled by "overriding reasons of national policy." But national visa rules would continue to regulate longer stays in the Schengen countries. The convention did not include lists of foreign countries whose nationals would be exempt from visa rules to enter Schengen, or rankings of countries by risk, or annexes of undesirables; those inventories remained concealed in the papers of the negotiating groups.[134]

The movement of goods, considered less freighted with security risks, occupied only a brief part of the convention. Free trade would be facilitated by "simplification" of regulations on the transit of merchandise across internal borders. The convention waived inspections for some goods, such as fresh fruit and cut flowers, while encouraging customs clearance inside each state, not at common borders, in order to accelerate procedures ranging from commercial transport permits to animal health checks. But it allowed states to retain robust controls aimed at stopping the transit of dangerous goods and the spread of disease. Where the convention did closely regulate goods, the rules supported crime prevention, blocking the traffic in illegal drugs and guns. There were detailed restrictions on acquiring, using, manufacturing, transporting, and dealing in firearms and ammunitions; prohibited devices included "automatic firearms" and "firearms normally used as weapons of war." Overall, however, the convention introduced modest technical adjustments to lift burdens on commerce: for goods carried across internal borders, it reduced the "number and intensity of checks," and for goods crossing external borders, it instructed harmonizing rules based on "uniform principles."[135]

Security was paramount in the procedures for ratifying the convention as well as for allowing accession to the treaty. The convention did not define common rules for ratification—simply providing for deposit of the affirming national instruments in Luxembourg and the treaty's entry into force within three months after the completion of ratification. But a joint declaration made implementation dependent on security, stipulating that the treaty would enter into force only when "checks at external borders are effective." The convention also provided for Schengen's geographical expansion through accession agreements, but accession was restricted to member states of the European Community, a limit consistent with Schengen's barriers against foreign migrants.[136]

Persons, goods, borders, security—in each area, the convention resolved the questions that had divided the treatymakers. It settled the disagreement on tracking the transit of foreigners by requiring declaration of entry into the territory of each Schengen state but allowing states to set terms for the declaration. Despite West Germany's opposition, it required checks at all external borders; and it required penalties for transport companies and any persons abetting illegal migration for "financial gain," despite the objections of the Netherlands. On cross-border pursuit by the police, called hot pursuit, it required ending the chase when requested by the state where it occurred, a compromise proposed by France that reconciled security with the inviolability of state territory, and that would advance accession by Italy and Spain, states with criminal justice systems at variance with procedures in the founding Schengen countries. On cross-border information flows, the convention called for harmonizing national civil liberties protection with common European principles.[137]

On asylum, the convention recognized the guidance of the European Community but stopped short of a common approach. A joint declaration stated the resolve of the Schengen countries to make "an inventory of national asylum policies with a view to the harmonization thereof," echoing a European Council conclusion of 1989.[138] Otherwise, the settlement reached on asylum simply allocated responsibility for reviewing asylum requests. The convention assigned responsibility to the country that granted a visa, but if no visa existed, to the country of first entry. When no proof of first entry existed, responsibility would lie with the country where the asylum request occurred.[139] With these common rules, the Schengen states aimed to stop asylum seekers from circulating in search of refuge while establishing accountability for arrivals within their borders, creating a duty to "take back an alien" who exited without authorization. While affirming international commitments under the Geneva principles, the convention imposed no standards for asylum decisions, deferring to state sovereignty.[140] Its rule of first entry was likewise the core principle of the 1990 Dublin Convention on asylum, framed by the European Community amid the Schengen treatymaking. But the Dublin Convention cited a "common humanitarian tradition" of refugee protection, as well as the aim of free movement—"the objective of an area without internal frontiers within which the free movement of persons will be guaranteed."[141] By contrast, the Schengen convention expressly declared a right to exclude—"to refuse entry or to expel asylum seekers"—and bound no Schengen country to offer refuge on its soil.[142]

What left no imprint on the Schengen convention was protest against its asylum rules—neither the criticisms raised at the Zeist refugee conference, nor the arguments made at a human rights convocation held in Strasbourg in the autumn of 1989, as migrants from Eastern Europe surged across the borders of the continent. The Council of Europe convened the Colloquy on Human Rights without Frontiers, attended by European dignitaries as well as by delegates from asylum agencies. A draft of the Schengen convention had found its way, unofficially, to colloquy participants, who claimed that its rules violated fundamental rights.[143] For the asylum principle embraced at the colloquy was *non-refoulement*—no return to a place of danger—a tenet of international law.[144] But that was not Schengen's principle, it was objected. Rather, with asylum seekers, European countries played "games of ping-pong in which they forget the balls are human beings," a cruel game that had become a "'philosophy'... in the draft agreement drawn up by the Schengen Group."[145] It was said that Schengen's "shadow" darkened the "European fortress."[146]

Evidently, the protest did not much redraw the terms of the convention, yet it gave further publicity to Schengen's paradoxes. Indeed, the outcry at the human rights colloquy was all the more notable because the meeting's host was the Schengen treatymaker Catherine Lalumière, who had become secretary general of the Council of Europe. Her address to the assembly of statespersons and advocates for asylum seekers dealt bluntly with the exclusion of foreigners from a borderless Europe. The impulse was "to put a brake on this immigration," she said, "by the Schengen group, for instance... avoiding being swamped by what is felt to be too great and dangerous an influx." It was worth remembering Europe's past—to take a "lesson from history and not confer the benefits of our major instruments mostly on nationals." Perhaps with a measure of resignation, however, she spoke of the limits of free movement: "We tend to keep human rights for our own nationals."[147]

On the day of the signing of the Schengen convention, a final act appended a set of declarations to the treaty. The declarations completed and clarified the provisions, as had the annexes added to the 1985 treaty listing the countries whose nationals were undesirable. Unlike the secret annexes, the convention declarations were public statements enshrined in the convention, covering everything from the trade in tulips to German reunification, checkpoints at external borders, and the catalog of national asylum practices. None affirmed the principle of *non-refoulement*. Nor did the term "human rights" appear in the convention.[148]

Almost a year after the signing of the convention, with the ritual return to the banks of the Moselle River, the central negotiating committee sent a dossier of materials on ratification to the parliaments of the Schengen countries. The dossier traced the emergence of the treaty, how a Schengen spirit arose from the Fontainebleau conclusions, developed as a pledge of intent under the 1985 accord, and became realized in the implementing convention. Without explaining the lengthy treatymaking, or the conflict that broke into the open after the fall of the Berlin Wall, it acclaimed Schengen as a "regime of free movement, valuable for all persons," which was created not as "an enclave within the borders of the European Community" but rather as a laboratory for a "vast space of freedom."[149]

By then, the Schengen countries included Italy, and the candidacies of Spain and Portugal were under consideration, and discussions with Austria had begun.[150] Germany, Austria's neighbor to the north, had been reunified into one country. When debate on the convention's ratification began in national parliaments, in 1991, the Schengen area extended east to the Oder River and south to the Mediterranean Sea. Countries whose nationals were classified as undesirable—Czechoslovakia and Poland to the east, Algeria, Libya, and Tunisia to the south, all designated security risks—were now proximate to the external borders of Schengen's space of freedom.[151]

At the time of the convention's signing, the difficulties of ratification had been foreseen. In his ceremonial address, Pieter Dankert had introduced a cautionary note, alluding to differences over asylum procedures and the legitimacy of the intergovernmental method.[152] While he spoke, a protest on the riverbanks agitated against racism and immigration restrictions.[153]

Ratification of the implementing convention would bring into the harsh light of parliamentary debate opposing views of Schengen—a cosmopolitan space embodying the principle of free movement or a European fortress abridging the guarantee of human rights.[154] It would involve a democratic public reckoning with the transformative measures negotiated behind closed doors, from abolishing internal frontiers to surveilling asylum seekers through cross-border information exchange. Starting in France, ratification would test whether the Schengen treaty conformed with both national law and international covenants.

4

A Problem of Sovereignty

"PARLIAMENT IS HERE, not on a boat!" objected a French law-maker. The National Assembly, the lower house of France's parliament, was in session in June 1991 in the Palais Bourbon in Paris, debating ratification of the Schengen treaty. The lawmaker denounced his own government for approving the implementing convention a year earlier, aboard a boat on the Moselle River. He was Pierre Mazeaud, a deputy from the neo-Gaullist Rally for the Republic, which claimed the mantle of French republicanism. The signing of the treaty aboard a boat, at the border of three countries, evoked for Schengen's authors the cosmopolitan spirit of the guarantee of free movement. For critics, however, it symbolized the flaws of the treatymaking process, as well as the dangers of a Pan-Europeanism that eroded national identity and democratic self-government. A riverboat was no replacement for parliament.[1]

The ratification process completed the treatymaking begun in 1985. It brought Schengen out from the shadows of diplomatic deliberation and into the spotlight of democratic debate. Dilemmas that had shaped the closed-door negotiations became overt in parliamentary encounters with the treaty, first in hortatory appeals from the European Parliament and then in formal consideration by national parliaments, which commenced in France in 1991. Those dilemmas—about sovereignty and democracy, national security and individual rights—figured in arguments both for and against Schengen.

Ultimately, no national parliament stood in the treaty's way. None rejected the terms of free movement as set forth in the implementing convention, not even the Dutch, whose delegation had expressed misgivings about endorsing the 1985 accord without parliamentary approval. All five original member states ratified the convention by the summer of 1993, allowing for its full entry into force in 1995, a decade after the first signing ceremony on the Moselle River, and five years after the reprise on the *Princesse Marie-Astrid*.[2]

But approval of the implementing convention was no banal bureaucratic process. It exposed tensions that marked the treaty's principal objectives—the pairing of freedom and security, and the joining of humanist and market justifications for European unification. As if forming a closing act to the short twentieth century, that time span from the outbreak of the First World War to the dissolution of the Soviet Union, the parliamentary debates that produced majorities for Schengen featured bitter disputes over the meaning of national sovereignty in a new international era inaugurated by the fall of the Berlin Wall.[3]

The conflict was most evident in France. It was the first Schengen country to take up ratification, in the summer of 1991. And it was the site of a court challenge to the treaty that summer, as well. The complaint, before the nation's highest constitutional authority, the Conseil Constitutionnel, drew on principles of national republicanism developed in the postwar era by the eminent jurist Michel Debré, a Gaullist who had drafted the 1958 French constitution.[4] France was also where Schengen's quiet diplomacy had first aroused outrage, capturing the attention of the press. *Le Figaro*, in the spring of 1989, had decried "the Schengen secret."[5] In the chambers of parliament, in the courtroom, and in the press, Schengen's guarantee of free movement made France host to dissension over the boundaries of democratic sovereignty and individual rights.

Opposition to the Schengen implementing convention was by no means limited to France. The European Parliament also scrutinized the treaty, concerned with matters ranging from the secret diplomacy to the status of asylum seekers. But nation-states controlled the fate of the intergovernmental agreement. Critics in Germany argued that the exclusionary terms of the treaty, the concept of the "undesirable," evoked their country's gravest sins. Belgium's Council of State, the country's highest administrative court, queried provisions of the convention granting decision-making authority to the Schengen Executive Committee, an unelected body of ministers from Schengen states. A similar body in the Netherlands, the Dutch Council of State, at first advised lawmakers not to ratify the treaty because of a rule requiring only the country of first entry to adjudicate an asylum claim. It was the first time that the council had advised against ratifying an international accord.[6]

The opposition to Schengen involved a common claim: that the treaty trespassed on state sovereignty. Critics on the left insisted on the need for state authority to welcome noncitizens—as refugees deserving of asylum. Critics on the right sought to preserve the authority of the state to exclude noncitizens—as unwanted immigrants. As Luxembourg's delegate, Robert Goebbels, recalled, "The left claimed we were building a 'Fortress Europe,' and the right saw the Schengen area as too open an area where criminals could circulate and where people could immigrate too easily."[7] Criticisms of the treaty appeared contradictory to its authors but shared a premise that Schengen undermined the sovereignty of the nation.

Ultimately, the opposition failed. The parliamentary dissenters in the Schengen countries could not overcome support for a borderless Europe. France's legal challenge foundered in court. In both France and Germany, the treaty's adoption brought constitutional reform of national asylum law. But the conflict over ratification laid bare the dualisms of Schengen's logic, producing democratic debate over free movement as a right of European nationals. The treatymakers had expected discord; as a French negotiator, Hubert Blanc, wrote in the *Revue du Marché commun et de l'Union européenne*, all who contributed to "the Schengen work had the feeling of facing a difficult challenge."[8] But they did not fully consider, despite the years of work drafting the rules, how the treaty would transform the powers and obligations of the Schengen states by dismantling internal borders. Nor did the treatymakers envision how the shifting boundaries of national authority—physical and

juridical—would give rise to nativist as well as humanitarian critiques of free movement.

———————————

Schengen's authors argued that the treaty embodied aspirations for
transnational citizenship. But the treaty never gained the approval
of a transnational demos. Because it was negotiated among member states, Schengen only required the endorsement of national
parliaments. It was not subject to the jurisdiction of the European
Community.

Still, the European Parliament, the sole Community institution
directly elected by citizens, did not fall silent on the accord. European
lawmakers issued a series of statements on Schengen, beginning
before the implementing convention became final. A pair of non-
binding resolutions expressed the body's evolving perspective on
Schengen, as disapproval gave way to qualified support for abolishing internal border controls. Anticipating the treaty's extension across
Europe, the lawmakers grappled with Schengen's consequences
for free movement and human rights. They also made evident the
absence of a democratic check on the Schengen regime commensu-
rate with its transnational reach.

In November 1989, at a moment of crisis for Schengen planning,
as the Berlin Wall came down and Germany prepared to ask its
partners for a delay in the signing of the implementing convention,
European parliamentarians implored national governments not to
approve the treaty, citing concerns over democracy and humanitarian law. A resolution adopted by the European Parliament warned of
the adversity of refugees and migrant workers controlled by "legislation of the most restrictive state." That would be the consequence
of harmonizing national immigration laws, with no state obliged
to offer more than minimum protections—whether in sheltering
refugees under the 1951 Geneva Convention or in safeguarding the
privacy of Schengen denizens, newly vulnerable to techniques of
surveillance and cross-border information sharing. Particularly,
the parliamentarians protested that the treaty, without democratic
input in its drafting and without provision for democratic oversight

in its operation, imposed rules designed to reassert control over the movements of people. Freedom of movement would be a dead letter, for some persons.[9]

The parliamentary resolution accused the treatymakers of cloaking their work, of seeking to "avoid a parliamentary and public debate on a vital question for the Europe we want to create and for the legal protection and fundamental rights of people living in the European Community." Members of the parliament condemned the hidden negotiations, claiming that the closed-door diplomacy contravened the practices of the European Community, "that secret debates, without democratic parliamentary control over questions of police, internal and external security and immigration . . . violate conventions and democratic principles." They warned that the erosion of humanitarian norms would grow more widespread, predicting that the treaty "would probably be adopted by the rest of the Community," with the achievement of the single market. By their lights, Schengen would become a laboratory for the breach of democratic principles and human rights.[10]

As the treatymaking continued, but on a continent transformed by the fall of the Berlin Wall, European lawmakers altered their stance. They did not go so far as to endorse ratification, but did not oppose it, either. As drafts of the implementing convention began to circulate informally, a new resolution of the European Parliament, put forth in March 1990, restated concerns about human rights, especially with respect to asylum and individual privacy. Yet it also offered the parliament's "collaboration and its support" in the realization of free movement while calling on other Community institutions to take a more active role in providing guidance. The parliamentary resolution advised the European Commission, as "guardian" of international treaties, to ensure respect for humanitarian law.[11]

The European Parliament therefore advanced claims about sovereignty, arguing that supranational institutions were necessary to protect human rights. Above all, it sought safeguards to balance new modes of cross-border security introduced by Schengen. The parliamentary resolution emphasized the "necessity of guaranteeing respect for human rights on the Community level, parallel to the development of cooperation among police services and the exchange of information." Notably, as the resolution stated, those very measures—police cooperation and information exchange— were among the aspects of the Schengen convention that had given rise to "important national reservations" requiring a delay in approval. Moreover, the parliament posited, Schengen was not the endpoint, but only "a preliminary step toward the free movement of persons," a path that would lead to freedoms extending across the European Community. Here, it invoked the conclusions on Citizens' Europe reached at Fontainebleau in 1984, describing free movement as a fulfillment of Fontainebleau's promise, and the civic principles of Citizens' Europe as a hedge against Schengen's illiberal tendencies.[12]

Concern about democracy animated the European Parliament's statements on Schengen. The concern would resonate with alarm voiced by lawmakers about "racism and xenophobia," amid debate about how to protect non-Europeans living in the Community.[13] Such debate culminated in a 1991 report by the European Parliament's Committee of Inquiry that examined human rights and free movement while expressly criticizing the drafting of the Schengen rules "behind closed doors," finding that the secret treatymaking both undermined democracy and gave priority to exclusion, making a travesty of free movement and fueling racism. "This not only hampers democratic control, but also gives the idea that the various bodies are working on a very delicate and huge problem, namely how to keep as much as possible new migrants, refugees and asylum seekers out of the Community," the report stated. "Migrants and ethnic minorities often use the expression 'Fortress Europe' to characterize the proposed policy." To entitle Europeans alone to free movement across borders "could well feed racist ideas and could be used to legitimize certain forms of racist behaviour." According to the report, Schengen put at risk matters of principle: "Policies related to freedom of movement are not merely administrative arrangements . . . but deal with fundamental human rights."[14]

Anxiety about democratic accountability echoed at the highest levels of European institutions. The European Commission's vice president, Martin Bangemann, delivered an indictment of Schengen's intergovernmental process in an appearance before the European Parliament in 1991. He directed blame at national governments for transforming the blueprint of Citizens' Europe into a treatymaking process that had allowed their own citizens no say in the making of Schengen. "Up to now, it has merely been a question of co-operation between governments," Bangemann said of the tougher anti-immigration laws that compensated for the removal of border controls. He told the parliament to be wary of the treaty's implementation: "You should be on the look-out for your real enemy," he said. "I would describe him as a died-in-the-wool bureaucrat from one of the national ministries."[15]

Emissaries from global institutions—not least the United Nations—also criticized the work of the Schengen treatymakers. A representative of the United Nations High Commissioner for Refugees lodged his objections with France's foreign affairs committee. Writing soon after the dossier of materials on ratification had arrived in the national legislatures of the Schengen states, Antoine Noël protested that adherence to international law would be hindered by the immigration restrictions introduced in the Schengen treaty—that refugees would have greater difficulty finding safety in Europe. "Our main concern," he wrote, "is to reconcile . . . the legitimate interest in providing greater freedom of movement for people on the one hand, and the very particular situation of the asylum seeker who does not necessarily and always have a passport, a proper entry visa, or adequate means of subsistence." From the vantage point of the international refugee agency, Schengen's provisions for free movement perversely appeared to present a danger to asylum rights.[16]

Such objections were shared by the world's foremost human rights organizations. Amnesty International raised concerns with national parliaments and European Community institutions about Schengen's inadequate protections for foreign migrants, "refugees and asylum seekers at risk of human rights violations." A report of June 1991, which marked the thirtieth anniversary of Amnesty's founding, highlighted the risks of the treaty's harmonizing of asylum and immigration rules that accompanied the dismantling of border controls. The report stated that the implementing convention was found lacking in "essential safeguards . . . to protect the rights of asylum-seekers and refugees." It also noted the lack of democratic process, "the absence of sufficient public discussion and parliamentary consultation."[17]

As the ratification process began, Amnesty International asked lawmakers in the Schengen countries not to approve the treaty, advising national governments to conduct a fuller consultation with independent legal experts. It disseminated guidance—a memorandum titled "Convention Implementing the Schengen Agreement: Concerns of Amnesty International"—that cataloged Schengen's threat to human rights, pointing to immigration rules that assigned asylum responsibility to the country of first entry, required penalties on anyone facilitating unlawful entry, and mandated uniform visa obligations. All this, Amnesty stated, formed an "obstacle to free access . . . for every asylum seeker . . . who seeks protection in one of the signatory states."[18] Arguments that the treatymaking was undemocratic thus joined appeals to reject Schengen as a violation of free movement and human rights.

France gave Schengen its first democratic endorsement. This marked a turning point in the accomplishment of free movement. But first, France played host to the beginning of a public encounter with the treaty, starting with salvos in the press. That set the stage for a rancorous parliamentary debate over the terms of free movement. The unfolding of the ratification process brought about a shift in the nature of the criticism aimed at Schengen. The European Parliament had laid stress on the treaty's flaws with respect to human rights. Some national lawmakers took up that cause. But their emphasis was on protecting national security and the authority of the nation-state.

Public awareness of Schengen emerged slowly due to the opaque and protracted treatymaking. Despite the momentous aims involved in guaranteeing free movement, the changes came in a piecemeal fashion. The Benelux states of Belgium, Luxembourg, and the Netherlands already had their own arrangement in place. The Saarbrücken agreement provided for free movement between France and West Germany, preceding the signing of the first Schengen treaty by about a year. Meanwhile, Schengen's authors described their objectives in occasional and laconic public communiqués. "We did not hide; we did not try to fool people," recalled Goebbels, Luxembourg's negotiator. "We did our job as junior ministers." But the work mostly went unnoticed.[19]

An unexpected discovery by a French lawmaker, however, momentarily turned Schengen into a cause célèbre. Paul Masson, a Rally for the Republic senator from the Loiret department in north-central France, demanded an explanation when he noticed details of Schengen planning in an interior ministry budget, which he happened upon in the spring of 1989. "It was as rapporteur for the interior's budget that my attention was drawn . . . to the mention made, on the back of one page, to agreements made in Schengen between France, the Federal Republic of Germany, Belgium, the Netherlands and Luxembourg," he told *Valeurs Actuelles*, a conservative weekly.[20] In response, a French minister, Edith Cresson, appeared in the French parliament, explaining how the European Community's stalled progress on free movement had impelled separate treatymaking by the Schengen states. "We wanted Schengen because the talks . . . didn't go fast enough," she said.[21] Unsatisfied, Masson predicted that violence would arise from the removal of border controls, recalling how Paris was convulsed in 1986 by a wave of terror that reached a climax in a bombing campaign aimed at the city hall, a police prefecture, a post office, and department stores and restaurants. He foresaw "entry on our territory of terrorist bands similar to those which bloodied Paris." His prophecy appeared in *Valeurs Actuelles*, in a story titled "The Secret about the Schengen Accords."[22]

Masson's allegations set off a spasm of panic. The right-wing press seethed. "Mitterrand's secretive policy destroys French sovereignty," blared a headline in *Présent*, a newspaper aligned with the National Front, which retold the story of Schengen's origins, as if revealing a scandal. The account of the dangers of free movement began with the treaty signing in 1985: "On a small boat moored in the Moselle . . . Catherine Lalumière, state secretary for European affairs, signed in the greatest secrecy . . . and together with her counterparts in Germany, Belgium, Holland and Luxembourg, agreements aimed at the outright removal, on January 1, 1990, of physical borders among the signatory states, and therefore of all possibility of controlling the movement of people and goods." The story took liberties with the treaty's details, but few readers knew better.[23] "Who knows of Schengen?" asked *Valeurs Actuelles*. "In France, no one, except some insiders. . . . Nobody, until the other week when Mr. Paul Masson . . . revealed its name." That was the effect of Schengen's undemocratic origins.[24]

Of course, it was untrue that no one knew of Schengen before Masson's findings and the ensuing outcry. The 1985 accord had been published in France's *Official Journal* in August 1986. But ignorance of the planning was so widespread that Pierre Joxe, the interior minister, was moved to affirm, in remarks before the National Assembly in 1989, during a debate on the entry of foreigners into France, that he was indeed familiar with the treatymaking. "First of all, I would like to reassure our Assembly," Joxe said, "by informing it that as interior minister I am perfectly aware of the Schengen Agreement." The assurance was necessary because of the "secrecy that surrounds this agreement," he acknowledged, explaining that the negotiations on the implementing convention were still ongoing and vowing that France's delegation would safeguard national sovereignty.[25] On behalf of Rally for the Republic, Masson wrote to Joxe, demanding that a text of the convention be transmitted to the French parliament. Meanwhile, as *Le Monde* reported, nongovernmental groups had become anxious "about the future fate of asylum seekers."[26]

France's government brought the implementing convention before parliament for ratification in May 1991, almost a year after the second treaty signing on the Moselle. The National Assembly began debate early in June. Mazeaud, the conservative deputy who decried the riverboat diplomacy, led the parliamentary assault on Schengen. The bloc backing him included some members of Rally for the Republic and the Union for French Democracy, two conservative parties that otherwise favored the agreement. For the most part, opposition to Schengen united the political extremes, joining the Communists and leaders of the National Front. The governing Socialists overwhelmingly backed the accord.[27]

"Very dense" was how a French diplomat described the parliamentary debate.[28] But that was rather an understatement for the torrent of words directed at Schengen. The intensity of the debate reflected its stakes for lawmakers acutely conscious of their country's position as the first to consider ratifying the treaty. "Why should we want France to be the first to approve this text?" protested a leading critic, Nicole Catala of Rally for the Republic. Conversely, Socialist proponents appealed to a sense of urgency. Appearing in the National Assembly to defend the treaty, Mitterrand's minister of European affairs, Élisabeth Guigou, impatiently asked, "Should we have stopped the Schengen train . . . at the risk of doing nothing and losing the momentum that had been created since 1985?" Her fellow Socialists cried out, "Of course not!" They argued, "That would have been the worst decision!" Meanwhile, Pierre Mazeaud reserved his harshest criticism for the process that produced Schengen: the secrecy, the intergovernmental rulemaking, the evasion of parliamentary oversight. In rebuttal, a Socialist deputy, Michel Pezet, noted that four legislators had attended a press conference in Schengen in 1985. Mazeaud retorted, "We are 577 deputies!"[29]

Oratory was interrupted; taunts flowed freely. Nothing could be conceded, as the debate turned to the meaning of a border. Speaking for the Union for French Democracy, the deputy Bernard Bosson defended Schengen, saying Europe had long since ceased to be a fortress, with its borders bearing no resemblance to the "Great Wall of China." Moreover, it was argued, an unpoliced border remained a "legal entity." But legal taxonomy alone did not carry the force of a barrier, as a Rally for the Republic lawmaker scoffed: "You confuse the nation and the land registry." The comparison drew laughter in the chamber.[30]

Sovereignty, security, asylum, individual freedoms—all were subjects of the legislative debate. Deputies favoring the treaty noted that France was already entwined with its neighbors, as a member of the European Community, and that Schengen would not erode national authority. "It is in Brussels that the objectives of agricultural policy are decided . . . in Luxembourg that disputes within the Community are settled," said François Loncle, a Socialist deputy. The European affairs minister, Guigou, described Schengen as a novel solution to intensifying problems of illegal immigration, citing measures restricting the entry and movement of foreign nationals, such as requiring that they announce themselves upon arrival in each Schengen state. At the same time, she denied any conflict between France's generous asylum laws—"France is traditionally a land of asylum and it intends to remain so"—and Schengen's rules for assigning responsibility for refugees to a single nation, the place of first entry. Likewise, she denied any infringement on national sovereignty, saying that the treaty entailed "not a single transfer of jurisdiction."[31]

The pairing of freedom and security promised by Schengen's advocates inspired intense opposition to the treaty. The right viewed the pairing as unworkable; the left argued that it was unethical. The National Front's Marie-France Stirbois spoke caustically of the influx of "new 'friends'"—singling out Zairians, Indonesians, and Iranians already residing in neighboring Schengen states, as she anticipated that undesirable foreigners would rush into France as borders disappeared. "Our country will no longer have its own borders," her allies claimed. By contrast, for the left, freedom was irreconcilable with intrusive policing procedures and restrictive asylum rules. Jean-Claude Lefort, a Communist, warned that tightened external security, including new obligations borne by transport companies to stem the entry of non-Europeans, involved an unlawful "transfer of police powers to private persons" and the "violation of human rights." He rejected the notion that assigning asylum claims to the country of first entry would still allow states to examine claims outside their remit, arguing that the treaty authorized ignoring asylum requests. "In the reductive logic of the text, can we seriously think that such a decision will frequently be made?" he asked. Rather, his prediction was that the Schengen countries would use the narrow assignment of national responsibility to shirk international humanitarian obligations.[32]

In the treaty, too, French lawmakers perceived conflicting prospects for embodying the ideals of Citizens' Europe in the Schengen area. At issue were opposing views of the treaty's origins as well as its role in Europe's economic integration. Did Schengen supply a humanist aspect to the market paradigm, or simply sustain the common market? Perspectives on this question were inseparable from partisan rivalry. Socialists supporting Mitterrand's civic aspirations for integration argued that Schengen gave moral legitimacy to the European project, adding a noneconomic dimension to the guarantee of free movement. "This agreement and this convention show that Europe is not only a market . . . it is above all a human Europe," argued the Socialist head of the National Assembly's foreign affairs committee, Michel Vauzelle, who viewed Schengen as the territorial basis for a "European legal area" where rights would reach across borders, and political liberties could be joined to market freedoms.[33]

But Schengen's critics cast the civic rationale as a cloak for the global market's penetration into domains of national autonomy and individual freedom. This rival view was put forward by Nicole Catala, a former law professor who had become influential in Rally for the Republic. She ridiculed the "seductive exterior of Citizens' Europe." She argued that Schengen ultimately derived from the Treaty of Rome, which allowed "the free movement of persons, but for economic purposes." Despite paeans to a human Europe, the market "raison d'être" endured, with Schengen threatening to render French borders "abstract, immaterial." The danger to French civic life and human freedom lay in Schengen's cosmopolitan rules, protested Mazeaud. Applause broke out in the chamber as he argued that France's constitution assured its people liberty by locating sovereignty in the nation: "This notion of national sovereignty is the affirmation of our freedom." But with Schengen, he said, "We bind our hands!"[34]

The nationalist argument against Schengen made a weapon of French history. Gaullists such as Mazeaud claimed to be guardians of an independent France, keepers of the supremacy of the nation, one and indivisible.[35] "You will understand that the Gaullist that I am . . . is attached to his country," Mazeaud said. "And being attached to one's country does not mean that one is against Europe! It simply means clarifying the conditions of the Europe of tomorrow." Schengen embodied a European future, he argued, that overlooked the lessons of the past—lessons reaching back long before the German occupation, almost to the start of recorded history. "Eighteen centuries have been necessary to realize our unity, the indivisibility of the Republic, to consecrate the notion of national sovereignty in our constitution," he told parliament, saying that Schengen would shackle France and desecrate that tradition.[36]

But in justifying free movement, Schengen's defenders hardly disavowed history. They celebrated a Europe without borders as a rectification for past wrongs. "The genius of the fathers of Europe was to imagine, for the first time in the history of the planet, this new structure . . . avoiding the formidable excesses of national-ism," said Bernard Bosson, who represented Haute-Savoie, on the border with Switzerland. Schengen's supranationalism stood as a moral rejoinder not only to the bloodshed of the Second World War but to the polarities of the Cold War, he argued. "In the West, we must accelerate the course of history," he pled, saying of the peoples of Eastern Europe and Central Europe, for whom history seemed stalled, that Schengen would lay the groundwork for a "political Europe capable of welcoming them." Jacques Toubon, a Rally for the Republic deputy, spoke for the pro-Schengen wing of the party in claiming that free movement would unite the continent's democ-racies as a counterforce against the Soviet Union's "tremendous pressure on Western Europe."[37] In this view, Schengen offered both redemption for Europe's past and a plan for future geopolitics.

Schengen's critics drew a different lesson from recent history, condemning the treaty as the undoing of French independence, wrested from the Axis Powers and secured in postwar constitutions. "I cannot accept that an authority other than the French state ensures our security," protested Christian Estrosi of Rally for the Republic. His adversaries accused him of echoing Jean-Marie Le Pen, the leader of the National Front. But Estrosi paid tribute to a dif-ferent figure—Charles Pasqua, the Gaullist interior minister whose name adorned a restrictive immigration law approved in 1986 but revoked three years later. "I am convinced of the need to build the Europe of tomorrow," Estrosi said. "But . . . we must first reinstate the Pasqua law in the area of security and immigration." His rea-soning anticipated the interplay between the Schengen provisions and the Pasqua measures that would define French debates over security, immigration, and human rights through the end of the century.[38]

Conflicting views of history also shaped debate on Schengen's meaning for the political transformations of the moment. Some expressed optimism that Western institutions could incorporate Eastern Europeans no longer cordoned off by the Iron Curtain.

The Gaullists were most adamant in opposing this view, fearing that the collapse of Cold War political geography would unleash migratory pressure that Western nations could not withstand. Rally for the Republic deputies cited a police report showing that the year 1990 had seen a 700 percent increase in the number of Soviet nationals residing illegally in France. The Socialists countered that the anti-Schengen bloc opposed the liberation of the eastern half of the continent. "You want to rebuild the Berlin Wall?" asked François Loncle, a Socialist advocate of the treaty. He placed Schengen within an inevitable European integration, arguing that parliament must

> situate the Schengen Convention in the context of European construction, in the guiding thread of a long march . . . from the Treaty of Rome to the Single Act . . . to the common market of January 1, 1993, to the political, economic and monetary union . . . in short, to a 'new European frontier,' to this European space, the best possible place for creating new relations among peoples, new answers to major demographic, ecological, scientific, cultural and human challenges.[39]

A critic replied that Schengen was instead a "milestone in the process of dissolving our national identity," making the French nation a relic of the past. Both sides claimed to speak for the "Europe of tomorrow."[40]

As grounds for their challenge, the dissenters invoked France's constitution of 1958, which inaugurated the Fifth Republic. "I am one of those who believe that the primacy of the constitution must prevail, especially in Parliament," Mazeaud proclaimed. "It is the Constitutional Council that will decide." Already, he foresaw, as head of the National Assembly's legal committee, a constitutional confrontation over Schengen.[41]

In the end, the National Assembly overwhelmingly approved Schengen's implementing convention, which passed 495 to 61 on June 3, 1991. Communists and members of the National Front remained steadfast in their opposition, but the political center formed a majority, with Mitterrand's Socialists capturing the support of the Union for French Democracy and Rally for the Republic, overcoming the dissent of a Gaullist bloc in their midst.[42] Approval followed in the Senate, the parliament's upper chamber.[43] Nevertheless, French legislators foresaw obstacles to the treaty's implementation. The National Assembly set up a *commission de contrôle* to oversee the process, authorizing it to correct mistakes in the drafting of the treaty, solicit public input, and incorporate the insights of government ministers. The commission also established priorities for French lawmakers arising from Schengen's ratification, including the containment of migratory flows, the control of external borders, and the protection of personal data.[44]

In the autumn of 1991, the commission sent a report to parliament, "Justifications," which examined the treaty's establishment. The rapporteur was Xavier de Villepin, a senator who belonged to the Union for French Democracy and who had fought in the Resistance. He wrote not just of border rules but of the "often tragic destiny of our continent." Like the treatymakers, he viewed Schengen as a laboratory of free movement that would incubate civic principles to supplement free trade. It would "make a Citizens' Europe"—not simply a "Europe of the common market." But the difficulty that would confront states preparing to implement Schengen arose from the equivalence between people and goods undergirding the treaty. "It may have been wrong to deal with the free movement of people as we dealt with the free movement of goods," de Villepin wrote. "Because people are not goods. They transport not only their identity and their nationality, but also their history, their language, their traditions, their religion, and also their fears or their fantasies." Ratification had begun a belated public reckoning with those most human traits of people in motion.[45]

Not even a month had passed since Schengen's ratification in Paris when French lawmakers who had failed to stop the treaty in parliament turned to the judiciary. At the end of June 1991, sixty deputies in the National Assembly brought a claim against Schengen to the Constitutional Council. As with the legislative opposition, the constitutional complaint united deputies across party lines, from the Communists to some in conservative factions to the National Front.

Schengen entailed an unconstitutional transfer of national sovereignty to foreign and supranational powers, the dissident deputies argued to the Constitutional Council. The council was established by the constitution of France's Fifth Republic, in 1958, as the nation's highest constitutional court, with the authority of judicial review over measures adopted by the French Parliament, to assure their adherence to constitutional principles. It sat in the Palais-Royal in Paris.

The complaint amplified claims made in the National Assembly that Schengen's dismantling of internal borders and imposition of compensatory security procedures violated France's constitution. According to the complaint, Schengen infringed on national sovereignty in three sectors: the state's duty to uphold the power of republican institutions; the state's need to control the composition of its population; and the state's responsibility to guarantee rights and freedoms to its citizens.[46] The first claim asserted that Schengen nullified the power of national institutions by rendering the domain of that power indistinct through the dismantling of borders. The second claim asserted that Schengen undermined France's nationality law, which made every child born on French soil a citizen. Invoking the "life of the nation" in conjuring fears of foreigners, the deputies argued that the birthright principle "was easily conceived when French authorities were masters of the control of the entry and exit of the territory; it is quite different with the Schengen agreements." The third claim asserted that Schengen's free movement guarantee and porous borders threatened France's social welfare system, "the survival of our social protection system," a bedrock of the social democratic state. If overwhelmed by foreign migrants, it was said, France would be unable to entitle its own citizens to health, material security, rest, and leisure.[47] The broader claim—that Schengen not only limited national authority but transferred sovereignty to undemocratic supranational institutions—rested particularly on the treaty's rules for asylum and cross-border policing. The objection was that the power to decide who could enter French territory would be ceded by the national police to officials of the first state entered by an "alien."[48]

The complaint alleged that Schengen's implementing convention violated France's constitution even more flagrantly than had the original treaty, adopted in 1985 without a procedure for ratification. It argued that the most serious constitutional failing of the implementing convention lay precisely in the measures that compensated for the deficits of the original pact. It cited the convention's rules on police and judicial cooperation as evidence of an admission that Schengen imperiled security. The deputies claimed that the "compensatory measures"—meant to prevent "the new area of freedom" from becoming a zone of lawlessness—succeeded only in undermining national sovereignty. They challenged the creation of a system of multilateral police cooperation that allowed authorities in one state to surveil and pursue a suspect in another state without prior permission. Allegedly, the system would permit foreign agents to take over the nondelegable duties of the state, representing an "amputation."[49]

The complaint further alleged that the convention trespassed on France's power not just to police its own borders but to open them to refugees, elaborating on the protest in parliament. The deputies objected that vagueness in the criteria for adjudicating asylum claims would deny legitimate refugees the protections of the 1951 Geneva Convention. Again, the problem was countervailing measures, overcompensation that violated rights in blocking asylum seekers from submitting claims in multiple states—from playing the market in a process of asylum tourism. "In particular, the compensatory mechanism for the principle of free movement intended to preserve public order and security appears manifestly disproportionate to the detriment of individual freedoms." In language more technical than the parliamentary debate, the complaint alleged that Schengen's pairing of free movement with security would cause unfreedom.[50]

Violation of individual privacy figured in the complaint as well. The deputies claimed that confidential information gathered about asylum seekers, passed among member states, might be mishandled, potentially reaching authorities in countries of origin. At the center of the privacy concerns lay the Schengen Information System, the computerized database designed to support police cooperation and external border control. The complaint argued that the promise to make records of criminal suspects available to participating states threatened the "right to respect for private and family life" enshrined in the European Convention on Human Rights.[51] It warned of abuse by "other State Parties that do not always guarantee an equivalent level of protection for individuals."[52] Here, too, the dissenting lawmakers returned to their central claim—that France was ceding control to other countries.

The legal case against Schengen reflected the political thought of Michel Debré, the author of the constitution said to prohibit the treaty. His name did not appear in the complaint, for he had left the National Assembly by the time of Schengen's ratification. Yet Debré's ideas on French sovereignty, expressed in his memoirs and reverential writings on French republicanism, shaped the arguments made before the Constitutional Council. A cavalry officer at the time of the war's outbreak, Debré was captured but escaped and joined the Resistance, assigned the responsibility by de Gaulle for naming replacements for Vichy officers in anticipation of liberation.[53] As the minister of justice in de Gaulle's first cabinet, he drafted the constitution of the Fifth Republic, became its first prime minister, and later led the country's ministries of justice, economy, foreign affairs, and defense. Thereafter, he was a long-serving deputy in the National Assembly. In his devotion to French sovereignty, Debré was said to be "more Gaullist than de Gaulle."[54] His final work, appearing in 1993, transcribed his conversations with de Gaulle, on such topics as decolonization and European integration. During the final weeks of the Algerian War in 1962, de Gaulle had asked Debré, then his prime minister, how he saw France's future as the nation lost its colonial possessions but gained increasing influence within the European Community. Debré expressed "deep pessimism," advising de Gaulle that European integration represented the "end of France."[55]

Debré's pessimism was forged in the Vichy years, when he began to associate individual freedom with national sovereignty. In *La mort de l'État républicain* (1947), he traced the downfall of democratic states, using Vichy as a case study. "A crime is being committed before our eyes: the state—our French state, our republican state—is dying, and it is being assassinated," he wrote.[56] But he insisted on France's complicity in the annihilation of its own nationhood, and he would soon point to self-destruction as the perverse impulse behind European union as well. For he rooted his rejection of Pan-Europeanism in a philosophy of constitutional sovereignty that viewed the nation as the direct expression of the popular will. His 1950 treatise on France's republican sovereignty,

FIGURE 4.1. Michel Debré, shown in 1976 at a meeting of the Gaullist Union for the Defense of the Republic, with portraits of De Gaulle and Georges Pompidou behind him, formulated criticism of Pan-Europeanism that figured in the legal and political opposition to Schengen. Credit: Keystone-France / GAMMA RAPHO

La République et son pouvoir, argued, "The nation is sovereign. It is represented by all living citizens old enough to reason. Each citizen is thus the ephemeral holder of a piece of sovereignty."[57] These ideals found expression in the constitution of the Fifth Republic, which began with a proclamation of "The French people" that affirmed, "National sovereignty shall vest in the people," a principle that offered authority for challenges to supranationalism, as would be wielded in the case against the Schengen treaty.[58]

For Debré, the constitutional right of self-government gave French citizens the power to resist absorption into Europe. He contrasted the ideals of Gaullism with the wrongs of a "supranational Europe," while championing a global French identity represented by the French Union, a successor to the colonial empire. European integration would erode French ties to its former colonies, he warned, fearing an internationalism that would "constrain France, which has taken and will always take a thousand faces, including in the past those of the Holy Roman Empire and the temporal power of the Papacy." He called on his compatriots to defend national autonomy, "a strong, free, respected republic," inveighing against European union in *Français choisissons l'espoir*, a 1979 polemic that recounted his efforts to narrow the terms of European unification by favoring Franco-German rapprochement but opposing economic and military harmonization. The story began after the war. An abortive European Defense Community was anathema to the "very idea of a French nation," he wrote. He advocated for France's independent nuclear deterrent, objecting to Euratom, a joint European market for nuclear power. And he assailed the economic aims of the Treaty of Rome, describing the European Community as an "internal customs disarmament." He called common market policy a "mutation," as his disciples would later decry Schengen as an "amputation."[59]

In his writings on French republicanism, Debré did not take account of Schengen, for its measures were still emergent as he was exiting public life. Yet, by the time he resigned from the National Assembly, in 1988, he had voiced his protest against opening borders through intergovernmental treatymaking. "The attack on national sovereignty is direct and unconstitutional," he objected to France's foreign ministry in 1986, deriding free movement guarantees as evidence that "supranational ideology blinds many minds." In reply, the foreign ministry countered Debré's assertion of national sovereignty through a procedural point, claiming that parliamentary consent was not constitutionally required because the treaties dealt only with "regulatory power" involving nothing more than "practical arrangements for border control of Community nationals."[60]

But internal government notes on the planning for free movement—an August 1986 foreign ministry report summing up a meeting on "circulation issues within the European framework"— acknowledged the validity of Debré's concerns about France's power to secure its borders. "Admittedly, it is regrettable" that Schengen provided for "immediately easing controls at the common frontiers before the harmonization of controls at the external borders has been negotiated," found the foreign ministry, envisaging the imple-

menting convention as "the instrument for realistically responding to the problem." Yet neither Debré nor the ministry could have
predicted that the compensatory security measures would awaken
new fears about restrictions on national sovereignty and free
movement.[61]

Debré's protest became public, though not the treatymaking he
denounced. *Le Monde* documented how Debré had come to see cosmopolitan free movement as "Europe against France." Nor was he
alone in calling for parliamentary oversight, drawing support from
the deputy Pierre Mazeaud, his Gaullist ally in Rally for the Republic. It was Mazeaud who would soon deplore the treaty signing on a
riverboat, leading the opposition to Schengen both in the National
Assembly and before the Constitutional Council.[62] When Mazeaud took up the case against Schengen, he had the endorsement
of Debré's sons, Bernard Debré and Jean-Louis Debré, who had
joined the National Assembly two years before their father resigned
from parliament. Both of their names appeared on the judicial
complaint brought in June 1991. French opposition to Schengen
was quite literally Debré's progeny.[63]

France's Constitutional Council took up the complaint against
Schengen on July 25, 1991, weighing whether the treaty on free
movement conformed with the constitution written by Debré.
An Algiers-born judge, Jacques Robert, who had taught law in
Morocco and Algeria before settling in Paris, where he joined the
law faculty of Paris-Panthéon-Assas and advocated for a national
referendum on fundamental rights, served as the case's rapporteur.
This made him responsible for investigating the complaint and
leading the court through an examination of its claims. His statement to the court began by tracing the treaty's history: the Fontainebleau conclusions, the long years of negotiations, the ceremonial signing. "The name of Schengen with the magical accents of
Viennese palaces is that of a small town in Luxembourg," he said.
"The idea of the free movement of people is simple. . . . The development of such an idea was long."[64]

The rapporteur began, as well, by defining the free movement of
people. He explained that it would differ for Europeans and non-
Europeans in the borderless space created by Schengen. "It consists
in allowing European citizens to move between different countries

in the same way as within their own national territory. . . . It hence-
forth establishes a space of freedom without any hindrance," he
said. "But such freedom could not be limited to Europeans alone.
In a space of freedom, it is necessary to take into account all the
people who circulate there or plan to circulate there." Therefore, a
different regime would exist for non-Europeans, for "the citizens of
third countries in order to regulate their entry into 'the space' and
then their free circulation within it." Explaining the treaty's restrictive rules for nonnationals, he offered the example of an Algerian
migrant entering the Schengen space, or a Pole in Germany, or
a Turk in Belgium. "Unlike Europeans, they will be subject to an
obligation of declaration," allowing countries to "make sure they do
not stay longer than three months and check the regularity of their
situation."[65] Accordingly, police cooperation would accompany free
movement and the dismantling of internal borders.

The statement of the rapporteur was anything but impartial;
forthrightly, he told his brethren on the court about his views of
the treaty's virtues, saying, "Schengen is the prefiguration of the
Europe of tomorrow." His exposition of the case said nothing
about a common market, or a single market, or any market at all.
Rather, it invoked the idea of Citizens' Europe, using a variant of
that title in stating, "Schengen is the Europe of people." In answer
to critics across the political spectrum, the rapporteur dismissed
claims about excessive freedom and excessive security, declaring:
"Schengen is neither a sieve nor a fortress."[66]

The court heard from the rapporteur a summary of the treaty's
purpose and an inventory of the objections. He outlined the five
major aims of Schengen's implementing convention in harmonizing
national laws: unifying visa rules; combating illegal immigration;
promoting police, judicial, and customs cooperation; expanding the
exchange of information; and clarifying asylum rights. He noted
approvingly that the treaty was already influencing the practices
of the wider European Community, whose 1990 Dublin regulation
adopted the rule assigning responsibility for asylum claims to the
country of first entry. But the court also learned of the opposition
to Schengen, as expressed in the complaint, and beyond in public
opinion. The rapporteur related fears that Schengen would create
"pipelines of illegal immigration," that Italy would become an "ante-

chamber" for Africans journeying to France, and that the Dutch would be disinclined to "drive back illegals."[67]

The court heard also of the lack of democratic process in the treatymaking, which had led to the initial opposition of the European Parliament. The absence was still more striking because of the question of sovereignty at stake, the rapporteur acknowledged. The treaty was "without democratic control at the stage of its elaboration," even though its 142 articles all concerned "the fundamental freedoms of the exercise of state sovereignty in essential fields," he said. "In the case of civil liberties, a priori democratic control would have been preferable."[68]

At times, the judges of the council appeared to reject the reasoning that reconciled the Schengen convention with the French constitution. They expressed their skepticism in colloquies with the rapporteur. "That leaves me dissatisfied," objected Francis Mollet-Viéville, a former president of the Paris bar, in response to an assurance that foreign police, authorized to operate on French territory, would follow French rules. At another point, he asked why the treaty did not speak of "national responsibility" to conduct border checks even as controls were lifted. The question prompted an explanation that Schengen involved no change to the rules governing checks within France, apparently satisfying Mollet-Viéville. The court's president, Robert Badinter, a former minister of justice under Mitterrand, was most wary of the procedures for collecting and exchanging data as part of the Schengen Information System, saying too little was known about measures that would protect privacy. He found reassurance, however, in the treaty's invocation of "'personal' liberty," rooted in the Declaration of the Rights of Man and of the Citizen, rather than the term "individual liberty," which the constitution of the Fifth Republic made contingent on vindication by a judge. Badinter approved of the "nuances" in the language.[69]

Mostly the judges discounted criticism of the treaty. Maurice Faure, a signer of the Rome Treaty, who had traveled a path from the French Resistance to service in France's foreign ministry to membership in Frances's parliament to a seat on the Constitutional Council, noted that the Gaullist dissenters were in the minority.[70] Dismissively, he remarked, "I never believed that Mr. Mazeaud would find his signatures," while also observing, "the prerogatives of parliamentarians are very limited since they cannot modify the treaty." Another judge criticized the contradictory nature of the complaint, noting that "on the one hand, it maintains that there is an attack on national sovereignty and, on the other, it argues that the right of asylum is ignored." He was Jacques Latscha, who later became president of the International Institute of Human Rights in Strasbourg. He called the complaint "bizarre."[71]

In explaining the treaty to the court, the rapporteur spoke matter-of-factly about Schengen's limits. It did not "create any new international organization," nor did the Schengen Executive Committee possess any lawmaking power, being merely a forum for intergovernmental consultation, its decisions subordinate to Community law. Furthermore, the treaty did not compel the complete harmonization of national law, serving rather as an "incentive" for additional coordination. Invoking a model for a federal system, he pointed across the Atlantic, saying the United States showed how Europe could "build a united space without compromising the constitutional particularities of the parties." His statement to the court did not examine the dilemmas of nation-states in an emergent international system, instead explaining the reconciliation of supranationalism with national sovereignty, and freedom with security in the Schengen expanse. "The principle of free movement is accompanied by measures of control at the external borders," the rapporteur said. "Borders are both the enclosure of nations and the scars of history."[72]

At the close of the hearing, the Constitutional Council rejected the complaint against the Schengen treaty, finding that the implementing convention did not violate the French constitution. Decisively, it ruled that the guarantee of the free movement of people across the internal borders of the Schengen states did not carry out a transfer of sovereignty or undermine national authority. Nor, it held, did the treaty abridge the rights and freedoms of citizens through the guarantee of security founded on rules governing foreign migrants, asylum process, policing, and information exchange. Nor would the harmonization of national laws impinge on the control of persons within a country. Supranationalism would not preempt nationalism. "The law authorizing the approval of the implementing convention of the Schengen agreement of June 14, 1985," the court decided, "is not contrary to the Constitution."[73]

The court's conclusion was brief, but in some sixty points of reasoning, the decision dismissed the claims of the deputies that Schengen was unconstitutional and therefore that parliamentary ratification of the treaty was unconstitutional as well. Again and again, the court found that the argument in the complaint "lacks in fact" and "can only be discarded"—and that Schengen's rules were in "no way contrary" to principles of nationhood, sovereignty, and individual rights. It rebuffed the grievances concerning France's sovereignty. It rejected the claim that Schengen violated the "territorial jurisdiction of the State," holding that free border crossing, "without the control of persons," was not tantamount to eliminating borders that delimit a country's boundaries. It denied that Schengen involved "a transfer of sovereignty," finding the claim "devoid of relevance," citing the powers reserved to France, including the authority to restrict border crossing "for reasons of public order or national security." It also denied that Schengen infringed on "the life of the Nation," concluding that the free movement of persons neither altered the attainment of French nationality nor negated national "control of migratory flows," noting that the abolition of border checks at internal frontiers was "not absolute" and would be paired with security rules fortified through "harmonization at the 'external borders.'" As for a threat to social welfare protection, the court found that France's provisions for health, leisure, and material security were unrelated to Schengen, discarding the claim as "inoperative."[74]

The court saw no merit at all in the pleas that the treaty would violate fundamental individual liberties. "As regards the rights and freedoms of citizens," it found that the opening of internal borders would not encroach on "the security of persons proclaimed by the Declaration of the Rights of Man and of the Citizen" or the duty of France "to ensure respect for the institutions of the Republic."[75] The decision affirmed the central logic of the implementing convention—the pairing of freedom with security. Not only would the treaty require restrictions at external borders to compensate for free movement inside the Schengen area, but it recognized police powers as an essential aspect of national sovereignty: "No change has been made to the legislation relating to the control of persons within the national territory."[76] Here, too, the court found no transfer of sovereignty.

Nor did Schengen's rules contravene rights of asylum and personal privacy lodged in France's fundamental law, the court held. On asylum, it noted the treaty's deference to the guarantees of the Geneva Convention relating to the protection of refugees as well the proviso that the first-entry principle of asylum obligation would not preclude another country from hearing the appeals of asylum seekers.[77] On privacy, the court dismissed the complaint that the creation of the Schengen Information System would invade the sphere of "individual freedoms" and deepen the vulnerability of asylum seekers, finding sufficient safeguards against the misuse of personal data in the treaty's "protective measures" for the gathering and exchange of information. Again, the decision stated that the complaint "lacks in fact."[78]

Still, the court did not deliver a wholesale endorsement of Schengen. While dismissing the constitutional claim, it insisted on limits to the treaty's implementation and affirmed the legal authority of the nation-state. Notably, it did not accept the independent authority of the Schengen Executive Committee, holding that national courts would retain jurisdiction over measures adopted by French officials to carry out committee decisions, meaning that the everyday implementation of free movement would be "subject to French law."[79] Judicial review would remain a matter of national sovereignty.

For the court, sovereignty—jurisdiction over the creation and adjudication of law—was the essential point. It ruled that neither the Schengen treaty nor its ratification was contrary to France's constitution because the dismantling of internal borders and the free movement of persons would not cause the transfer of sovereignty away from national courts and parliaments to supranational institutions. Guaranteeing the right of free movement, policing borders, and controlling persons would still belong to the sovereignty of France. At the hearing, the court had signaled the significance of this authority. Its president, Robert Badinter, made explicit that no lawmaking power would be ceded to the Schengen regime, but rather that its implementing measures would "be subject to judicial review." On that point, he said, "You have to be vigilant."[80]

And at the hearing, too, the chief judge asked the court to set out its assurances on national sovereignty to the public, "to provide some clarifications . . . and include them in the press release."[81] No longer would Schengen's implementation be obscure to the French people. Two days later, a story on the judgment appeared in *Le Monde* titled "The Construction of Europe under the Control of the Constitutional Council: The Schengen Agreements Do Not Imply a Transfer of Sovereignty." Bluntly, the story depicted the boundaries of sovereignty defined by the court. Acerbically, however, *Le Monde* noted that the latitude for judicial review was really quite narrow, the declaration of national sovereignty being all that the court "could allow itself." For had France imposed greater limits, the treaty would become a dead letter, unratified by other Schengen states. "Measured approval becomes a refusal."[82]

But that was not the court's last word on the question of sovereignty raised by Schengen or the treaty's rules on free movement. Again, two years later, it was asked to review the rule of country of first entry in examining a restrictive measure passed by the French parliament, a new Pasqua law that cited Schengen's implementing convention in denying asylum seekers a right to bring pleas for refuge in France rather than in the country of first entry. The court struck down the law as a violation of the right of asylum guaranteed in France's constitution. In a decision of August 1993, it recognized that France had authority to control its borders, and that "no constitutional principle or rule guarantees aliens general and absolute rights of access and residence in the national territory." But it found that the Pasqua law was contrary to the constitution's guarantee that "any man persecuted in virtue of his actions in favor of liberty may claim the right of asylum upon the territories of the Republic."[83]

Again, too, the court affirmed the breadth of the right of free movement, a right granted to foreigners as well as citizens of France, declaring that non-Europeans were entitled to "individual freedom . . . notably the freedom to come and go"—and that free movement belonged to "the fundamental rights and freedoms secured by the Constitution to all persons residing in the territory of the Republic." It ruled that "aliens . . . must be able to exercise the right of redress to enforce their rights and freedoms," relying on the provisions of France's constitution but also citing the Geneva Convention and the principles of universal human dignity and equal protection proclaimed in the Declaration of the Rights of Man and of the Citizen.[84]

An amendment to France's constitution settled any seeming conflict between Schengen's rule of first entry and the right of asylum guaranteed in the nation's fundamental law, establishing anew the sovereignty of France over the control of persons within its borders. Article 53–1, adopted by the parliament in November 1993, expressly allowed France to enter into treaties allocating responsibility for asylum claims but preserved the power of France to grant refuge to any asylum seeker in its territory. "The Republic may enter into agreements with European States . . . for the purpose of determining their respective jurisdiction as regards requests for asylum," the amendment stated. "The authorities of the Republic shall remain empowered to grant asylum to any foreigner who is persecuted for his action in pursuit of freedom or who seeks the protection of France on other grounds."[85] Affirming the country's humanitarian obligations to asylum seekers in search of liberty, France's constitution codified the principle that Schengen carried no transfer of sovereignty.

The problem of sovereignty also confronted other Schengen countries in ratifying the treaty. Among France's partners, too, debate over the implementing convention led to democratic scrutiny of the scope of national autonomy, the limits of supranational interdependence, and the terms of free movement for Europeans and non-Europeans. Ratification came last in Germany, prolonged by constitutional reform that became a condition of parliamentary approval of the treaty. The debate in the Bundestag centered on one category of people seeking free movement: asylum seekers.

Of the Benelux states, the Netherlands presented the greatest obstacle to Schengen. At the start of the treatymaking, the Dutch delegation had expressed reservations about signing the 1985 accord without parliamentary approval, and the Dutch were alone in submitting the original accord, after signing, to their legislature. After the signing of the implementing convention in 1990, the Dutch government's supreme advisory council, the Raad van State, warned parliament not to ratify the agreement because of the procedure for deciding responsibility for asylum claims. The first entry rule, the council found, allowed the Netherlands "to delegate to another State the task of determining whether an individual is a refugee."[86]

It was the first time in Dutch history that the council had advised the government against approving an international treaty.[87] Inspired by the advisory opinion, a Labor member of parliament, Maarten van Traa, contacted lawmakers in Belgium and Germany, proposing to develop an alternative text for Schengen, as *Statewatch* reported in the summer of 1991. His aim was to strengthen the treaty's commitment to political asylum and the protection of privacy in the exchange of police data. He also sought to set up a European court capable of resolving disputes arising from the new Schengen procedures.[88] But the Dutch government pressed ahead, and, ultimately, the advisory council reversed its position and endorsed ratification.[89] The initial expression of disapproval was nonetheless consequential, as *Statewatch* observed, for it spoke to "splits between the hardliners and the more liberal national authorities"—between those who sought to make Schengen an instrument of policing and counterterrorism and those who sought greater protections for civil liberties. Their disagreements spoke to the ambiguities of Schengen as a testing ground for free movement.[90]

Plans for the Schengen Executive Committee, the intergovernmental body assigned control over the convention's implementation, also evoked skepticism echoing concerns raised by France's Constitutional Council. The Dutch advisory council objected to the executive committee's vast powers, which appeared to combine executive, legislative, and judicial authority, in an unelected, supranational apparatus. The highest administrative court in Belgium, the Conseil d'État, was distrustful as well.[91] The Dutch parliament secured veto power over decisions taken by the executive committee. As part of the ratification process, in 1992, it adopted a resolution suggesting that a supranational authority, such as the European Court of Justice, be granted jurisdiction over disputes among the member states.[92] The proposal met a mixed reception, gaining the support of certain political factions within other member states, such as the center-left Social Democratic Party in Germany.[93] A decade earlier, drafting the Schengen treaty had entailed pairing freedom and security. But the prospect of implementing free movement required determining how conflict between freedom and security would be resolved in practice and delineating the boundaries of national and cosmopolitan jurisdiction.

By the time France amended its constitution to reconcile intergovernmental treatymaking with the supremacy of humanitarian principles, all Schengen countries had ratified the implementing convention. But in Germany, the cleavage between national sovereignty and supranationalism had widened over asylum adjudication, drawing out ratification in the Bundestag for more than a year. It was not complete until 1993. Protest against the treaty's asylum rules was especially divisive in Germany, whose delegation, during the long negotiations over the convention, had driven the adoption of the rule limiting the obligation to hear asylum claims to the Schengen country of first entry. The Bundestag debate was underlain too by what Germans called *Vergangenheitsbewältigung*, the effort of reckoning with the past.[94]

Support for Schengen united Helmut Kohl's center-right Christian Democrats with their main opposition, the center-left Social Democrats. The rival lawmakers joined in casting the treaty as a cornerstone of German progress—and the free movement of people as fundamental to European unification and the achievement of the internal market. "Europe becomes one," the interior minister, Rudolf Seiters, told the Bundestag, urging ratification to grant Europeans "a measure of free movement that appeared inconceivable just a few years ago." Consideration of the treaty was "a crossroads for German domestic politics," he said. "We debate about the Schengen Agreement—a preliminary stage and test bed for the cooperation . . . in the common internal market."[95] The Social Democrats celebrated the treaty as a culmination of the work begun by Kohl at Fontainebleau, in alliance with the Socialists of France. "One remembers the walk that the Chancellor took with President Mitterrand," recalled an SPD member from Berlin. "Both considered that in anticipation of a European solution, freedom of movement for persons should be created." Schengen was "a magnificent thing," he said, "created under a *Europaeuphorie*."[96] That was to say the treaty expressed European euphoria.

From the outset, however, calls for constitutional reform attached to the Bundestag debate on ratification, and the European euphoria was tempered by anxiety about the free movement of non-Europeans, the border crossing of asylum seekers in the Schengen territory. Germany's constitution, the Basic Law adopted in 1949, protected the asylum rights of all persons, stating in Article 16: "Persons persecuted on political grounds shall have the right of asylum."[97] That guarantee reflected the country's postwar endeavor of atonement for its Nazi past. But by the time of the ratification debate, Germany was under pressure from a surge of asylum seekers. The number of asylum claims in Germany was rising, reaching 438,000 in 1992—an increase of 70 percent from the prior year. By 1992, as the Bundestag was debating Schengen's abolition of internal border controls, Germany was absorbing more than two-thirds of all refugees in the European Community.[98] Increasing attacks on foreigners accompanied the migratory flow. Human Rights Watch documented an upsurge of "xenophobia and racist violence in Germany." A 1992 report found the terror aimed at refugees reminiscent of the atrocities of Nazism. "Rioting skinheads throwing Molotov cocktails at refugee shelters, onlookers applauding and cheering, slogans such as 'foreigners out' and 'Germany for Germans,' inevitably recall images of Nazi terror during the Third Reich. Physical injury, fear and humiliation have become a daily experience for foreigners in unified Germany." The Christian Democrats, along with their Bavarian sister party, the Christian Social Union, sought a constitutional amendment that would narrow Germany's obligations to asylum seekers.[99]

The Bundestag debate on ratification thus turned the defense of sovereignty into a pursuit of constitutional reform. For against the backdrop of Schengen's open borders, the free movement of asylum seekers posed a burden unanticipated in the German Basic Law's protection of all people claiming refuge from political persecution. Germany would become the "reserve asylum country on this continent" as other Schengen states applied the rule of first entry, warned Erwin Marschewski, a Christian Democratic spokesman for domestic policy. A member of the Christian Social Union, Wolfgang Zeitlmann, agreed, "We are now basically in an asylum debate, and that is because, as a result of the abolition of border controls, it will be easier for asylum seekers to migrate to another member state." The proposal was for a change to the Basic Law that would deny refuge to asylum seekers crossing into Germany from other Schengen countries or from anywhere in the European Community or from any nation with robust humanitarian protections.[100]

For the conservatives, Schengen's ratification was conditional on constitutional reform of Germany's asylum guarantee. As the minister president of Bavaria, Edmund Stoiber, argued, "Ratification without a sufficient change in the constitution makes it possible for other contracting parties to unload at our expense."[101] By this reasoning, adhering to the Schengen country-of-first-entry rule compelled restricting Germany's grounds for asylum, a change said to uphold Germany's autonomy by safeguarding the nation from an influx of foreigners.

But limiting asylum rights through amendment of the Basic Law drew opposition from lawmakers who saw risks to Germany's humanitarian commitments. By their lights, the European euphoria embodied in Schengen meant pairing free movement with security, but also protecting the right to asylum as a fundamental freedom of all persons. It was principally members of center-left and liberal parties who argued for ratification without abridging asylum rights, rejecting proposals for constitutional reform. "We Free Democrats say yes to the Schengen Agreement, to the implementation of the Schengen Convention, yes without any ifs or buts, without any addition," proclaimed Wolfgang Lüder of the liberal Free Democrats. On the left, the burden of providing for foreign migrants that was deepened by Schengen's removal of borders did not go unrecognized. "We no longer have borders to the west; we have open and in any case no longer controllable borders to the east. . . . The magnitude of the immigration overwhelms local authorities," an SPD member said. "It also clearly overwhelms the emotional balance of broad sections of the population." But the answer for many in the left-liberal coalition was not to limit a right to refuge in Germany. That outcome, said a member of Alliance 90 /

The Greens, would mark a "dark day in the young history of our reunified country."[102]

The argument against constitutional reform invoked the German past, holding that the country must never forget its moral obligation to persecuted peoples. It called on the Bundestag not to betray this obligation—not to restrict the right of free movement to Europeans—but rather to open its borders to asylum seekers from across the world, to all people fleeing political persecution and also to economic refugees. It recounted why the right to asylum appeared in the Basic Law. A spokesperson for Alliance 90 / The Greens, Konrad Weiß, a civil rights activist from the former East Germany, set out the argument to the Bundestag. "A human right, a fundamental right, which the best German men and women fought for with their blood and at unspeakable sacrifices, is here today carelessly being made disposable. 'People persecuted politically enjoy the right to asylum.' . . . This was and is one of the most precious sentences ever written in the German language," he said. At length, he recalled the history of guilt and atonement written into the Basic Law's article on asylum:

> It was written from the direct experience of guilt, persecution and suffering. It could be written because German women and men had experienced in their own souls what it means to find refuge when persecuted, to be welcomed as an outcast, to be respected as an outlaw. It had to be written because German men and women were deeply shaken by the guilt in which they shared silently, acquiescently, or actively. It was allowed to be written because they wanted to start a better Germany, a Germany that doesn't build walls.
>
> For six decades, this country had to suffer from the madness of those who had made being German a religion and persecuted, expelled and destroyed everything that was 'un-German,' as they called it. The result was a destroyed and divided country, millions of people were dead, ostracized, and disdained. Have we forgotten how infinitely difficult it was before we Germans found respect and trust again, until we were able to return home to the family of nations, until this country became a democratic Germany?

To narrow the breadth of the Basic Law's protection for refugees was to cast off Germany's distinctive humanitarian burden, to exclude "un-German" people who crossed into the country after entering another Schengen territory from claiming asylum rights. Always, the opposition to amending Article 16 drew on the weight of history: "The conclusions that were drawn from the period between 1933 and 1945," as a Left party member said. "People who were being persecuted by the Nazis were dependent not only on leaving their country, but above all on finding political asylum in another country." Some spoke simply of a return to "German nationalism and racism."[103]

But arguments directed toward past wrongs did not prevail in a Bundestag preoccupied with securing Germany against the free movement of foreigners. The counterclaim was that Germany could not stand alone in granting a broad constitutional right to asylum once other Schengen countries had followed the treaty's rule of first entry in disowning asylum responsibility. "Nonsense" and "a moralizing speech" were the replies given in the chamber to a question from Weiß: "Do you want to build a new wall around Germany, a wall around Europe?" Some in the governing conservative bloc flatly denied the existence of an absolute right to asylum, untroubled by the image of a German fortress inside the borders of the Schengen territory. "If you think," said Edmund Stoiber, the Bavarian minister, "that there is a fundamental right of asylum in Europe, then I say to you: You are enormously mistaken." Others argued that asylum rights would be unthreatened by constitutional reform. "Asylum will continue to exist," the Bundestag's vice president, Hans Klein, promised. Still others stressed the need to reconcile national rules with the multinational treaty. Even this "fundamental right," said Johannes Gerster, a leader of the conservative bloc, "must be adapted to international agreements." The chairman of the conservative parliamentary group, Wolfgang Schäuble, warned that embracing Schengen without embarking on asylum reform meant Germany would "only assume the obligations without making use of the authority in this respect." Based on this logic, German membership in the Schengen world of free movement would hinge on the curtailment of the constitutional right of foreigners to refuge.[104]

As the debate in the Bundestag continued, asylum claims mounted in Germany, as did violence against foreigners. Since the signing of the Schengen implementing convention, the number of attacks on non-Europeans had risen 800 percent.[105] Those developments alarmed lawmakers across the political spectrum. "Asylum seekers, immigrants, family reunification, legal guest workers, illegal ones . . . we are approaching the 1 million mark this year," as an SPD member said. "Immigration has reached levels that are no longer sustainable."[106] By the end of 1992, the Social Democratic leadership had finally consented to constitutional reform, in exchange for a promised liberalization of German naturalization rules: as the right to seek asylum narrowed, the right to seek citizenship would broaden.[107] Accordingly, the government mustered the two-thirds majority for altering the Basic Law. The amendment, a new Article 16a, reaffirmed the grant of asylum rights—"Persons persecuted on political grounds shall have the right of asylum." But it limited the grant by virtue of country of first entry, stating that the right to asylum on German soil could "not be invoked by a person who enters the federal territory from a member state of the European Communities" or from any state that applied international conventions on refugees and on human rights and freedoms.[108] No longer would politically persecuted people have an unqualified right to seek asylum in Germany. Not if the asylum seeker had first entered another European country, then moved freely across Schengen's internal borders, arriving in Germany.

In July 1993, the Bundestag at last ratified the Schengen treaty. Earlier that summer, the amendment to the constitutional right of asylum had become part of the Basic Law, which cleared the way for the ratification of Schengen's implementing convention. The amendment spoke neither of Schengen nor the country of first entry, but implicitly it, too, ratified the treaty's rules, absolving Germany of the obligation to adjudicate all asylum claims. Paradoxically, approval of Schengen's supranational rules led to new assertions of German sovereignty designed to turn back the tide of asylum seekers. In the words of Germany's interior minister, "Whoever says yes to a Europe without borders must also say yes to a common European asylum policy."[109]

––––––––––––––––––––

Three years after the return to the Moselle River for the signing of the Schengen implementing convention aboard the riverboat, all signatory states had ratified the treaty. Parliaments gave a democratic hearing to its terms while courts in Schengen's member countries provided judicial review. What particularly concerned the legislators and jurists about free movement in a borderless Europe and the harmonizing of security measures was encroachment on both national sovereignty and individual rights, set in relief by the claims of asylum seekers in transit across the Schengen countries.

France was first to ratify, Germany last. In both countries, however, ratification gave rise to constitutional reform of national asylum law, as lawmakers confronted the Schengen rule assigning asylum responsibility to the country of first entry. A new Article 53-1, adopted by France, expressly preserved the power of the nation to grant refuge to any asylum seeker in its territory. A new Article 16a, adopted by Germany, gave the nation power to refuse any asylum seeker who had first entered another Schengen country or any country with robust protection for asylum rights. In contrasting ways, the constitutional reform arising from Schengen's ratification affirmed national sovereignty.

The signing of the Schengen treaties had given an unremarkable village in Luxembourg the aura of legend. But during the prolonged ratification process, as conflict in parliaments and courts brought Schengen's rules more fully into public view, the legend took on opposing meanings. Laboratory of free movement. Embodiment of Citizens' Europe. Sieve Europe. Fortress Europe. Debating ratification entailed probing into the details of a supranational regime devised behind closed doors, a disclosure that made Schengen a symbol of the most vexed aspects of European union—sovereignty and human rights, migration and asylum, market rules and civic bonds. As the Churches Committee for Migrants in Europe observed in 1993, the "realisation of a Europe without internal borders has proved to be a lot more complex and complicated than its promoters had imagined." And among the complexities were "questions of respect for human rights."[110]

The conflict made evident the ambiguities of all that Schengen had come to symbolize in the years since the first treaty signing on the Moselle River. "Schengen is becoming a myth," a conservative deputy declared in the National Assembly during the ratifying debate in France. But it was undeserving of the aura of other European landmarks, places of conquest and glory. "After all, it is neither Alesia, nor Pavia, nor Versailles, nor Rapallo, nor Rome," he said, but simply "a good way to build Europe" and to safeguard "the sovereignty of our country, the security of the French."[111]

But reconciling European cosmopolitanism with national sovereignty had indeed proved complicated. In France, the problem of sovereignty had led parliament to look back at the country's history of national republicanism; in Germany, it led the Bundestag to return to the crimes of the Nazi era. The ratification of the treaty, however, ensured that Schengen's symbolism would carry practical force. Schengen was not a site of an armed battle. No sovereign had gained or lost an empire there. But within its borders, the nature of sovereignty would change, as supranational measures of security compensated for the dismantling of internal frontiers. Precisely because Schengen was a place of free movement, it was a place of risk. Under the treaty, security would be lodged not in physical checkpoints but rather in digital information. As a Bundestag member said, Schengen marked a "step into the European surveillance state."[112]

5

A Place of Risk

MARKS & SPENCER, the British emporium of choice for everything from haberdashery to haricot beans, opened its first international store in Paris in 1975. It stood on the Boulevard Haussmann, a street teeming with commerce, an artery cut through the warren of ancient streets by Georges-Eugène Haussmann in the renovation of the city a century earlier. The Paris store was a brick-and-mortar emblem of transnational retail—a bedrock of the globalizing post-war economy.[1]

A decade after the migration of Marks & Spencer to France, at the moment when European treatymakers were devising the Schengen accord, a bomb exploded inside the Parisian outpost of the British department store. It detonated in the food department early on a February morning in 1985, just after the doors had opened to shoppers. It killed one person and wounded fifteen.[2] The 15 May Organization, a Palestinian terrorist group, claimed responsibility for the bombing.[3] It began a wave of violence that would convulse the French capital for more than a year and extend to other nations. As Schengen took shape, Paris became the epicenter of a European confrontation with terror that—like commerce—crossed borders.[4]

The bloodshed had profound geopolitical consequences, pervading the project of European union and influencing Schengen's creation—making brutally palpable that a territory of free movement was a place of risk. From its inception, Schengen was understood to be a site of dualisms, where freedom would join with security, and cosmopolitanism with the exclusion of non-Europeans. From

FIGURE 5.1. The detonation of a bomb at the Marks & Spencer store in Paris on February 23, 1985, killed one person and wounded fifteen. The attack, carried out by a Palestinian extremist group, brought attention to cross-border terrorism as Schengen treatymakers devised compensatory measures for free movement. Credit: Michel Baret / GAMMA RAPHO

the drafting of the first treaty to the ratifying of the implementing convention, the abolition of internal borders was hedged by concerns about the risks of free movement across the expanse of the Schengen area.

The Schengen Information System would manage that risk. It stood at the center of Schengen's security apparatus and policing infrastructure, a mechanism for gathering, storing, and exchanging information, with tentacles branching across the Schengen countries. The treatymakers designed the system to consist of a vast computerized file, which would pair surveillance with free movement, compensating for the lifting of physical borders with the collection and distribution of personal data. Along with the treaty's requirements for harmonizing immigration rules, cooperating on external border control, and keeping a shared list of countries whose nationals were to be excluded, the information system would rely on common procedures for tracking persons denied entry, principally through techniques of international data exchange.[5]

Detection, therefore, would be achieved through digital surveillance, a transnational instrument of police power aimed at arresting illegal immigration. A declaration by ministers and state secretaries appended to Schengen's implementing convention stated that "risks in the fields of security and illegal immigration" required external border controls and "harmonization of working methods for surveillance."[6] Such surveillance would not only detect unlawful asylum seeking, by claimants seeking refuge in multiple countries, but also augment protections against acts of terrorism, such as the bombing at the Paris department store. The treatymaking that produced the Schengen security architecture would, in turn, shape the founding of Europol, the European Union Agency for Law Enforcement Cooperation. As Schengen institutionalized the conflicting principles of free movement and state security, it expressed the aims of policing a transnational place of risk well before Europol began operating as a multinational crime-fighting agency in 1994. To this day, the Schengen Information System remains integral to European policing. With "no internal borders between Schengen countries," as the European Commission has explained, it became a "cooperation tool for . . . immigration, police, customs," a system that "compensates for borders," so that "people and objects can be located."[7]

From the Schengen laboratory, then, emerged a transnational panopticon of the information age—a security instrument that substituted for control at territorial borders with cross-border information flows augmenting the state's police power. And in the Schengen area, the guarantee of security was etched not at the borders between nations but at the boundary between Europeans

and non-Europeans. The arcana of the prolonged treatymaking—
the meeting notes and diplomatic telegrams—recorded the construction of the surveillance system. It also recorded treatymakers' confrontation with the conflict between digital surveillance
and individual privacy, the protection of a right to informational
self-determination. Again, too, the problem was to reconcile state
authority with transnational institutions, in this instance state
control of the administration of justice with cross-border surveillance and policing. For the power lodged in the Schengen Information System trenched also on democratic self-determination.
A transnational information system designed to secure the
Schengen territory against the risks of free movement put at risk
both individual privacy and state sovereignty, core aspects of
self-determination.[8]

Within the borderless interior of the Schengen area, the surveillance system challenged venerable doctrines that defined security as coterminous with physical territory.[9] Transnational policing
also underlay the effort of the Schengen countries to redefine the
principles of associational life, the elements of what the political
philosopher Michael Walzer has termed "*communities of character*, historically stable, ongoing associations of men and women
with some special commitment to one another and some special
sense of their common life."[10] In Schengen, with European belonging constituted by the dismantling of internal frontiers, common
life depended on other markers of identity, and, by proxy, race—
distinctions that would be maintained by a web of digital surveillance reaching from the interior of states to Schengen's external
borders to the home countries of migrants deemed "undesirable." If
state administration depended on "knowledge of the files," to borrow Max Weber's classic's phrase, Schengen made the files a mode
of transnational policing.[11]

The risks posed by the information system were deepened by
Schengen's strange character as an intergovernmental creature.
Schengen had no government of its own; it was founded as a place
without a legislature or a judiciary—and yet it would have a powerful transnational security apparatus. Therefore, Schengen was a
place of risk in a double sense—risks posed by the free movement
of people across borders, and risks posed to individual freedom

by a security system subject to no countervailing transnational institutions that would either protect individual rights or curb the police power of nation-states enhanced by new techniques of surveillance. Schengen's strangeness was bluntly summed up, soon after the treaty entered into force, by none other than the director of the Schengen Secretariat, a quasi-administrative body with no substantive executive powers. "The term 'Schengen institution' is itself a paradox," said the director, Wouter van de Rijt. "This tremendous tool that is Schengen, a tool for police cooperation and free movement, does not have institutions in the forms with which we're familiar. . . . Schengen is not presided over by a government that leads, a parliament that votes, or a court that judges." Of this peculiar system of power, he observed, "Montesquieu would probably have had any number of reasons to roll over in his grave in encountering a dynamic process like Schengen."[12]

The Schengen Information System began its working life in a rural corner of Strasbourg in 1995. The data files took shape on a dead-end street called rue de Schengen, in the French city bordering Germany. A small, nondescript building housed two computers and 2.3 million files of the apparatus known as the SIS.[13]

Half of the files concerned foreigners classified as "undesirable," along with other unwanted persons; the other half had to do with stolen objects—vehicles, weapons, banknotes, identity papers. Twenty-eight information technology specialists, all French, tended the files. Each of the Schengen countries also sent a representative to oversee the central database, which transmitted information to national networks when alerts were entered by authorities throughout the Schengen area. Police then acted on the digital intelligence.[14]

Supervisors of the SIS boasted of the speed of the information exchange enabled by the technical machinery. "We are able to respond to a request for information from a national center in less than five minutes," the director in Strasbourg, Bernard Kirch, told *Le Monde*, whose story on the inauguration of the SIS offered a tour into "the heart of the information system."[15]

At its heart, the system operated to give Schengen countries knowledge of the people crossing their borders. The Schengen implementing convention explained how the knowledge would travel almost instantaneously, the computer files allowing authorities, "by means of an automated search procedure, to have access to alerts on persons and property." The purpose of the knowledge, the treaty stated, was to enable "the administration of legislation on aliens in the context of . . . the movement of persons," the enforcement of national law in matters such as asylum, visas, and residence permits. Within the borders of the Schengen territory, digital alerts would replace physical barriers in checking the free movement of foreigners.[16]

This was the panopticon built by Schengen. The site in Strasbourg had no watchtower. Its instruments of surveillance were not "architecture and geometry," as Foucault famously wrote of Bentham's prison. Its axis of knowledge and power did not rest on eyesight. Instead, Schengen's non-corporeal information system used digital intelligence stored in millions of computer files as mechanisms of discipline and exclusion—recording all people, categorizing all objects, and linking Strasbourg with Europe's periphery. Yet it, too, relied on permanent registration, as a political technology of surveillance, replacing physical restraint with the speed and ubiquity of the digital files.[17] The observation was not of a prisoner locked in a cell but rather of a foreigner moving across the Schengen area.

Transnational surveillance under the data system reintroduced techniques of separation and exclusion in a space cleared of physical borders. Without chains, locks, or internal checkpoints, this new machine enforced the distinction between insider and outsider, national and foreigner. The "undesirable" was a new category of abnormal, made into an object of knowledge stored in the building in Strasbourg.[18]

The debut of Schengen's information system had been delayed by some technical problems as well as political maneuvering by the countries preparing to bring Schengen into force in 1995. The system's creators were too sanguine about the setup, which involved blending German computer equipment and French software. It cost 40 million francs.[19] A plan for the mechanics of the database had been spelled out by the Schengen implementing convention a half-decade earlier. The central file in Strasbourg would support national branches in each of the Schengen countries. The system would function according to a hit / no-hit mechanism, allowing authorities to determine if the database held an alert on a person. A hit meant policing instructions would follow. Possible instructions included arrest, extradition, and "discreet surveillance."[20]

The blueprint for the system had developed slowly, drafted over the course of the five years of treatymaking that produced the implementing convention. The SIS fulfilled a pledge, set forth in the 1985 accord, to "improve the exchange of information," particularly in the "fight against crime" and to "prevent the unauthorized entry and residence of persons." The pledge on information exchange formed part of a broader resolve among the Schengen countries "to ensure the protection of the entire territory . . . against illegal immigration and the activities which could jeopardize security." But the document was bare of specifics, deferring the details to negotiations on the implementing convention that would develop further "compensatory measures." The name "Schengen Information System" was not yet in use.[21]

Always, however, Schengen's treatymakers foresaw that the removal of internal borders would create a new territory of risk, proposing to compensate for free movement and the elimination of physical controls with enhanced information exchange. At a Bonn meeting of the police and security working group in March 1985, before the initial accord was finalized, delegates discussed how data could bolster cross-border crime control. "One of the key areas for improving collaboration will be the establishment of information exchange," noted a summary of the meeting prepared by the West German delegation. Shared data would be a weapon against unwanted movement, reinforcing the "fight against illegal entry."[22]

But data was a tricky subject. The risk it carried, foreseen by the treatymakers from the outset, lay in the intrusion on civil liberties—above all, on the right to privacy. At the Bonn meeting, the negotiators acknowledged that certain categories of information "must lead to a restriction of personal liberty." Together, legal and technical obstacles would make automatic linking of data files "impossible," they concluded. The dilemmas appeared pervasive—"all states face serious legal problems inherent in the protection of computerized data"—leading the negotiators to point to the need for a "specific convention of public international law" that would clarify the rules for transnational data linkages. "This goal cannot be achieved in the short term," the meeting's draft summary found, underscoring that the "need for information and the nature of its transmission . . . will have to be decided in detail in future meetings."[23]

The treatymakers did not wait long to make information exchange a formal prong of Schengen planning. Soon after the signing of the 1985 treaty, as the discussion of the implementing convention started, they agreed to consider using electronic equipment to facilitate the exchange of information among Schengen countries. The proposal came from West Germany's delegation. The idea was to study "not only the technical but also the legal aspects" involved in allowing transnational and instant access to data about people as well as goods.[24] That was the seed of the information system.

Architects of the information system found templates in national webs of data exchange, but also marked differences in the practices of Schengen countries. The most instructive model was in West Germany, a federal republic with a powerful police force, which had authority, for example, to use an advanced file-matching strategy, called *Rasterfahndung*, to identify terrorists affiliated with the Red Army Faction.[25] An information system for the police, called *Informationssystem der Polizei*, or INPOL, had begun operating in 1972, administered jointly by the federal government and the *Länder*, or states. The Bundeskriminalamt served as a central clearinghouse for data exchange, hosting a network in Wiesbaden with links to files in each of the states. Authorities could consult the network to check travelers entering the country.[26] France maintained a pair of central sites for storing information, one with the National Police and the other with the National Gendarmerie, with both agencies equipped to draw on common data to refuse entry to ineligible persons. Automated systems also already managed roughly 40 percent of France's cross-border freight traffic. The Benelux states used a shared file in monitoring their external borders, though it was not computerized.[27]

A permanent Schengen working group on information exchange formed in December 1987. The aim was to plan for the "search union." That was the shorthand used by police and security officials in a report to the central Schengen negotiating group; such a search union would bind together member states whose internal borders were projected to "lose their filter character after the removal of controls."[28] Early the next year, the Standing Working Group on the Schengen Information System began its deliberations. Negotiations proceeded in a common language, English, rather than in translation, as had been customary for prior Schengen planning. Members of the working group included information technology experts as well as police officials from each country.[29]

The working group's first task was studying the feasibility of digital information exchange and its technical composition. Consensus came quickly on the basics. The group found that a multinational file was technically attainable, defining the purpose as storing and exchanging data for use in crime control as well as in decisions on visas, residency requests, and work permits. It advised setting up files for each Schengen country, all anchored in a central database. National authorities could report persons or goods in the system, as needed by considerations of public order and national security. An alert would then appear across the entire network, signaling how police should proceed with a suspect— whether, for example, to pursue immediate arrest for extradition, or refuse entry because of nonadmission in another member state, or seize goods, or perform discreet checks as part of a surveillance request.[30] Access to the files would exist every hour of the day, for use by police, border control, customs, and judicial, visa, and vehicle registration officials in all Schengen countries as well as by certain European agencies.[31]

The planning on information exchange to offset free movement found parallels within European Community institutions. Here, too, Schengen offered a laboratory. The Community's anti-terrorism committee, known as the Trevi group, based a study of a common automatic system of data exchange "on the model of Schengen," according to the European Commission.[32] The Community's justice and interior ministers supported a cross-border network for police cooperation, but met resistance from national policing officials "jealous for their sovereignty," as *Le Républicain Lorrain*, a regional French newspaper, reported in 1987, noting that the development of transnational surveillance was more advanced at the intergovernmental level, where "significant progress in the exchange of information" was laying the groundwork for a "European super-police."[33]

By then, a European super-police had come to appear necessary because of the rising threat posed by international terrorism. Just days after the signing of the first Schengen treaty, in June 1985, a bomb had blasted through a departure hall in the Frankfurt airport, killing three people, with responsibility later traced to a militant Palestinian group.[34] Evidence mounted of border crossings by terrorist groups. Members of the Red Brigades, a terrorist group that carried out murders, kidnappings, and sabotage, moved from Italy into France.[35] Lebanese terrorists, linked to a network that had visited violence on Paris, were arrested in Frankfurt. The mobility of terror led to a Paris summit on counterterrorism in 1987.[36] It was followed by another in Venice, where European leaders confronted the statistics of violence: nearly eight hundred acts of international terrorism committed the prior year, with some two thousand casualties.[37] Illegal traffic in contraband goods also crossed national frontiers, including stolen and forged passports circulating in an international black market.[38] All of which fueled calls for surveilling the transit of people and goods, as borders lost their force as sites of interdiction. As the *Deutsches Allgemeines Sonntagsblatt* observed, "the border barrier is to be replaced by the computer terminal."[39]

Schengen promised to become a new locus of police cooperation. As the working group on the information system drafted the procedures for digital surveillance, it defined data sharing as a basis for transnational policing. A memo prepared by France's inter-ministry coordinator for free movement, Émile Cazimajou, assessing the "status of work on implementing the agreement" as of February 1989, explained why the control of persons hinged on information exchange. "The contracting parties considered that one of the conditions for the abolition of checks at the common borders was the creation of a common system enabling police authorities, by means of a computerized query procedure, to have alerts for the purposes of search for objects and persons, with a view to questioning or monitoring them during police checks carried out in in accordance with national law," Cazimajou wrote. The police checks would occur "at the external borders and within the country," and rules would be developed for cross-border observation and cross-border pursuit.[40] As the French foreign ministry's secretary general affirmed, "discreet surveillance" would equip authorities to convey information—a suspect's location, a vehicle used, objects transported—"on the occasion of police checks."[41]

Of all the treaty's articles, however, the sections on surveillance, data exchange, and police operations proved most difficult to draft. In a handwritten memo of December 1989, Cazimajou indicated that the work was still unfinished, while again stressing the importance of the computerized file. He wrote of the "extreme attention" paid to realizing the database, "an essential aspect regarding the abolition of controls at common borders." But that attention also brought adverse scrutiny, not least from French regulators concerned with personal data protection, Cazimajou noted. The surveillance architecture was itself, he wrote, "under strict surveillance by the Commission nationale de l'informatique et des libertés, or National Commission on Informatics and Liberty, France's data protection authority. Nonetheless, he expected a "constructive solution," heartened that the regulators had not expressed opposition to a transnational information system.[42] Indeed, the Informatics Commission expressed no intention of blocking police cooperation "through cross-border information systems."[43] It found no conflict, in principle, between the protection of personal data and a common information system in Schengen's zone of free movement.

But devising the provisions was a fractious process within the working group. Among the most vexed issues was speed: how quickly information transmitted by one country would be available to the others and for what purpose. France pressed for delayed transmission, especially of information underwriting extradition. West Germany argued that this would introduce unnecessary chokeholds into a system designed to overcome barriers to information sharing.[44] Ultimately, the decision was against delay, providing instead for the "rapid and effective transmission of data."[45] There was also division on the scope of the information system and control of the national files, stemming in part from differing traditions of personal data protection among the Schengen countries. Belgium stressed that any reference to international norms on the processing of personal data would have "value in principle, but no effect in positive law." The Dutch sought language clarifying that the purpose of SIS extended beyond police checks to cover immigration and customs control. West Germany objected to provisions recognizing the independence of national files from the central database, while France disputed language indicating that the central system "controls the national files."[46] Compromises were reached on "Data on aliens," including use of alerts for refusal of entry, removal, and deportation.[47] There were debates over single words—*dangerous*, as applied to criminals; *extremely*, as applied to crimes—with *dangerous* deleted as excessively vague, but *extremely* retained as regarding alerts for crimes.[48]

The greatest conflict emerged over harmonizing rules governing data use for extradition. The Netherlands and West Germany defended broad and rapid information exchange—"automatic incorporation of alerts"—to support extradition requests. The French government sought limitations, making the entry of extradition data into the system subject to the express agreement of the country from which the suspect would be extradited, "not taking the risk of arresting a person whom one does not wish to extradite."[49] But that rule, it was claimed, would thwart the principle of rapid data exchange, "emptying the information system of its meaning."[50] Luxembourg proposed a "variable" system allowing acceptance of data alerts for extradition to some requested states but not others, which the Netherlands rejected as contrary to the "uniformity of the system." West Germany's delegation offered a compromise that would create obligations for every country seeking data use for extradition to verify that the request complied with the national law of the country from which extradition was requested. The working group further sought to appease France by drafting a specific stipulation for extradition from its national territory.[51] The course of the negotiations on such vexed issues reflected the priorities of the most senior leaders of the Schengen states. In the fall of 1989, a Mitterrand adviser wrote to France's chief negotiator on Schengen to convey the president's position on key criminal justice priorities. Mitterrand directed his diplomats not to yield on a high threshold for extradition requests. But he gave ground on the issue of hot pursuit, reasoning, as his adviser quoted his conclusion, that, "Europeans (and the police) must learn to live together." The observation wryly acknowledged that European cosmopolitanism required European police cooperation.[52]

Even the computer equipment, which was to reflect Schengen's cosmopolitan ambitions, evoked disagreement. The working group sifted through proposals, leaning toward a French-American consortium. But the governments of the Schengen countries insisted on using domestic companies for a project meant to signify European identity. They selected the French computer company Groupe Bull and Germany's Siemens Nixdorf Informationssysteme, along with the Anglo-French IT company Sema Group.[53]

Finally, the location of the central terminal required compromise. The French initially submitted Paris as the capital of the Schengen search union, saying that the city had "a high-quality computer environment." The Benelux states favored Luxembourg.[54] Then, the Grand Duchy withdrew in exchange for a concession from the French on hot pursuit.[55] The Germans appeared poised to suggest their country given its "IT environment." So, in place of Paris, the French put forward Strasbourg, which lay closer to the German border.[56]

What the treatymakers fully agreed on was the value of the information system in a space without borders—on the use of digital surveillance to enable free movement by ensuring security and preventing crime across the expanse of the Schengen countries. The implementing convention declared: "The purpose of the Schengen Information System shall be . . . to maintain public policy and public security, including national security, in the territories of the Contracting Parties and to apply the provisions of this Convention relating to the movement of persons in those territories, using information communicated via this system."[57] The articles on the data files included myriad provisions dealing with crime and criminal process.

When Schengen's information system became the cornerstone of enhanced police cooperation, the use of supranational institutions to curb criminal activity already had a long history in Europe. For a century, maintaining public security had involved joint state efforts to suppress violence by non-state actors. Global in scale, these efforts accelerated after the First World War and were formalized with the founding of the International Criminal Police Organization, or Interpol, after the Second World War. But the advent of free movement in Western Europe beginning with the Rome Treaty, and the abolition of internal border controls in the Schengen area, hastened deeper European security cooperation.[58]

The origins of joint European policing traced back to the late nineteenth century, when fears of anarchist terrorism swept the continent. From Paris to Barcelona to Geneva, acts of anarchist violence claimed European lives, and European nations enacted anti-anarchist laws. In 1898, a Pan-European anti-anarchist conference met in Rome. Delegates from twenty-one nations gathered for a month at the Corsini Palace, in a convocation titled the International Conference of Rome for the Social Defense against Anarchists. The conference began with a call for "universal recognition of the necessity for common action against the Anarchists"; it ended with resolves for European police cooperation and information exchange, with common action particularly directed to measures for extraditing anarchists.[59] In 1914, the first International Criminal Police Congress met in Monaco, addressing crime prevention, surveillance, and extradition. In 1923, aspirations for collective policing were further institutionalized at a Vienna conference that created the International Criminal Police Commission. The countries participating in the Vienna conference were primarily European, but there were also delegates from Egypt, Japan, and the United States. Arrests, extradition, fingerprinting techniques, recordkeeping—all were fields for common action. The rise of Nazism ended the commission, but after the war Belgian police led the way in its revival. In 1956, at a Vienna conference, the commission became Interpol.[60]

Interpol was based in Paris, but it was truly global. Dedicated to principles of both universality and national sovereignty, it was founded by some fifty countries—from Argentina, Australia, Austria, Belgium, Britain, and Cuba to India, Iran, Italy, Israel, and Japan; from Libya, Mexico, the Netherlands, Norway, Pakistan, the

Philippines, and Portugal to Spain, Sudan, Sweden, Syria, Thailand, Turkey, the United States, West Germany, Venezuela, and Yugoslavia. Interpol's statement of principles explained that police cooperation was founded on the action of each national police force operating within its national territory and adhering to national law. At the same time, Interpol would enable "any country to cooperate with another country" in combating international crime, "without setting geographical limits to co-operation."[61]

By 1989, as the Schengen treatymakers crafted plans for the information system, Interpol had reached a membership of 150 countries, increasing its presence in Africa, Asia, and the Americas. It was still centered in France, but in Lyon, not Paris.[62] Some of the provisions of its founding constitution had been updated. But the declaration of Interpol's fundamental policing aims was unchanged: "To ensure and promote the widest possible mutual assistance between all criminal police authorities within the limits of the laws existing in the different countries and in the spirit of the Universal Declaration of Human Rights. . . . To establish and develop all institutions likely to contribute effectively to the prevention and suppression of ordinary law crimes."[63] The cooperation was built on a system of color-coded notices, alerting authorities to everything from missing persons to suspects wanted for serious crimes.[64]

But Interpol's inadequacies became increasingly apparent to European nations, which accounted for the majority of the police communications in the system.[65] Some of the problems were technical. Interpol was still relying on Morse code as the basis of an expansive radio network when the Schengen negotiations began. Behind the transmission of urgent policing priorities sat operators punching telegraph keys by hand. Upgrades were too costly, straining a budget that drew on contributions from individual states.[66] "Interpol was a post office," said Jürgen Storbeck, a West German police official who worked there from 1980 to 1983—meaning it was an organization unsuited for combating cross-border terrorism and drug trafficking.[67] That concern had arisen years earlier in West Germany, at a meeting of the Bund Deutscher Kriminalbeamter, an association of criminal investigative officers. The central criticism was that Interpol was inadequately equipped to address the threats evolving from free border crossings within the common market, as mandated by the Rome Treaty. The association's director, Rolf Grunert, broached a plan for greater European police cooperation, including deputizing European agents with investigative powers.[68]

At first, such planning developed within the Interpol network, but the progress of the European Community toward the free movement of goods and persons gave impetus to new forms of European police cooperation. As dissatisfaction with Interpol's central apparatus deepened, meetings of the agency's European Regional Conference took on greater importance. At a conference in 1981, Interpol agents from West Germany proposed amalgamating the police activity of various National Central Bureaus into a single regional bureau. A working group formed by the European Regional Conference took up the task of examining the proposal, issuing a report in 1984, the same year that West German and French leaders met in Saarbrücken to announce the lifting of checks at their common border—a bilateral accord that also promised joint action to combat "drugs, crime, and the irregular entry of people."[69]

Saarbrücken, the most consequential of all precursors to Schengen, was also a landmark in the planning for ever-closer police cooperation. In the wake of Saarbrücken, police officials gathered in Paris, pledging, as Jürgen Storbeck later recalled, to "fight to overcome the risk of open borders." Despite the accord's resolutions about combating crime, he said, Saarbrücken's authors had paid insufficient attention to the scale of the risk—and to the practical details of integrating West German and French police forces. "They hadn't thought about the security risks," said Storbeck, who was then leading a unit of the Bundeskriminalamt, West Germany's criminal police office. "We came up with it."[70]

At that time, European police coordination occurred mostly informally. As a senior official in the Bundeskriminalamt, Storbeck recalled, he sent a deputy to Paris to learn about France's response to Action Directe, a radical-left terrorist organization that resembled the Baader-Meinhof Group in West Germany. The German deputy frequented a café near the Élysée Palace where French officers went for coffee. Their conversations led to policing advice. Such casual exchange was also how police chiefs coordinated their activities at the tripoint joining Aachen in Germany,

Liège in Belgium, and Maastricht in the Netherlands. Authorities met monthly to share notes about detecting suspects on their most-wanted lists.[71]

Schengen's creation appeared to present still greater security risks from free movement across open borders. The liberty of coming and going—though held, in principle, only by Europeans—made the vast territory of five countries a place of unprecedented risk. And it imposed new security burdens on the police. As a police commissioner and member of France's negotiating group put it, "The abolition of internal borders between the member states of the Schengen accord cannot put at risk the internal security of those states."[72] Along with the intergovernmental planning for cross-border policing, ad hoc methods of surveillance persisted. A joint French-Dutch initiative stationed officers from the two countries at major border crossings, where they kept watch with binoculars to detect unauthorized immigrants. As *Statewatch* described the surveillance, "Schengen does not allow any systematic controls on the borders, so the police and *Koninklijke Marechaussee* have come up with a creative solution." The detection explicitly relied on racial markers. "Yes, the colour of the skin did play a role in this process, as a helpful marechaussee officer explained to inquiring journalists."[73]

After the signing of the first Schengen treaty, police officials went ahead rapidly with forming greater European cooperation. The European Regional Conference acted on the proposals of its working group, creating a European Secretariat, alongside a Technical Committee for Cooperation in Europe. By 1986, proposals for common European policing developed alongside the drafting of the Schengen implementing convention. As Storbeck recalled, "Suddenly, Europe specifically was the agenda."[74]

Schengen contributed decisively to the police agenda. During the expedited talks that yielded the 1985 accord, the working group on security had already foreseen cross-border police cooperation extending beyond Interpol—a system to be based on information exchange. A meeting of the working group in Bonn, in March 1985, clarified the agenda. Minutes from the meeting, sent from West Germany's interior ministry to ministries in the partner countries, described the existing cooperation, which occurred mainly between local police authorities who happened to operate in adjacent districts. "Police collaboration will have to be accentuated as the border controls are reduced," the working group concluded, stressing "contacts between immigration services." The removal of foreign migrants posed a particular problem of policing. "Illegal immigrants cannot be returned to another EC member state, but must be returned to their countries of origin," the working group determined, proposing cooperation between border police and immigration officials to ensure that migrants barred from one state could not enter others. The conclusions of the working group expressly found that Interpol networks were insufficient for joint action on illegal immigration: "Collaboration must go beyond the framework of Interpol and become much more formal." Schengen became a platform for going beyond Interpol's framework with a European policing agenda aimed especially at illegal border crossing.[75]

As outlined by the Schengen treatymakers, a common European police system would enhance the power of each state rather than amalgamating the power of all into a central authority. A principal author of the 1985 treaty was Gilbert Guillaume, the director of legal affairs in France's foreign ministry, who prepared a penultimate draft with a provision on police cooperation declaring member states would "strengthen cooperation among their customs and police authorities, notably in the fight against crime . . . against the irregular entry and stay of people and against customs fraud and contraband." It also provided for data exchange, instructing that states, "in compliance with their internal legislation . . . shall endeavor to improve the exchange of information." This became Article 9. Later, Guillaume elaborated the principle of state security underlying the text. In an article in the *International and Comparative Law Quarterly*, he explained that the globalization of terrorism had "propelled States to the forefront of the international arena." He wrote of the power of nation-states, which "alone are entitled to deploy violence legitimately." There would be no transfer of sovereignty to European institutions; rather, the legitimate deployment of violent police power would remain the sole prerogative of nation-states. As the Schengen states prepared to remove internal borders, the capability of each would be augmented through mutual legal assistance, extradition agreements, information exchange, and criminal pursuit at common borders. In Schengen, cross-border networks would enhance national police power.[76]

Meanwhile, bilateral plans emerged to suppress terrorism, as government ministers in West Germany and France directed attention to the acceleration of cross-border movement. In 1987, Friedrich Zimmermann, West Germany's interior minister, joined his French counterpart, Charles Pasqua, to announce the launching of cross-border pursuit of criminals and information exchange. "For a long time, criminals have not been deterred by our borders," said Zimmermann, who had been a lieutenant in the German army during the Second World War, and "recent terrorist events . . . have highlighted the ideological and technical rapprochement of terrorist groups." As violence traveled across borders, it was "necessary to establish an equally close collaboration of the police, especially in the operational field." Acting together, France and West Germany would be "an engine, and an example," he said, "for intensified cooperation between Western European police."[77]

For the Trevi group, the Franco-German effort offered a model of the cross-border European police cooperation projected in Schengen. European Commission documents spoke of a "Trevi-Schengen group," as ministers of the Schengen states met to complete the drafting of the treaty's sections on criminal law.[78] The Trevi group brought together representatives from justice and home affairs ministries in European Community countries in an intergovernmental body formed to counter terrorism. It was founded in Rome in 1976, taking its name from the city's majestic fountain.[79] Just as anarchist violence had led Europe's diplomats to meet in Rome a century earlier, so the Trevi group tracked the threat of terrorism. But it was only with Schengen's guarantee of the free movement of persons that Trevi's purview came to include immigration.[80] A highly anticipated Trevi meeting in Brussels in April 1987, just after the Franco-German anti-terrorism pact became public, addressed information exchange, illegal immigration, police cooperation, and hot pursuit. The ministers explored ways of detecting foreign nationals at borders. Finally, they examined the law of extradition, increasingly viewed as a lynchpin of criminal justice.[81]

As the Trevi group dwelled on the movement of people across borders, Schengen's imprint grew more pronounced.[82] The treatymaking overlapped with the counterterrorism agenda of cross-border police cooperation. The European press remarked how migration had become a Trevi concern, but also how common rules proved hard to define. As *La Libre Belgique* noted, "Drugs, terrorism and . . . immigration: European ministers would like to harmonize procedures. Simple?"[83] The same issues preoccupied the Schengen treatymakers, as did the task of harmonizing criminal procedures. At a Schengen meeting in Berlin in 1987, which commemorated the city's 750th anniversary, policing and security were paramount: mutual legal aid in pursuing terrorists and drug traffickers; surveilling Schengen's external borders to block illegal entry; tracking the movements of foreign nationals inside the territory; data sharing.[84] Trevi officials recognized Schengen as a site, quite literally, for converting their advisory responsibilities into concrete measures. By 1989, the Trevi group and Schengen diplomats held joint meetings, examining the risks of free movement and open borders: "The consequences of the bringing down of internal border controls for the movements of terrorists."[85] The aim was to address security at the "political level," with Schengen providing a basis for intergovernmental cooperation across Western Europe.[86]

From that dialogue emerged a Trevi working group on the security challenges posed by the free movement of people. It was titled Trevi '92, the year of the single market's expected completion, and drew on the principles defined by the committees drafting the Schengen implementing convention.[87] The Trevi studies, wrote Hubert Blanc, a French delegate at the Schengen meetings, "are naturally inspired by Schengen's solutions and align with them on the essentials."[88] By 1990, Trevi had issued an "Action Programme," which echoed the Schengen principles in calling for multilateral police training and data exchange.[89]

Meanwhile, as the long work of drafting the Schengen convention drew to a close, the matter of police cooperation remained a priority but also a point of conflict. The fall of the Berlin Wall had slowed the convention's completion, but so too did disagreement over the procedures for common policing. Particularly, there was division on incorporating Interpol into Schengen as a supranational policing force. In April 1989, France's foreign affairs ministry took stock of the progress of the treatymaking, which Paris was chairing at the time, as well as of the European Council's concern with security matters.[90] The ministry's legal office prepared a report—"Free Movement of Persons in Europe"—for an interministerial Schengen meeting. Annexed to the report was a memorandum titled "Observations on the Notion of a 'European Federal Police.'" The memorandum explained that federal policing in Europe would require enacting federal legislation, and it cited models for a European unit ranging from the West German Bundeskriminalamt to the American Federal Bureau of Investigation. It also explained that a European federal police would entail a "definition of a European legal person," whom federal police could pursue and federal authorities could investigate. And this would require cosmopolitan legal institutions—"Federal Court, Federal Prosecutor's Office"—to try the accused as well as a "responsible political authority" to oversee a federal police agency. Without offering a verdict on the notion, the French memorandum cataloged the obstacles to forming a supranational European police force—a transfer of sovereignty unforeseen in Schengen's creation.[91]

Again, as final drafts of the implementing convention circulated, the treatymakers turned away from proposing a transfer of police power to a supranational authority. Indeed, they explicitly refused to assign Interpol that authority in Schengen. A draft text of an article on police cooperation came under scrutiny at a meeting of the Schengen central negotiating group at the end of 1989. The phrasing was still unsettled. It was Belgium that moved to deny Interpol a place in Schengen, deleting it from the text. At that point, the compromise reached on joint policing was to replace the term "Interpol" with the phrase "an authority to be determined." But the implementing convention signed at last in June 1990 did not include that phrase. It provided for police cooperation among the Schengen states but not a common police authority. In pairing free movement with cross-border security, the treaty bypassed the problem of a supranational police power.[92]

Of the 142 articles in the Schengen implementing convention, more than half dealt with security and information exchange. There were chapters on the establishment of the Schengen Information

System, and on police cooperation and mutual assistance in criminal matters. There were chapters on data security and personal data
protection, and on extradition, drug trafficking, and illicit gun use.
There were chapters on crossing internal and external borders. And
there was a chapter on the conditions governing the movement of
aliens. All of which contained procedures for surveillance.[93]

At the time of the convention's signing, the representatives of
the Schengen countries adopted declarations announcing both the
progress and the risks of free movement. The treaty was "an important step towards creating an area without internal borders . . .
a basis for further activities amongst the Member States of the
European Communities," the signatories affirmed, while warning
of "risks in the fields of security and illegal immigration." Therefore,
the declarations stressed the need for gathering information about
the movement of foreigners—procedures to "ascertain the circumstances under which a third-country national has entered the territories" of Schengen—and for "border surveillance."[94]

Alone, the articles of the convention on the Schengen Information System created an entirely new apparatus. The treaty's rules on
internal borders were novel in abolishing, removing, and eliminating barriers, not in forming new structures. The measures on police
cooperation provided for joint prevention of illegal immigration
and pursuit of crime prevention, but did not establish a new police
authority. The provisions for forming an executive committee to
implement the treaty, with each Schengen state having a delegate,
borrowed from the model of the central negotiating committee; it
did not establish a new political body with powers of enforcement
and adjudication.[95] Purely advisory, the executive committee did
not oversee a legislature or judiciary, nor establish supranational
law. Only the Schengen Information System was a fully new institution, creating a surveillance architecture.

Throughout, the treaty reflected the principle that freedom
and security were an inseparable pair, with restraints on the border crossing of foreigners—a priority in preserving national security. Affirmations of free movement that had been intoned by the
treatymakers—"at the borders, pass, pass, pass"—became attached
in the implementing convention to measures fortifying external
border controls, instructing the use of checks to block entry, and
imposing "cross-border surveillance."[96]

Nowhere were the limits on cross-border movement more plain than in the provisions on asylum. On the one hand, the convention preserved the right of all Schengen states to process asylum requests, despite the country-of-first-entry rule, thereby not completely excluding asylum seekers from the freedom to cross internal borders. On the other, the convention protected the absolute right of nation-states to exclude foreign migrants, expressly recognizing the authority of states to control their borders, stipulating that each state "shall retain the right to refuse entry or to expel asylum seekers to a third State on the basis of its national provisions and in accordance with its international commitments."[97] It also provided for cooperation in asylum recordkeeping, in sharing "statistical data on the monthly arrivals of asylum seekers, indicating the main countries of origin," as well as "gathering information on the situation in the asylum seekers' countries of origin." The information exchange also included data on identity—names, aliases, age, nationality, family members, routes traveled—and "any other details needed to establish the asylum seeker's identity."[98]

Extradition, of course, also presupposed restraint on movement, operating through cross border surveillance and data exchange, pairing police cooperation with respect for the authority of national law. The Schengen convention supplemented the European Convention on Extradition, which was adopted in 1957, alongside the Treaty of Rome's rules for free movement in the common market. It stated that the Schengen nations shall "extradite between themselves persons being prosecuted by the judicial authorities" of the member nation for extraditable crimes. But cross-border surveillance of suspects accused of an extraditable crime could occur only where a Schengen nation allowed the police of another to enter its territory (except in cases of great urgency, and then only for a few hours) and where the surveillance procedures complied with national law. Under the Schengen convention, arrests pursuant to extradition could immediately be set in motion via alerts entered into the Schengen Information System, alerts carrying "the same force" as formal requests under the European Convention.[99]

Throughout, too, the treaty gave deference to national sovereignty. That was especially evident in the chapter on police cooperation. It began by declaring that the Schengen countries "undertake to ensure that their police authorities shall, in compliance with national law and within the scope of their powers, assist each other for the purposes of preventing and detecting criminal offences." It further established the primacy of national law by stating that alerts seeking police assistance could occur "in so far as national law does not stipulate that the request has to be made and channeled via the judicial authorities." The treaty imposed significant conditions on cross-border surveillance, protecting the right of the Schengen countries to control persons and exercise plenary police power within their national borders. It specified not only the offenses that could trigger such surveillance—high crimes such as murder, rape, human trafficking, kidnapping and hostage taking, arson, and extortion—but also the office to conduct it in each country: the Criminal Investigation Department in Belgium; the Federal Crime Office in West Germany; the Central Headquarters of the Criminal Police in France; the Principal State Prosecutor in Luxembourg; the National Public Prosecutor in the Netherlands.[100]

Nowhere was the supremacy of national law more plain than in the limits set on cross-border hot pursuit within Schengen. The treaty allowed such pursuit where suspects were caught in the act of committing high crimes. But it restricted the parameters, only authorizing the pursuit across land borders, requiring immediate notice to officials in the country where it was carried out, barring entry into homes and other private spaces, instructing that the action cease as soon as requested by the country where it was occurring, and empowering only local authorities to make arrests. Again guaranteeing the authority of national law, the treaty stated that "pursuing officers shall not have the right to apprehend the pursued person."[101]

At the same time, however, the treaty directed the Schengen countries to promote joint policing via information exchange—by installing telephone, radio, and telex equipment at border areas to accelerate the "transmission of information"—which would operate to facilitate "cross-border surveillance and hot pursuit." It also identified other technologies for improving police communication throughout the Schengen area, from widening the frequency bands in border areas to using standardized communications systems. It advised broad forms of cooperation, calling for the deployment of liaison officers to deepen transnational networks, and it prescribed detailed recordkeeping to support criminal investigation and identity detection, requiring European nationals housing foreigners to "see to it that aliens accommodated therein . . . complete and sign registration forms and confirm their identity."[102]

Across the fields addressed in the Schengen treaty—surveillance, hot pursuit, extradition, asylum, illegal immigration, identity detection, information gathering, data sharing—the Schengen Information System undergirded the prevention of risks to national security and the restraints on the free movement of foreigners. The implementing convention provided in great specificity for the technical details of the information system. It covered everything from the establishment of the file, the mechanics of its operation, and the costs of its maintenance to the rules for the protection of personal data and compliance with the Council of Europe Convention for the Protection of Individuals with regard to Automatic Processing of Personal Data. In operating this system, the Schengen states would each run a national section, with the files arranged uniformly, all supported by a technical service apparatus based in Strasbourg. Throughout the Schengen territory, the system would maintain "national security . . . relating to the movement of persons."[103]

The core of the information system was the machinery of alerts on persons and property that set in motion surveillance and information exchange. It was through the system's automated search procedure that the Schengen states had access to the alerts, for administration of national law "on aliens," external border checks, cross-border surveillance and pursuit, and other acts of joint policing. Each state could issue alerts to refuse entry based on a threat to national security, or to prevent criminal acts, or to seek extradition or arrests, or in cases where "the alien" was subject to deportation, or other forms of forced removal.[104]

At length, the treaty set forth the procedures for "discreet surveillance" and use of the alerts for gathering information, which could trigger "specific checks" whereby persons, vehicles, and objects could be "searched in accordance with national law." If national law disallowed a specific check, the alert would revert to signaling discreet surveillance. Discreet surveillance allowed data to be conveyed to the Schengen state issuing the alert. This would be information about the location of a person subject to an alert; the objects carried; the vehicle used; the circumstances of the detection; the place, time, or reason for a check; the "route and destination of the journey." Uncannily, the convention echoed the description, in *Discipline and Punish*, of techniques of surveillance "absolutely 'discreet'" and "always alert," that operated "like a piece of machinery" and "largely in silence." The treaty required covert vigilance: "During the collection of this information steps must be taken not to jeopardize the discreet nature of the surveillance."[105]

Under the treaty, the Schengen states had wide latitude over the alerts placed in the information system and the data exchanged. The network would contain only information supplied by the states, which had authority to decide when a case was "important enough to warrant entry of the alert." But no state had the power to search the data files of other states; a national section's files were the exclusive domain of that state. Here, too, the treaty protected national autonomy. However, it imposed certain limits on the type of data that could be entered into the system—particularly concerning persons. That information could include no more than certain fundamental details, such as name, sex, nationality, date and place of birth, whether the person was armed or violent, reason for the alert, and certain other markers: "Any specific objective physical characteristics not subject to change." Otherwise, the national law of each Schengen state governed the alerts and data stored in its national section. If a state objected to data in an alert, as inconsistent with "its national law, its international obligations or essential national interests," it could add a "flag" in the data system warning that action on the alert would not occur in its territory, but the alert would apply elsewhere until withdrawn by the issuing country. Time limits controlled sensitive personal data used for "tracing persons"; such information could be kept in the system only as long as the surveillance lasted and for no more than three years. Data on identity papers could be held for five years. It fell to the member states as well to maintain data security, preventing unauthorized access to and use of the files.[106]

Overall, the treaty entrusted the Schengen states with sweeping authority over the information in the transnational system. The state entering an alert had sole responsibility for ensuring that its data was accurate, lawful, and up-to-date, and only that state had the power to alter, correct, or delete the data, unless the alert exceeded the time limits. Each state was to set up an authority responsible for managing the data in its national section. That authority would exercise "independent supervision" of the file, in keeping with national law. Among its responsibilities was data security and personal data protection—assuring that use of the information, the alerts, and exchange of data did not abridge individual rights. A brief directive stated that the national "supervisory authority" would carry out "checking that the processing and use of data entered in the Schengen Information System does not violate the rights of the data subject." But it listed no protocols for rights protection.[107]

It was in more general terms that the treaty recognized the rights of data subjects, while reinforcing national sovereignty. It directed the Schengen countries to adopt national provisions equivalent to European Community safeguards banning data collection on race, political beliefs, religious faith, health, and sexual life, but did not compel ratification of transnational agreements: neither the 1982 Council of Europe Convention for the Protection of Individuals with regard to Automatic Processing of Personal Data nor a 1987 Recommendation of the Committee of Ministers of the Council of Europe regulating the use of personal data in the police sector.[108] It provided for assertions of individual rights, vesting "any person" with the power to seek redress concerning personal data stored in the system, "to correct, delete, or obtain information . . . in connection with an alert involving them." It stated, "Any person shall have the right to ask the supervisory authorities to check data entered in the Schengen Information System which concern them and the use made of such data." It vested the power to decide claims about cross-border data-sharing not with a supranational authority but with national bodies—a court or authority "competent under national law." Invocation of data protection rights would rest strictly on national law.[109]

Under the Schengen treaty, therefore, the creation of a transnational surveillance architecture was not paired with new norms of data protection or new guarantees of individual rights or new forms of governance. Schengen's information system constituted an unprecedented concentration of power to detect, classify, record, and exclude. But the new security institution was overseen by supranational authorities with only advisory power. It vastly expanded cross-border policing with control lodged in the autonomous states that formed the Schengen territory. The implementing convention provided for a "joint supervisory authority" to manage the data system's technical support function, a body consisting of two delegates from each member state, with responsibility to settle interstate disputes about alerts and information use. But it had no enforcement power; nor did the executive committee, established to supervise the treaty's implementation and determine procedures for surveillance and external border checks.[110] Carrying no transfer of sovereignty, the treaty created no supranational legal institutions—no political authority to govern the area, no federal police to prevent security risks, no cosmopolitan courts to adjudicate the rights claims of data subjects.

Influenced by the making of Schengen, however, by the opening of internal borders and the years of intergovernmental dialogue on cross-border policing, a Pan-European police agency emerged. Europol, the European Union Agency for Law Enforcement Cooperation, began operating in 1994. Its legal authority derived from the Maastricht Treaty, which founded the European Union, in 1992. The Schengen treatymaking opened up new conditions of possibility for forming a common European police, which would act as a counterpart of the common market, mitigating the risks of the free movement of goods and people across Europe's frontiers. Within a decade, Schengen's information system—the computer files and alert procedures—would serve as an axis of cross-border surveillance in Europol's operation.[111]

A year after the signing of the Schengen convention, as the ratification process began, the German chancellor Helmet Kohl proposed the creation of the European policing unit. At a European Council meeting in Luxembourg in June 1991, as the delegates tired of debate late one evening, he set out a plan for a Central European Criminal Investigation Office.[112] Earlier, in the midst of the Schengen negotiations, he had raised the idea of a "European federal police." It was explored by the treatymakers, though not adopted, given the limits of Schengen's supranational authority. Kohl's idea, "attractive as an objective . . . implies institutional, constitutional and political prerequisites, which still seem distant," explained a report prepared by the French foreign ministry's office on the free movement of persons.[113] But at the Luxembourg meeting, the European Council approved the plan; annexed to the Council's conclusions was a commitment to establishing a supranational policing unit termed "Europol" by the end of 1993.[114] "Kohl wanted to be a forerunner," recalled Jürgen Storbeck, who would become Europol's first director.[115]

Europol would develop in two stages, starting with information exchange and leading to police action, according to the Council's planning. The first would involve installing relay stations for data exchange as well as sharing expertise among national police forces. The second would empower agents of Europol to act within Community countries to suppress crime. A working group developed the plans, which became part of the conclusions reached in Maastricht in 1992, when the notion of a European Information System also came under consideration. Echoing the Schengen treaty, in compensating for risk with security measures aimed at fortifying external borders and blocking the entry of foreigners, the Maastricht Treaty declared: "For the purposes of achieving the objectives of the Union, in particular the free movement of persons, Member States shall regard the following areas as matters of common interest . . . rules governing the crossing by persons of the external borders of the Member States and the exercise of controls thereon . . . conditions of entry and movement by nationals of third countries . . . combatting unauthorized immigration . . . organization of a Union-wide system for exchanging information within a European Police Office (Europol)."[116] Like Schengen, Maastricht paired free movement with cross-border policing and information exchange. Unlike Schengen, it authorized a supranational police power.

A Europol convention gained approval from European Union countries in 1995, the year the Schengen Information System began operating.[117] By the century's end, Europol would reside at the same site in Strasbourg as the Schengen Information System, police sharing space with the computerized files. Soon an amendment to the convention would make the Schengen data available to Europol. Ultimately, EU institutions would authorize Europol to issue alerts in the Schengen system based on data transmitted from countries worldwide.[118] The aim was to stop acts of terror that "exploit the advantages brought about by globalisation and mobility."[119] Today, the European Commission calls the Schengen system "the most widely used and largest information sharing system for security and border management in Europe."[120]

But the power embodied in the Schengen Information System was manifest at its inception. As the provisions of the treaty became public, as ratification unfolded, the capabilities of the information system as a center of gravity for cross-border surveillance became evident to the public as well. "It changes everything," the French weekly *La Tribune* remarked of Schengen in 1991, noting that it portended "a common police, a sort of European FBI," and would be "an embryo of a European army."[121] *L'Humanité*, once controlled by the French Communist Party, found that an agreement to lift borders had built "a new wall in Europe."[122] From across the English Channel, the *Guardian* observed, "Interpol, the long-standing body for handling legal and policing matters, is being bypassed."[123] Meanwhile, European police officials marveled at the technical capacities of Schengen's surveillance system. Writing in a publication of Germany's Bundeskriminalamt, in a manual titled *Verbrechensbekämpfung in europäischer Dimension* (Fighting crime in a European dimension), a French police official, Michel Giot-Mikkelsen, who oversaw transnational technical security cooperation at France's interior ministry, explained that no other system had gone as far in "merging and exploiting operational information." Schengen was the "world premiere."[124]

Well before the treatymaking finished, as drafts began to circulate, it became clear that an information system designed to counter the risks of open borders would create risks to freedom in the countries it guarded. The prospect of discreet surveillance across Schengen's borderless interior and at its external frontiers, making a particular target of the movement of foreign migrants and operating in the absence of cosmopolitan constitutional rules, brought protests that the treaty put at risk both individual liberty and national autonomy—risks said to represent a crisis of democratic self-determination.

Consider the claims of the president of France's human rights league, Yves Jouffa, a French Jew who had evaded Nazi capture as a member of the Resistance and began practicing law after the war. Writing about Schengen in *Le Monde* in May 1989, he warned of the perils of the information system and the lack of judicial controls. A new project was absorbing the treatymakers in "a very discreet if not secret examination. . . . It envisages the creation of a data system." He criticized the "spatial extension" of police power, which would render "the control of justice more difficult," making a dead letter of existing rules. A cross-border data system would restrict free movement, enabling the Schengen states to remove or refuse entry to undesirable migrants, "to turn back any person considered non grata by one of its partners." The exclusion would "conflict with the rights of asylum."[125]

Jouffa's piece was titled "Controlling the Police." It highlighted the novel quality of the Schengen surveillance system, drawing attention to the transcendence of territoriality as a basis for police power and the intangible form of that power, especially as asserted in identity checks. The effect, he argued, was to erode national sovereignty. "The very nature of these powers—for example the quasi-discretionary nature of the power of the police to carry out identity checks—deprives the judiciary of any substance over which to exercise its control. It can no doubt punish physical violence that may have occurred on occasion, but that is therefore something other than identity checks," Jouffa wrote. "The deterritorialization of police power . . . renders the current control procedures practically ineffective." Moreover, the treaty would "envisage for the future the right of pursuit by the police from one territory to another." That pursuit would "pose problems of sovereignty."[126]

Ultimately, the argument rested on human rights. Against the power of the police, "and therefore of the State," must act "a counter-power." Jouffa wrote, "This is the very logic of human rights . . . no power without control, a counter-power." In the face of "coercion," there must be a guarantee "in terms of freedoms." The violation of rights and the problems of sovereignty were all the more dire because Schengen was "obviously a test bed" for the entire European community. "What is an authoritarian regime if not a regime in which the police take precedence over justice?" he argued. "This is a vital democratic issue."[127]

Earlier that year, the risks of the information system had led delegates from data protection agencies in the Schengen states to convene in Luxembourg. Their mission was to define freedoms countering the power that would lie in the new supranational mechanism of data exchange. From the National Commission on Informatics and Liberty in France, the Federal Commissioner for Data Protection and Freedom of Information in West Germany, the Advisory Commission in Luxembourg, and the Ministries of Justice in Belgium and the Netherlands emerged a joint statement calling for the protection of individual privacy. Regarding the Schengen plan for "common automated police files," the commissioners resolved that "the establishment of this system go hand in hand with effective protection of personal data."[128]

The concern of the Luxembourg summit was with "the rights of citizens." It produced a *Declaration on the Matter of the Protection of Personal Data in Relation to the Project for a Common Information System of the Signatory States of the Schengen Accord*, dated March 16, 1989. The declaration expressed no opposition, in principle, to data flows across Schengen but set out principles for safeguarding individual privacy against police surveillance. "It is not the intention of data protection officials to frustrate the objective of improving, in a Europe of open borders, international police collaboration through cross-border information systems," the declaration began, but then acknowledged the risks of information exchange. "The projected information system is likely to affect, in a very sensitive way, the rights of citizens. It will indeed not only serve to signal suspicious persons to be arrested, but also to search for missing persons . . . and stolen identity documents, to investigate the whereabouts of persons, to collect, in a more or less hidden way, information in all fields, to turn back or extradite undesirable foreigners." Therefore, rights guarantees must be attached to the creation of the information system, affirming the protections of the Council of Europe's convention on personal data as "minimum binding obligations."[129]

As a hedge against the power projected in the Schengen data system, the Luxembourg declaration proposed rules for both self-determination and supranational oversight. It enumerated conditions for the treaty to enter into force. Those included precise definitions for the content, purpose, and use of the common data banks; a personal right to access information about oneself, correct inaccuracies and delete irrelevant data; oversight of the system by a "common body," along with "independent bodies" in each Schengen state, to address "common problems, in terms of control." The Schengen states would also have to provide greater safeguards regarding immigration and asylum, where "the exchange of data will take on a new dimension." That would require surveilling the surveillance system on behalf of individual rights: "Data protection officers will need to be vigilant in all areas so that new cross-border data flows and international information systems can only be implemented if the fundamental conditions for the protection of personal data are fulfilled." Precisely because the notion was to expand the system to all European Community countries, and because the cross-border exchange of personal data would soon extend beyond police search to "identification services or to data relating to all crimes, suspects, and periods of incarceration," vigilance in terms of rights must act as a counterforce to the police power amplified by Schengen's data system.[130]

Data protection would thus advance the cause of freedom promised in the Schengen treaty. That was the argument of the director of France's National Commission on Informatics and Liberty. Reflecting on the Luxembourg data summit, the director, Jacques Fauvet, wrote to the French treatymaker Émile Cazimajou: "It is important for public opinion to perceive the Schengen Agreement as creating an area of freedom more than a police area." And to instill that view of freedom, data protection was essential: "Recognizing a right of access and rectification," which would also assure "the quality of the information recorded." But safeguarding individual rights would entail overcoming differences in national law; therefore, he advised that data commissions, not national governments, should have the authority to choose members of the independent, multinational body that would oversee Schengen's information exchange. No less important was opening the treatymaking on the data system "not only to computer experts" but also to "representatives of protective authorities." Fauvet wrote that the necessary principles to govern the Schengen files were to be found in the Luxembourg declaration, which drew on the tenets of the Council of Europe's data convention.[131]

The Council of Europe convention was the first legally binding international instrument of data protection—a charter guaranteeing a human right to privacy in a world where data flowed freely across international borders. The Convention for the Protection of Individuals with regard to Automatic Processing of Personal Data was signed in Strasbourg in 1981. Known as Convention No. 108, it began with a declaration of the need "to reconcile the fundamental values of the respect for privacy and the free flow of information between peoples." The convention at once recognized a "right to privacy" and "freedom of information regardless of frontiers." It presupposed a flow of information across borders as free as the movement of people, goods, and capital. But it laid down "safeguards for everyone's rights and fundamental freedoms, and in particular the right to the respect for privacy, taking account of the increasing flow across frontiers of personal data undergoing automatic processing."[132]

The data convention required member countries to conform national law with the principles of privacy and freedom, giving effect to data protection. It defined personal data, any information relating to a "data subject," while barring data on race, sexuality, religion, and political belief except to protect security and safety as consistent with the rules of domestic law and democratic society. It provided for forming a "consultative committee" composed of representatives from Community countries. It expressly authorized "transborder flows of personal data" but entitled all persons to know of being a data subject, to access the data in their files, and to gain "rectification or erasure" of the data. Such were the freedoms of information exchange and the rights of data privacy.[133]

The right to access and rectify information about oneself—to assert data privacy—became couched in the language of self-determination. In West Germany, *Selbstbestimmung* had entered the lexicon of privacy debates by 1983, the year the country's Constitutional Court suspended the taking of a census, finding potential for abuse in the collecting and processing of personal data. At risk was *Selbstbestimmung*, or self-determination, the court stated. It held that rights guaranteed by Germany's constitution included protection against "unlimited collection, storage, use and disclosure of his / her personal data." That meant a "capacity of the individual to determine in principle the disclosure and use of his / her personal data." Here, the freedom of self-determination figured as a personal right of data privacy, not as a collective anti-colonial autonomy.[134]

But not all the Schengen countries affirmed informational self-determination or adhered to the European data convention, which deepened concerns about the risks to freedoms posed by founding the treaty's security measures on the creation of a cross-border information system. France had ratified the data convention in 1983, West Germany in 1985, and Luxembourg in 1988. But Belgium and the Netherlands had not.[135] National law on data collection and individual privacy also varied widely across the Schengen countries. France and West Germany had comprehensive legislation regulating police files. Luxembourg had a statement of principles, and the Netherlands was drafting a measure at the time of the treatymaking. But Belgium had no applicable rules on data privacy.[136]

It was the problem of reconciling plans for Schengen's data system with national law that first exposed the provisions for cross-border surveillance to the scrutiny of data protection authorities while delaying the treatymaking. In the autumn of 1988, France's delegation asked to suspend discussions of information exchange in order to seek guidance from its National Commission on Informatics and Liberty about developing a position on individual data rights and national authority. "For this reason, we had to ask for a pause in the negotiations," explained memoranda prepared by Émile Cazimajou, underscoring the significance of data protection.[137]

The French commission's review of the surveillance apparatus centered on individual privacy, as well as on national sovereignty. "The system raises a legal problem, which is currently being examined: It concerns its compatibility with existing legislation on the protection of privacy," Cazimajou wrote, noting that France's data privacy protections were more stringent than were those in other

Schengen states, "certainly the most comprehensive and rigorous," and that a 1978 French law required that any development of police files must be approved by the commission. This led the French treatymakers and civil liberties authorities to "enter into discussions."[138] As a diplomat in France's foreign ministry later told the prime minister's office, the discussions produced guidance on rights reflecting "a dual concern for the protection of individual freedom and respect for national sovereignty."[139]

The commission's statement—"Note on the Draft Convention Treaty in the Field of Data Protection Concerning the Schengen Information System"—assessed the risks presented by both free movement and cross-border policing. It found that the opening of internal borders "leading to a liberalization of the movement of people and goods . . . will make it more difficult for the police services of each state to maintain order and public security." It noted the complexities of deploying a computerized data exchange system for joint policing, explaining that a "Permanent working group on the Schengen Information System" had drawn up the treaty's draft measures under review. But it pointed to a set of problems with the system, above all the discrepancies in national rules, which put individual freedom at risk. The Schengen countries lacked "the same level of data protection," the commission stressed. It warned of "Different rights. . . . The rights of individuals will be determined by national legislation. They will be different for the same person according to territories." It cited the absence of safeguards in Belgium, where a suspect would have no claim to "the right to access and rectify information" in the Schengen system. It pointed to vagueness in the provisions, which failed to distinguish among perpetrators, victims, and witnesses as subjects of discreet surveillance. It found the legal procedures unclear, whether registry of data subjects in the system would occur from requests of the "judicial police" or "intelligence activities," varying by national rules. It forecast difficulty in harmonizing rights because the European data convention had not been universally ratified in the Schengen area.[140]

By the spring of 1989, the mechanics of the information system still remained unsettled points of the treatymaking. And, by then, the Luxembourg declaration calling for adherence to rights principles had influenced the negotiations, highlighting how risks to freedom coincided with risks to security in the Schengen area. As Jacques Fauvet, the director of France's Informatics Commission, told his country's treatymakers, the essential finding of the Luxembourg meeting was that Schengen must be *un espace de liberté*— "an area of freedom."[141] An assurance came from France's foreign ministry, promising to give priority to personal data protection in the Schengen system: "Despite its difficulties, the construction of a common space must be an opportunity for progress and not for regression in the field of public freedoms."[142] But the difficulties were substantial, and making a priority of liberty stalled the treatymaking. "Origin of the difficulty: France," admitted France's treatymakers, in a communiqué titled "Schengen Negotiation: Points to be Negotiated at Ministerial Level."[143]

There were several sticking points related to data exchange, as France sought to attach greater protection for personal information to the surveillance process. It aimed to reconcile the Schengen system with a French data protection law that established an individual right to object to the processing of one's personal data. It also proposed allowing a delay in the transmission of data following an alert, giving police time to ensure their actions complied with national law, for as long as fifteen days in extradition cases. This would "further preserve the sovereignty of the French authorities in the exercise of their police powers," as the delegation informed the prime minister's office.[144] But the other Schengen countries refused the delay, providing for instant data sharing to expedite cross-border policing.[145]

"It is in the field of police and security that the negotiations confront the greatest number of serious difficulties," Émile Cazimajou told the French government, reporting on a meeting of the central negotiating group in May 1989.[146] Although only advisory, the Luxembourg declaration had led to further consideration of privacy risks. A meeting of the subgroup on information exchange, held just days after the declaration was sent to the Schengen countries, expressed consensus on "the need to emphasize the concepts of privacy and personal liberty." It approved language to recognize rights of access and rectification, and to mandate protections in keeping with the principles named by the Council of Europe data convention.[147] But other objectives went unrealized. Notably, treatymakers did not specify how members of the joint supervisory authority responsible for overseeing Schengen's information system would be chosen, allowing national governments to decide on its composition rather than requiring a role for data commissions.[148] Nor did they adopt particular safeguards with respect to immigration. Delay of automatic data transmission remained a flashpoint of conflict.[149]

Always, arguments about risk in Schengen concerned the dual aspects of sovereignty—the collective power of nations to self-govern and the personal right to be sovereign over oneself. And as the treatymaking continued, the significance of Schengen as a laboratory for rulemaking on the transborder flow of data grew more apparent. In June 1989, the European Council adopted the Palma Document— on the "Free Movement of Persons"—a set of measures anticipating the opening of internal frontiers across the European Community to achieve the single market and endorsing greater intergovernmental cooperation in policing, surveillance, and information exchange to combat illegal immigration and cross-border crime. The Palma catalog of "*essential*" measures included developing "a system of surveillance at external frontiers" and "a system for exchanging information on persons" and "a common system of search and information." Among the "*desirable*" measures were a "Data bank" and "Computerisation of the exchange of information."[150] Nothing was said of the Schengen treaty. But Schengen treatymakers were acutely aware of the Palma Document, suggesting it "was inspired by the Schengen Information System," while noting it failed to envision rules for information exchange. Therefore, in establishing a body of data rules—"to protect the fundamental freedoms of individuals, and in particular the right to privacy"—Schengen would serve as a European model.[151]

Indeed, Schengen became a point of reference for data protection authorities worldwide. At a Berlin meeting in August 1989, the International Conference of Data Protection Commissioners addressed the intensifying transit of personal data in global networks and warned of insufficient legal controls. Founded a decade earlier, the conference brought together national privacy regulators in annual meetings. The Berlin meeting focused on the asymmetry between data flows across borders and a diversity of national laws: "The problem of safeguarding the position of those individuals whose details are transmitted around the world." It called for countermeasures connecting the work of privacy authorities, so that "greater risks, entailed by international exchanges of data, to the rights of individuals . . . are counterbalanced by international co-operation among data protection commissioners."[152] Schengen was a case in point. "Some Community nations are already working on a pilot project to establish common police 'wanted persons' files (the Schengen Information System)," as a statement from the European commissioners stressed in calling for the creation of an independent Pan-European data authority.[153]

In the wake of the Berlin conference, the significance of Schengen's information system as a model drew further attention from data protection officials. But a model of what? Cross-border surveillance? Data privacy protection? Risks to individual freedom? That was the question raised by a French senator and officer of France's Informatics Commission. The international flow of personal data "finds an illustration in the Schengen accord," wrote Jacques Thyraud, "The Schengen accord is the first experience of a broad exchange of sensitive data on an international level." He traced the development of the treaty, how it had gone from obscurity to public controversy, "about its consequences for public safety, immigration, and the right to asylum," and how it "might be feared that the entire population will be subject to numerous checks," compelling awareness of "the need to respect the principles of the law on data processing, files and freedom in the Schengen Information System." He wrote of protecting rights against the instruments of surveillance in the Schengen territory—of an "imperative need not to transform an area of freedom into an area of permanent control through the excessive use of automated data processing systems." He dwelled on the ironies of free movement, observing, "It would be paradoxical if the desire . . . to create a space for the free movement of people resulted in increased surveillance of these people." Schengen put Europe at a crossroads— on a path toward "the implementation of protective legislation" or a path toward "control over individuals." Of the risks to freedom, he wrote, "It's not too early to worry about it."[154]

The plans for Schengen's information exchange, however, satisfied the European Commission, the powerful executive branch of the European Community, which endorsed the computerized file as a model and discounted concerns about data protection. According to the Commission's vice president, Martin Bangemann, the information system was "the key to the security aspect," enabling "in-depth cooperation between the police services," which would "compensate for the abolition of checks at the borders." Objections about breaches of privacy "must not block the system."[155] The Commission's president, Jacques Delors, was untroubled as well; an adviser in his cabinet expressed confidence in the Schengen system in assessing the progress of European integration early in 1990. Alarm about "fundamental rights," the adviser found, was a "false trial."[156]

Nonetheless, the rules for the Schengen Information System continued to vex the treatymakers. The negotiations had paused after the fall of the Berlin Wall, resuming in the spring of 1990, as West Germany secured guarantees relating to German reunification. Again, however, the question of data protection arose, leading to amendments to the draft treaty. A statement from West Germany's delegation stressed the "protection of private life," seeking further to balance information exchange with legal safeguards and national authority. Specifically, it proposed language clarifying that discreet surveillance and data transmission could only occur in accordance with national law, "from the point of view of protection of privacy."[157]

Yet still the treaty's title on the protection of personal data remained unfinished. It was finally a meeting of privacy experts in Brussels, in late May, that settled the last details for exchanging and deploying data. Elaboration of the rights of access and rectification proposed by West Germany were rejected. Notably, however, the meeting yielded compromise language about adherence to the Council of Europe convention on the automatic processing of personal data—a priority set by the Luxembourg declaration a year earlier. That compromise, not requiring the Schengen states to ratify the convention but compelling them to adopt national measures with equivalent protections, harmonized supranational rules with national sovereignty.[158]

Even among the treatymakers, it was hardly expected that the signing of Schengen's implementing convention would end the conflict over the information system. A report titled *After Schengen* anticipated obstacles to the cross-border flow of data. Appearing at the end of the summer of 1990, it was prepared by France's foreign ministry, as the database would be located in Strasbourg, and France was poised to inherit responsibility for Schengen planning. It noted a timeline for ratification of the treaty by the Schengen countries, as well as the projected accession of other European Community countries. It stated a pledge of the French presidency to develop the data file: *Le dossier système d'information de Schengen*. Bluntly, it admitted that the dossier would be "very delicate (administrative and technical coordination, data processing . . .) but our partners are urging us to move forward quickly."[159]

Meanwhile, criticisms of the information system flowed across the borders of the Schengen countries, in a transnational circuit of protest. The arguments centered on a common claim—that Schengen's cross-border modes of surveillance could not be controlled by existing institutions, thereby eroding principles of self-government and the autonomy of individuals founded on both privacy and free movement. Consider the reasoning of a West German lawyer, Thilo Weichert, who had represented the Greens in the state parliament of Baden-Württemberg and become an authority on data use in criminal investigations. Writing about Schengen in the journal *Computer und Recht* (Computers and Law) in 1990, he warned of the abridgement of individual freedom and democracy from "a Europeanization of law enforcement," a concentration of power that "conflicts with the national constitutional order." The treaty's rules for data exchange were "not suitable to ensure a constitutionally required minimum standard for protection of informational self-determination," he argued. "Democratic control . . . is impossible."[160] Schengen thus violated the self-determination constituted by personal freedom and national sovereignty.

Free movement across open borders made Schengen a place of risk. So acute was the perception of that risk that late in the treatymaking, there was conjecture about deleting the set of measures on abolishing internal border controls and enabling movement inside the Schengen area—leaving only the security measures. In April 1990, the Netherlands put forward the idea. The Dutch prime minister, Ruud Lubbers, proposed limiting Schengen's implementing convention to "the aspects most essential to security," stripping it of all but "the aspects relating to police cooperation and the information system." France replied with a rhetorical question, suggesting the perverseness of the proposition: "Why compensate for the abolition of border controls if we no longer abolish border controls?" Such illogic would destroy the spirit of the treaty, nullifying the ideal of free movement at the heart of European union, transforming Schengen into a dossier society. "Schengen would risk no longer appearing . . . within the framework of Citizens' Europe, but as the beginning of a Europe of files." Again, France posed a rhetorical question, "Can we envision a reduced Schengen?"[161]

But outside the forum of treatymaking, the idea that Schengen would become a space not of freedom but of unfreedom did not appear unimaginable—however perverse. And it was the power lodged in the surveillance architecture of Schengen's information system that embodied that risk, a supranational police power against which no cosmopolitan counterpower of rights protections existed. It was not until the Treaty of Amsterdam, in 1997, which did not enter into force until 1999, that Schengen became integrated into European Union law, coming within the jurisdiction of the European Court of Justice, but even then the court's authority was limited in matters of migration, border control, and asylum.[162] Protecting rights of privacy and freedom against the intergovernmental power asserted via cross-border policing would continue to depend on national law.

Therefore, Schengen remained a place of risk. A year after the Schengen treaty came into force, and the data system began operating in Strasbourg, a lawyer with Belgium's human rights league described how freedom was abridged in the Schengen space. Writing in 1996, Jean-Yves Carlier protested a "double negative," with the opening of internal borders meaning that "freedoms are infringed"—the "privacy of people inside this space" and also the "freedom of movement of people outside . . . as it is very difficult for them to enter." Along with "surveillance in the interior," Schengen had set "a padlock on the outside door." Put simply, "free movement has not been achieved."[163] But the risks to free movement had been evident since the signing of the treaty. As *Jeune Afrique Économie*, an African news magazine, asked in 1990: "Will the doors of Europe be more difficult to open?"[164]

A *Sans-papiers* Claim to Free Movement as a Human Right

ON JUNE 28, 1996, undocumented immigrants in Paris began an occupation of Saint-Bernard de la Chapelle, a church in a neighborhood known as *Goutte d'Or*, or Drop of Gold, long home to the city's working classes. The insurgents were nationals of countries mainly in West Africa—countries on the Schengen lists of undesirables. The occupation would last for almost two months, as hundreds gathered in the church. They were men and women, young and old, entire families—migrants who labored as cleaners, caterers, construction workers, and computer technicians. Some had been denied asylum. Others had overstayed their visas or had family members born in France. Within the resplendent neo-Gothic church, the migrants claimed a space for themselves in a territory where they were called *clandestins*, or illegal.[1]

What the migrants called themselves were the *sans-papiers*, or "without papers"—the documents authorizing residence in France and granting permission to work. It was this lack, this *sans*, that the migrants put at the center of their self-conception. And it was this lack, the condition of non-belonging in Europe, that would prompt the claim of the sans-papiers across the Schengen area to free movement as a human right. Such a right would untether the free movement of persons from citizenship, whether national or cosmopolitan.

As sans-papiers, the migrants in the Saint-Bernard church claimed the inheritance of the sans-culottes, urban workers who had turned their lack of trousers into a symbol of egalitarian aspirations and natural rights principles in the age of the French Revolution. Excluded from the guarantees of Citizens' Europe, sans-papiers in the Schengen area lacked the right of free movement across its internal borders. They bore the brunt of restrictions meant to mitigate the risks of open borders, the security measures enforced by the Schengen Information System and Europol, which extended from heightened controls at external frontiers to policing that penetrated inside workplaces, homes, and houses of worship. The undocumented were rendered "illegal" as Europe realized a single market promoting the free circulation of people, goods, capital, and services. Schengen was a territory of unfree movement for people who were sans-papiers.

In occupying the Saint-Bernard church, the sans-papiers aimed their protest not only, or always, at the rules of the Schengen system. Yet Schengen was its terrain—as a place generative of European integration and as a symbol of the pairing of freedom and exclusion. The occupation challenged the Pasqua laws, a set of repressive immigration codes adopted by France to compensate for Schengen's abolition of internal borders. The legislation sought "zero immigration," including by restricting naturalization and expediting deportation. As Schengen's formation fueled a nativist turn, the sans-papiers emerged from the shadows of illegality to seek recognition, a quest that involved matters of papers, but also of free movement. A sans-papiers spokesperson from Senegal, Madjiguène Cissé, put it simply. "Every human being has the right," she said, "to travel, to migrate, to circulate, to receive and be received."[2]

At the Saint-Bernard church, then, the sans-papiers claimed a place for themselves in Citizens' Europe, a place denied to people classified as aliens, as undesirables, as illegals, as *clandestins*. There, in the church, they built in a few weeks' time what became known as *La ville des sans-papiers*, or "The city of the sans-papiers."[3] In a sense, the sans-papiers represented nothing less than outcasts seeking a "right to have rights," in the classic formulation of Hannah Arendt concerning the condition of stateless refugees after the Second World War. As Arendt wrote, "The fundamental deprivation of human rights is manifested first and above all in the deprivation of a place in the world."[4] Rights entailed a place to be—but also a place within which to move. As the sans-papiers claimed, to migrate, to circulate, was a human right.

On August 23, 1996, the police forcibly expelled the sans-papiers from their refuge in the Saint-Bernard church. At the order of France's interior minister, the church door was rammed open, and police arrested the men, women, and children inside. That night, twenty thousand people marched through Paris, opposing the evacuation.[5] It was a landmark in the uprising of the sans-papiers, which reached out from the sanctuary of the parish church into the city's public spaces and moved across the borders of Western Europe, throughout the Schengen countries. As the movement took root in Germany, the outcry became *Kein Mensch ist illegal*—"No one is illegal."[6] The transnational protest of unfree migrants has persisted, compelling attention to the contrast between their status and the free flow of commodities and capital in an era of ascendant globalization.[7] And their protest illustrates how the barriers against the movement of persons bear the stamp of European colonialism. It exposes the racial hierarchies that still structure the continent's zone of free movement.[8] Writing on the "geography of anger," the anthropologist Arjun Appadurai has observed how practice and theory must join "to make globalization work for those who need it most and enjoy it least, the poor, the dispossessed."[9]

The transnational insurgency of the sans-papiers—their claim to free movement as a human right—reflects such a unity of practice and theory. The acts of the sans-papiers occurred in places as sacred as churches, as profane as the streets of Paris, and as consequential as the European Court of Human Rights. Their speech, or *parole*, was recorded in judicial decisions, newspapers, and autobiographical accounts. It told of conflict over Schengen's logic of freedom and exclusion. It examined the balance between the protections of international law and the rules of national security, and it condemned the subaltern status of former colonial subjects in European countries. The words of the principal sans-papiers spokespersons at the Saint-Bernard church, Ababacar Diop and Madjiguène Cissé, offer evidence of the discriminatory guarantee of free movement, as attached not to personhood but to European citizenship. There was a tendency to "forget that the world is a crowded place," wrote Edward Said in his 1993 book *Culture and Imperialism*, despairing of the "re-emergence of racist politics in Europe."[10] The book appeared the same year as France's Pasqua laws. The sans-papiers testified to the wrongs of such forgetting reflected in the Schengen treaty.

The mobilization of the sans-papiers thus belongs to Schengen's history, a countermovement to the animus against non-Europeans aroused by the opening of borders. From the creation of a transnational territory of free movement emerged a transnational protest against unfree movement. And from that agitation emerged human rights claims that would find affirmation in the work of moral and political philosophers who theorized about self-determination in the postcolonial world. As the Schengen treaty entered into force, the unrest of the sans-papiers became a laboratory of rival ideas about the free movement of people.

The August storming of the Saint-Bernard church by the Parisian police marked the climax of a conflict between the sans-papiers and the French government that had been intensifying for almost half a year. The strife arose from efforts by France's interior ministry to tighten controls over immigration and asylum as internal border controls came down within the Schengen area.

In the quartier Saint-Ambroise, a neighborhood not far from the Goutte d'Or, the battle lines had been drawn. There, in the church of Saint-Ambroise, hundreds of Africans living in Paris without papers gathered on March 18, 1996.[11] The immigrants had come mainly from Mali, but also from Mauritania, Côte d'Ivoire, Senegal, and Guinea. They sought the regularization of their immigration status and the right to work without the risk of arrest and deportation, asserting a common claim to belonging in France as the "African collective of Saint-Ambroise."[12] Some began a hunger strike.[13] The occupation lasted four days, until police conducted a raid at dawn.[14] "Even a church is no longer a place of welcome for people," lamented a Catholic cleric.[15]

The Saint-Ambroise occupation came in response to the enforcement of restrictive immigration laws that bore the name of Charles Pasqua, the interior minister who had crafted the legislation. Pasqua was a Gaullist who justified the measures by pointing to the abolition of border controls under the Schengen treaty and the grant of free movement. As he argued to the National Assembly in 1993, the European integration achieved by "the Schengen group" required a national policy of "more rigorous and better-coordinated actions," including the denial of legal residence and work permits to undocumented migrants.[16]

The Pasqua laws advanced the French government's aims, two decades in the making, to arrest the tide of immigration that had brought workers from North Africa and other former colonies. That labor source had fueled postwar economic recovery in France, which had promoted permanent immigration based on the prospect of naturalization, rather than temporary guest worker programs.[17] However, by the 1970s, as the oil crisis slowed growth, nations across Western Europe closed their doors to foreign workers.[18] France suspended labor migration from outside the European Community in 1974, a ban reflecting a new political consensus under the administration of Valéry Giscard d'Estaing that the country had reached its *seuil de tolérance* or "threshold of tolerance."[19] Still, the restriction was not absolute, as the government allowed that certain industries—such as mining and construction—needed a stream of cheap labor. Meanwhile, France's population of racial and ethnic minorities continued to increase through reproduction and family reunification. The risk of deportation also increased, with the suppression of migration flows. Random identity checks became commonplace.[20]

The rigors of the Pasqua laws brought greater repression and greater risk to the undocumented. Notably, the legislation came alongside Schengen's formation. A first Pasqua law appeared in 1986, a year after the signing of the original Schengen treaty. It tightened residency rules, facilitated deportations, and expanded police powers.[21] A second Pasqua law appeared in 1993, registering the completion of Europe's internal market that year and anticipating

Schengen's entry into force. It made attaining legal status more difficult for migrants, and, to discourage their settlement in France, also withheld social care and restricted the appeals process for unfavorable immigration decisions.[22] Moreover, the legislation marked a major shift in French nationality law. It required most children born in France to immigrant parents to request citizenship, rather than conferring it upon adulthood, moving away from the principle of *jus soli* and revoking a right guaranteed for more than a century.[23] A coda to the Pasqua laws was approved in 1997, bearing the name of the new interior minister, Jean-Louis Debré, a son of former prime minister Michel Debré. The Debré law required citizens who sheltered non-European immigrants to inform the government of their presence, augmenting regulations that made harboring immigrants deemed illegal a criminal offense; other provisions included expanding identity checks to prevent the illegal employment of foreign labor. It was enacted in the aftermath of the Saint-Bernard uprising, evidently intended to subdue support for the sans-papiers. And it reflected rising concern that immigrants would surge into France as a consequence of Schengen at last coming into force in 1995.[24] A draft of the legislation presented to the French parliament explained how exclusion balanced freedom, "a compromise that is constantly desired between firmness against illegal immigration and respect for individual human rights."[25]

The purpose of the Pasqua and Debré laws was unequivocal: halting immigration, punishing the undocumented, and blocking the transit of non-Europeans across borders. "France has been a country of immigration; it doesn't want to be one anymore," Pasqua argued in 1993.[26] The restrictive measures reduced immigration by 40 percent between 1992 and 1995.[27] At the same time, the revocation of unconditional birthright citizenship caused the population of the undocumented to soar.[28] Deportations reached more than ten thousand annually but remained only a fraction of those ordered by French prefects yet never enforced due to inadequate documentation of countries of origin. The crackdown on immigration intensified against the backdrop of the rising influence of the National Front, the anti-immigrant party led by Jean-Marie Le Pen, the patriarch of the French far right, a nationalist who would be convicted of racism in the nation's courts.[29]

Schengen stood at the center of the restrictive legislation, meaning that free movement always was at issue. Debate in the National Assembly recorded how the Pasqua laws were intended to offset the removal of border controls. Conservative deputies spoke of European integration eroding existing national regulations, echoing arguments about French sovereignty directed against Schengen during the debate over the treaty's ratification. "It was useless to confuse freedom of movement with lack of control," said Jacques Myard, a deputy with Rally for the Republic, warning against eliminating "the controls at the internal borders too quickly." As applause rang out among the chamber's Gaullists, Myard praised the Pasqua measures as a model of immigration restriction that should be adopted across the continent—"we must set an example at the European level"—just as Schengen served as a model of free movement. "The Schengen Agreement," he said, "is a good agreement but that seems to me to have gaps." Others described fraudulent asylum schemes that abused French munificence. As a deputy with the Union for French Democracy said, Schengen posed challenges for the "control of migratory flows."[30]

Pasqua appeared in the assembly to argue for the restrictions, offering a précis of France's obligations to liberty and to law. He drew on his authority as Minister of the Interior and Territorial Planning, which gave him jurisdiction over the physical integrity of the nation. "France is a republican state," Pasqua said. "France is also a state of law." He reminded the chamber that France was "a country conscious of its history . . . and proud of the idea that it represents, in the eyes of other countries, that which invented the rights of man and the rights of peoples to self-determination." But liberty had limits, and France could not be the refuge for the outcast and the exiled worldwide. "France is not an El Dorado for all," Pasqua said, nor could its rights protections redress "all the misfortunes of the world." Rather, France must maintain "mastery over its identity"—to control national belonging and "define for itself the situation, the nature, the origin of those who are or will be associated with the national community, in the spirit of the Republic's values." Pasqua's arguments recalled the Euroskeptic polemics of the elder Debré. As self-professed guardians of the Gaullist tradition, both statesmen understood republicanism to entitle the French people to determine the composition of their national community. Self-government, Pasqua reasoned, gave the state the power to exclude.[31]

Still, the sovereign power to exclude had limits, particularly in the realm of asylum rights. Defenders of Pasqua's law spoke of preserving the balance between immigration restriction and international human rights norms. The aim was said to be clarifying France's authority to prevent abuse of its humanitarian guarantees. Pasqua made a point of assuring the assembly that the legislation would not affect the right to asylum established by the 1951 Geneva convention and incorporated into French law. Stressing how international agreements served to elucidate the scope of national responsibility, he recognized Schengen as the source of the principle, inscribed in the Dublin convention, that the country of first entry bears responsibility for adjudicating the claims of asylum seekers. National law regulating the movement of people became all the more essential, Pasqua said, with the advent of a "common European policy."[32]

The debate therefore made evident how new national rules of immigration control emerged from the Schengen principles of free movement and open borders. It was Pasqua who foresaw a Central Directorate for Immigration Control having "a role to play in the application of the Schengen accords." France, he pledged bluntly, would refuse "to allow the free movement of people to be transformed into the free movement of crooks, of delinquents and of drugs."[33]

Tested in the French courts, however, Pasqua's legislation was partly negated, an outcome that would ultimately yield a constitutional amendment affirming its thrust. The Constitutional Council in 1993 struck down several provisions, including regulations for investigating marriages alleged to have involved expediency. The most significant part of the judgment concerned asylum. The council found that France could not refuse to examine an asylum claim rejected in another country, thereby also casting into question Schengen's first-entry doctrine and the Dublin rule. When Pasqua appealed the opinion to the Conseil d'État, France's highest administrative tribunal, the court held that only an amendment to the Fifth Republic Constitution of 1958 would release France from the obligation to hear an asylum claim already considered by another European state. By the end of the year, French legislators had adopted a constitutional amendment allowing the country's entry into international agreements on asylum jurisdiction while also providing that France was entitled—but not obliged—to review asylum claims already examined by other European nations. This aligned French law with Schengen's asylum rules.[34]

France was hardly alone in responding to Schengen's creation with new immigration restrictions. A 1993 European Commission report on immigration highlighted the "stringent attitudes" of member states, finding that national governments approached the opening of internal borders by asserting "a necessary limitation of freedom of movement . . . for persons from non-Community countries," with a "focus being on asylum seekers." In Luxembourg, security concerns—centering on the border crossing of undocumented migrants—prompted legislation to apply penalties to transporters bringing foreigners without proper papers into the Schengen area. The Commission report also identified Schengen as the impetus for a Luxembourg plan that would create restrictions exceeding common European rules by excluding migrants who had received at least a year's prison sentence or posed a threat to public order, national security, or the international relations of another European Union member state. In Belgium, too, Schengen's implementation was understood to imperil the free movement of non-European residents. In West Germany, as in France, a constitutional amendment—a revision of the postwar Basic Law— adhered to the Schengen asylum rules and sought to prevent abuse of asylum rights. Across the Schengen countries, new expulsion measures overcame the resistance mounted by countries of origin to the return of migrants.[35]

The Pasqua laws were the most infamous of the restrictions, drawing public condemnation. A parody in the French magazine *Globe Hebdo* put on display the racist cast of the legislation in the summer of 1993, caricaturing Pasqua as a North African. The image appeared on the cover, with text explaining how easily a "real Frenchman can be transformed into a foreigner and thus into a potential victim of discrimination." The cartoon circulated across borders, reproduced in the German press, with *Der Spiegel* observing how the transfiguration of the neo-Gaullist interior minister aptly served to protest the tightening of French immigration laws to form a quota of "zero."[36] The European Commission report on immigration offered more oblique criticism of Pasqua's regulations on nationality, identity checks, and immigration control: "Never before had legislation on immigration been so radically changed in such a short space of time."[37] Only a few years earlier, the journal *Race and Class*, published by the Britain-based Institute of Race Relations, had produced a special issue titled "Europe: Variations on a Theme of Racism." The editor was Ambalavaner Sivanandan, the institute's director, a Sri Lankan-born intellectual, activist, and author of a magisterial novel about his native Sri Lanka, *When Memory Dies*.[38] Sivanandan warned that the "inter-state treaty makers of Schengen" had created a regime stained by a "common culture of European racism, which defines all Third World people as immigrants and refugees, and all immigrants and refugees as terrorists"—a regime unable to distinguish "a citizen from an immigrant or an immigrant from a refugee, let alone one black from another. They all carry their passports on their faces."[39] That was the regime depicted by the *Globe Hebdo* cartoon.

The most explicit and searing critique of the Pasqua program came in a United Nations report that identified a "wave of xenophobia currently sweeping over France," fed by a tide of legislation that bore its author's name: "Xenophobia in France is today sustained by the Pasqua Acts." The report was prepared for the United Nations Human Rights Commission in 1996 by a Beninese jurist, Maurice Glélé-Ahanhanzo, who deplored a politics that scapegoated foreigners, "particularly if they are Black, Arab or Muslim." The report described how the Pasqua laws—"the peremptorily enacted laws on immigration, the right of asylum and the forced repatriation of 'illegal' entrants"—violated the moral responsibility of nations to defend human rights and stained France's global image as "the original homeland of human rights and the rights of the citizen." It told of a French "crisis of society" occurring amid the development of integration in "a greater Europe" that stood against foreigners "as a fortress." The report asked, "What has become of human dignity?"[40]

That was the question raised by the sans-papiers of Paris—surveilled, driven from workplaces—who stole through the streets of the city seeking refuge, until their unfree movement surged out into open defiance of the Pasqua laws. It was a scene that Le Monde described as a "national psychodrama."[41] Turmoil arose from the expulsion of the sans-papiers from the Saint-Ambroise church, in the spring of 1996: street protests; arrests; deportations of immigrants from Mali, Senegal, Guinea, and Burkina Faso; remonstrances from SOS-Racisme and other humanitarian organizations; forcible evictions from other places of shelter. "If the mayoralty does not find us any room, we will find it ourselves," declared a spokesperson for Droits Devant, a humanitarian organization. The prefect of police oversaw the expulsions. "We went out," a sans-papiers said. "We had no choice."[42]

At the time of the Saint-Ambroise strife in 1996, it was elsewhere in the city, at the Luxembourg Palace in the chamber of France's Senate, that the national government marked the first anniversary of Schengen's entry into force. A minister for European affairs spoke of the progress made in implementing free movement: "The practical details for crossing internal borders are on the way to becoming satisfactory."[43] Meanwhile, the country's interior minister, Jean-Louis Debré, defended the expulsions at Saint-Ambroise as compelled by the rule of law. Yielding to the undocumented was to accept lawbreaking, Debré said, "to construct a society based on force . . . a society that turns its back on the principles of the Republic and of democracy."[44] Or, as France's president, Jacques Chirac, stated, "with free movement" there could be no "lax legislation."[45]

Thus emerged the unrest of the sans-papiers, who circulated from place to place across Paris—the Gymnase Japy, a sports hall that had been a wartime internment center for Jews; a union headquarters; a communist bookshop; a theater, La Cartoucherie, that was once a munitions factory; the Saint-Hippolyte church; the Halle Pajol, at that time a disused railway warehouse—before occupying the Saint-Bernard church as a place of refuge at the end of June.[46] In the name of democratic republicanism and the rule of law, the French government justified the exclusion of migrants despised as illegal. But the sans-papiers claimed a place within Citizens'

Europe, meaning also a right of free movement across the Schengen territory.

———————————

A day after the Saint-Ambroise evacuation, a thousand people gathered outside the district's town hall, proclaiming, "We are all 'sans-papiers.'"[47] The protest drew support from neighbors in places that sheltered the undocumented, and from priests and their parishioners, and from trade unionists, artists, and intellectuals, and was recorded in newspaper accounts and a filmic journal of the insurgency, *La Ballade des sans-papiers.*[48] It would be amplified by human rights organizations and echo across Europe. It expressed aspirations for regularization of status, for residence, and for lawful employment—as guarantees that would protect all the undocumented—and a collective refusal to be categorized as illegal. By the time of the Saint-Bernard occupation, those aspirations had public spokespersons: the sans-papiers Ababacar Diop and Madjiguène Cissé, immigrants from Senegal.

The mobilization of the sans papiers was born in the homes of immigrants, in the housing projects of eastern Paris, near the Saint-Ambroise church. The undocumented drew on lessons that had been learned through encounters with associations seeking housing rights and workplace justice, and the church occupations kindled a sense of collective will. No longer would individual pleas to the prefecture be the path toward regularization of status. "So we said to ourselves, 'We have to mobilize, we have to get informed, we have to regroup, we have to come together,'" as a sans-papiers explained.[49] The resolve deepened after the Saint-Ambroise expulsion, despite the risk of arrest and detention, as the sans-papiers migrated among places of refuge in acts of open civil disobedience. The evident intent was to "put themselves in danger of deportation," said witnesses to the protests in accounts of the confrontation of "'Illegals' and the State."[50]

It was the threat of deportation that led the undocumented to declare their lack of papers, making this absence the core of their political revolt. They chose to become the "sans-papiers" following an expulsion from the Gymnase Japy just days after the Saint-

Ambroise evacuation. As Ababacar Diop explained, the aim was not just obtaining papers. Rather, the name captured the idea of securing a "new space of liberty"—hence the allusion to the sans-culottes.[51] What they sought to transform was not a despotic ancien regime but a cosmopolitan Citizens' Europe that excluded the sans-papiers. That liberatory aim began with repeal of the Pasqua laws that codified the wrongs of being "sans." As Madjiguène Cissé said, "It's because of these laws that we're here."[52]

The sans-papiers' search for recognition gained allies offering many forms of support, from physical protection to political mediation. Trade unions at Air France denounced the use of company aircraft in the deportations, and the postal and telecommunications union provided shelter at its Paris headquarters. The General Confederation of Labor, the French Democratic Confederation of Labor, and other national unions joined with the Human Rights League of France to launch a common appeal against the Pasqua laws, as the sans-papiers sought to convey to the public that undocumented immigrants were not the cause, but the "first victims," of economic dislocation.[53] The theater director Ariane Mnouchkine sheltered the sans-papiers in the halls of La Cartoucherie, where Molière's *Tartuffe* was being staged at the time.[54] Humanitarian associations—Droits Devant, Médecins du Monde, SOS-Racisme—organized demonstrations as influential figures in French intellectual life, with Étienne Balibar and Pierre Bourdieu at the forefront, issued an "appeal in solidarity with foreigners."[55] A mediation proposal put forth by Mnouchkine and a public health advocate, Léon Schwartzenberg, drew a renowned French diplomat, Stéphane Hessel, into the conflict.[56]

During the weeks after the Saint-Ambroise expulsion, a sans-papiers social movement developed alongside the efforts of mediation. Decision-making was democratic, the work of a sans-papiers general assembly, with elected delegates. Among other forms of neighborhood organizing and public protest, women in the movement came forward to highlight their suffering through a "women's march." In a communiqué to the press on May 9, 1996, they announced themselves as "the female sans-papiers of Saint-Ambroise," saying they had been "fighting for almost two months to obtain our papers and thus to live legally on French soil" and

FIGURE 6.1. Female sans-papiers, shown marching for regularization of their status in 1996, took a lead role in the immigrant uprising—organizing the movement's internal deliberations and issuing press communiqués that highlighted their plight. Credit: Duclos / Stevens / GAMMA RAPHO

condemning French law as "racist and sexist." Their aspirations extended beyond their legal status. Affirming universal principles of asylum and mobility, the sans-papiers women claimed "refugee status for all" and the "right of free movement for all."[57]

Meanwhile, Stéphane Hessel pursued mediation, interceding between the interior ministry and the sans-papiers. A cosmopolitan, Hessel was born in Berlin, became a citizen of France, served in the Resistance during the war, escaped death in the Nazi camps, aided in the creation of the Universal Declaration of Human Rights, and advanced global humanitarianism as a French diplomat.[58] He worked with an eminent committee of mediators, including the philosophers Paul Ricœur and Edgar Morin; a journalist, Noël Copin, who was president of France's branch of Reporters without Borders; the priest André Costes, a pastor to immigrants; and Antoine Sanguinetti, a former admiral who was president of the Rights and Freedoms Committee in the Military and had helped found Ras l'front to contest the rise of the National Front.[59]

Initially, mediation seemed to produce concessions: the ministry agreed that the review of immigrant dossiers in regularization decisions would take account of illness, family bonds, and immersion in French society; in exchange, the sans-papiers ended a hunger strike.[60]

But the ministry proved intransigent, and the waiting useless. By June, papers had been granted to only forty-eight Parisian sans-papiers of the hundreds seeking regularization. On June 28, after a protest at the Place de la République, the sans-papiers crossed the city and entered the Saint-Bernard church. As the occupation began, the call went out for a moratorium on deportations and a renewal of negotiations. Meanwhile, demonstrations erupted across Paris. Inside the Saint-Bernard church, a new hunger strike commenced. Henri Coindé, christened the "priest of the sans-papiers" for opening his church to the migrants, preached of the glory of those who "reestablish in the law those who have been outlawed."[61] Among the ten sans-papiers refusing food was a Mauritanian named Camara Hamady, who said, "We demand our rights, that's all."[62]

Still, the government did not yield. Refusing the appeals of the sans-papiers, and defending his ministry's enforcement of the Pasqua rules, Jean-Louis Debré stated, "The application of the law is nonnegotiable." Toward the end of August, Debré went to the Conseil d'État, seeking an opinion that would uphold the denial of regularization.[63] The court found that none of the cases required regularization but also determined that the Pasqua laws did not prevent the government from regularizing the immigrants.[64] Accordingly, the prime minister, Alain Juppé, vowed to end the occupation.[65] On August 22, in a televised appearance, he pledged that Debré's ministry would examine each case individually, sustaining humanitarian principles but not illegality. Never would a mother be separated from her children, he said. Nor would a gravely ill person be expelled from France. Instead, the government would avert such cases by reinforcing the barriers against unlawful entry. But first the prime minister would end the spectacle at Saint-Bernard.[66]

The sans-papiers expected a raid, and many stayed awake throughout that night. On August 23, just after 7 a.m., more than a thousand police officers broke through metal barricades outside

FIGURE 6.2. Madjiguène Cissé and Ababacar Diop, the two principal spokespersons for the sans-papiers in Paris, address the media outside the Saint-Bernard church in August 1996. They would soon be expelled from their refuge by the police. Credit: Sébastien Dufour / GAMMA RAPHO

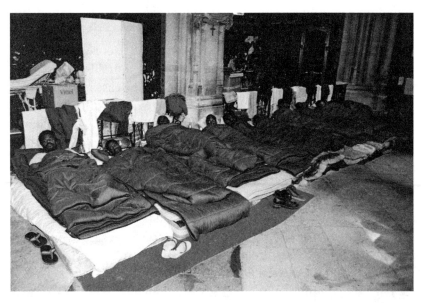

FIGURE 6.3. Sans-papiers occupying the Saint-Bernard church in Paris before a police raid on August 23, 1996. Credit: Alexis Duclos / GAMMA RAPHO

the church, past protesters chanting, "French, immigrants, solidarity!" The police used axes to break down the church door while Father Coindé led Mass inside, speaking of the "bread of tomorrow" that would feed "every mouth"—consecrated as the "product of the longest, the most difficult human struggle." As the police entered the nave, seizing people of color from among the white parishioners and aid workers, violence filled the sacred space. Some pleaded, "Do not touch the hunger strikers, not them!" Children choked on tear gas. Later that day, Debré said of the sans-papiers' expulsion from the Saint-Bernard church, "The moment had come to apply the law."[67]

Yet the police action did not end the uprising. That night some fifteen thousand people marched in Paris, in solidarity with the sans-papiers. A national coordinating committee of the undocumented called for continuing resistance: street protests, church occupations, and collaboration with humanitarian organizations. "Juppé surrender your papers to us," sans-papiers protested at a vigil in the Place de la République, marking the death of a Saint-Bernard hunger striker.[68] So, too, the drowning of an Angolan living in Paris who had fled an identity check became a symbol of sans-papiers suffering. Civil liberties groups monitoring human rights abuses linked the "flurry of anti-'immigrant' activity," as *Statewatch* reported, to "ratifying the Schengen Agreement," exposing the connection between free movement and the sans-papiers crisis.[69]

A documentary project of the sans-papiers movement unfolded as the protests continued. IM'média, a press agency with roots in immigration and housing struggles, worked with REFLEX, part of an anti-fascist network, to portray the aims, breadth, and theory of the uprising: *Chroniques d'un mouvement*. The account revealed how immigrants from across the world joined with Africans from former French colonies in the sans-papiers mobilization. "We are sans-papiers, so we are there," explained a Chinese immigrant who belonged to a contingent that had come from Wenzhou, a coastal city near Shanghai, in a wave of immigration spurred by the Tiananmen Square protests. "Papers. Papers!" she said. "We want to be regularized." A critique of "Social Apartheid" termed the internal market a "new mode of capitalist exploitation" based on the "economic thought of Fordism . . . the ideas of Keynes." A

FIGURE 6.4. The cover of *Chroniques*, a booklet documenting the unfolding of the sans-papiers uprising in Paris in 1996, copublished by IM'média, a press agency specializing in immigration and social movements, and an anti-fascist group called REFLEX. Credit: IM'média and REFLEX

polemic against "Precarity" attacked the "misdeeds of neoliberalism" and "xenophobic politics." *Chroniques* asked, "What about the free movement of individuals in a Europe that is closing in like a fortress?"[70]

A year after the Saint-Ambroise occupation, as Paris streets became a space for commemorative events of protests, the philosopher Étienne Balibar reflected on the meaning of the sans-papiers uprising for democratic life. He spoke at a solidarity demonstration organized by a filmmakers' union, just as he had joined an appeal the year before on behalf of foreigners. For Balibar, the problem was one of rights and obligations, of politics and ethics: "What We Owe to the 'Sans-papiers.'" He argued that France was indebted to the sans-papiers, who had refused "clandestineness" and "recreated citizenship among us" by claiming a "right to stay." Because the sans-papiers made the wrongs of immigration restriction "circulate in public space," challenging "border institutions," exposing "*institutional racism*," and showing how the state created the "regime of illegality," Balibar said, "We owe them." Their rights claims gave "political activity the transnational dimension . . . prospects for social transformation and civility in the era of globalization." That activity elucidated, he said, "what democracy is," and therefore France owed the sans-papiers the justice of "recognition."[71]

But recognition would not be granted to the sans-papiers under Debré's ministry, in the Gaullist government of Juppé and Chirac. Rather, Pasqua's rules were reinforced by Debré's measures, which expanded identity checks and imposed further restrictions on sheltering non-European immigrants. As the mediator Sanguinetti, the military man-cum-civil libertarian, observed contemptuously of Debré: "He follows orders and he follows them stupidly."[72] Nor would the situation of the sans-papiers change significantly with the forming of a cohabitation government in the summer of 1997, as the national legislature newly led by parties of the left shared power with Chirac's administration, amid the rising influence of the anti-immigrant National Front. The cohabitation government took a piecemeal approach, rejecting full repeal of the Pasqua and Debré laws while adopting some reforms, including restoring citizenship under certain conditions to children born in France to foreigners and ruling more favorably on regularization applications.[73] A legislative package of 1998, sponsored by Debré's successor as interior minister, Jean-Pierre Chevènement, enabled family reunification but made regularization harder for single migrants. The changes appeased few in French society.[74]

By century's end, most of the sans-papiers of Paris had slipped back into the shadows of the city's immigrant neighborhoods. Those who gained regularization took menial jobs to obtain the pay stubs validating their stay. Across France, the tenor of public debate had shifted, becoming more permissive of anti-immigrant views and more hostile to open borders; according to a poll released in 1998 by the CSA Institute, 18 percent of French citizens saw themselves as "racist," and 40 percent as "a little" racist or "tempted by racism," believing there to be too many people of color and Arabs in the country, and finding France unrecognizable.[75] Although symbolic acts of church occupation continued, by the third anniversary of the Saint-Bernard expulsion, the turnout for solidarity demonstrations had fallen, and the epithet "forgotten" joined the label "sans-papiers."[76]

Across Europe, however, the cause of the sans-papiers took root, and the protest assumed new forms as it extended to other Schengen countries and beyond. Always the lack of papers became a symbol of the deprivations attached to being "illegal"—surveillance, unfree movement, denial of asylum, denial of work, family separation, deportation. In one of the most evocative acts of transnational mobilization, sans-papiers in France traveled to greet a caravan of migrants journeying through Germany. On a September day in 1998, they met at a bridge, Pont de l'Europe, which crosses the Rhine, connecting France and Germany, an iconic site of postwar reconciliation that first opened for travel in September 1960. The pilgrimage symbolized their lack of a right to free movement across Europe's borders. *Kein Mensch ist illegal* ("no one is illegal") was the outcry in Germany.[77]

At first, transnational efforts sought mainly to gather new allies and audiences for the sans-papiers in France, who developed contacts with anti-racism, human rights, and feminist groups across Europe. There were solidarity protests outside French consulates, and sans-papiers declarations were translated into several languages;

invitations to tell of the movement came from throughout the continent.[78] Films documented the story of the sans-papiers, such as *Wir sind schon da* (We are already there), made by German feminists, who went to Paris to collect footage. As borders fell, "bridges have been built," Cissé wrote, and organizing "took on a European dimension."[79]

From the epicenter in Paris, an expansive network developed, with the unrest of undocumented migrants shaped by legacies of colonialism and the global effects of neoliberal reform. Across the Schengen area—which included Spain, Portugal, Italy, and Austria by the end of the century—the harmonization of restrictive immigration measures accompanying the fall of interior borders spurred transnational campaigns.[80] Calls came from the Netherlands for support in the "Struggle for 'Sans Papiers' and 'Illegalized' people." A Dutch anti-racist group, Nederland Bekent Kleur, sent out a notice describing "a struggle with our government to legalize a group of 'sans papiers'" who were stripped of rights under a new law, the *Koppelingswet*:

> Now the illegalized have started to defend their rights: two separate hunger strikes are going on, one of 15 women and one of 31 men. We feel that pressure from abroad would certainly help our cause.[81]

Demonstrations in Germany, Italy, and Spain also were inspired by the French example. In Spain, the undocumented demanded regularization for all and targeted *Ley de Estranjería* ("a law on foreigners"). A Madrid group with forty-nine allied social organizations formed Papeles para todos y para todas (or Papers for All). In Barcelona, a collective of the undocumented took the name Assemblea papers per tothom (or Assembly Papers for Everyone). And the movement extended beyond the Schengen countries: in Britain, human rights and anti-racism associations protested to Parliament against the expulsion of asylum seekers under the Dublin rule of first entry; in Japan, where immigrant unrest had little precedent, the demands of the undocumented led to the mobilization of what a French scholar called "les sans-papiers au Japon."[82]

The influence of the sans-papiers traveled through a then-novel channel of communication: the Internet. Mobile telephones, digital mailing lists, webmail services—cyberspace became a new terrain of political mobilization allowing instant contact across neighbor-hoods and the borders of nations. As European policymaking has-tened globalization, and digital surveillance proceeded under the Schengen Information System, the Internet enabled globalization from below, brought on by undocumented immigrants who became brokers of a new digital politics. At the Saint-Bernard church, sans-papiers waited for the police holding mobile phones, more than a decade before the "networked protest" of the Arab Spring.[83] "It's quite strange to get in contact with people you have never seen before," a German activist said, noting how the web fostered "the complexity and diversity of the movement."[84]

In Germany, the insurgency produced *Kein Mensch ist illegal*, a campaign inspired by the refusal of the sans-papiers to be named illegal. It borrowed from the language of the Holocaust survivor Elie Wiesel, who had said of refugees: "You who are so-called illegal aliens must know that no human being is illegal."[85] The organizing arose from a "media laboratory" staged at the contemporary art exhibition *Documenta X* in the city of Kassel in 1997, a setting sug-gestive of redemption and resistance, for *Documenta* was founded after the war to bring the public the modern art condemned as "degenerate" by the Nazis.[86] As the exhibition guidebook explained, *Documenta*'s advent belonged to "the now-vanished era of post-war Europe, shaped by the cold war . . . and brought to a close by the fall of the Berlin wall"—an era ended by the "age of globalisation and . . . sometimes violent social, economic, and cultural transformations." At the century's close, therefore, *Documenta* explored a new set of "great ethical and aesthetic questions . . . the urban realm, ter-ritory, identity, new forms of citizenship, the national social state and its aftermath, racism and the state, the globalisation of markets and national policy."[87] At the exhibition, the documentary project became fused to the cause of the undocumented.

Kein Mensch ist illegal emerged from this fusion of politics and art, agitating for rights of regularization and free movement. The media laboratory—created by artists, physicians, lawyers, jour-nalists, many with experience in the antinuclear movement—assembled a network of humanitarian and anti-racist groups, bringing a sans-papiers delegation from France.[88] "All of us felt that the struggle of the sans-papiers represents a completely new quality," a German artist, Florian Schneider, said. "Our first aim was to establish a connection to Paris." Among the laboratory's transgressive works at the *Documenta* exhibition was a passport exchange office that invited spectators to relinquish their passports to migrants lacking papers. "Is this art or not?" the police asked.[89] More systematic work followed the exhibition, devised less by migrants than by their allies, unlike in France.[90] Against the backdrop of Germany's immigration restrictions—"the ship is full to the brim," it was said—*Kein Mensch ist illegal* built a transnational network, pursued a politics of direct action rather than dialogue with the government, and helped migrants cross borders.[91]

The German group became part of a "No Border Network," a Pan-European association supporting a universal right of free movement, in opposition to the restrictive harmonization of immigration law. It began as "Admission Free," aimed at a European Council meeting in Amsterdam in 1997—the summit that brought Schengen into European law. Outside the meeting, anti-racism groups protested Schengen's perils for foreigners.[92] The opposition cohered in the "No Border Network," which worked with immigrants' rights organizations worldwide; among their principal models was Justice for Janitors, a labor union campaign for workplace rights, with a constituency of thousands of undocumented immigrants in American cities.[93] No Border's organizing gained momentum in 1999, when the Amsterdam Treaty entered into force, completing the European Union's absorption of Schengen's principles. Its network led protests that year at the EU summit in Tampere, Finland, where member states agreed to harmonize the rules for suppressing "asylum tourism" and the terms of a common European arrest warrant, matters of criminal justice that had come to the fore in implementing Schengen.[94] Coordination of the Finland protests took place at Helsinki's contemporary art museum, recalling the genesis of *Kein Mensch ist illegal* at the *Documenta X* exhibition in Kassel.[95]

Under No Border's aegis, direct action would continue through the turn of the century, often taking aim at sites symbolic of Schengen's contradictions. Strasbourg, the center of the Schengen Information System, was the site of an exemplary occupation in July 2002. Some three thousand people gathered in an encampment for ten days in the French city bordering Germany. "No Border," they protested. "The Schengen Information System serves as an electronic, supranational instrument of exclusion and deportation first and foremost against migrants but also against all people." Condemning the rules of exclusion, they declared, "We oppose a more and more 'harmonised' migration policy."[96]

Not far from the No Border protest was the Pont de l'Europe. There, at the bridge spanning the Rhine, sans-papiers crossing France had met their counterparts traveling across Germany, subversive journeys meant to exhibit their lack of the right to free movement within the Schengen territory. As Cissé said of the legacies of the Parisian church occupations, "The undocumented people of France started the fight against fortress Europe."[97]

In 1998, the labors of the sans-papiers achieved recognition—not from the government of France, nor from other European Community countries, but from the International Federation for Human Rights. The ceremony marked the half-century anniversary of the Universal Declaration of Human Rights, as LIGA, a German branch of the international rights league, honored the *Zivilcourage*, "moral courage," of France's undocumented migrants. By then, the sans-papiers spokespersons, Ababacar Diop and Madjiguène Cissé, had begun theorizing the abjection of the undocumented and their aspirations to human rights. Theirs was a revolt against laws "denying the right to exist," Diop wrote.[98] Of Saint-Bernard's lessons, Cissé stated:

> Little by little the masses of people understood that our struggle raised questions that go beyond the regularization of the 'Sans-Papiers.' New questions have gradually emerged: "Do you agree to live in a France where fundamental human rights are scorned?"[99]

The point was that to protest as sans-papiers was to claim human rights.

In the work of both Diop and Cissé, memoir fused with critique, as each bore witness to the sans-papiers revolt—inside the churches, outside in the streets, the desperation of families, the failure of negotiations, the hunger strikes, the arrests, the experience of political awakening—and analyzed their own condition as rightless persons. Diop's account, *Dans la peau d'un sans-papiers* (In the skin of a sans-papiers), appeared a year after the Saint-Ambroise occupation, in 1997. Cissé set out her thoughts following the Saint-Bernard occupation in "Sans-papiers: First Lessons," an essay printed in the journal *Politique, la revue*, and then developed her ideas in *Parole de sans-papiers* (A sans-papier speaks), published in 1999.[100] Diop's writing is more personal, Cissé's more analytical. Yet both spoke of Africa and Europe; of race, colonialism, citizenship, and illegality; and of rights, borders, and free movement.

"I lived, before the beginning of this struggle, the life of a sans-papiers in a tragic way," Diop wrote in the opening of his memoir. He described always fearing arrest, and the humiliation of hiding and lying, which was to live in the skin of a sans-papiers: "Vivre m'était difficile [Living was difficult for me]." He explained his reasons for writing the book. One was to create a record of the insurrectionary sans-papiers, to give migrants a place in the history of the nation: "To testify directly so that the experience lived within the context of this struggle rests in the collective memory that translates into the history of a nation." The other was to undertake self-transformation. "This book is part of the process," Diop wrote, "and perhaps I will be able at last to cast off this skin of the sans-papiers in which I am forced to live."[101] To write the book was to free himself of sans-papiers skin.

Diop was raised among fisherman on the Atlantic coast of Senegal, in the city of Saint-Louis, once the capital under French colonial rule. Swept up in political activism that placed him under government surveillance, he left in 1988. To enter France, he obtained a visa, although the immigration rules were tightening, as conceived in the Schengen laboratory. At first, he did not seek asylum, viewing France as an "open country" with a debt to its former colonies. But when his visa was expiring, he filed an asylum claim, which gave him temporary access to a work authorization that he used to find a job as a cleaner. This was the beginning of what Diop called his "period of papers." But when his asylum claim was rejected, in 1990, he learned the meaning of lacking papers, a lack all the more acute because he had just attained professional credentials in computer technology. Being denied "the right," Diop wrote, "to be here; to be able to enter the labor market, but not to have the possibility of going out into the open," he experienced what "the authorities call 'clandestin,' and what we call 'sans-papiers.'"[102]

As a sans-papiers, Diop disappeared into the shadowy life of France's undocumented immigrants, "neither seen, nor known." He appealed to the Conseil d'État, but a refugee commission denied him sanctuary in 1995. In the past, he learned, he would have been allowed residence due simply to his many years on French soil, seven at that point. But the Pasqua laws had revoked that privilege, distorting the concept of justice as "blind."[103]

"One was nothing," Diop wrote of himself. And that awareness led him to "exit the shadows." He described joining the Saint-Ambroise occupation, how he left his home and went to the church, after seeing televised images of the protest: "Several hundred African sans-papiers had overtaken a place of worship." He wrote of the significance of language, recalling how the "clandestins" became the "sans-papiers," in a liberatory change of vocabulary: "We stopped speaking of 'clandestins' to speak of 'sans-papiers.' The sans-papiers took form and shape; they became the defenders of a more exalted liberty, a more exalted democracy: the contemporary sans-culottes." Of the violence of the Saint-Bernard expulsion, Diop wrote: "Was this Satan?"[104]

As Diop set his own life story into the record of sans-papiers unrest, his account argued for vindicating rights but also for establishing historical truth. Both required confronting the influence of colonialism, he wrote, as it existed in the past and endured in the present, ordering the lives of undocumented migrants. "We are not here by chance," he insisted. "We did not come to France by chance." Rather, the sans-papiers' unwanted presence reflected the relations of colonial exploitation that had bound the countries of Africa to France. "Our countries have suffered and continue to suffer from colonization," he wrote. "Our riches have been and are still being exploited by France, as well as by other European countries." Therefore, Diop insisted, African migrants had powerful claims to recognition, in France and throughout Europe: "It is legitimate for nationals of our blood-drained countries to come and find enough to subsist here." But they faced laws enforcing "'zero' immigration, the warhorse of Pasqua." Their movement across borders

FIGURE 6.5. Ababacar Diop, right, strategizes with the priest Abbé Pierre during the Saint Bernard church occupation of 1996. Credit: Alexis Duclos / GAMMA RAPHO

was blocked by a politics of exclusion, "the formidable machine to exclude which has a grip on France."[105]

Living in the skin of a sans-papiers, then, was to bear the mark of colonialism's wrongs and of laws that violated fundamental rights. As Diop wrote, "The story of the sans-papiers of Saint-Bernard reveals the unbearable nature of the conditions generated by the legislation on foreigners." He illustrated the liberatory meaning of the church occupation by telling of a ritual of exorcism in Senegal. When someone was possessed by demons, drums were beaten and incantations recited, and the possessed became filled with agitation, in a *ndeup*, an exorcism organized by the community, until the "demons, attacked by so many incantations, freed the victim who, little by little, regained his senses." That was the feeling of occupying the church, as if the demons were leaving him, "as if the *ndeup* were beginning." He wrote of seeking self-liberation in the sans-papiers movement: "To get out of the shackles . . . to be able to exist with my true black skin, of which I am very proud."[106]

For Diop, release from the sans-papiers shackles meant full enfranchisement, not simply regularization—an enfranchisement carrying rights of political belonging and participation in common life. The migrants were owed recognition faithful to the heritage of the sans-culottes, he argued: "Never forget, we are citizens of France, and above all citizens by law." Such recognition entailed ending the criminalization of France's immigrant population, addressing colonialism by acting, in the "face of racism, to renovate the collective memory," and promoting the independence of associations asserting political power. Still more, Diop argued for suffrage rights for nonnationals in local elections in exchange for their economic contributions, applying the natural law of reason to the claims of African migrants: "'Cogito ergo sum' . . . Eh bien, 'I pay my taxes, therefore I vote.'" Here lay the recovery of "historical truth," he wrote, "France of the Declaration of the Rights of Man, of tolerance, of liberty."[107]

But chief among Diop's propositions was a guarantee of free movement as a human right. At the close of his account, enumerating the sans-papiers' aspirations to freedom, he began with *se déplacer*—to move, to circulate, to travel, to change places. He wrote, "allow everyone to move freely." Next, he turned to racism, regularization, and political agency. Prior, then, to residence or work or suffrage was a basic right of free movement, a right fundamental to personal dignity and belonging in common life. "I long to be able to go wherever I want," he wrote of the impulse to cross the world's borders. "I don't see why ideas would circulate whereas human beings are condemned to limit their horizon." For a sans-papiers, therefore, exiting the "shadow cast by the laws" obliged seeking free movement as a human right.[108]

That argument coursed through Cissé's book, *Parole de sans-papiers*, animating her defense of the rights of undocumented migrants. She recounted the story of the sans-papiers uprising— day by day, month by month, describing its passage beyond France—and offered a critical history of immigration law, giving scathing attention to Schengen's rules. Her work was less a memoir than an anatomy of a social movement and an indictment of human rights violations. She began by addressing free movement as coeval with humanity, and migration with social existence. "At

FIGURE 6.6. Madjiguène Cissé, the sans-papiers spokesperson
who returned to her native Senegal, pictured in 2006. Credit:
Sébastien Dolidon

all times, in all places, human populations have defied the worst
conditions, crossed deserts, oceans, mountains to be together," she
wrote, maintaining that the "history of the human species is inter-
twined from the start with such migration. . . . Making and crossing borders has always been one of the ways in which societies are
built." Thus, Cissé derived a rights argument: "Every human has
the right, in the continuity of one's ancestors, to travel, to migrate."
And she explained that the sans-papiers sought just this, *la liberté
de circulation*—"freedom of movement."[109]

Cissé grew up in Pikine, a city near Senegal's seaport capital of
Dakar that was founded in the last years of French colonial rule.
It emerged from a slum clearance project in the capital, hous-
ing displaced residents, and remained scarred by poverty and

unemployment.[110] She left to study in West Germany, on an academic exchange program; earlier, as a lycée student, she had followed the events of May 1968 in Europe, as she read Sartre, Lenin, Lumumba, Malcolm X, and Mao. After completing her degree in Saarbrücken, Cissé returned to Senegal to be a teacher but in 1993 made her way to Paris, where she found work and settled, though she held only a temporary tourist visa.[111] She, too, lived in the skin of a sans-papiers and experienced the afterlives of colonialism. "We are all bearers of a story. Memories of our fathers, our ancestors, stories of the slave trade and colonization," she wrote. "We have all experienced the images and situations of neo-colonialism. We relive them, as one bad nightmare in the heart of the City of Light." She recalled being inside the church—the disorder of the first days, the organization of the hunger strike, the government's intransigence ("Pasqua was watching"), the attention to everyday needs—and becoming a spokesperson for the sans-papiers, affirming the refusal "to return to the shadows." To be visible, from Saint-Ambroise to Saint-Bernard, saying "we insist on staying," was to transform the African migrant from a "pariah" to a rights claimant endowed with "sans papiers citizenship."[112]

Cissé set her analysis of the mobilization of the sans-papiers within the context of a global political economy that she said was defined by principles of neocolonialism and neoliberalism. That system, she argued, maintained European dominion and the imperatives of capitalist development, dividing the world into rich and poor countries, and defined African migrants as both alien and necessary to wealth accumulation, reproducing relations of colonial subjection in the situation of the sans-papiers. "African countries are thus considered as minor children under tutelage, while their difficulties are the consequences of several centuries of colonialism and neo-colonialism, whose mantle is taken up by the unbridled liberalism of today," she wrote. European integration reflected the same rapacious dynamic, she argued. "The commercial concept of European construction is wreaking havoc," she wrote, warning that, "The implosion of social relations . . . is the main risk of trauma from the dynamics of capitalist accumulation." She assailed the effect on African countries of "neoliberal policies leaving little chance for the flourishing and freedom of peoples," stressing the connections to the sans-papiers rebellion: "A jolt, a revolt to say: 'We no longer want France to continue to submit us to the same relations that it maintains with the states of our countries of origin built on exploitation, contempt and paternalism.'"[113] This was colonial conflict in the heart of the metropole.

And free movement lay at the heart of the conflict, according to Cissé's account. Again and again, she contrasted the barriers against human migration with capital's unfettered flow, as she argued for free movement as a human right. "By claiming and granting ourselves freedom of movement, we wanted to say that this freedom could not be limited to capital and merchandise. . . . In a world where everything circulates—information, capital, commodities, music, culture—should people accept being deprived of freedom of movement, one of their most fundamental rights, one of the rights they have exercised since time immemorial?" she wrote. "To fight for obtaining freedom of movement is a way of fighting against savage liberalism." Indeed, for capital to travel the world, the movement of people must be forbidden, she claimed. "To better organize exploitation at the global level . . . to better control the labor market . . . the 'rich' countries erect borders where they deem it necessary, open them halfway or shut them again depending on the economic conditions. While capital circulates freely, wealthy countries seek to impede the free movement of nationals of 'poor' countries." Such restraint, she wrote, took the form of "quotidian violence."[114]

Always, *Parole de sans-papiers* counted free movement as a right possessed by virtue of being human. This freedom was not to be limited by borders or citizenship, Cissé argued. "For there are human rights, rights that we hold simply for being human. . . . Freedom of movement is not a fiction. It consecrates a state of fact." She condemned the European Community countries, and France particularly, for violating the rights of foreigners protected by international conventions, as she counterposed the laws of states with human rights. "Expel the maximum. Close, control, master, repress," she wrote. "Does the law that the nation-state applies to the foreigner superimpose itself on the intrinsic rights of the individual?" In subverting the laws of Pasqua and Debré—"godless laws"—the sans-papiers enshrined "'papers for all' . . . the idea of freedom of movement for all people on the planet."[115]

For Cissé, Schengen's creation brought into force the brutal paradoxes of free movement. In her account, Schengen was a laboratory of sans-papiers unfreedom, a space embodying both the principle of exclusion and a commercial construct of Europe, where migratory flows were controlled, capital mobility assured, and human rights denied. It was where the tightening of external borders balanced the opening of internal frontiers, and where the harmonization of laws regulating foreigners enforced the "non-rights of men." She surveyed the history of immigration restriction in the European Community, from the Treaty of Rome to the Treaty of Amsterdam, tracing the commitment to ending illegal immigration and illegal residence. "From the outset, the principle of exclusion haunted the project, the texts and the objectives of the European space," she wrote. Yet Schengen was a turning point in that project, she argued, as a territory created to free the border crossings of goods and Europeans but not of foreigners, where member states regulated sans-papiers as "people without rights," establishing models— laboratories—for the European Community. "The Schengen agreements," she wrote, "were immediately followed by the enactment of laws on the immigration of workers in the various countries of the European Union, then by a whole series of treaties and conventions on the control of migratory flows, the movement of foreigners and the right of asylum." Accordingly, in the Schengen states, the question of papers became a conflict over transnational freedom of movement.[116]

First in Cissé's citation of Schengen's wrongs was the Schengen Information System. She described how the flow of data among the Schengen countries underpinned the suppression of the sans-papiers, enabling their detection and expulsion, making their shadowy existence more unsafe, stopping their border crossing, inhibiting their movement. "The Schengen Information System, an enormous computer file, is created, establishing police cooperation: 'undesirable' foreigners in a country are registered in this file, they thus become undesirable in all Schengen signatory countries." Through the computerized system, the xenophobia of one state could travel across the entire Schengen bloc, forming a regime "anachronistic with respect to the desire for democratic construction," she wrote. "The Schengen agreements . . . base the European construction on phobia of the foreigner. . . . A space made in this way will bear the scars of totalitarianism." Thus, the circulation of data became a cornerstone of fortress Europe: "Once the principle of free movement was acquired for nationals of member countries of the European space," she reasoned, the aim became to "protect this same space from the 'invasion' of outsiders, often in defiance of the most basic human rights." An information network buttressed Schengen's "asylum prisons": the detention centers, walls, watchtowers, and barbed wire.[117]

Cissé's account became most personal in telling of her own arrest, imprisonment, and trial after the Saint-Bernard evacuation. She recalled the axes breaking down the church door; the police forcing her out; the order to show her papers; the handcuffs; being held at a detention center, police headquarters, and the prefecture; being separated from her daughter; stripped naked and searched; fingerprinted, weighed, measured, photographed, and locked into a cell. She wrote of "the humiliation . . . the powerlessness." She was questioned about her identity but would not answer. "That is the spokeswoman" for the sans-papiers, the police said, "who lost her speech."[118]

But in the Correctional Court, a criminal tribunal, Cissé spoke. She stood accused of being a sans-papiers—that on the day of the church evacuation, August 23, 1996, she was found to have stayed in France without a residence permit and trespassed on French territory as a foreigner. She recalled the court asking, "Do you want to be judged today?" She answered, "Yes," taking the floor to speak in self-defense about the relationship between Africa and France:

> I say how France colonized my country of origin, how our countries were impoverished by colonization, neo-colonization. How these countries are crumbling under the weight of debt. How these Africans, whose relations with the state administration are judged today, are treated in this country. How our grandparents had fought alongside French soldiers to repel the Nazi occupation.

She wrote of being punished with a two-month suspended sentence, a judgment hanging over her "like the sword of Damocles," so that she came to live in a sans-papiers' skin, "without authorization in the country of the rights of man." She was "made guilty." To tell of her trial was to show how refusing to be illegal meant claiming free movement as a human right.[119]

———————————

In 1998, Cissé's case came before the European Court of Human Rights. By then, her pleas had been dismissed by the French judiciary; an appeals court upheld her conviction, adding an order excluding her from France for three years. A higher court refused to reconsider the ruling. It fell to the European court to determine the balance between human rights protected by international covenants and the power of a sovereign nation to secure order in its territory. At issue in *Cissé v. France* was the freedom of sans-papiers to assemble, circulate, and claim a place in a country where they were outlaws.[120]

A set of prior cases involving deportation orders in the Schengen states suggested that the European human rights court might be receptive to Cissé's claims. The cases tested the balance between the free movement of foreign migrants and the power of nations to exclude, asking the court to review the enforcement of immigration laws. Notably, however, the claimants in these cases did not invoke the free movement guarantee of the European Convention on Human Rights—the 1963 protocol granting everyone the "right to liberty of movement and freedom to choose his residence"—for that right did not reach across the borders of countries and continents but was expressly limited to persons "lawfully within the territory of a State" and to movement within "the territory of a State."[121] Nor did they appeal to the European Court of Justice, which had recognized a right to cross borders for employment training in the *Gravier* case, because Community law did not protect foreign nationals. Their arguments did not invoke Schengen's affirmation of the asylum rights guaranteed by the Geneva Convention. Rather, their claims rested on family ties, in which the European human rights court found merit.

As a barrier to deportation—unfree movement—the migrants cited the European Convention's protection of family life. Article 8, section 1 of the convention stated: "Everyone has the right to respect for his private and family life." The convention protected that right against state interference, except for the limitation clause providing for restrictions "necessary in a democratic society" and required to maintain "national security, public safety or the economic well-being of the country" and prevent "disorder or crime"—security imperatives that took on still greater prominence with Schengen's removal of internal border controls.[122] In the deportation cases, therefore, the problem before the European human rights court was reconciling national security not with individual free movement but with the integrity of family relations.

Less than a year before the Paris church occupations began, a ruling came down in *Nasri v. France*, blocking the expulsion of an Algerian national living with his parents in Nanterre. In reaching that judgment, the European human rights court examined the terms of the Pasqua legislation, the bane of the sans-papiers. The court noted that the first Pasqua law, in 1986, removed the word "serious" from the provisions of the national code authorizing the interior minister to order a deportation "if the aliens' presence on French territory constitutes a serious threat to public order." The qualification was reinstated in 1990, applying to the dispute over separating Mohamed Nasri from his parents under a deportation order.[123]

That qualification—whether there was a serious threat to public order—mattered as the court weighed Nasri's right to family life against the state's interest in banishing him. Deaf and mute, Nasri had come to France with his family; but he was expelled from school and unable to stay employed as a house painter, accumulating a criminal record—for theft, attempted theft, theft with violence, receipt of stolen goods, assault of a public official, and gang rape. Pasqua ordered his deportation, declaring his presence a threat to public order. An administrative tribunal struck down the order, finding that Nasri's criminal convictions predated the Pasqua law of 1986 that loosened the serious-threat standard for deportations. Following a series of appeals in France, the European Commission of Human Rights stayed the deportation order, sending the case to the European human rights court.[124]

The court ruled in the immigrant's favor, finding that deporting him—and forcing him to move away from his family—would violate his rights under the European Convention. It found no compelling justification for the expulsion—"necessary in a democratic society"— that would overcome the Algerian's right to remain with his family. Yet it did not deny France's authority to order deportations, recognizing the power to exclude as core to state sovereignty. "It is for the Contracting States to maintain public order . . . to control the entry and residence of aliens and notably to order the expulsion of aliens convicted of criminal offences," the court affirmed, echoing other international tribunals in upholding national control of domestic policy affecting migrants. Rather, in *Nasri*, the court elucidated the constraints on state power, holding that its exercise in a democracy must be "justified by a pressing social need and, in particular, proportionate to the legitimate aim pursued." Because his disabilities made Nasri's family bonds essential, while mitigating his criminal liability, the rupture of family life was disproportionate to the public good derived from his deportation, the court held. His capabilities, his prospects for "achieving a minimum psychological and social equilibrium," were possible "only within his family, the majority of whose members are French nationals." By this reasoning, the primacy of family unity merged with ties of nationality to limit the state's authority to exclude non-Europeans.[125]

The decision in *Nasri v. France* drew on precedent developed in expulsion cases that reached the European court from countries across the Schengen area. Notably, the litigation emerged as Schengen members tightened immigration rules in response to the dismantling of internal borders. In 1988, the court barred the Netherlands from deporting a Moroccan national, Abdellah Berrehab, finding that his ties to his daughter still merited protection although he no longer lived with her, following his divorce from his Dutch wife.[126] The court applied the protective doctrine to immigrants enmeshed in a range of family bonds, to both adults and children, and to those with criminal records as well as those without. In 1991, it held that Abderrahman Moustaquim, a Moroccan national who had come to Belgium as a child, could not be deported even though he was classified as a "real danger to society," appearing before the juvenile court nearly 150 times.[127] A year later, it blocked France from deporting an Algerian national with a criminal history. Born in France to Algerian parents, Mohand Beldjoudi lost his birthright citizenship when Algeria gained independence and his parents chose not to retain French citizenship. He married a French national. Convicted of crimes including theft, weapons possession, and assault and battery, he was imprisoned for several years. But the European court held that his deportation order did not meet the proportionality standard, finding France in violation of Article 8 of the human rights convention.[128]

Family, then, stood as a bulwark against unfree movement, affording nonnationals a measure of protection against forced removal even in states where the transnational guarantee of free movement depended on European citizenship. As the European Court of Human Rights became an arbiter of the competing claims of family life and state sovereignty, its jurisprudence entitled even the "undesirable" to a form of protected movement otherwise withheld from non-Europeans in the Schengen territory. Appeals to a human right to family life hedged the state power of deportation to secure the European community.

The problem posed by *Cissé v. France* was different: an appeal not for residence based on family bonds, but for a judgment safeguarding the right of a sans-papiers to occupy the Saint-Bernard church against the power asserted by France to maintain public order. Again, the European court had to balance a claim of human rights against an exercise of state sovereignty. And, again, the rights claim did not rest on the European Convention's free movement protocol, for that protection did not belong to a sans-papiers unlawfully within the territory of France.

Instead, Cissé challenged her subjection to forcible movement— her evacuation from the church, imprisonment, and order of deportation—by invoking the right to free assembly and association guaranteed in the European Convention. She rooted her claim in Article 11 of the international covenant, which stated, "Everyone has the right to freedom of peaceful assembly and to freedom of association with others," and which barred state restriction of that freedom, except as necessary, under the limitation clause, for protecting "national security or public safety" and preventing "disorder or crime" in a democracy. Unlike the family guarantee, it included a clause expressly allowing the exercise of state police power: "Imposition of lawful restrictions . . . by members of the armed forces, of the police or of the administration of the State."[129] It also differed from the free movement protocol in imposing no requirement of lawful presence within the territory of a state as a condition of holding the associative right. Under the European Convention, a sans-papiers unentitled to free movement nonetheless possessed a right to free assembly and association.

Therefore, Cissé claimed in the European court that France had violated her human right to assemble and associate by occupying the Saint-Bernard church. She argued that the evacuation was illegal, justified by neither a valid purpose nor the rule of proportionality. She maintained that illegal immigrants were entitled to assemble, that their assembly was not violent, and that the priest and parish council supported the gathering of the sans-papiers inside the church. She argued that their presence never disrupted the rituals of religious worship or disobeyed safety regulations, and that the French government had no authority to determine a church's interests. She claimed that the police commissioner was not empowered "to deploy the armed forces to defeat the right of asylum through forcible eviction of people who had, as a last resort, taken refuge in a place of worship," that the charges of disorder were "just a pretext," and that the police "had merely implemented a decision taken by the President of the Republic and the Prime Minister in an attempt to avoid giving the public the impression that they had been weakened by the challenge to the Government posed by the 'sans papiers' in their pursuit of a review of their immigration status." She argued that France had breached her right to assemble peacefully with other foreigners.[130]

What Cissé's argument left unsaid was that a right to assemble and associate entailed mobility: a capacity to circulate, to migrate, a right to come and go. It was this idea that she introduced at the opening of *Parole de sans-papiers*, as she wrote that human beings "at all times, in all places . . . crossed deserts, oceans, mountains to be together."[131] As a sans-papiers, seeking vindication of her rights, but unlawfully within the territory of France, she could not argue that point to the European court, for the European Convention recognized no claim to free movement by an undocumented immigrant. Yet the liberties were inseparable, as she illustrated outside the courtroom: Associative freedom implied a right to free movement.

For the French government, the task was justifying the Saint-Bernard evacuation, the arrest of the sans-papiers, and Cissé's sentencing in the nation's courts. All were necessary to preserve public order and prevent crime, the argument went, and consistent with democratic practices and the protection of national security. No right to unlawful assembly existed under European human rights doctrine, the government maintained, and because the intent of the church occupation was legitimizing the violation of French immigration law, the "unlawfulness of the assembly was therefore particularly flagrant and the very purpose of that assembly in itself entailed a breach of public order," and could not be considered "peaceful." Nor was the police action unwarranted, the government argued, citing a law dating from the era of the French Revolution—Ordinance of 12 Messidor, Year VIII—that gave the Paris police commissioner "full powers to maintain public order." Moreover, the occupation, continuing for months, not only disrupted worship but also blocked passage through nearby streets due to the barricades erected around the church. "The installations that had been set up outside the church obstructed the free flow of traffic," stated the government, invoking free movement with unintended irony in justifying the forcible removal of the sans-papiers.[132]

Finally, the government claimed that an undocumented immigrant had no right to freedom of assembly. Cissé was "in breach of the immigration rules," having been instructed to leave France, and by occupying the church, the government argued, "contravened by her conduct" a French law, a century old, on free assembly, thereby deserving her punishment: her arrest, detention, and exclusion from France for a term of three years ordered by the Paris appeals court. Allegedly, as a sans-papiers, she had lost a right not only to free movement but to free assembly.[133]

In 2002, the European Court of Human Rights at last decided *Cissé v. France*. In balancing her freedoms with France's sovereignty—finding what was proportionate and necessary to a democracy—the court handed down a balanced judgment. Again, it affirmed that non-Europeans were entitled to protections under the European Convention, and that even "illegal immigrants" possessed a right of free assembly, meaning that a sans-papiers, in principle, could claim associative freedom everywhere within the

European community. But it held that the circumstances of the Saint-Bernard occupation by foreigners without papers justified the government's forcible interference, meaning that France had not violated Cissé's human rights.[134]

The court reviewed the facts of the case, finding that Cissé was a Senegalese national and spokesperson for the assembly of the sans-papiers—"a group of aliens without residence permits"—who had occupied the church in a "collective action" to demonstrate their difficulties in regularizing their immigration status, and that the Paris police commissioner had ordered an evacuation because of "public-order risks." The court described how the police had set up a checkpoint to identify immigrants who lacked papers "authorizing them to stay and circulate in the territory" and were punished with detention and deportation, noting that a sans-papiers had no claim to free movement. It also noted the differential treatment of the races: "Whites were immediately released while the police assembled all the dark-skinned occupants." It found that Cissé had no papers and was duly arrested, tried, and convicted as an "illegal immigrant" without "family reasons" for staying in France.[135]

But the court rejected France's argument that Cissé's illegal status placed her beyond the pale of enforceable rights. It held that her status as a sans-papiers did not strip her of the right to free assembly and recognized that her expulsion from the Saint-Bernard church infringed on her associative rights. "The Court does not share the Government's view that the fact that the applicant was an illegal immigrant sufficed to justify a breach of her right to freedom of assembly," the judgment stated. "The Court finds that the evacuation of the church amounted to an interference in the exercise of the applicant's right to freedom of peaceful assembly." Nor was a peaceful protest—even against immigration rules openly disobeyed—a sufficient reason for "a restriction on liberty" under the European Convention's associative guarantee.[136]

Yet none of this exculpated Cissé or meant that France had violated her rights. To the contrary, the court found that the protection of public order justified France's evacuation of the Saint-Bernard sans-papiers—that the state pursued legitimate aims, that the circumstances of the long occupation made interference with her freedom of assembly necessary, and that the use of state power against an undocumented immigrant met the test of proportionality. The judgment declared unequivocally: "The evacuation was ordered to put an end to the continuing occupation of a place of worship by persons, including the applicant, who had broken French law. The interference therefore pursued a legitimate aim, namely the prevention of disorder." While recognizing that the police raid was uninvited by the parish priest, unannounced, and "indiscriminate," the court found that authority to supervise religious practices belonged to the government and that the prolonged hunger strike and inadequate sanitary conditions had posed public health risks raising reasonable "fear that the situation might deteriorate rapidly and could not be allowed to continue much longer." Furthermore, the occupation had been allowed its polemical purpose, the court stated: "The symbolic and testimonial value of the applicant's and other immigrants' presence had been tolerated sufficiently long enough." The sans-papiers had made their point; it was time for the state to act.[137]

The court therefore affirmed the lawfulness of Cissé's expulsion from France—her unfree movement. It upheld the interference with her right to freedom of assembly, finding the state's imposition of restrictions, "in the light of all the circumstances," both necessary in a democracy and "not . . . disproportionate" under Article 11 of the European Convention.[138] In the eyes of the court, as it balanced security and freedom, her circulation as a sans-papiers posed a greater risk to public order in France than did the presence of non-Europeans with criminal records whose family ties blocked their deportation. Deferring to state sovereignty, the court unanimously dismissed her claim.

By the time the European human rights court delivered its judgment, Cissé had returned to Senegal, obeying her deportation order. Earlier, however, while her case was pending, she had traveled from Paris to Berlin, where, on behalf of the sans-papiers, she accepted the prize for moral courage awarded by the German league of the International Federation for Human Rights.[139] As a sans-papiers spokesperson, beginning with the church occupations, Cissé expressed a claim to free movement that countered Schengen's principles by defining border crossing as a human right transcending nationality. No court—neither France's tribunals nor Europe's human rights court—allowed her that freedom. Ruling for France, the European court recognized the right of an undocumented immigrant to have rights but affirmed the power of a nation-state to subject her to unfree movement.

———————————

The Paris unrest of the sans-papiers inspired a transnational movement of undocumented migrants but brought no change to the law governing the undocumented. The church occupations left the rules of regularization unchanged. The border encampments failed to influence Schengen's harmonization of immigration laws. Cissé's appeals altered neither criminal justice in France nor the status of migrants in Europe. Yet the protest of the sans-papiers recast understandings of the guarantee of free movement—and therefore of human rights claims and principles of entitlement and exclusion based on citizenship—becoming jurisgenerative outside the formal space of courtrooms.[140]

The conflict at the Saint-Bernard church was a turning point. It might be thought of as an *évènement*, to borrow from the ideas of the philosopher Paul Ricœur, himself a member of the sans-papiers mediating committee, who used the term to explain historical and conceptual transformation. An *évènement* signifies a rupture, an event of history, brought about by human actors, which creates an "epistemic gap" requiring further explication to draw out unstated meaning.[141] Saint-Bernard—and its afterlives—represented such an *évènement*.

As sans-papiers spokespersons, Diop and Cissé gave meaning to the events of the church occupations, theorizing in their memoirs about the situation of undocumented migrants and the boundaries of free movement, as shaped by the colonial past and the project of European union advanced by Schengen's creation. So, too, did France's philosophers find meaning in the cause of the sans-papiers as their insurgency unfolded in Parisian neighborhoods and reached across Europe.[142] Their thought about possessing human rights—having a right to have rights irrespective of citizenship—affirmed sans-papiers claims to free movement and asylum, vindicating arguments rejected by the courts.

"But what are the 'sans-papiers' lacking?" asked Jacques Derrida, speaking at a mass demonstration in Paris in December 1996. He confessed to finding "sans-papiers," just the term itself, "terrifying." The language was frightful in expressing how a piece of paper had become synonymous with a right—not just any right, but "the right to a right," the Algerian-born philosopher said. "The 'sans-papiers' is in the end '*sans droit*,' 'without right' and virtually outside the law." And to be placed outside the law was to be "naked and exposed, without right, without recourse, deficient in the essential." It was to lack "*dignity*," he said, because of the French state's "derelictions of a right to justice."[143]

Months earlier, just after the Saint-Ambroise evacuation, when the sans-papiers wandered through Paris seeking refuge, the physician-cum-social theorist Didier Fassin had begun making sense of the events. "Humanitarian considerations weighed little against repressive logics," he wrote of the "'Illegals' and the State." His essay, appearing in *Le Monde*, began by observing, simply, that there was "meaning in the action taken by these men, women and children without papers who believed they could find refuge in a church"—that it allowed "some truth to emerge on the issue of foreigners in an irregular situation." Fassin refused to speak for the sans-papiers about the meaning of their protest, saying it would be "improper to claim to express it in place of those who have thus deliberately put themselves in danger of being removed from the territory." But he condemned the "situation of juridical exclusion." He wrote of the "merciless repression against irregular immigration," arguing that the state both produced and forbade the condition of "irregularity." This was signified by the usage of *clandestin*, which "judges and punishes."[144]

In speaking of the sans-papiers' lack, Derrida elaborated the critique of the state's dereliction of justice. But he, too, made a point of saying that he did not speak for the sans-papiers, because they spoke for themselves. "We are here to protest and to act first by speaking," he said to his listeners in a Paris theater. "This means by raising our voice for the 'sans-papiers' . . . but not *for them* in the sense of *in their place*. They have spoken and they speak for themselves, we hear them." He said of sans-papiers speech: "We are here to hear them and to listen to them tell us what they have to tell us, to speak with them, and not only, therefore, to speak about them."[145]

In hearing the sans-papiers, Derrida spoke of the lack of a right to free movement. He told his listeners about the borders and laws that enabled the exclusion and expulsion of foreigners from the states of the European community, "in defiance of the rights of man." European countries, he said, were "turning their borders into new iron curtains. Borders are no longer places of passage; they are places of interdiction . . . of banishment, of persecution." He described how state authority, "discriminating, filtering out, hunting down, expelling" under the Pasqua and Debré laws—"a police system of inquisition, of record-keeping"—reduced a human being to a "subject 'without papers,'" as if lacking papers defined the entirety of one's being.[146]

This critique pointed to the systemic correspondence between state repression of paperless migrants and the mobility of capital worldwide. He protested the sans-papiers' subjection as a problem both particular and universal—"a singular human tragedy" but also the "exemplary symptom of what happens to the geo-political sphere in what one calls the *globalization* of the market under the domination of neo-liberalism." Here Derrida cited European integration—"the Schengen accords, for example"—as evidence of the "calculated mystifications" of "so-called globalization," where sans-papiers lacked freedom to cross borders. The need, then, was for annulling the rules of lack and illegality, for "changing the law" by recognizing the sans-papiers as bearers of "the *rights of man.*"[147]

It was this problem of lack that underlay Étienne Balibar's judgment about the freedom owed to the sans-papiers. For to ask what was owed was another way of stating what was lacking. Seeking, a year after the advent of the protest, to find what was due to the sans-papers as actors in democratic life—"for being seen and heard"—he treated the Saint-Bernard occupation as an *évènement*. His language was of rupture and transformation, as he drew out the meaning of Saint-Bernard in his speech at the Paris solidarity demonstration in 1997. "Broken," "shattered," "recreated," "renewing," "breathing life back into democracy" was how he described the acts of the sans-papiers in "reestablishing the truth of the history and condition of humans . . . and engaging the universality of rights."[148]

Balibar elaborated on the civic contributions of the sans-papiers in an essay two years later—"*Droit de cité* or Apartheid?"—in which he counterposed the rights of immigrants to a violent system of racial exclusion. He argued that European unification had advanced a "European apartheid," a form of "recolonialization" or "specifically 'European' racism," constituted by the new guarantee of transnational citizenship conferred only on European nationals.[149] By contrast, the protest of the sans-papiers enacted "active citizenship," refusing the exclusionary citizenship enshrined by European treatymaking in seeking the "*democratization of borders and of the freedom of movement.*"[150]

Over time, Balibar would develop this moral critique, singling out Schengen for condemnation while placing free moment as sought by the sans-papiers at the center of aspirations for transnational democracy and justice. In a lecture celebrating the inauguration of a degree in humanitarian action at the University of Geneva, he sketched a "Topography of Cruelty," with European institutions standing as landmarks. Schengen, he wrote, combined "modern techniques of identification and recording with good old 'racial profiling.'" The humanitarian project, then, was to create a "*desegregated Europe*, that is, a democratic Europe."[151] In that project, he would later recall the Saint-Bernard occupation as an "emblematic moment" as he abjured the use of repression in "Schengen-area Europe . . . to block the influx of migrants." Again, the philosopher affirmed the claim of the sans-papiers to free movement: "A new right for the circulation of people . . . above and beyond national borders."[152]

At Saint-Bernard, and in that moment's aftermath, the sans-papiers provoked a reimagining of free movement as a human right to cross national borders as well as profound doubt about the legitimacy of Schengen's rules of exclusion. Their lives in the shadows of illegality became more precarious as internal borders opened in the Schengen countries. To be a foreign migrant without papers was to lack a place in the cosmopolitan space of the European community, where rights remained attached to nationality and colonialism's past marked the derelictions of justice. Yet outside the forum of legislatures and courts, the sans-papiers won vindication in claiming, in Cissé's words, a "right to come and go, to settle . . . imprescriptible rights of the human being, without the guarantee of which one cannot speak of Humanity."[153] The chant of protesters traversing Paris—"We are all 'sans-papiers'"—recognized free movement as a human right owed to the sans-papiers.[154]

Epilogue

ON JUNE 13, 2010, the Musée européen Schengen opened its doors for the first time to celebrate the signing of the Schengen treaty a quarter-century earlier. The museum stands on the banks of the Moselle River; it is a plain building, made of gray cement and glass, with no adornments other than jagged stars carved into the front wall. The stars symbolize the founding states of Schengen.[1]

The museum holds artifacts of the creation of a borderless Europe: the treaty signed in 1985, obsolete customs equipment, fragments of a border wall. A permanent exhibition portrays Schengen's history and the rise and fall of frontiers across the continent; it also depicts the use of the Schengen Information System and visa rules for non-Europeans. Maps illustrate how the Schengen area expanded over time, eventually extending from Italy, Spain, and Greece to the Scandinavian countries and east to Poland, Slovenia, Hungary, and the Baltic states. On display is the everyday value of removing borders—how the "free movement of people within the Schengen Area and the new external borders have changed the lives of Europeans," and how Schengen "put into practice one of the four foundational European freedoms set down in the 1957 Treaty of Rome."[2]

Outside the museum are pieces of the Berlin Wall, ruins symbolizing free movement. Nearby, a monument rises from the riverbank, a set of steles cut into by stars, honoring the Schengen treaty.[3] Otherwise, the landscape is quite as it was before the village of Schengen gave its name to the territory of free movement.

Vineyards still cover the hillsides that rise from the river where the treaty was signed.

Dignitaries from across Europe attended the museum's opening: the royalty of Luxembourg, officers of the European Parliament and the European Commission, and representatives from European Union member states. The Schengen treatymakers returned for the event, celebrating the long years "we worked to build Europe."[4]

It was a particular point of celebration that the museum would offer the public a history of a cosmopolitan project, with Schengen as a landmark of Citizens' Europe and a model of free movement. The account of historical change on display would highlight the demise of borders, the demolition of walls, the downfall of the Iron Curtain. The exhibitions would show what was "progressively left behind: closure and withdrawal, confrontation and war . . . and a continent cut in half," as Luxembourg's foreign minister said. "It is the first museum of its kind having as an object one of the great achievements of the European construction that traces the path from a Europe of borders to Citizens' Europe." It would portray how Schengen marked "the beginning of a greater Europe of the free movement of people." But the museum would also make evident the barriers against foreigners, "our external borders, our security." Its purpose was to exhibit a common European space, "of belonging to a territory, a culture."[5]

The museum's dedication was the most visible of commemorations, yet other anniversaries of European integration also became moments for considering Schengen's emergence as the continent's laboratory of free movement. Those reflections recalled the past but also contemplated the future, surveying Schengen's place in a Europe no longer divided by borders between sovereign nations, where humanist values lent legitimacy to free market mechanisms and multilateral security measures protected the liberties of European nationals. Appraisals of free movement began almost as soon as the Schengen treaty entered into force in 1995.

An authoritative reckoning came in a *Report of the High Level Panel on the Free Movement of Persons*, prepared for the European Commission in 1997. That year marked the fortieth anniversary of the signing of the Rome Treaty; it also witnessed the signing of the Treaty of Amsterdam, which incorporated Schengen into European

FIGURE 7.1. Simone Veil, a Holocaust survivor and French health minister who was the first woman chosen as president of the European Parliament, in 1979, is shown here campaigning for elections to the transnational body that year, based on the slogan, "I love France. I choose Europe." Veil's vision of European integration, as articulated in 1997, on the fiftieth anniversary of the Rome Treaty, was a humanistic endeavor transcending the market. Credit: Keystone-France / GAMMA RAPHO

Union law. The chairperson of the Commission panel was Simone Veil, a Holocaust survivor who became a preeminent advocate of European unification, serving for many years in the European Parliament and holding its presidency for a term.[6] She had endured unfree movement across Europe's borders, for she had been deported from her home in France to Auschwitz in Poland, and then to Bergen-Belsen in Germany. Never would she forget, she said, seeing "the sky clouded by the smoke of the crematoria."[7]

The Veil report traced the arc of free movement since the war, citing Schengen as a model for the entire European Union. By 1997, eight countries had acceded to the treaty: Italy in 1990, Spain and Portugal in 1991, Greece in 1992, Austria in 1995, and Denmark, Finland, and Sweden in 1996. Examining border crossing throughout the expanse of Schengen, the report declared the unhindered circulation of European nationals an essential aspect of common citizenship: "The free movement of persons is of major importance in bringing the peoples of the Union closer together and in making them increasingly aware of their European citizenship."[8]

The recasting of free movement appeared especially valuable—the turn away from a purely market paradigm—as a principle not only of border crossing but of unification itself. Situating Schengen in the development of the European Union, from the Rome Treaty to the Maastricht Treaty, the Veil report celebrated how free movement had come to reach all European nationals as persons, not simply as economic actors, in a progression from "human resources as a factor of production" to the "free movement of citizens." It charted how a "fully integrated single market has given way to a Union." In a preface to the report, Veil wrote of Europe as a humanistic achievement: "The Union is not simply a market but also a body of men and women united by values and a common destiny."[9]

But this was not enough. Fully realizing the free movement of persons as a principle of cosmopolitan citizenship required expanding the Schengen area across the entire European community, the Veil report found. Precisely because open borders created a "sense of belonging to a common area," it advised that Schengen "ought to be extended as far as possible," for if barriers disappeared on only part of the continent, there would be "fragmentation of the area of free movement between Schengen and non-Schengen countries." Noting that controls persisted at certain common borders, including identity checks, it urged strict enforcement of the rights of all European nationals. But the report did not address fortifying external borders in arguing for Schengen's expansion, simply concluding that "the principle whereby people may move freely without being checked at internal borders should be extended to all EU Member States."[10]

The Veil findings on free movement—particularly the virtues of transcending the market as the basis of European unity—won the endorsement of the European Commission. "This area without frontiers must not be confined to economic aspects," affirmed a Commission civil liberties committee.[11] And a Commission recommendation to the European Parliament echoed the Veil report in recognizing freedom of movement as a heritage of all European citizens, "irrespective of whether they pursue an economic activity."[12] That meant extending the Schengen area.

Thus Schengen became a touchstone in official representations of the past and future of the European Union that stressed the breadth of free movement. For it embodied the advance beyond the Rome Treaty's economism, a space where border crossing was no longer a byproduct of commerce, nor limited to vendors of labor, but a liberty of all Europeans as citizens of a community that was not just a market.

The half-century anniversary of the Rome Treaty brought new reflections on European integration. Across the continent and worldwide, in 2007, there were exhibits and seminars and festivals acclaiming the progress from a "common market to Citizens' Europe."[13] As the philosopher Bernard-Henri Lévy wrote at the time, Europe was "a mindset which transcends frontiers," an exceptional place: "It can only be a stranger to the language of borders."[14] Among the many commemorative events was a symposium held by the Financial Economics Association, on themes ranging from postnational identity to monetary theory, with contributions by international bankers, scholars, European statespersons, and directors of Europhile foundations. Among the speakers was Catherine Lalumière, the Schengen treatymaker.[15]

But hers was an account of declension—of humanism subordinated by the market. Lalumière spoke from a vantage point shaped by her illustrious experience; after her work on the Schengen treaty, she became secretary general to the Council of Europe, and then a member and later the vice president of the European Parliament. At the time of the finance symposium, she was president of La Maison de l'Europe de Paris, an association promoting European citizenship.[16] In considering the legacies of the Rome Treaty, however, Lalumière offered a bleak appraisal of the relationship between the single market and Citizens' Europe. She portrayed a debasement of the ethos of Europeanism, a descent from idealism to materialism, from the values of democratic pluralism animating reconciliation after the Second World War to the goals of neoliberalism—Europe as "triumphant capitalism," an instrument of "economic liberalism," the "consequence of 'globalization.'" Just after the war, she recalled, Pan-Europeanism was "a cultural project based on a humanist philosophy," aimed at securing peace, protecting freedom, and blocking totalitarianism. But with the Rome Treaty, Europe became a "big economic project," developing prosperity but taking on, "over time, an image more and more materialistic, finally cold and without human warmth."[17]

It was an arc of change that contrasted with triumphalist origin stories of Citizens' Europe. Lalumière did not address Schengen's expansion, or the difference between persons and workers as beneficiaries of free movement, or the security of Europe's external borders. Instead, she argued for restoring "a soul for Europe," which required looking outward to "external relations with the rest of the world" and adhering to "humanist values" in global commitments: "One glimpses all that must be imagined, fathomed, deepened in the setting of globalization, a new reunified Europe, and a society in full transformation."[18] And for that, Schengen did not offer a model.

———————————

By the time of the Schengen museum's dedication, the sans-papiers spokesman Ababacar Diop had returned to Senegal, where he promoted the free circulation of people and information through networks of exchange between Africa and Europe. A onetime asylum seeker, he had traveled a remarkable path, his fortunes rising and falling after the expulsion of the sans-papiers from their refuge in the Paris church. The rules of asylum had been a flashpoint of conflict in Schengen's emergence, bringing into question the protection of rights and principles of national sovereignty. In Diop's journeys, asylum seeking became a laboratory for ventures meant to democratize the economic value of free movement.[19]

His return to Senegal was voluntary. Earlier, when still in Paris, Diop had finally secured residence papers. Yet he continued to advocate for the sans-papiers while finding work as a computer technician. He remained preoccupied with the effects of colonialism and with migratory flows, free and unfree.[20] In Paris, he created Terrou, an association that aided deported African migrants by providing retraining in their home countries. And to protest their expulsion, he organized a "charter of friendship" in which thirty French nationals handcuffed themselves and flew to Dakar in homage to the sans-papiers deported from France.[21] In 2000, he opened a cybercafe in Paris, near the Saint-Bernard church, calling it Vis@Vis and forming a partnership with a cybercafe in Dakar: for five francs a minute, migrants in France could video-conference with family in Africa, a venture enabling digital border crossings. From a trademark dispute, he became wealthy, winning eight million francs in a settlement with a French media company.[22] He founded a real estate firm, Migrance Universalis, to help immigrants access property, and envisioned creating a "bank for the sans-papiers" that would grant loans to "those who have nothing and allow them to afford to move."[23] His aim was to become an "ambassador of the sans-papiers."[24]

Soon he returned to Senegal to invest his fortune in his home-land. He started a transport firm with a fleet of buses brought from France and opened cybercafes in Dakar and Saint-Louis to bring the Internet to "the poorest."[25] By 2007, however, his projects had faltered, and he was briefly held in a Saint-Louis jail for an alleged breach of a promise to procure travel documents for a man bound for Europe. After that, his path became obscure, and in Paris, it was said that the migrant movement had lost track of its former spokesman.[26]

Meanwhile, sans-papiers in Europe continued to protest the wrongs of unfree movement. Their civil disobedience was transna-tional; migrants without papers traveled across Schengen's common borders, occupied the streets of Europe's capitals, erected encampments outside the European Parliament, and staged demonstrations at refugee holding centers. In the summer of 2014, a March for Freedom neared the village of Schengen. The journey had begun in Strasbourg and would end in Brussels, crossing France, Germany, Luxembourg, and Belgium, a countermovement to the construction of a fortress Europe. "We will exercise our basic right of freedom of movement," the migrants declared. "We are asylum seekers, refugees, undocumented migrants . . . who have no full privilege of citizenship."[27]

The freedom march brought together a Pan-European set of sans-papiers, drawing support along the route from immigrant rights groups in Germany, France, the Netherlands, Belgium, Austria, and Italy.[28] It emerged from the occupation of a public space in Berlin, Oranienplatz, a tree-lined square in the Kreuzberg neighborhood, where asylum seekers gathered, beginning in the autumn of 2012, pitching tents, calling for the right of all sans-papiers to stay. But its roots reached back earlier, to the Paris occupation of the Saint-Bernard church, and a *Kein Mensch ist illegal* encampment set up at the German-Polish border in 1998, which became a model for border camps across the Schengen area, such as in Strasbourg, near the European Parliament, in 2002, and in Vienna, at the Sigmund Freud Park, in 2012.[29]

All the encampments rested on the principles: "No one is illegal" and "Freedom of movement for all." But the Oranienplatz protest was extraordinary in lasting almost two years, and taking over a public square in the center of the German capital, close to where the Berlin Wall once stood. It set forth three central demands: abolition of *Residenzpflicht*, rules restricting the free movement of asylum seekers; abolition of *Lagers*, refugee camps; and an end to deportations. It was born out of a protest march, from a *Lager* in Würzburg, through the forested hills of Bavaria and the flatlands of lower Saxony, and across the Elbe River northeast to Berlin. As a Sudanese asylum seeker, Napuli Langa, explained, Oranienplatz was "the political symbol of the struggle in the street." In April 2014, the tent camp was cleared from Oranienplatz; a month later, the freedom march began.[30]

The passage on foot across the Schengen area took about a month. Along the way, there were demonstrations at places evocative of the history of European unification, from Saarbrücken to Brussels. About four hundred sans-papiers and asylum seekers made the journey. Their outcry was: "Freedom of movement is everybody's right."[31] As the asylum seeker Langa described the protest: "We were crossing the borders. . . . We moved from town to town. . . . We want the freedom for work, to go everywhere without permission." And the backdrop for their search for asylum was "colonialism, capitalism, racism, and imperialism."[32] Another spokesperson for the migrants declared, "We are not considered to be human. We are the trash of capitalism!"[33]

The village of Schengen held special symbolism for the migrants. Claiming a right to free movement, they crossed the Moselle River from Germany into Luxembourg—"breaking the border"—and enacted a rewriting of the Schengen treaty. Some crossed the river by boat, portraying the danger of voyaging on the Mediterranean Sea to reach the coasts of Europe, and jumped into the water before

FIGURE 7.2. A ceremonial crossing of the Moselle River in Schengen, to draw attention to the dangers of reaching the Schengen area by sea, during the 2014 March for Freedom. Credit: Unknown, in Heinz Nigg, "Sans-Papiers on Their March for Freedom 2014: How Refugees and Undocumented Migrants Challenge Fortress Europe," *Interface: A Journal for and about Social Movements* 7, no. 1 (May 2015): 271.

reaching the riverbank to memorialize the deaths of the thousands of migrants who had drowned at sea. A Turkish migrant described the Moselle crossing:

> We do not recognize the travel ban and borders imposed on refugees and immigrants. . . . There were some of us who had traveled by boat before. . . . We applied the red paint we carried with us to our faces and bodies. With this action, we aimed to reveal the lives of refugees who drowned in the sea while trying to escape to Europe due to imperial wars. We wanted to expose murder organizations like Frontex.

On land, in the village of Schengen, the journey paused, as the migrants hung barbed-wire fences on the star-etched monument that honored the Schengen treaty, chaining themselves to the fences with handcuffs. Pictures of sans-papiers who had died crossing borders formed a makeshift exhibition outside the Schengen museum.[34]

In Brussels, a seat of the European Union, the freedom march ended with protests demanding a global regularization of all migrants without papers. A tent camp was set up near the Schaerbeek neighborhood, home to immigrants from North Africa and Turkey. By design, the journey's end coincided with a summit meeting of the European Council. The pilgrimage was for the "freedom of hundreds and thousands . . . from Africa, from Syria, from Palestine, Libya, Tunisia." The migrants declared, "And even if you place armed forces at the border of the Mediterranean Sea, you will not be able to stop the free movement of people."[35]

The rights claims of the migrants, from the theory conceived at the Saint-Bernard church to the protest of the freedom march, refused the history taught in the Schengen museum—of European integration prevailing to create a world of cosmopolitan liberty and postnational peace. Aspirations to free movement as a human right, as enacted by sans-papiers and asylum seekers, cast into cruel relief the boundaries of exclusion that protected the open borders inside Schengen.

When Madjiguène Cissé left France, obeying her deportation order, she pled a final time on behalf of the sans-papiers, for their right to come and go freely. On her return to Senegal, in 2000, she took up the cause of sustainable development in Africa, condemning a neocolonial order that simultaneously produced and blocked refugees seeking entry into Europe. It was soon after her return that a final judgment in her case denied that the Saint-Bernard evacuation had violated her fundamental rights. But *Cissé v. France* would become a landmark in the law of freedom of assembly. Paradoxically, the European Court of Human Rights invoked her case in upholding a right to freedom of assembly in protests involving entry into Europe.[36]

At issue was not a tide of undesirable migrants flowing in from beyond the Schengen zone of free movement, but a bid by a nation at Schengen's edge to join in closer union with Europe. The protests were the Maidan uprising, named for the central square in Kyiv where Ukrainians came to defend the path of their country toward the European Union. From the autumn of 2013 through the winter of 2014, thousands of protesters gathered in the square, opposing the authoritarian regime of Viktor Yanukovych and his postponement of a Ukrainian association agreement with the European Union. The protesters set up tents, occupied government buildings, and erected barricades. The police sought to suppress the unrest, clearing the square, using clubs, tear gas, stun grenades, and guns. About a hundred protesters died, a thousand were injured, and a great many were arrested. The protesters declared, "The Maidan is Europe."[37]

At the very moment of the Oranienplatz occupation in Berlin, the Maidan uprising in Kyiv drew the world's attention to the eastward movement of Pan-Europeanism. By the spring, Ukraine's pro-Russia regime had collapsed; the Maidan was thus a postscript to the disintegration of the Soviet Bloc but also a prelude to deepening conflict with Russia over Ukraine's orientation toward Europe. For Ukraine shared a 330-mile land border with Poland, a country once ranked on the Schengen undesirable lists that had joined the European Union in 2004.[38]

But it was not geopolitics that figured in the case arising from the Maidan protests that came before the European Court of Human Rights. In *Shmorgunov and Others v. Ukraine*, the plaintiffs alleged that the suppression of the protests violated the guarantees of the European Convention on Human Rights—the prohibitions against torture and unjust detention, and the right to freedom of assembly. As a signatory of the convention, Ukraine fell within the jurisdiction of the European human rights court.[39] The plaintiffs claimed the freedom to assemble in peaceful protest as a fundamental right of democratic society. Their aim in the Maidan, as even criminal prosecutors recognized, was "eliminating the threat to Ukraine's constitutional order, sovereignty and independence, and to citizens' right of movement . . . freedom of speech and peaceful assembly."[40] From the Maidan protest emerged arguments linking free movement in Ukraine with the European project.

In *Cissé v. France*, the European human rights court denied the appeal of a sans-papiers on behalf of free movement, finding that France's dispersal of the Saint-Bernard protest was a valid protection of public order. Yet the court affirmed the right of free assembly under Article 11 of the European human rights convention—even for a migrant without papers. It rejected the notion that the status of being "an illegal immigrant sufficed to justify a breach of her right to freedom of assembly." Nor could the right to free assembly be lost by an act of civil disobedience—"peaceful protest against legislation which has been contravened." Neither circumstance would "constitute a legitimate aim for a restriction on liberty."[41]

That judgment—that circumstances of illegality alone do not warrant infringement on free assembly—turned *Cissé v. France* into a landmark of European human rights jurisprudence. It has come to stand as a precedent in cases vindicating the right to freedom of assembly in countries across Europe, from the claims of the dissident Aleksei Navalny in Russia to those of squatters in the Netherlands and political protesters in Hungary.[42]

So it was with the Maidan. The European human rights court ruled that the government of Ukraine violated the protesters' right to free assembly, drawing on *Cissé v. France* to find that, "An unlawful situation, such as the staging of a demonstration without prior authorization, does not necessarily justify an interference with a person's right to freedom of assembly." The court held that the brutal police raids, and the arrests and detentions, were unwarranted by the protests: "Interferences with the freedom of peaceful assembly . . . disproportionate to any legitimate aims . . . thus were not 'necessary in a democratic society.'" In violation of Article 11, the state violence at the Maidan abridged fundamental freedoms, so as "to deter the protesters and the public at large from taking part in the protests and more generally from participating in open political debate."[43] A doctrine forged in the crucible of protests by people inside Europe but excluded from its guarantees came to vindicate protests by people outside Europe's borders seeking participation in its guarantees. Such was the ironic afterlife of Cissé's failed claim to freedom of assembly.

Where the legacy of *Cissé v. France* had no place was in the claims of migrants barred from entering Europe. Many of their cases that reached the European human rights court involved the sea passage across the Mediterranean, the crossing reenacted by the freedom march on the Moselle River. At issue in those cases was not freedom of assembly but humanitarian principles of non-refoulement and the right to challenge deportation, to be free from torture and inhuman treatment, and to enjoy liberty and security. There was the case of Somalian and Eritrean asylum seekers, who left Libya on a voyage intercepted by the Italian coastguard, which forced their return to Libya, a violation of the principle of non-refoulement.[44] There was the case of migrants who traveled from Iran to Turkey and took a boat to Italy, where they were placed in a holding center, and then fled to Austria and went to Switzerland, where they challenged their deportation order.[45] A case dramatizing the dilemmas that maritime migrants posed for Europe involved Tunisians escaping from the strife of the Arab Spring who were detected by the Italian coastguard while crossing the Mediterranean at night. Taken to the island of Lampedusa, they were confined in a dirty, crowded holding center, and kept under police surveillance. When a revolt broke out among the migrants, and the holding center was set on fire, the Tunisians joined in the street protests mounted by thousands of migrants. Rounded up, they were sent back to Tunisia. Italy's defense was that the flow of migrants onto its shores was a humanitarian crisis burdening all of Europe. In *Khlaifia and Others v. Italy*, the European human rights court found that the migrants had been wrongfully deported.[46]

The case of the Tunisian migrants had everything to do with Schengen. For the island of Lampedusa was a threshold of entry into Europe, just as the Schengen area was a corridor of free movement across the continent. Protecting internal European freedom meant fortifying Italy's external borders against maritime migrants from Africa and the Middle East; and the removal of the Tunisians was shaped by rules originating in Schengen. Surveillance of the seas, migrant holding centers, deportations—all derived from the border safeguards of the Schengen treaty. The influx by sea, observed the European human rights court in *Khlaifia*, had aroused "tensions with France and a serious reassessment of freedom of movement in the Schengen area."[47]

Over time, as countries that once lay behind the Iron Curtain joined the European Union, and as the Schengen area of free movement expanded, so did the barriers against the entry of migrants by sea and on land. By 2006, the European Union had adopted a

Schengen Borders Code governing a vast borderless space, which allowed internal controls to be reintroduced temporarily for security reasons and required arrests to "apprehend individuals crossing the border illegally," while also recognizing the principle of non-refoulement.[48] That year, as well, a set of member states new to the European Union—Poland, Hungary, the Czech Republic, Slovakia, Slovenia, Estonia, Latvia, Lithuania, and Malta—underwent inspection prior to joining Schengen, with close scrutiny of fortifications at the outer perimeter, "controls at land, sea and air borders." At a cost to the European Union of nearly one billion euros, new security barriers and surveillance systems would run along Schengen's lengthy borders with Russia, Belarus, Serbia, Croatia, and Ukraine.[49]

Meanwhile, human rights organizations counted the deaths of migrants at Europe's border crossings. As the death toll rose, the European community confronted a growing humanitarian crisis, while at the same time aiming to stem the flow of clandestine immigration across its borders.[50] The deadliest passage was the sea journey on the Mediterranean, though the count was inexact because the boats often sank without a trace, explained the United Nations refugee agency. As the European Union celebrated the Rome Treaty's half-century anniversary, the refugee agency estimated that five hundred migrants died crossing the Mediterranean that year, with nongovernmental groups counting closer to a thousand.[51] The year of the freedom march through the Schengen countries, 2014, was one of the deadliest for migrants on the Mediterranean, the refugee agency found: more than three thousand lives were lost at sea.[52] That year, recordkeeping began by the Missing Migrants Project, a United Nations inventory of death and disappearance.[53]

But the gathering of the evidence had started earlier, in the midst of the Schengen treatymaking. Lists of migrant deaths at European border crossings began to appear on a portal titled Fortress Europe in 1988. Some of the first entries reported: a shipwreck near Cadiz, ten dead; migrants shot crossing the border near Trieste, one dead; a body of a Ghanian found in a ship sailing from Cameroon. The death lists lengthened year by year, gruesomely repetitive, as in examples from 1996, the year of the sans-papiers uprising in Paris:

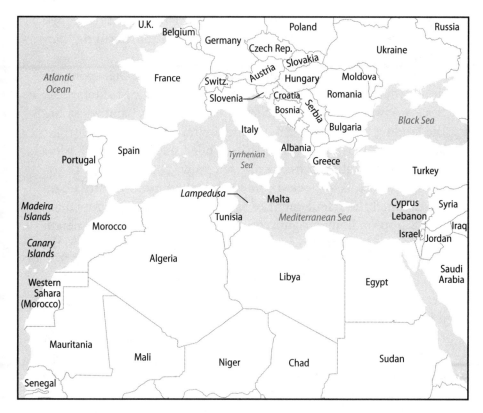

MAP 3. Western / Northern Africa and Southern Europe, with the island of Lampedusa shown at the midway point between North Africa and Italy.

two dead fleeing from the border police while crossing into Germany; bodies found of migrants drowned while crossing the Oder River into Germany; a frozen body found in the undercarriage of a plane landing in Italy; 283 migrants drowned after a collision of boats on the Mediterranean; a shipwreck near Lampedusa, one dead and nineteen missing.[54]

In Senegal, ballads were sung about the fateful claim to free movement—risking death to reach Europe. "Nothing will stop us to reach Europe or die trying," sang rap musicians.[55] The music honored Senegalese migratory cultural traditions, offering homage to those who navigated wooden fishing boats in making the ocean journey from the western coast of Africa to Spain.[56] By 2006, this voyage had become a common route of the crossing to Europe; and "Barca wala Barsakh," became a hit song in Senegal, meaning "Barcelona or Death."[57]

Nowhere was the humanitarian crisis more acute than along the deadly route to the island of Lampedusa. Lying in the Mediterranean Sea, a midway point between North Africa and Italy, Lampedusa was the landing place of most maritime migrants en route to Europe; and as land barriers were fortified under the Schengen Borders Code, the migratory pressures by sea grew. The European Union set up sea patrols to block the flow, while the European Parliament condemned the refoulement of asylum seekers from Lampedusa, and European human rights committees toured the island's detention centers to examine safeguards for the migrants.[58] It was in the coastal waters of Lampedusa, on October 3, 2013, that a boat from Libya sank, and 368 people died in sight of the shoreline, one of the deadliest migrant shipwrecks then recorded.[59] Among the corpses, a newborn was found, still attached to his mother by the umbilical cord.[60] It was Lampedusa that became the symbol of Europe or death. "Immigrants dying at sea, in boats which were vehicles of hope and became vehicles of death," Pope Francis lamented in a homily on Lampedusa. "In this globalized world, we have fallen into globalized indifference."[61]

And it was Lampedusa that symbolized unfree movement, "a synonym for Europe's borders, for the immigration rules . . . for the European policy on asylum, for the colonial heritage," wrote Napuli Langa, the Sudanese migrant who joined the sans-papiers freedom march across the Schengen territory. "A synonym for the borders which continue within the *European Union*."[62]

Amid the deepening migrant crisis, the fortification of borders within Europe came into conflict with single-market doctrine, splitting asunder the parts of the Schengen treaty—the guarantee of free movement and the protection of national security. A severe test for Schengen arose with the entry of more than a million migrants through its borders in 2015, the largest human displacement in Europe since the Second World War. They arrived in flight from conflict and persecution in Syria, Afghanistan, and Iraq—all on the Schengen lists of undesirable countries. The main route had shifted from the Mediterranean to the Aegean, and by land across Greece and Turkey, and up through the Balkans.[63]

A principal destination was Germany, whose borders stayed open until the autumn of 2015. At one point, as many as thirteen thousand migrants crossed into the country each day—a humanitarian moment that became known as the second fall of the Wall. It was said to be part of the country's long work of reckoning with the past, *Vergangenheitsbewältigung*, of fulfilling a moral duty to persecuted peoples and asylum seekers worldwide. Migrants traveling from Serbia through Hungary and across Austria were welcomed in Germany, which at the time seemed flush with "pro-refugee euphoria."[64] From there, they were free to cross Schengen's internal borders.

But the tides turned. By the end of the year, internal border controls went up across the Schengen area, a set of exceptional measures adopted for reasons of national security, as public anxiety increased about the burdens on host countries, and as anti-immigrant populism surged across the European Union. Germany was the first to restore temporary checkpoints at all internal borders, followed by France, Denmark, Austria, and other Schengen states.[65] Meanwhile, the Netherlands increased the frequency of spot checks, and France continued to send hundreds of migrants back to Italy each day.[66] Terrorist attacks in Paris by Islamic State militants in November heightened the backlash against free movement.[67] As divisions grew among European countries over the distribution of the refugees, the Schengen principles appeared at risk.[68] "Two decades of open borders in the EU ended," warned the United Nations.[69] A year later, mounting Euroskepticism proved politically explosive with the Brexit vote by Britain, never a Schengen member, to leave the European Union.[70]

The tide of nationalist reaction countered the decades-in-the-making European effort to transform a continent ravaged by world war into an expanse of liberty and commercial prosperity. Indeed, the hardening of Schengen's internal borders to stop the circulation of migrants threatened to break apart the borderless area. By 2016, a report on *Schengen Border Controls*, commissioned by the European Parliament, warned of the harms to economic life. "The integrity of the Single market could eventually be damaged," it found, stressing that Schengen was "one of the most valued accomplishments of the integration process: the free movements of individuals in an area with no internal border checks." It concluded: "The reintroduction of ID-checks at internal Schengen area borders entails a negative impact on the economies of the European Union."[71] If free movement had costs, so did its abridgement.

Those dual costs—of opening all internal borders and restoring barriers at times of exceptional risk—soon became still clearer with the onset of the coronavirus pandemic. As the deadly pathogen spread, the Schengen countries closed their borders altogether. German soldiers stood guard at the bridge across the Moselle River into Schengen, evoking memories of wartime. "It was like a dystopia," recalled the Schengen museum's director.[72] A European Parliament report on the *Coronavirus and the Cost of Non-Europe* explored the economic losses from the prolonged border closures, warning of a fragmenting of the single market and the disintegration of Schengen, a "mortal threat" to Europe.[73]

By no means, then, had Europe become a stranger to the language of borders; rather, the curbs on free movement reappearing at Schengen's internal crossings registered constant global crisis— the mass migrations of asylum seekers, the spasms of terrorism, the pandemic's arrival, the outbreak of war. In the name of security, the Schengen states repeatedly claimed authority to restore controls temporarily at internal borders, and as the area of free movement expanded, Europe's newly opened common frontiers again became sites of restraint, "in exceptional circumstances."[74] The refugee crisis of 2015 was scarcely the first time, or the pandemic the last, that internal checkpoints returned, as allowed by the rules of the Schengen Borders Code. "Continuous big influx of persons seeking international protections"; "persistent terrorist threat"; "Mediterranean migratory flow"; "coronavirus COVID-19"; "irregular migration"; "threats to public order and internal security in the EU, the situation in the Middle East and in Ukraine"—such were the reasons for resurrecting land, sea, and air borders inside the expanse of the Schengen territory.[75]

And the costs of abridging free movement were understood to transcend economic values. That was the finding of the European

Court of Justice, in a case concerning a years-long restoration of a checkpoint at an internal Schengen border—a case that required the court to balance security interests against the right to freedom of movement. At issue was a land border between Austria and Slovenia. Austria restored controls at that border in 2015, citing the influx of refugees, renewing the checks repeatedly, on the grounds of security, for a time longer than the limit of two years set by the Schengen Borders Code. Known simply as NW, the plaintiff was stopped there, while crossing into Austria, and asked for his papers. His rights claim—that the border check infringed on free movement—reached the European Court of Justice. The court did not question that open borders made Schengen a place of risk. Nor did it discount the difficulty of balancing security and freedom. But holding that prolonged internal barriers struck at the heart of the European project, the court affirmed Schengen's place in the history of Pan-Europeanism: "The creation of an area in which the free movement of persons without internal border control is ensured is one of the main achievements of the European Union."[76]

Within Schengen, border checkpoints blocking the right to free movement "should remain an exception . . . a measure of last resort," instructed the European Court of Justice. But the right would remain restricted to Europeans, "citizens of the Union." The word "market" did not appear in the ruling.[77]

———————————

As I write the last pages of this book, I turn from reports of Europe's internal borders now hardening yet again to a letter from a Schengen treatymaker defending the guarantee of free moment. The reports tell of constant migratory pressure by sea and land, the security situation in the Middle East, uncertainty due to the war in Ukraine, a fatal attack by a Tunisian asylum seeker in Belgium who had traveled across Europe after landing in Lampedusa—and of a belief expressed in the European Council that Schengen "isn't dead but broken."[78] The treatymaker's letter reflects on the crisis, saying that "the Schengen agreements were not at the origin of all the problems."[79] Still, I wonder about Schengen's death by a thousand cuts.

This book is about origins, not outcomes. It challenges legends of Schengen's creation—contrasting legends, Schengen as Europe's laboratory of freedom and Schengen as fortress Europe. Both are too simple; each is incomplete. Schengen at once lifted the stamp of economism from free movement, advancing the development of Citizens' Europe along with the single market, and set down powerful barriers to bar the entry of non-Europeans. Never were all persons meant to circulate as freely within its borders as were goods and capital; Pan-European humanism joined with both principles of neoliberalism and practices of neocolonialism in the making of Schengen.

Always, the opening of borders inside Schengen intended free movement only for European citizens. It never promised border crossing as a human right. From its inception, Schengen paired cosmopolitan freedom with exclusion enforced by sovereign nations. The free movement of persons—even nonworkers—always was designed to add value to Europe's single market, lending moral legitimacy to economic union. As the Schengen area expanded, migrant holding centers grew more crowded at Europe's edges. The dualisms defy stories of progress or declension.[80]

So, too, a history of Schengen's creation is incomplete without taking account of dissident odysseys: individual journeys, such as the itineraries of Ababacar Diop and Madjiguène Cissé, and collective pilgrimages, such as the freedom march across Europe on behalf of exiles, asylum seekers, and migrant workers. The world made by Schengen was never a Europe without borders—not for the sans-papiers. Nor did it break with the imperatives of the market that propelled European union. Nor was it meant to be otherwise by the treatymakers.

On September 19, 2015, death rites for free movement were performed outside the Schengen museum. The ritual was enacted by the National Front, the nativist French party, memorializing the restoration of checkpoints at Schengen's internal borders as the refugee crisis deepened that autumn.[81] By then, the party was warning against migratory flows by preaching of the *Grand Remplacement*, and it came to the Moselle Valley to make the village of Schengen a symbol of the demise of internationalism.[82] The riverbank figured as a graveyard, with a funeral wreath laid on the star-etched monument to the Schengen treaty. So, in response, the museum erected a sculpture proclaiming Schengen's vitality: "#schengenisalive," an affirmation that came to adorn placards posted across the village. A year later, as internal checkpoints remained in place, stopping migrants from moving through Europe, the ceiling of the Schengen museum collapsed. The village mayor denied any symbolism, saying only, "It's a sign. . . . that we need to do some repairs."[83]

ACKNOWLEDGMENTS

MANY PEOPLE, ACROSS many borders, lent support to this project, and I thank them here.

I begin with Paul Betts, who not only offered the most acute guidance in my study of Europe but also understood the challenges of my double life as a historian and journalist. I thank him for his high standards and his humanity. For counsel at Oxford, I also thank Patricia Clavin, Martin Conway, Anne Deighton, Timothy Garton Ash, Kalypso Nicolaïdis, Kevin O'Rourke, and Stephen Weatherill. I presented an early version of chapter 5 of this book at the Weizsäcker Conference in May 2019 at Oxford, and learned a great deal from the discussions, especially from the comments of Martin Geyer, the conference organizer. For financial support, I'm grateful to the Rhodes Trust; and for all kinds of advice at Oxford, I thank Mary Eaton. At Yale, a point that Timothy Snyder made about the market's nonmarket foundations would later help me frame a key claim in this book. These pages also reflect lessons from Jean-Christophe Agnew, Akhil Amar, Richard Avidon, John Burghardt, George Chauncey, Anne Fadiman, Gilbert Joseph, Jim Sleeper, Harry Stout, Jenifer Van Vleck, and John Witt. I wish John Merriman were here to see how his teachings about French history and politics have stayed with me. I think of him often.

This project was possible only because of archivists across Europe. My thanks to Sylvie Prudon at the diplomatic archives in La Courneuve; Herbert Karbach and Lukas Herbeck at the Political Archive of the Federal Foreign Office in Berlin; Carlos Van Lerberghe at the archives of the Council of the European Union in Brussels; and Ruth Meyer at the Historical Archives of the European Union in Florence. I also thank the Schengen treatymakers—and those who experienced its guarantee of free movement in illuminating ways—who shared their recollections with me, particularly Robert Goebbels, Françoise Gravier, Catherine Lalumière, Amira Suleiman, and Guy Van Hyfte.

Several people read parts of this manuscript in draft form and offered invaluable insights. For their queries and criticisms, I thank Alice Baumgartner, Seyla Benhabib, Martin Conway, Thomas Meaney, Kevin O'Rourke, Kiran Klaus Patel, Becca Rothfeld, and Tara Zahra, as well as two anonymous readers for Princeton University Press. At Princeton, Priya Nelson has been full of thought-provoking enthusiasm for this project, which has been guided into print with the help of Lachlan Brooks, Kathleen Cioffi, Carl Denton, and Emma Wagh.

It's been said that journalism is the first draft of history. My work on this book was greatly enhanced by the simultaneous reporting I was doing for the *Washington Post* in Europe. I will always be grateful to the editors who dispatched me to Berlin in the summer of 2017, especially Cameron Barr, Tracy Grant, and Doug Jehl, and to other editors who've made the *Post* my professional home in the years since, including Tim Elfrink, Matea Gold, Roz Helderman, Phil Rucker, Steve Smith, and Griff Witte. Particular thanks to Peter Wallsten, who always understood why I was writing this book and how it emerged from my reporting on the migration crisis. I also thank Bob Woodward, who early on offered stern instruction about going to the scene and returning repeatedly to my sources—methods that translate to researching and writing history.

From Oxford to Berlin to Washington, I've been lucky to have as interlocutors David Adler, Isaac Arnsdorf, Rachel Benoit, Lilly Bussmann, Sewell Chan, Rachel Colonomos, Lorraine Daston, Dan Diamond, Zach Fine, Chiara Focacci, Mikaela Gerwin, Julian Gewirtz, Gerd Gigerenzer, Kazumi Hoshino-Macdonald, Jerry Kleiner, Moritz Kramer, Claire Leibowicz, Jon Levy, Ruth Marcus, Barnaby Martin, Pablo Ponce de Leon, Beth Reinhard, Noah Remnick, Alexandra Rojkov, Tony Romm, David Shribman, Glenn Stanley, Lee Stanley, Perry Stein, Lena Sun, Sarah Waltcher, Kristin Warbasse, Zac Weisz, Yvonne Wingett Sanchez, and Wesley Yiin.

There will always be a special place in my heart for the Hinksey Outdoor Pool in Oxford, which kept me afloat during a critical stage of work on this project.

I could never adequately thank my brother, Tom Stanley-Becker, or my parents, Amy Dru Stanley and Craig Becker, who have discussed ideas with me for as long as I can remember. They made writing this book seem possible, and everything good in it is for them.

APPENDIX

Countries Whose Nationals Were Classified as "Undesirable" in Confidential Lists Annexed to the 1985 Schengen Accord

Countries Whose Nationals Posed "a Problem of Migratory Flows":

Afghanistan
Algérie (Algeria)
Angola
Bangladesh
Cap-Vert (Cape Verde)
Chine (République Populaire) (People's Republic of China)
Comores (Comoros)
Dominique (Dominica)
Ethiopie (Ethiopia)
Ghana
Guinée (Guinea)
Guinée-Bissau (Guinea-Bissau)
Guyana (Guiana)
Haïti (Haiti)
Hong-Kong
Ile Maurice (Mauritius)
Inde (India)
Indonésie (Indonesia)
Irak (Iraq)
Iran
Liban* (Lebanon)
Madagascar
Malaisie (Malaysia)
Maroc (Morocco)
Mozambique
Nigéria (Nigeria)
Pakistan
Pologne (Poland)
République Dominicaine (Dominican Republic)

* *y compris les Palestiniens munis de titres de voyage libanais* (including Palestinians with Lebanese travel documents)

Sainte-Lucie (Saint Lucia)
Saint-Vincent et Grenadines (Saint Vincent and the Grenadines)
Singapour (Singapore)
Soudan (Sudan)
Sri Lanka
Surinam (Suriname)
Tunisie (Tunisia)
Turquie (Turkey)
Yougoslavie (Yugoslavia)
Zaïre (Zaire)

Countries Whose Nationals Posed a Problem of "Security":

Afghanistan
Afrique du Sud (South Africa)
Albanie (Albania)
Algérie (Algeria)
République Démocratique Allemande (German Democratic Republic)
Arabie Saoudite (Saudi Arabia)
Bahreïn (Bahrain)
Bulgarie (Bulgaria)
Cambodge (Cambodia)
Chine (République Populaire) (People's Republic of China)
Colombie (Colombia)
Corée du Nord (North Korea)
Cuba
Egypte (Egypt)
Emirats Arabes Unis (United Arab Emirates)
Ethiopie (Ethiopia)
Hongrie (Hungary)
Irak (Iraq)
Iran
Jordanie (Jordan)
Koweit (Kuwait)
Laos
Liban (Lebanon)
Libye (Libya)
Maroc (Morocco)
Mongolie (Mongolia)
Oman
Pakistan
Pologne (Poland)
Qatar
Roumanie (Romania)

Somalie (Somalia)
Surinam (Suriname)
Soudan (Sudan)
Syrie (Syria)
Taiwan
Tchécoslovaquie (Czechoslovakia)
Tunisie (Tunisia)
Turquie (Turkey)
Union des Républiques Socialistes Soviétiques (Soviet Union)
Vietnam
Yemen du Sud (South Yemen)
Yemen du Nord (North Yemen)
Yougoslavie (Yugoslavia)
Zaïre (Zaire)

Source: "Projet d'accord à caractère confidentiel complémentaire à l'accord entre les gouvernements des États de l'Union Économique Benelux, de la République fédéral d'Allemagne et de la République française relative à la suppression graduelle des contrôles aux frontières communes," June 4, 1985, Binder 1b BNL-D-F + gc red cc BNL, 1984–1985, Central Archives of the Council of the European Union, Brussels, Belgium.

NOTES

Introduction

1. In using the language of abolishing borders and Europe without borders, I borrow the vocabulary of the treatymakers and of European institutions. By no means is this to suggest the actual redrawing of the map of Europe, but rather to designate the practical effect of lifting checkpoints. See Elpida Papahatzi, *Free Movement of Persons in the European Union: Specific Issues*, European Parliament Directorate General for Research, Civil Liberties Series, Working Document PE167.028 (Brussels, May 1999), 5.

2. Directorate-General X, European Commission, "Free Movement of People," Factsheet, March 23, 1995, Europe des Citoyens, Femmes d'Europe Fonds 158, Historical Archives of the European Union, Florence, Italy (hereafter HAEU).

3. Accord relatif à la suppression graduelle des contrôles aux frontières communes du Benelux, de la République fédérale d'Allemagne et de la France, June 14, 1985, OJ (L239) (2000) [s.l.] (hereafter Schengen Agreement), preamble. I have translated into English all quotations from foreign-language sources.

4. On liberal internationalism and its critics, see Tara Zahra, *Against the World: Anti-Globalism and Mass Politics between the World Wars* (New York, 2023); Glenda Sluga, *Internationalism in the Age of Nationalism* (Philadelphia, 2015); Saskia Sassen, *Globalization and Its Discontents* (New York, 1998); Mark Mazower, *Governing the World: The History of an Idea, 1815 to the Present* (New York, 2012); Charles S. Maier, *The Project-State and Its Rivals: A New History of the Twentieth and Twenty-First Centuries* (Cambridge, MA, 2023). On institutions securing the free market, see Quinn Slobodian, *Globalists: The End of Empire and the Birth of Neoliberalism* (Cambridge, MA, 2018); Jamie Martin, *The Meddlers: Sovereignty, Empire, and the Birth of Global Economic Governance* (Cambridge, MA, 2022); Turkuler Isiksel, "The Dream of Commercial Peace," in *After the Storm: How to Save Democracy in Europe*, ed. Luuk van Middelaar and Philippe Van Parijs (Tielt, 2015), 27–40; Patricia Clavin, *Securing the World Economy: The Reinvention of the League of Nations, 1920–1946* (Oxford, 2013). On the EU and Cold War geopolitics, see Corine Defrance, *Entre guerre froide et intégration européenne: Reconstruction et intégration, 1945–1963* (Villeneuve-d'Ascq, 2012); John van Oudenaren, *Uniting Europe: European Integration and the Post-Cold War World* (Lanham, MD, 2000); Andrew Moravcsik, *European Union and World Politics* (London, 2006).

5. "Schengen: The First Three Months," *Statewatch*, May–June 1995, accessed October 21, 2021, https://www.statewatch.org/statewatch-database/schengen-the -first-three-months/.

6. Catherine Lalumière, "La Construction européenne au-delà de l'économie," in "50 ans après le Traité de Rome," special issue, *Revue d'économie financière* 88 (April 2007): 197.

7. See Eckart Wagner, "The Integration of Schengen into the Framework of the European Union," *Legal Issues of Economic Integration* 25, no. 2 (1998): 1–60; Monica Den Boer, ed., *Schengen's Final Days? The Incorporation of Schengen into the New TEU, External Borders and Information Systems* (Maastricht, 1998).

8. On the European Union and colonialism, see Giuliano Garavini, *After Empires: European Integration, Decolonization and the Challenge from the Global South: 1957–1986* (Oxford, 2012); Peo Hansen and Stefan Jonsson, *Eurafrica: The Untold History of European Integration and Colonialism* (London, 2014); Megan Brown, *The Seventh Member States: Algeria, France, and the European Community* (Cambridge, MA, 2022); Hans Kundnani, *Eurowhiteness: Culture, Empire and Race in the European Project* (New York, 2023); Herman Lebovics, *Bringing the Empire Back Home: France in the Global Age* (Durham, NC, 2004); Emily Marker, *Black France, White Europe: Youth, Race, and Belonging in the Postwar Era* (Ithaca, NY, 2022); Muriam Haleh Davis, *Markets of Civilization: Islam and Racial Capitalism in Algeria* (Durham, NC, 2022). On human rights, global institutions, and European integration, see Mark Mazower, *No Enchanted Palace: The End of Empire and the Ideological Origins of the United Nations* (Princeton, NJ, 2009); Kiran Klaus Patel, *Projekt Europa: Eine kritische Geschichte* (Munich, 2018). On how a market-based principle of free movement became a right encompassing more than economic pursuits, see Stephen Weatherill, *The Internal Market as a Legal Concept* (Oxford, 2017), 7. For critical assessments of human rights doctrine, see Samuel Moyn, *The Last Utopia* (Cambridge, MA, 2010); Adom Getachew, "Universalism after the Post-Colonial Turn," *Political Theory* 44, no. 6 (December 2016): 821–45.

9. On the operation of Schengen after its entry into force, see Evelien Brouwer, *Digital Borders and Real Rights: Effective Remedies for Third-Country Nationals in the Schengen Information System* (Leiden, 2008); Elspeth Guild et al., eds., *In Search of Europe's Borders* (The Hague, 2003), especially Kees Groen, "New Borders Behind Old Ones: Post-Schengen Controls Behind the Internal Borders and Inside the Netherlands and Germany," 131–46. On Schengen's eastward expansion, see Konrad H. Jarausch *Out of Ashes: A New History of Europe in the Twentieth Century* (Princeton, NJ, 2015), 526, 687; Heather Grabbe, "The Sharp Edges of Europe: Extending Schengen Eastwards," *International Affairs* 76, no. 3 (July 2000): 519–36; Olga Potemkina, "A 'Friendly Schengen Border' and Illegal Migration: The Case of the EU and Its Direct Neighbourhood," in *Soft or Hard Borders? Managing the Divide in an Enlarged Europe*, ed. Joan DeBardeleben (Aldershot, 2005), 165–82. On free movement and labor migration after enlargement, see Martin Kahanec and Klaus F. Zimmerman, eds., *EU Labor Markets after Post-Enlargement Migration* (Berlin, 2010). On the twenty-first century refugee crisis, see Matthew Carr, *Fortress Europe: Dispatches from a Closed Continent* (New York, 2012); Patrick Kingsley, *The New Odyssey: The Story of Europe's Refugee Crisis* (London, 2016); Daniel Trilling, *Lights in the Distance: Exile and Refuge at the Borders of Europe* (London, 2018); Robin Alexander, *Die Getriebenen: Merkel und die Flüchtlingspolitik; Report aus dem Inneren der Macht* (Munich, 2017); Akram Belkaïd and Cécile Marin, "Mortelle Méditerranée," *Le Monde Diplomatique*, August–September 2021; Isaac Stanley-Becker,

"How McKinsey Quietly Shaped Europe's Response to the Refugee Crisis," *Washington Post*, July 24, 2017.

10. Formative works on the EU's history and significance include John Gillingham, *European Integration, 1950–2003: Superstate or New Market Economy?* (Cambridge, UK, 2003); Andrew Moravcsik, *The Choice for Europe: Social Purpose and State Power from Messina to Maastricht* (Ithaca, NY, 1999); Luuk van Middelaar, *The Passage to Europe: How a Continent Became a Union*, trans. Liz Waters (New Haven, CT, 2013); Desmond Dinan, *Europe Recast: A History of European Union* (Basingstoke, UK, 2004); Jürgen Habermas, *The Crisis of the European Union: A Response*, trans. Ciaran Cronin (Cambridge, UK, 2012); Konrad H. Jarausch, *Embattled Europe: A Progressive Alternative* (Princeton, NJ, 2021); Harold James, *Europe Contested: From the Kaiser to Brexit* (London, 2019). See also Anthony Teasdale and Timothy Bainbridge, *The Penguin Companion to European Union* (New York, 1995); Andrew Knapp, *Government and Politics in Western Europe: Britain, France, Italy, Germany* (New York, 1998).

11. On migration and free movement in postwar European integration, and on restrictions embedded in that project, see Didier Bigo and Elspeth Guild, eds., *Controlling Frontiers: Free Movement into and within Europe* (Aldershot, UK, 2005); Malcolm Anderson and Eberhard Bort, eds., *The Frontiers of Europe* (London, 1998); Peter Gatrell, *The Unsettling of Europe: How Migration Reshaped a Continent* (New York, 2019). On the centrality of free movement to citizenship and democratic self-government, see Willem Maas, ed., *Democratic Citizenship and the Free Movement of People* (Leiden, 2013), especially Matthew Longo, "Right of Way? Defining Freedom of Movement within Democratic Societies," 31–56. On globalization, migration, and cosmopolitan citizenship, see Seyla Benhabib, *The Claims of Culture: Equality and Diversity in the Global Era* (Princeton, NJ, 2002), especially 153; Rita Chin, *The Crisis of Multiculturalism in Europe: A History* (Princeton, NJ, 2017); Ruth Mandel, *Cosmopolitan Anxieties: Turkish Challenges to Citizenship and Belonging in Germany* (Durham, NC, 2008).

12. Treaty Establishing the European Economic Community, March 25, 1957, 298 UNTS 11 (1958) (hereafter Rome Treaty).

13. See Slobodian, *Globalists*, especially 20, 93, 208–14; Wolfgang Streeck, *How Will Capitalism End?: Essays on a Failing System* (London, 2016), especially 26, 156–57; David Harvey, *A Brief History of Neoliberalism* (Oxford, 2005); Gary Gerstle, *The Rise and Fall of the Neoliberal Order: America and the World in the Free Market Era* (Oxford, 2022), especially 5, 177, 275; David Theo Goldberg, *The Threat of Race: Reflections on Racial Neoliberalism* (Malden, MA, 2008).

14. Présidence de la République, Service de Presse, "Conférence de Presse de Monsieur François Mitterrand, Président de la République Française, à l'Issue du Conseil Européen," June 26, 1984, 8, BAC no. 49 (1984), dossier 44, vol. 1, Historical Archives, European Commission, Brussels (hereafter Commission Archives).

15. "Bericht der Bundesregierung zur Lage der Nation im geteilten Deutschland," *Bulletin des Presse- und Informationsamtes der Bundesregierung*, no. 30 (March 1984): 267.

16. William Blackstone, *Commentaries on the Laws of England in Four Books with Notes Selected from the Editions of Archbold, Christian, Coleridge, Chitty, Stewart, Kerr, and Others, Barron Field's Analysis, and Additional Notes, and a Life of the Author by George Sharswood*, vol. 1, book 1 (Philadelphia, 1893), 134.

17. Madjiguène Cissé, *Parole de sans-papiers* (Paris, 1999), 9.

18. Schengen Agreement, preamble; Rome Treaty, art. 48.

19. Universal Declaration of Human Rights, G.A. Res. 217A (III), U.N. Doc. A / 810 (1948) (hereafter UDHR), art. 13; Protocol No. 4 to the Convention for the Protection of Human Rights and Fundamental Freedoms, Securing Certain Rights and Freedoms Other than Those Already Included in the Convention and in the First Protocol Thereto, September 16, 1963, E.T.S. No. 46, art. 42.

20. On the nonmarket foundations of market principles, see Emma Rothschild, "Global Commerce and the Question of Sovereignty in the Eighteenth-Century Provinces," *Modern Intellectual History* 1, no. 1 (April 2004): 3–25.

21. Schengen Agreement, preamble. On the yoking of human rights to national citizenship, see Hannah Arendt, *The Origins of Totalitarianism* (New York, 1951), 290–302.

22. Allègement des contrôles aux frontières: Réunion à Paris le 12 mars 1985 du "Group central de négociation," March 7, 1985, 2, binder 1a BNL-D-F + gc red cc BNL, 1984–1985 (hereafter BNL), Central Archives of the Council of the European Union, Brussels, Belgium (hereafter Council Archives). On the stigmatizing of undesirable migrants, see Michel Agier, *Gérer les indésirables: Des Camps de réfugiés au gouvernement humanitaire* (Paris, 2008).

23. Convention Implementing the Schengen Agreement, June 19, 1990, art. 1, chapter 4 (hereafter Schengen Convention); Jean-Paul Anglès, "Réunion à Paris le 12 mars 1985 du 'Groupe Central de Négociation,'" March 7, 1985, 2–5, binder 1a BNL, Council Archives.

24. On transnational European policing, see David Fernández-Rojo, *EU Migration Agencies The Operation and Cooperation of FRONTEX, EASO and EUROPOL* (Cheltenham, UK, 2021); Andrew W. Neal, "Securitization and Risk at the EU Border: The Origins of FRONTEX," *Journal of Common Market Studies* 47, no. 2 (March 2009): 333–56; Elspeth Guild, "Danger—Borders under Construction: Assessing the First Five Years of Border Policy in an Area of Freedom, Security and Justice," in *Freedom, Security and Justice in the European Union: Implementation of the Hague Programme*, ed. Jaap W. de Zwaan and Flora A.N.J. Goudappel (The Hague, 2006), 45–72; Didier Bigo, *Polices en Réseaux: L'Expérience européenne* (Paris, 1996).

25. On race-based exclusion in the European project, see Étienne Balibar, *We, the People of Europe? Reflections on Transnational Citizenship*, trans. James Swenson (Princeton, NJ, 2004), especially 44, 116, 121, 123, 162, 171; Andrew S. Rosenberg, *Undesirable Immigrants: Why Racism Persists in International Migration* (Princeton, NJ, 2022); and Tyler Stovall, *White Freedom: The Racial History of an Idea* (Princeton, NJ, 2021).

26. On the sans-papiers, see Smaïn Laacher, *Mythologie du sans-papiers* (Paris, 2009); Johanna Siméant, *La Cause des sans-papiers* (Paris, 1998); Gatrell, *Unset-*

tling of Europe, 248, 330; Anne McNevin, "Political Belonging in a Neoliberal Era: The Struggle of the Sans-Papiers," *Citizenship Studies* 10, no. 2 (May 2006), 135–51; Holk Stobbe, *Undokumentierte Migration in Deutschland und den Vereinigten Staaten: Interne Migrationskontrollen und die Handlungsspielräume von Sans Papiers* (Göttingen, 2004).

27. On Schengen and the Great Replacement theory, see Karina Piser, "What a Foiled Plot to Execute Muslims Reveals about Islamophobia in France," *The Nation*, July 10, 2018. On reproduction, race, and immigration, see Judith Surkis, "Minor Threats and the Biopolitics of Youth," *Comparative Studies of South Asia, Africa and the Middle East* 41, no. 3 (December 2021): 413–21. On neofascism and its intellectual underpinnings, see Douglas R. Holmes, *Integral Europe: Fast-Capitalism, Multiculturalism, Neofascism* (Princeton, NJ, 2000). On transnational circulation of far-right ideology, see Isaac Stanley-Becker, "Election Fraud, QAnon, Jan. 6: Far-Right Extremists in Germany Read from a Pro-Trump Script," *Washington Post*, September 25, 2021.

28. Papahatzi, *Free Movement of Persons*, 7.

29. The modern European Union came about with the 1992 Maastricht Treaty, on the basis of the European Economic Community along with the European Coal and Steel Community and the European Atomic Energy Community. Treaty on European Union, 7 February 1992, 31 ILM 247 (hereafter Maastricht Treaty).

30. Bulgaria and Romania became the twenty-eighth and twenty-ninth Schengen member countries in March 2024, with checks coming down at internal sea and air borders and a decision expected later on internal land borders. See "Schengen Area," EU Immigration Portal, accessed March 31, 2024, https://home-affairs.ec.europa.eu /policies/schengen-borders-and-visa/schengen-area_en.

31. "Fact Sheets on the European Union," European Parliament, accessed October 3, 2018, http://www.europarl.europa.eu/factsheets/en/home.

32. See Finn Laursen, ed., *Designing the European Union: From Paris to Lisbon* (Basingstoke, UK, 2012); John O'Brennan, *The Eastern Enlargement of the European Union* (London, 2006); Harold James, *Making the European Monetary Union* (Cambridge, MA, 2012).

33. See Moravcsik, *Choice for Europe*, 342, 346, 475–477; Philipp Ther, *Europe since 1989: A History* (Princeton, NJ, 2016), 126. Schengen goes unmentioned in van Middelaar, *Passage to Europe*; Gillingham, *European Integration*.

34. See Charles S. Maier, *Once within Borders: Territories of Power, Wealth, and Belonging Since 1500* (Cambridge, MA, 2016); Mabel Berezin and Martin Schain, eds., *Europe without Borders: Remapping Territory, Citizenship, and Identity in a Transnational Age* (Baltimore, 2003); Alan S. Milward, *The European Rescue of the Nation-State* (London, 1992); Chin, *Crisis of Multiculturalism*; Mark Mazower, *Dark Continent: Europe's Twentieth Century* (New York, 1999); Gatrell, *Unsettling of Europe*.

35. Tony Judt, *Postwar: A History of Europe since 1945* (London, 2005), 718.

36. On EU historiography, see Kiran Klaus Patel, "Widening and Deepening? Recent Advances in European Integration History," *Neue Politische Literatur* 64, no. 2 (July 2019): 327–57. On Schengen's operation, see Andreas Pudlat, *Schengen: zur*

Manifestation von Grenze und Grenzschutz in Europa (Hildesheim, 2013); Angela Siebold, *Zwischen Grenzen: Die Geschichte des Schengen-Raums aus deutschen, französischen und polnischen Perspektiven* (Paderborn, 2013).

37. See Carr, *Fortress Europe*. On security and *Sicherheitshysterie*, see Heiner Busch, "Europa—ein 'Mekka der Kriminalität?'" EG-Grenzöffnung und international Polizei-kooperation," *Kritische Justiz* 23, no. 1 (1990): 1; Bertrand Wert, "Security Governance in the Largest Border-Metropolis of the Schengen Area: The Lille 'Eurodistrict' Case Study," *Journal of Borderlands Studies* 23, no. 3 (September 2008): 95–108; Hans Heiner Kühne, *Kriminalitätsbekämpfung durch innereuropäische Grenzkontrollen?* (Berlin, 1991); Johannes Velling, "Schengen, Dublin und Maastricht—Etappen auf dem Weg zu einer europäischen Immigrationspolitik," ZEW Discussion Papers, no. 93–11, 1993. On Schengen and the internal market, see Moravcsik, *Choice for Europe*, 353, 474–77. On Schengen and internationalism, see Peo Hansen and Sandy Brian Hager, *The Politics of European Citizenship: Deepening Contradictions in Social Rights & Migration Policy* (New York, 2010); Willem Maas, *Creating European Citizens* (Lanham, MD, 2006). Schengen is treated extensively in testing theories of border formation; see Ruben Zaiotti, *Cultures of Border Control: Schengen and the Evolution of European Frontiers* (Chicago, 2011). My understanding of Schengen, the single market, and the exclusion of non-Europeans is informed by the landmark work of Elspeth Guild; see Elspeth Guild, "The Single Market, Movement of Persons and Borders," in *The Law of the Single European Market: Unpacking the Premises*, ed. Catherine Barnard and Joanne Scott (Oxford, 2002), 295–310; Elspeth Guild, *Security and Migration in the 21st Century* (Cambridge, UK, 2009), especially 181–88; Didier Bigo and Elspeth Guild, *La Mise à l'écart des étrangers: La Logique du Visa Schengen* (Paris, 2003).

38. See Jeffry A. Frieden, *Global Capitalism: Its Fall and Rise in the Twentieth Century* (New York, 2006); Rawi Abdelal, *Capital Rules: The Construction of Global Finance* (Cambridge, MA, 2007); Harvey, *A Brief History of Neoliberalism*.

39. My periodization of the postwar era, as extending into the late twentieth century, draws on Judt's *Postwar*, which identifies the 1980s as a crucial period in Europe's postwar experience, shaped by refugees, guest workers, and the afterlives of colonialism; see Judt, *Postwar*, 9. See also Chin, *Crisis of Multiculturalism*, especially 138–91; Jarausch, *Out of Ashes*, especially 522–32, 732–40, 783–85; Eric Hobsbawm, *The Age of Extremes: The Short Twentieth Century, 1914–1991* (London, 1994).

40. See Isaac Stanley-Becker, "Border Camps Show the Schengen Zone Only Ever Promised Europeans Free Movement," *New Statesman*, July 5, 2018; Brian Barry and Robert E. Goodin, eds., *Free Movement: Ethical Issues in the Transnational Migration of People and Money* (University Park, PA, 1992); Chiara Cordelli and Jonathan Levy, "The Ethics of Global Capital Mobility," *American Political Science Review* 116, no. 2 (May 2022): 439–52.

41. Piet Dankert, "Discours de Piet Dankert sur la convention d'application de l'accord de Schengen," *Bulletin de documentation du Service Information et Presse, Ministère d'État*, no. 3 (Luxembourg, June 19, 1990).

42. On postwar regeneration, see Paul Betts, *Ruin and Renewal: Civilizing Europe after World War II* (New York, 2020).

Chapter 1. A Market Paradigm of Free Movement

1. Présidence de la République, Service de Presse, "Conférence de Presse," 9, 17.

2. "Conclusions du Conseil européen de Fontainebleau" (June 25 and 26, 1984), *Bulletin des Communautés européennes*, no. 6 (Luxembourg: Office des publications officielles des Communautés européennes), 3, available at Centre virtuel de la connaissance sur l'Europe, accessed June 16, 2019, https://www.cvce.eu/obj/conclusions _du_conseil_europeen_de_fontainebleau_25_et_26_juin_1984-fr-ba12c4fa-48d1 -4e00-96cc-a19e4fa5c704.html.

3. On Rome as a framework for future regulations, see Judt, *Postwar*, 303.

4. See Niall Ferguson, "Crisis, What Crisis? The 1970s and the Shock of the Global," in *The Shock of the Global: The 1970s in Perspective*, ed. Niall Ferguson et al. (Cambridge, MA, 2010), 1–24; and, in the same volume, Charles S. Maier, "'Malaise': The Crisis of Capitalism in the 1970s," 25–48.

5. "L'Europe des Citoyens: Suites à donner aux conclusions du Conseil européen de Fontainebleau," Commission des Communautés Européennes, September 24, 1984, 2, BAC no. 50 (1984–85), dossier 44, vol. 2, Commission Archives (hereafter Fontainebleau conclusions). "L'Europe des citoyens" is sometimes translated as "People's Europe," but drawing on the civic aspirations evident at Fontainebleau, I use the more literal "Citizens' Europe."

6. My account differs from those that treat Fontainebleau's significance in terms of fiscal policymaking and "Citizens' Europe" as a Mitterrand gambit; see Geoffrey Denton, "Re-structuring the EC Budget: Implications of the Fontainebleau Agreement," *Journal of Common Market Studies* 23, no. 2 (December 1984): 117–40; Nils Jansen, *Binnenmarkt, Privatrecht und europäische Identität: Eiene historische und methodische Bestandsaufnahme* (Tübingen, 2004); Michael Burgess, *Federalism and European Union: Political Ideas, Influences, and Strategies in the European Community, 1972–1987* (London, 1991), especially 116.

7. Influential scholarship on the EU's legal development that gives little consideration to *Gravier* includes Antione Vauchez, *Brokering Europe: Euro-Lawyers and the Making of a Transnational Polity* (New York, 2015); Alec Stone-Sweet, *The Judicial Construction of Europe* (New York, 2004); Gareth Davies, *Nationality Discrimination in the European Internal Market* (The Hague, 2003); J.H.H. Weiler, "A Quiet Revolution: The European Court of Justice and Its Interlocutors," *Comparative Political Studies* 26, no. 4 (January 1994): 510–34. *Gravier* is most extensively addressed in Gisella Gori, "Mademoiselle Gravier and Equal Access to Education: Success and Boundaries of European Integration," in *EU Law Stories: Contextual and Critical Histories of European Jurisprudence*, ed. Fernanda Nicola and Bill Davies (Cambridge, UK, 2017), 446–70. The case also receives some treatment in legal journals; see Philippa Watson, "Case 293 / 83, *Gravier v. City of Liège*," *Common Market Law Review* 24, no. 1 (1987): 89–97; Peter Wytinck, "The Application of Community Law in Belgium," *Common Market Law Review* 30, no. 5 (1993): 981–1020. On Community-wide education policy, see Nigel Johnson, "From Vocational Training to Education: The Development of a No-Frontiers Education Policy for Europe?," *Education and the*

Law 11, no. 3 (1999): 199–213; Stine Jørgensen, "The Right to Cross-Border Education in the European Union," *Common Market Law Review* 46, no. 5 (2009): 1567–90.

    8. *Gravier v. City of Liège*, Case 293 / 83, [1985], ECR 593.

    9. Rome Treaty, art. 48.

    10. Some aspects of Citizens' Europe, such as a European flag, were quickly implemented. Others took longer; not until 1992 was European citizenship enshrined in the Maastricht Treaty.

    11. Philippe Lemaitre, "La Reliance de l'Europe au sommet de Fontainebleau," *Le Monde*, June 26, 1984. See also Johannes Lindner, *Conflict and Change in EU Budgetary Politics* (Abingdon, UK, 2006), especially 125.

    12. Fontainebleau conclusions.

    13. Fontainebleau conclusions, 2.

    14. Fontainebleau conclusions, annex, 2. On culture and European union, see Cris Shore, *Building Europe: The Cultural Politics of European Integration* (London, 2000).

    15. Fontainebleau conclusions, annex, 1.

    16. On Mitterrand's past and partnership with West Germany, see Philip Short, *Mitterrand: A Study in Ambiguity* (London, 2014), 86; Ulrich Lappenküper, "Le Plus Germanophile des chefs d'dtat Français? François Mitterrand und Deutschland, 1916–1996," *Historische Zeitschrift* 297, no. 2 (2013): 390–416; Antoine Halff, "When Mitterrand Cozied up to Marshal Petain: French in a Furor over a President's Secret Past," *Forward*, September 9, 1994. On Kohl and the European project, see Hanns Jürgen Küsters, "Helmut Kohl und Frankreich: Einführung," *Historisch-Politische, Mitteilungen* 20, no. 1 (2013): 229–42; Helmut Kohl, *Deutschlands Zukunft in Europa: Reden und Beiträge des Bundeskanzlers* (Herford, Germany, 1990). On Kohl's past, see "Verschwiegene Enteignung," *Der Spiegel*, September 14, 1986.

    17. Speech by François Mitterrand to the European Parliament, May 24, 1984, *Official Journal of the European Communities*, Debates of the European Parliament, 24.05.1984, no. 1–314, 2, 8, 2.

    18. The National Front came to power in Dreux in 1983 and, days before the 1984 Fontainebleau summit, won ten seats and more than 11 percent of the French vote in European elections. See Françoise Gaspard, *Une Petite Ville en France* (Paris, 1990); Pierre Bréchon and Subrata Kumar Mitra, "The National Front in France: The Emergence of an Extreme Right Protest Movement," *Comparative Politics* 25, no. 1 (October 1992): 65; Lebovics, *Bringing the Empire Back Home*, 8–9.

    19. Speech by François Mitterrand to the European Parliament, 7.

    20. "Discours du Chancelier à l'Europa-Union," March 12, 1984, folder 3 "Mouvements Européens," box 1971 "Direction d'Europe, 1981–1985," Ministère de l'Europe et des Affaires Étrangères, La Courneuve, Seine-Saint-Denis, France (hereafter MEAE).

    21. Fontainebleau conclusions, especially 3.

    22. "Leo Tindemans, Statesman, 1922–2014," *Financial Times*, December 28, 2014; Leo Cendrowicz, "Leo Tindemans: Former Belgian Prime Minister," *Independent*, January 1, 2015; Leo Tindemans, *De memoires: Gedreven door een overtuiging* (Tielt, 2002), 589.

23. Leo Tindemans, *Report on European Union, Presented to the European Council, December 29, 1975*, supplement 1, *Bulletin of the European Communities* (1976): 2, 18. See Reiner Marcowitz and Andreas Wilkens, eds., *Une "Europe des Citoyens": Société civile et identité européenne de 1945 à nos jours* (Bern, 2014).

24. Tindemans, *Report on European Union*, 18, 19, 20, 3. On democracy and technocracy, see Martin Shapiro, "'Deliberative,' 'Independent' Technocracy vs. Democratic Politics: Will the Globe Echo the EU?," *Law and Contemporary Problems* 68, nos. 3–4 (Summer–Autumn 2005): 341–56.

25. See Alexandre M. Cunha and Carlos Eduardo Suprinyak, eds., *Political Economy and the International Order in Interwar Europe* (Cham, 2021); Peter Stirk, *A History of European Integration Since 1914* (London, 1996).

26. Quoted in Luisa Passerini, "From the Ironies of Identity to the Identities of Irony," in *The Idea of Europe: From Antiquity to the European Union*, ed. Anthony Pagden (Cambridge, UK, 2002), 177.

27. Immanuel Kant, "Perpetual Peace," in *Political Writings*, ed. Hans Reiss, trans. H. B. Nisbet, 2nd ed. (Cambridge, UK, 1991), 104.

28. Immanuel Kant, "Idea for a Universal History with a Cosmopolitan Purpose," in *Political Writings*, ed. Hans Reiss, trans. H. B. Nisbet, 2nd ed. (Cambridge, UK, 1991), 51.

29. "Foreign and Colonial," *The Spectator*, August 25, 1849, 793.

30. Quoted in Shane Weller, *The Idea of Europe: A Critical History* (Cambridge, UK, 2021), 116–18; Gilbert Rist, *The History of Development: From Western Origins to Global Faith* (London: 1997), 51.

31. Richard N. Coudenhove-Kalergi, "Das paneuropäische Manifest," in *Die Idee Europa, 1300–1946: Quellen zur Geschichte der politischen Einigung*, ed. Rolf Hellmut Foerster (Munich, 1963), 226, 234, 228, 227, 228, 229, 236, 234, 228. On defining European identity vis-à-vis American economic and military might, see Lebovics, *Bringing the Empire Back Home*.

32. Coudenhove-Kalergi, "Das paneuropäische Manifest," 236.

33. Richard N. Coudenhove-Kalergi, *Pan-Europe*, anonymous translation (New York, 1926), xii, 7, 17. On core-periphery frameworks and the "Pan-European world," see Immanuel Wallerstein, *World-Systems Analysis: An Introduction* (Durham, NC, 2004), especially 8.

34. Coudenhove-Kalergi, *Pan-Europe*, 21.

35. Richard N. Coudenhove-Kalergi, condensed statement, Foreign Policy Association Luncheon, October 31, 1925, PAN / EU-2 1925–1935, HAEU. This effort to establish a union of democracies serves as a prehistory to the era of democratic flourishing after 1945; see Martin Conway, *Western Europe's Democratic Age, 1945–1968* (Princeton, NJ, 2020), 11.

36. Coudenhove-Kaleri, *Pan-Europe*, 169–70.

37. Martyn Bond, *Hitler's Cosmopolitan Bastard: Count Richard Coudenhove-Kalergi and His Vision of Europe* (Montreal, 2011), 5.

38. R. N. Coudenhove-Kalergi, "Afrika," 1929, 1, 3, 1, PAN / EU-28 1920–1934, HAEU. See also Hansen and Jonsson, *Eurafrica*, especially 28.

39. Weller, *The Idea of Europe*, 163.

40. A. Einstein to R. N. Coudenhove-Kalergi, July 6, 1932, PAN / EU-10 1928–1935, HAEU.

41. Katiana Orluc, "Decline or Renaissance: The Transformation of European Consciousness after the First World War," in *Europe and the Other and Europe as the Other*, ed. Bo Stråth (Brussels, 2000), 151.

42. Robert Boyce, *The Great Interwar Crisis and the Collapse of Globalization* (New York, 2009), 200–201. See Victoria de Grazia, *Irresistible Empire: America's Advance through Twentieth-Century Europe* (Cambridge, MA, 2005).

43. Willy Buschak, "Enthusiasm for Europe and Europeanization in the Labor Movement of the 1920s," in *Reconsidering Europeanization: Ideas and Practices of (Dis-)Integrating Europe since the Nineteenth Century*, ed. Florian Greiner et al. (Berlin, 2022), 328. See also Willy Buschak, *Die vereinigten Staaten von Europa sind unser Ziel: Arbeiterbewegung und Europa im frühen 20. Jahrhundert* (Essen, 2014); Christian Krell, *Sozialdemokratie und Europa: Die Europapolitik von SPD, Labour Party und Parti Socialiste* (Wiesbaden, 2009).

44. Sozialdemokratischen Partei Deutschlands, *Das Heidelberger Programm* (Heidelberg, 1925), reproduced on Marxists Internet Archive, accessed October 3, 2023, https://www.marxists.org/deutsch/geschichte/deutsch/spd/1925/heidelberg.htm.

45. Bond, *Hitler's Cosmopolitan Bastard*, 5.

46. Richard Nicolaus Graf von Coudenhove-Kalergi, *Crusade for Pan-Europe: Autobiography of a Man and a Movement* (New York, 1943), 8, 200.

47. Letter from Paul-Henri Spaak, September 9, 1944, translation available from Centre virtuel de la connaissance sur l'Europe, accessed November 18, 2023, https://www.cvce.eu/en/obj/circular_letter_from_paul_henri_spaak_london_9_september_1944-en-7360a69f-943d-442f-98a5-b0feeb017a91.html.

48. Denis de Rougement, "Message to Europeans," May 10, 1948, available at Centre virtuel de la connaissance sur l'Europe, accessed October 8, 2023, https://www.cvce.eu/content/publication/1997/10/13/b14649e7-c8b1-46a9-a9a1-cdad800bccc8/publishable_en.pdf.

49. Richard Coudenhove-Kalergi, "Memorandum on the Organization of a Parliament for Europe," February 12, 1947, available at Centre virtuel de la connaissance sur l'Europe, accessed November 19, 2023, https://www.cvce.eu/content/publication/2003/10/8/4a3090c1-8247-4fd3-ad6b-2c9adb4b2203/publishable_en.pdf. On democracy in postwar Europe, see Conway, *Western Europe's Democratic Age*, 142–51.

50. Aurélie Dianara Andry, *Social Europe, the Road not Taken: The Left and European Integration in the Long 1970s* (Oxford, 2022), 30–31. See also Sergio Pistone, *The Union of European Federalists: From the Foundation to the Decision on Direct Election of the European Parliament* (Milan, 2008), especially 91; Walter Lipgens, *A History of European Integration* (Oxford, 1982); François Denord and Antoine Schwartz, "L'Économie (très) politique du traité de Rome," *Politix*, no. 89 (April 2010): 35–56. On the Mont Pelerin Society, see Ben Jackson, "At the Origins of Neo-Liberalism: The Free Economy and the Strong State, 1930–1947," *The Historical Journal* 53, no. 1 (January 2010): 129–51; Angus Burgin, *The Great Persuasion: Reinventing Free Markets since the Depression* (Cambridge, MA, 2012).

51. "Altiero Spinello: An Unrelenting Federalist," European Commission, n.d., accessed February 23, 2023, https://european-union.europa.eu/system/files/2021-07/eu-pioneers-altiero-spinelli_en.pdf.

52. On the island and how discussions with fellow socialist radicals Eugenio Colorni and Ursula Hirschmann informed the manifesto, see Nancy Jachec, *Europe's Intellectuals and the Cold War: The European Society of Culture, Post-War Politics, and International Relations* (London, 2015), 25–26.

53. Altiero Spinelli and Ernesto Rossi, *The Ventotene Manifesto*, June 1941, 7, available at Centre virtuel de la connaissance sur l'Europe, accessed February 23, 2023, https://www.cvce.eu/obj/the_manifesto_of_ventotene_1941-en-316aa96c-e7ff-4b9e-b43a-958e96afbecc.html. On federalist visions for Europe, see Kalypso Nicolaïdis and Robert Howse, eds., *The Federal Vision: Legitimacy and Levels of Governance in the United States and the European Union* (Oxford, 2001); Paul Michael Lützeler and Michael Gehler, eds., *Die Europäische Union zwischen Konfusion und Vision* (Vienna, 2021).

54. Jachec, *Europe's Intellectuals and the Cold War*, 25–27.

55. Quoted in Pagden, *The Idea of Europe*, 18–19; Altiero Spinelli, "L'Union européenne des fédéralistes en 1952," La voix fédéraliste, Organe de l'Organisation Luxembourgeoise du Mouvement Européen, no. 1 (Luxembourg: Organisation Luxembourgeoise du Mouvement Européen), 3, available at Centre virtuel de la connaissance sur l'Europe, accessed October 26, 2023, https://www.cvce.eu/en/obj/altiero_spinelli_the_union_of_european_federalists_in_1952-en-a3cbcc45-033e-4fb9-9cce-49ebf371d786.html.

56. "La C.E.D. est rejetée," *L'Humanité*, August 31, 1954; "Council of Europe: European Political Community," *International Organization* 9, no. 2 (May 1955): 301–2. See Turkuler Isiksel, "Cosmopolitanism and International Economic Institutions," *Journal of Politics* 82, no. 1 (January 2020): 211–24.

57. Central to the European Defense Community's parliamentary defeat was the opposition of Michel Debré, a Gaullist senator and future prime minister who counterposed France's authority in overseas territories, formalized in the French Union as a successor to the colonial empire, to incipient plans for European union. On colonial prerogatives in France's rejection of the EDC, see Brown, *The Seventh Member State*, 81–91. On Debré's role, see Brown, *The Seventh Member State*, 95; Marker, *Black France, White Europe*, 2–4. On Debré and colonialism, see Lebovics, *Bringing the Empire Back Home*, 25–29. On the French Union, see Avner Ofrath, *Colonial Algeria and the Politics of Citizenship* (London, 2023), especially 15; Todd Shepard, *The Invention of Decolonization: The Algerian War and the Remaking of France* (Ithaca, NY, 2006).

58. Paul-Henri Spaak, *The Brussels Report on the General Common Market* (referred to as the Spaak Report), Unofficial translation of the main portions of the report on the common market prepared by the Intergovernmental Committee on European Integration, Information Service, High Authority of the European Community for Coal and Steel, June 1956, 1, accessed October 14, 2023, http://aei.pitt.edu/995/1/Spaak_report.pdf. See also Paul-Henri Spaak, "The Integration of Europe: Dreams and Realities," *Foreign Affairs*, October 1950, 94–100; Paul-Henri Spaak,

"Europe in a Western Community," *Annals of the American Academy of Political and Social Science* 282, no. 1 (July 1952): 45–52; Pierre-Henri Laurent, "Paul-Henri Spaak and the Diplomatic Origins of the Common Market, 1955–1956," *Political Science Quarterly* 85, no. 3 (September 1970): 373–96; Andrew Moravcsik, ed., *Europe Without Illusions: The Paul-Henri Spaak Lectures, 1994–1999* (Lanham, MD, 2005).

59. Quoted in Piero Graglia, *Altiero Spinelli* (Bologna, 2008), 389. See also Thomas McStay Adams, *Europe's Welfare Traditions since 1500: Reform without End*, vol. 2, *1700–2000* (London, 2023), 337–38. On Spaak and the "return to the market," see John Gillingham, *European Integration, 1950–2003: Superstate or New Market Economy?* (Cambridge, UK, 2003), 43.

60. Spaak Report, 1; Spinelli, "L'Union européenne des fédéralistes en 1952," 4.

61. Spaak Report, 1, 3, 7, 10, 19; Resolution adopted by the Foreign Ministers of the ECSC Member States at Messina, June 1–3, 1955, translation available at Centre virtuel de la connaissance sur l'Europe, accessed November 18, 2023, 2, 3, https://www.cvce .eu/obj/resolution_adopted_by_the_foreign_ministers_of_the_ecsc_member_states _messina_1_to_3_june_1955-en-d1086bae-0c13-4a00-8608-73c75ce54fad.html.

62. Spaak Report, 3, 9, 10, 19.

63. F. A. Hayek, "The Economic Conditions of Interstate Federalism," in *Individualism and Economic Order* (Chicago, 1980), 255, 269, 266, 267. See Slobodian, *Globalists,* 99–104.

64. Hayek, "Economic Conditions," 270, 268, 258.

65. Rome Treaty, preamble, art. 2. See Robert Schütze, *European Union Law* (Cambridge, UK, 2015), 13. Also signed on March 25, 1957, alongside the treaty establishing the European Economic Community, better known as the Rome Treaty, was the treaty establishing the European Atomic Energy Community, which set up Euratom to delevop a European market for nuclear power. Euratom reflected imperial anxiety about the security of extra-European energy sources and anticipated the sharing of technical knowledge under Schengen and later Europol. See Brown, *The Seventh Member State*, 112; Judt, *Postwar*, 302; Jean-Marie Palayret, *Une Université pour l'Europe: Préhistoire de l'Institute Universitaire Européen de Florence (1948–1976)* (Florence, 1996), 49–61.

66. Rome Treaty, art. 3, preamble, art. 2, preamble, art. 117.

67. Rome Treaty, title III, art. 48, 68, 51, 123, 52, 118.

68. Rome Treaty, art. 220.

69. See "Paris Summit Achieved Nothing, Says Haughey," *Irish Times*, December 14, 1974; "Soviet Announces New Internal Passport System," *New York Times*, December 26, 1974.

70. See Christoph Rass, "Temporary Labour Migration and State-Run Recruitment of Foreign Workers in Europe, 1919–1975: A New Migration Regime?," *International Review of Social History* 57, no. S20 (2012): 191–224.

71. "Paris Summit, Final Communiqué," *Bulletin of the European Communities* 12 (December 9–10, 1974): 3.

72. "Commission Report on the Implementation of a Passport Union," *Bulletin of the European Communities*, supplement 7 (July 3, 1975).

73. "Commission Report on the Implementation of a Passport Union," 2.

74. See Thomas Christiansen and Christine Reh, *Constitutionalizing the European Union* (New York, 2009), 55; Michael Longo, *Constitutionalising Europe: Process and Practices* (New York, 2006), 101–2.

75. *Draft Treaty Establishing the European Union, Bulletin of the European Communities* 2 (February 1984): 4–7.

76. A. Spinelli, "La beffa del Mercato comune," in *L'Europa non cade dal cielo* (Bologna, 1960), 282–87, as quoted in Graglia, *Altiero Spinelli*, 389.

77. *Draft Treaty Establishing the European Union*, 6–7, 4.

78. *Draft Treaty Establishing the European Union*, 5, 8. On citizenship and state power, see Saskia Sassen, "The Repositioning of Citizenship and Alienage: Emergent Subjects and Spaces for Politics," *Globalizations* 2, no. 1 (2005): 79–94.

79. *Draft Treaty Establishing the European Union*, 17.

80. Christiansen and Reh, *Constitutionalizing the European Union*, 55.

81. Présidence de la République, Service de Presse, "Conférence de Presse," 15, 8.

82. Fontainebleau conclusions, 2.

83. Fontainebleau conclusions, 5, 11, 2.

84. Alan Osborn, "Preparing for the First Euro-Citizen," *Daily Telegraph*, June 28, 1984.

85. Pierre Beylau, "L'Obsession de Mitterrand," *Le Quotidien de Paris*, June 25, 1984.

86. "'L'Inventaire' de l'Europe du Citoyen," *Le Matin*, June 27, 1984; Jacques Prévert, "Inventory," quoted in William F. Baker, *Jacques Prévert* (New York, 1967), 88–89.

87. "Rapport du Comité ad hoc 'Europe des citoyens,' Rapport adressé au Conseil européen de Bruxelles," March 29 and 30, 1985, in *Bulletin des Communautés européennes*, no. 3; "Rapport du comité pour l'Europe des citoyens remis au Conseil européen de Milan," June 28–29, 1985, in *Bulletin des Communautés européennes*, supplement 7 / 85. The free-passage decal resembled the original emblem of the Union of European Federalists; see Sergio Pistone, *The Union of European Federalists: From the Foundation to the Decision on Direct Election of the European Parliament (1946-1974)* (Milan, 2008), 161.

88. "Rapport du Comité ad hoc 'Europe des citoyens,'" 2.

89. "Rapport du Comité ad hoc 'Europe des citoyens,'" 8–9.

90. "Pietro Adonnino," European Parliament, accessed October 12, 2023, https:// www.europarl.europa.eu/meps/en/957/PIETRO_ADONNINO/history/1; Consiglio dell'Ordine degli Avvocati di Roma, minutes no. 14 of the meeting of March 28, 2013, accessed March 25, 2024, https://www.ordineavvocatiroma.it/wp-content/uploads /2022/04/28%20marzo%202013%20n.%2014.pdf; Emanuele Isidori, *Pedagogia, Sport e Relazioni Internazionali: Dall'analisi del Contesto alla Metodologia di Sviluppo* (Rome, 2016), 18.

91. Pietro Adonnino to Dr. Garret FitzGerald, n.d., BAC 224 / 1994, no. 1159 (1985), L'Europe des Citoyens, Commission Archives. See Carl Boggs and David Plotke, eds., *The Politics of Eurocommunism: Socialism in Transition* (Montreal, 1980).

92. Introductory letter from the Chairman to the President of the European Council, in "A People's Europe: Reports from the Ad Hoc Committee," *Bulletin of the European Communities*, supplement 7 / 85, 8.

93. Reports from the Ad Hoc Committee to the European Council, Brussels, March 29 and 30, 1985, 9.

94. Reports from the Ad Hoc Committee, Milan, June 28 and 29, 1985, 18.

95. "Rapport du Comité ad hoc 'Europe des citoyens,'" 2.

96. "Compte-rendu de la 9ème réunion du Comité ad hoc 'Europe des citoyens' des 4 et 5 mars 1985," March 6, 1985, BAC 201 / 1989, no. 375 (1984–1985), L'Europe des Citoyens, Commission Archives.

97. Ad Hoc Committee on a People's Europe, *Report to the European Council*, March 29 and 30, 1985, 5, BAC 224 / 1994, no. 1159 (1985), L'Europe des Citoyens, Commission Archives.

98. "Rapport du Comité ad hoc 'Europe des citoyens,'" 4.

99. "Rapport du Comité ad hoc 'Europe des citoyens,'" 2.

100. Statement by Jacques Delors, President of the Commission, to the European Parliament and his reply to the ensuing debate, March 12, 1985, in *Bulletin of the European Communities*, supplement 4 / 85, 11, 17, 19.

101. "Rapport du Comité ad hoc 'Europe des citoyens,'" 2.

102. "Rapport du Comité ad hoc 'Europe des citoyens,'" 8.

103. "Rapport du Comité ad hoc 'Europe des citoyens,'" 8.

104. See Steven King and Anne Winter, eds., *Migration, Settlement and Belonging in Europe, 1500–1930s: Comparative Perspectives* (New York, 2013); Anne Winter, "Caught between Law and Practice: Migrants and Settlement Legislation in the Southern Low Countries in a Comparative Perspective, c. 1700–1900," *Rural History* 19, no. 2 (October 2008): 137–62.

105. "Rapport du Comité ad hoc 'Europe des citoyens,'" 8.

106. "Rapport du Comité ad hoc 'Europe des citoyens,'" 8.

107. "Rapport du comité pour l'Europe des citoyens remis au Conseil européen de Milan," 6.

108. "Rapport du comité pour l'Europe des citoyens remis au Conseil européen de Milan," 5.

109. "Rapport du comité pour l'Europe des citoyens remis au Conseil européen de Milan," 10, 11.

110. "Rapport du comité pour l'Europe des citoyens remis au Conseil européen de Milan," 15, 16.

111. "Rapport du comité pour l'Europe des citoyens remis au Conseil européen de Milan," 16.

112. Reports from the Ad Hoc Committee, European Council Conclusions, Brussels, March 29 and 30, 1985, 15.

113. Reports from the Ad Hoc Committee, European Council Conclusions, Milan, June 28 and 29, 1985, 31.

114. "Conclusions of the Milan European Council," extract on the completion of the internal market, June 28 and 29, 1985, *Bulletin of the European Communities*, no. 6.

115. *Completing the Internal Market: White Paper from the Commission to the European Council, June 14, 1985,* COM(85) 310 final, especially 18–20, 26–28, accessed June 17, 2022, http://europa.eu/documents/comm/white_papers/pdf/com1985_0310_f_en.pdf.

116. "Projet de communications de la commission au conseil consacrée aux suites à donner aux conclusions de Fontainebleau relatives à l'Europe des Citoyens," n.d., BAC 314-2014 no. 50, dossier 44, vol. 2, Fontainebleau, Commission Archives.

117. Reports from the Ad Hoc Committee, European Council Conclusions, Milan, June 28 and 29, 31; Statement by Jacques Delors, 53.

118. Commission of the European Communities, Consolidating the Internal Market (Communication from the Commission to the European Council, Fontainebleau, 25–26 June, 1984), COM (84) / 350 final (9 July 1984), 4, 2, accessed June 29, 2022, http://aei.pitt.edu/2803/1/2803.pdf.

119. "Projet de communications de la commission au conseil consacrée aux suites à donner aux conclusions de Fontainebleau relatives à l'Europe des Citoyens," n.d., 2, BAC 314-2014, no. 50, dossier 44, vol. 2, Fontainebleau, Commission Archives.

120. Reports from the Ad Hoc Committee, European Council Conclusions, Milan, June 28 and 29, 31.

121. Memo for the members of the Commission, meeting of the Committee of Permanent Representatives, European Commission, September 27, 1985, 4–5, BAC 224 / 1994, no. 1159 (1985), L'Europe des Citoyens, Commission Archives.

122. "La rencontre Kohl-Mitterrand à Konstanz—preparation pour Milan," n.d., B18779 / 16 Cooperation Politique Européenne 1984–1985, Archives Diplomatiques, Affaires Etrangères, Commerce Extérieur et Coopération au Développement, Brussels. See Antje Wiener, "Forging Flexibility—the British 'No' to Schengen," *European Journal of Migration and Law* 1, no. 4 (January 1999): 441–63.

123. "Disunited Europe," *Irish Times*, July 1, 1985, 11; Nigel Hawkes, "Defeat for Britain in EEC Split on Reform," *The Observer*, June 30, 1985, 2.

124. Memo for the members of the Commission.

125. Memo for the members of the Commission, 2

126. Memo for the members of the Commission, 1–5; Directory of the Commission of the European Communities, June 1985, 9, accessed October 14, 2023, http://aei.pitt.edu/75545/.

127. Memo for the members of the Commission, 2.

128. Affaire 293 / 83, *F. Gravier contre Ville de Liège* (1985), Procédure écrite, Instruction, Demande: le 28.12.1983, 2, Historical Archives, Court of Justice of the European Union, Luxembourg (hereafter ECJ). See Académie Royale des Beaux-Arts de Liège ESAHR, accessed November 19, 2023, https://www.academieroyaledesbeauxartsliege.be/historique/.

129. *Gravier*, 608.

130. T. Koopmans, "Rapport d'audience dans l'affaire 293 / 83," 2–6, ECJ.

131. Luc Misson, *Observations Présentées par Mademoiselle Gravier*, March 10, 1984, 1, 2, 5, ECJ.

132. Françoise Gravier, interview with the author, September 13, 2023 (hereafter Gravier Oral History).

133. Gravier Oral History.

134. *Gravier*, 608–9; Misson, *Observations*, 1–2; Koopmans, "Rapport d'audience," 2.

135. See Morten Broberg and Niels Fenger, *Preliminary References to the European Court of Justice* (Oxford, 2010).

136. *Gravier*, 610; *Sandro Forcheri and His Wife Marisa Forcheri, Née Marino v. Belgian State and asbl Institut Supérieur de Sciences Humaines Appliquées—Ecole Ouvrière Supérieure*, Case 152 / 82, 1983, ECR, 2325–26. See also Protocol on Privileges and Immunities of the European Communities, Brussels, 8 April 1965, 1348 UNTS 14, 13.

137. *Forcheri*, 2335. Regarding *Forcheri*, see also Anne de Moor, "Article 7 of Treaty of Rome Bites," *The Modern Law Review* 48, no. 4 (July 1985): 452–59.

138. Misson, *Observations*, 5.

139. *Gravier*, 606, 607; Affaire 293 / 83, Procédure écrite, 2–3.

140. Rome Treaty, art. 7, title III, especially arts. 48–66.

141. *Gravier*, 608–9.

142. Rome Treaty, art. 128; *Gravier*, 612.

143. "Mémoire par la Commission des Communautés Européennes dans l'affaire 293 / 83," March 16, 1984, 22, ECJ; Misson, *Observations*.

144. Misson, *Observations*, 11, 17.

145. *Gravier*, 608, 609; Misson, *Observations*, 1, 2, 5, 20.

146. Rome Treaty, art. 48.

147. Luc Misson, "Réponse de Mademoiselle Gravier à la question posée par la cour de justice," August 29, 1984, 9, 6, ECJ.

148. Advocate General Sir Gordon Slynn, [Opinion] 596 (1985), *Gravier v. City of Liège*, Case 293 / 83, 1985, ECR 596.

149. Misson, *Observations*, 16.

150. Misson, *Observations*, 6, and see also 7–9.

151. Misson, *Observations*, 18, 20.

152. Misson, "Réponse," 1, 5, 2.

153. On the court's request to all parties, see, e.g., Laurids Mikaelsen, "Besvarelse af Domstolens spørgsmål i sag 293 / 83, Gravier mod Bylen Liège," August 28, 1984, 1, ECJ; "Réponse du Royaume de Belgique à la Question Posée par la Cour de Justice des Communautés Européennes, 293 / 83," 1, ECJ; Mission, "Réponse," 1.

154. Misson, "Réponse," 6, 4; Commission des Communautés Européennes, "Réponse à la question posée par la cour dans l'affaire 293 / 83," September 4, 1984, 5, 4, ECJ. The court's question concerned the Rome Treaty's Article 58 regarding firms without a "profit motive."

155. Bernard Perin, "Réponse du Royaume de Belgique à la question posée par la cour de justice," September 10, 1984, 3, ECJ.

156. Perin, "Réponse," 2–4.

157. Mikaelsen, "Besvarelse af Domstolens spørgsmål i sag 293 / 83," 6. On the Danish view, see also Laurids Mikaelsen, "Indlaeg fra den danske regering i sag 293 / 83, F. Gravier mod Byen Liège," March 23, 1984, ECJ.

158. J.R.J. Braggins, "Answer of the United Kingdom to the Court's Question, Case No. 293 / 83," October 8, 1984, 2, 3, ECJ.

159. J.R.J. Braggins, "Written Observations by the United Kingdom, Case no. 293 / 83," March 27, 1984, 15, ECJ.

160. Braggins, "Written Observations," 10; Braggins, "Answer," 3.

161. Braggins, "Written Observations," 14–15.

162. Braggins, "Answer," 2.

163. Braggins, "Written Observations," 17.

164. "Mémoire par la Commission des Communautés Européennes," 19.

165. "Mémoire par la Commission des Communautés Européennes," 12, 14, 16, 17, 19, 36, 41, 43.

166. "Mémoire par la Commission des Communautés Européennes," 43; Commission, "Réponse," 4. See also Koopmans, "Rapport d'audience," 22.

167. Koopmans, "Rapport d'audience," 7, 10.

168. "See Court of Justice," available at Centre virtuel de la connaissance sur l'Europe, accessed May 2, 2019, https://www.cvce.eu/en/education/unit-content /-/unit/d5906df5-4f83-4603-85f7-0cabc24b9fe1/c89b0195-280c-4fbb-bcb1 -ac400d20852d.

169. Alexander Mackenzie Stuart, "The European Communities and the Rule of Law," delivered at the Institute of Advanced Legal Studies, London, 1977, 77.

170. *Gravier*, 613, 612.

171. Simon Kuper, "Tintin and the War," *Financial Times*, October 21, 2011.

172. *Gravier*, 615, 611, 613.

173. The Council of Ministers, formally the Council of the European Communities and later the Council of the European Union, is composed of national ministers from the bloc's member countries and shares legislative responsibilities with the European Parliament. It differs from the European Council, composed of leaders of the bloc's member countries and charged with setting its overarching priorities.

174. *Gravier*, 612, 614. The court referred to 63 / 266 / EEC, council decision of April 2, 1963 laying down general principles for implementing a common vocational training policy (OJ 63 20.04.1963, 25, 27, ELI, http://data.europa.eu/eli/dec/1963 /266/oj). See also "General Guidelines for Drawing Up a Community Action Programme on Vocational Training," *Official Journal* C 081, 12 / 08 / 1971 P. 0005–0011, https://eur-lex.europa.eu/legal-content/EN/TXT/?uri=CELEX%3A31971Y0812.

175. *Gravier*, 614. See "General Guidelines for Drawing Up a Community Action Programme on Vocational Training."

176. Rome Treaty, art. 129, 210, 220.

177. UDHR, art. 22, 26, 29. See Loukēs G. Loukaidēs, *Essays on the Developing Law of Human Rights* (Dordrecht, 1995), 84; Loukēs G. Loukaidēs, "Personality and Privacy under the European Convention on Human Rights," *British Yearbook of International Law* 61, no. 1 (January 1991); Council of Europe, *Yearbook of the European*

Convention on Human Rights (The Hague, 1976), 379; Edward J. Eberle, "Observations on the Development of Human Dignity and Personality in German Constitutional Law: An Overview," *Liverpool Law Review* 33, no. 3 (November 2012): 201–33.

178. David Edward, "Lord Mackenzie-Stuart of Dean," Royal Society of Edinburgh, accessed May 10, 2019, https://www.rse.org.uk/cms/files/fellows/obits_alpha/mackenzie-stuart_lord.pdf.

179. Mackenzie Stuart, "European Communities and the Rule of Law," 5.

180. Mackenzie Stuart, "European Communities and the Rule of Law," 1, 3, and see also 2–3, 11.

181. Mackenzie Stuart, "European Communities and the Rule of Law," 6, 104, 112, 117.

182. Mackenzie Stuart, "European Communities and the Rule of Law," 16, 18.

183. Mackenzie Stuart, "European Communities and the Rule of Law," 2, 20; *Van Gen den Loos v. Nederlandse Administratie der Belastingen*, Case 26 / 62, 1963, ECR 1.

184. Mackenzie Stuart, "European Communities and the Rule of Law," 23.

185. Mackenzie Stuart, "European Communities and the Rule of Law," 106, 5, 23, 115, 117; see also 15, 19, 62, 73–74, 91–94, 105. On the market mechanism and "negative integration," see Gillingham, *European Integration*, xiii. A vast literature addresses competing visions of Europe—a political and social community or a framework for the functioning of the market; see Aurélie Dianara Andry, *Social Europe, the Road not Taken: The Left and European Integration in the Long 1970s* (Oxford, 2022); Moravcsik, *Choice for Europe*; Daniel Yergin and Joseph Stanislaw, *The Commanding Heights: The Battle between Government and the Marketplace That Is Remaking the Modern World* (New York, 1998).

186. Mackenzie Stuart, "European Communities and the Rule of Law," 116, 117.

187. Ulrich Everling, "The Court of Justice as a Decisionmaking Authority," *Michigan Law Review* 82, no. 5 / 6 (April–May 1984): 1305, 1309, 1294, 1308.

188. On jurisgenerativity, see Seyla Benhabib, *Dignity in Adversity: Human Rights in Troubled Times* (Cambridge, UK, 2011), especially 15, 93–137.

189. "Prof. Tim Koopmans," Universiteit Leiden, accessed May 12, 2019, https://www.universiteitleiden.nl/en/law/institute-of-public-law/tim-koopmans; "Prof. Tim Koopmans Passed Away on Christmas Eve," *European Public Law Organization*, January 2, 2016, accessed May 12, 2019, https://www1.eplo.int/newsitem/764/prof.-tim-koopmans-passed-away-on-christmas-eve.

190. Thijmen Koopmans, "The Judicial System Envisaged in the Draft Treaty" EUI Working Paper no. 85 / 145, 1985, 29, 17.

191. Koopmans, "The Judicial System Envisaged in the Draft Treaty," 30.

192. *Gravier*, 613, 614. The ECJ would soon find that state-funded education was not a service; see *Belgian State v. Humbel*, Case 263 / 86, 1988, ECR 5388.

193. On EU law and individual rights, see Jason Coppel and Aidan O'Neill, "The European Court of Justice: Taking Rights Seriously?," *Common Market Law Review* 29 (1992): 669–92. On constitutionalizing the Rome Treaty, see Stone-Sweet, *Judicial Construction*, 65.

194. *Gravier*, 613.

195. On European courts as agents of political and economic change, see Karen Alter, *The European Court's Political Power: Selected Essays* (Oxford, 2009); Christian Joppke, "Evolution of Alien Rights in the United States, Germany, and the European Union," in *Citizenship Today: Global Perspectives and Practices*, ed. T. Alexander Aleinikoff and Douglas Klusmeyer (Washington, DC, 2001), 36–62. On vocational training and human rights, see Val D. Rust, "The Right to Education for Employment and Mobility: Norway and Yugoslavia," in *Human Rights & Education*, ed. N. Bernstein Tarrow (Oxford, 1987), 121–38. On rights as a "battle cry" of free-market conservatism, see Moyn, *Last Utopia*, 35.

196. Gravier Oral History.

197. The Erasmus program opened in the 1987–88 academic year, under European Commission authority as recognized by *Gravier's* broad construction of vocational training; see Benjamin Feyen and Ewa Krzaklewska, "Generation ERASMUS—The New Europeans? A Reflection," in *The ERASMUS Phenomenon—Symbol of a New European Generation?*, ed. Benjamin Feyen and Ewa Krzaklewska (Frankfurt am Main, 2013), 229–42; Sacha Garben, *EU Higher Education Law: The Bologna Process and Harmonization by Stealth* (Alphen aan den Rijn, The Netherlands, 2011), 60. The decision prompted other foreign nationals to seek recovery of enrollment payments; see *Blaizot v. University of Liège*, Case 24 / 86, 1988, ECR.

198. Koopmans, "The Judicial System Envisaged in the Draft Treaty," 5.

199. Georges Kremlis, interview with the author, February 19, 2018. Kremlis led the European Commission's work on the *Gravier* case.

200. "L'Europe des Citoyens: Suites à donner aux conclusions du Conseil européen de Fontainebleau," September 24, 1984, 5.

Chapter 2. A Treaty Signed on the Moselle River

1. Octavius Rooke, *The Life of the Moselle* (London, 1858), 1, 9. See also Jörg Schmitt-Kilian, *Von Koblenz zu Rhein und Mosel: Orte an und über dem Wasser* (Messkirch: 2012); Michel Caffier, *La Moselle: Une Rivière et ses hommes* (Nancy, 1985).

2. Communiqué de Presse, Schengen, 14 June 1985, folder "Allègement des contrôles aux frontières, signature du traité (accord à 5)," box 2 "Coordination interministérielle pour l'allègement des contrôles aux frontières, 1984–1989 and Coordination interministérielle pour l'allègement des contrôles aux frontières: Dossiers de MM. Plaisant, Beaux, Cazimajou et Angles 1914INVA" (hereafter "Coordination"), MEAE.

3. That summer, Luxembourg held the central negotiating group's presidency and chose a place for the Schengen signing. See "Allègement des contrôles aux frontières: Réunion à cinq du 14 mai 1985 à Bruxelles," Télégramme du départ, Ministère des Relations Extérieures, May 17, 1985, 4, folder "Allègement des contrôles aux frontières: Réunion au niveau ministériel (Bruxelles) 14 mai 1985," box 5 "Mouvement des coordonnateurs libre circulation, 1985–1989" (hereafter "Mouvement"), MEAE.

4. "Unterzeichnung des Abkommens D-F-Benelux über den schrittweisen Abbau der Grenzkontrollen," June 10, 1985, box 17318, shelf 284 "Abbau der Grenzkontrollen,

Deutschland-Frankreich-Benelux—von Schengen-Abkommen, 1985–1986" (hereafter Grenzkontrollen), Politisches Archiv des Auswärtigen Amts, Berlin, Germany (hereafter PA); Catherine Lalumière, interview with the author, October 19, 2017 (hereafter Lalumière Oral History).

5. Communiqué de Presse, 1.

6. "Discours de Monsieur Robert Goebbels, Secrétaire d'État aux Affaires étrangères sur l'accord relatif à la suppression graduelle des contrôles aux frontières communes du Benelux, de la République Fédérale d'Allemagne et de la France," *Bulletin de documentation. dir. de publ. Service Information et Presse-Ministère d'État*, no. 4 (June–July-August 1985), 32–33 (hereafter Discours Goebbels), available at Centre virtuel de la connaissance sur l'Europe, accessed October 19, 2023, https://www.cvce.eu/en/obj/address_given_by_robert_goebbels_on_the_schengen_agreement_14_june_1985-en-1a3cf916-c898-4b1e-9356-f2ac3a19816c.html.

7. On the shift in EU law from a market-based to a rights-based conception of free movement, see Stephen Weatherill, *The Internal Market as a Legal Concept* (Oxford, 2017), 6–7.

8. UDHR; Protocol no. 4.

9. Communiqué de Presse, 2; Schengen Agreement, art. 17; Discours Goebbels.

10. Discours Goebbels.

11. Robert de Suzannet, "Europe: Allégement des contrôles routiers," *Le Figaro*, June 15, 1985.

12. Robert Goebbels, interview with the author, November 1, 2021 (hereafter Goebbels Oral History).

13. Lalumière Oral History

14. "No school of thought can be identified that would explore Schengen systematically," according to Markéta Novotná, "Schengen Cooperation: What Scholars Make of It," *Journal of Borderlands Studies* (April 2018): 2. Schengen began to feature in scholarship on issues of asylum and free movement with the implementing convention's adoption in 1990; see Alex Gerlach, "Dubliner Asylrechtskonvention und Schengener Abkommen: Lohnt sich die Ratifikation?," *Zeitschrift für Rechtspolitik* 26, no. 5 (May 1993): 164–66. Existing accounts focus on particular member states; see Simone Paoli, "France and the Origins of Schengen: An Interpretation," in "Peoples and Borders: Seventy Years of Migration in Europe, from Europe, to Europe, 1945–2015," ed. Elena Calandri, Simone Paoli, and Antonio Varsori, special issue, *Journal of European Integration History* (2017): 255–79; Simone Paoli, *Frontiera Sud: L'Italia e la nascita dell'Europa di Schengen* (Florence, 2018); Emmanuel Comte, *The History of the European Migration Regime: Germany's Strategic Hegemony* (Abingdon, UK, 2018); Ferruccio Pastore, Paola Monzini, and Giuseppe Sciortino, "Schengen's Soft Underbelly?," *International Migration* 44, no. 4 (2006): 95–119; Wiener, "Forging Flexibility—the British 'No' to Schengen." International relations theorists have explored derogations from the open-border mandate, and economists have quantified the commercial costs of restricting free movement; see Jacqueline Hellman and María José Molina García, "La erosión del proceso de integración europea como consecuencia de ciertas restricciones a la libre circulación

de personas," *Revista Universitaria Europea*, no. 22 (June 2015): especially 33; Andreu Olesti Rayo, "El Espacio Schengen y la reinstauración de los controles en las fronteras interiores de los Estados miembros de la Unión Europea," *Revista d'estudis autonòmics i federals*, no. 15 (2012): 33. The 2015 refugee crisis spurred research on Schengen, much of it predictive; see Serio Carrera et al., *Die Zukunft des Schengen-Raums: Aktuelle Entwicklungen und Herausforderungen des Schengen-Regelungsrahmens seit 2016* (Brussels, 2018).

15. Vendelin Hreblay, *La Libre circulation des personnes: Les Accords de Schengen* (Paris, 1994), 7.

16. Hreblay, *Libre circulation*, 5–6.

17. Hreblay, *Libre circulation*, 9, 6, 7, 32. See Isaac Stanley-Becker, "'An Inseparable Pair': Freedom and Security in the Schengen Space," in *Sites of Modernity—Places of Risk: Risk and Security in Germany since the 1970s*, ed. Martin Geyer (New York, 2023), 150–70.

18. Discours Goebbels.

19. François Mitterrand to Helmut Kohl, n.d., 1–2, box 14930, shelf 238 "Europäischer Rat in Fontainebleau," PA.

20. Schengen Agreement, preamble.

21. Discours Goebbels.

22. Treaty Instituting the Benelux Economic Union, February 3, 1958, 381, UNTS. 165 (hereafter Benelux Treaty); "Benelux," Luxembourg Government, accessed October 21, 2023, https://gouvernement.lu/en/dossiers/2018/benelux.html.

23. Benelux Treaty; Hreblay, *Libre circulation*, 2–5.

24. "Abkommen zwischen Deutschland, Frankreich und Benelux über den schrittweisen Abbau der Grenzkontrollen," 2, appended to "Unterzeichnung des Abkommens," June 10, 1985.

25. "Wir müssen wie Wölfe sein," *Der Spiegel*, February 26, 1984.

26. Guy Van Hyfte, interview with the author, August 16, 2023 (hereafter Van Hyfte Oral History).

27. Claude Debons and Joël Le Coq, *Routiers, les raisons de la colère* (Paris, 1997), 170.

28. "Wir müssen wie Wölfe sein."

29. Michael Dobbs, "Europe Sinks into Paralysis," *Washington Post*, February 26, 1984; K. N. Malik, "Blockades Paralyse French Borders," *Times of India*, February 24, 1984; John Vinocur, "French Act to End Truck Blockades," *New York Times*, February 19, 1984.

30. "Wir müssen wie Wölfe sein." See Marci McDonald, "The Truckers' Highway Revolt," *Maclean's*, March 5, 1984, 27.

31. "Wir müssen wie Wölfe sein." On the phenomenon of Happenings, see Jon Erickson, "The Spectacle of the Anti-Spectacle: Happenings and the Situationist International," *Discourse* 14, no. 2 (Spring 1992): 36–58.

32. "Wir müssen wie Wölfe sein"; Vinocur, "French Act to End Truck Blockades." See also E. S. Phelps and J.-P. Fitoussi, "Causes of the 1980s Slump in Europe" (Brookings Papers on Economic Activity, no. 2, 1987), 487–520.

33. Ernst and Whinney, *Research on the "Cost of Non-Europe": Basic Findings*, vol. 4 (Luxembourg, 1988), 3, accessed October 21, 2023, http://aei.pitt.edu/47966/1/A9311.pdf.

34. "Wir müssen wie Wölfe sein."

35. "Wir müssen wie Wölfe sein."

36. Roland Dumas, "Progress of European Cooperation," Council of Europe, Committee of Ministers, 74th session, May 10, 1984, 7, box 14930, shelf 238 "Europäischer Rat in Fontainebleau," PA.

37. Mechthild Bauman, *Der deutsche Fingerabdruck: Die Rolle der deutschen Bundesregierung bei der Europäisierung der Grenzpolitik* (Baden-Baden, 2006), 56–57.

38. "Bericht der Bundesregierung zur Lage der Nation im geteilten Deutschland," *Bulletin des Presse- und Informationsamtes der Bundesregierung*, no. 30 (March 1984): 267.

39. "Präsident Mitterrand und Bundeskanzler Dr. Kohl, Pressekonferenz, Paris," May 29, 1984, box 17318, shelf 284 "Grenzkontrollen," PA; Ambassade de France, Bonn, June 25, 1984, box 17318, shelf 284 "Grenzkontrollen," PA; Hans-Hagen Bremer, "Bald ohne Grenzkontrollen," *Frankfurter Rundschau*, May 30, 1984.

40. "Keine Grenzkontrollen," *Bild*, June 18, 1984.

41. Saarbrücken Accord, July 13, 1984, 1401 UNTS 167 (hereafter Saarbrücken Accord), preamble, art. 3, 5, preamble.

42. See Andreas Pudlat, "Der lange Weg zum Schengen-Raum: Ein Prozess im Vier-Phasen-Modell," *Journal of European Integration History* 17, no. 2 (2011): 311–12; Hreblay, *Libre circulation*, 311.

43. Memorandum to Paul Cousseran, "Zusammenarbeit zwischen der Republik Frankreich und der Bundesrepublik Deutschland auf grenzpolizeilichem Gebiet," September 30, 1983, box 17318, shelf 284 "Grenzkontrollen," PAA.

44. "Polizeigewerkschaft befürwortet Abbau der Grenzkontrollen," *Der Deutsche Depeschendienst*, June 25, 1984, box 17318, shelf 284 "Grenzkontrollen," PAA.

45. "Mitteilung von Jean-Louis Bianco an Waldemar Schreckenberg," n.d., box 17318, shelf 284 "Grenzkontrollen," PAA.

46. Saarbrücken Accord, preamble, art. 10, 9.

47. Frances M. B. Lynch, "De Gaulle's First Veto: France, the Rueff Plan and the Free Trade Area," *Contemporary European History* 9, no. 1 (March 2000): 132; Jeffrey Glen Giauque, *Grand Designs and Visions of Unity: The Atlantic Powers and the Reorganization of Western Europe, 1955–1963* (Chapel Hill, NC, 2002), 62–67.

48. "Erklärung von Bundeskanzler Helmut Kohl und Staatspräsident François Mitterrand zum Abbau der Grenzkontrollen anlässlich der deutsch-französischen Konsultationen am 29. und 30. Oktober 1984 in Bad Kreuznach," *Bulletin des Presse- und Informationsamtes der Bundesregierung*, no. 131 (November 1984): 1154.

49. Irene-Maria Eich, interview with the author, August 31, 2023 (hereafter Eich Oral History).

50. Willi Carl, interview with the author, July 22, 2023.

51. Memorandum, December 12, 1984, binder 1a BNL, Council Archives.

52. "Objectifs de l'Accord du 13 juillet," December 13, 1984, 3, folder "Allègement des contrôles aux frontières: Consultations Franco-allemandes (1984)," box 1 "Coordination," MEAE.

53. "Objectifs de l'Accord du 13 juillet."

54. Communiqué to the press, Brussels, February 27, 1985, folder "Allègement des contrôles aux Frontières: Réunion du 27 fév. 1985 à Bruxelles," box 5 "Mouvement," MEAE.

55. Discours Goebbels.

56. "Robert Goebbels," Europa Nu, accessed October 21, 2021, https://www.europa-nu.nl/id/vhzna0ij85u3/robert_goebbels.

57. "Catherine Lalumière," Maison de l'Europe de Paris, accessed December 30, 2023, https://paris-europe.eu/catherine-lalumiere-presidente/.

58. "Mit seiner Unterschrift unter das Schengen-Abkommen schrieb er Geschichte," *Rhein-Neckar-Zeitung*, August 8, 2017.

59. "Paul De Keersmaeker," Vlaams Parlement, accessed December 30, 2023, https://www.vlaamsparlement.be/nl/vlaamse-volksvertegenwoordigers-het-vlaams-parlement/paul-de-keersmaeker.

60. "Ex-staatssecretaris Virginie Korte-van Hemel overleden," *NU*, April 5, 2014.

61. "Wim van Eekelen," Indonesia-Nederland Society, accessed October 8, 2021, https://www.indonesia-nederland.org/about-us/board-of-trustees/wim-van-eekelen/.

62. Memorandum, December 12, 1984.

63. E. Kaufhold to E.D.J. Kruytbosch, July 27, 1984, binder 1a BNL, Council Archives.

64. "Note du Comité de rédaction au Comité de Direction de l'Union économique Benelux," Conseil de l'Union économique, Comité de rédaction, January 15, 1985, binder 1a BNL, Council Archives; "Note aux membres du Conseil de l'Union économique," February 5, 1985, Conseil de l'Union économique, Comité de rédaction, 1, binder 1a BNL, Council Archives; "Juxtaposition des textes du 'Mémorandum Benelux' et des propositions officieuses franco-allemandes (télux du 19.2.85) en matière de simplification des formalités aux frontières, confidentiel," February 27, 1985, Binder 1a BNL, Council Archives (hereafter "Juxtaposition des textes du 'Mémorandum Benelux'").

65. "Document de travail franco-allemand mis au point le 14 fevrier 1985 à Bonn en prévision de la négociation France-RFA-Benelux sur l'allègement des contrôles aux frontières," February 27, 1985, 1, binder 1a BNL, Council Archives.

66. Memorandum, December 12, 1984.

67. "Note du Comité de rédaction au Comité de Direction de l'Union économique Benelux," 1.

68. "Note aux membres du Conseil de l'Union économique," 2.

69. "Conclusions de la réunion tenue à Bruxelles le 27 février 1985," March 6, 1985, folder "Allègement des contrôles aux frontières: Réunion du 27 fév. 1985 à Bruxelles," box 5 "Mouvement," MEAE.

70. "Ouverture des négociations avec le Benelux, Fiche télégraphique," February 28, 1985, folder "Allègement des contrôles aux Frontières, reunion du 27 fév. 1985 à Bruxelles," box 5 "Mouvement," MEAE.

71. "Conclusions de la réunion," 3.

72. Communiqué to the press, Brussels, February 27, 1985, included with "Conclusions de la réunion tenue à Bruxelles, le 27 février 1985," folder "Allègement des contrôles aux Frontières, réunion du 27 fév. 1985 à Bruxelles," box 5 "Mouvement," MEAE.

73. "Report from the Ad Hoc Committee on a People's Europe to the European Council, Brussels," March 29 and 30, 1985, in *Bulletin of the European Communities*, supplement 7 / 85, 9–14.

74. Basil de Ferranti to James Dooge, February 5, 1985, box 12463, shelf 203 "Grenzkontrollen," PA.

75. "Conclusions de la réunion," 2. See Fontainebleau conclusions, 3.

76. "Conclusions de la réunion," 3. On Schengen as a boon for travelers, see Jarausch, *Out of Ashes*, 523.

77. "Conclusions de la réunion," 3.

78. "Demandeurs d'asile en RFA," Fiche Télégraphique à M. Anglès, February 20, 1985, folder "Allègement des contrôles aux frontières: Négociations franco-allemandes," box 2 "Coordination," MEAE.

79. "Demandeurs d'asile en RFA."

80. "Juxtaposition des textes du 'Mémorandum Benelux.'"

81. "Juxtaposition des textes du 'Mémorandum Benelux.'"

82. "Juxtaposition des textes du 'Mémorandum Benelux'"; "Note aux membres du Conseil de l'Union économique, Conseil de l'Union économique," February 5, 1985, binder 1a BNL, Council Archives; Jean-Claude Prevel, "Message pour l'Ambassadeur Représentant Permanent de la France auprès des Communautés Européennes," May 28, 1985, folder "Marché Intérieur: Session du 10 juin 1985," box 349 "Secrétaire d'État auprès du Mre Chargé des Affaires Européennes: Mme Catherine Lalumière, 7 décembre 1984–17 mars 1986" (hereafter "Lalumière Papers"), MEAE. On the disjuncture between human flows and capital flows, see Barry and Goodin, eds., *Free Movement*.

83. Jean-Paul Anglès, "Allègement des contrôles aux frontières: Réunion à Paris le 12 mars 1985 du 'Groupe Central de Négociation,'" March 7, 1985, 1–5, binder 1a BNL, Council Archives.

84. Point 3.b, "Du Projet d'Ordre du Jour de la Réunion du Comité de Direction du 15 Avril 1985, Note au Comité de direction de l'Union économique, Union Économique Benelux," April 10, 1985, binder 1a BNL, Council Archives.

85. ChBk to AA, "Abschluss eines Abkommens zum Abbau von Grenzkontrollen zwischen der Bundesrepublik Deutschland, Frankreich und den Benelux-Staaten," May 3, 1985, 1, 2, file 505.MV 820 "Staatsvertrag über die Verlegung der Personenkontrollen an die Außengrenzen" (hereafter "Staatsvertrag"), PA; "Note à l'attention de Monsieur Jean-Paul Anglès," May 7, 1985, folder "Marché Intérieur: Session du 10 juin 1985," box 349 "Lalumière Papers," MEAE.

86. ChBk, ref. 211, "Verhandlungen D-F-Beneluks über Abbau der Grenzkontrollen," May 17, 1985, 2, 3, file 505.MV 820 "Staatsvertrag," PA.

87. ChBk, ref. 211, "Verhandlungen D-F-Beneluks über Abbau der Grenzkontrollen."

88. Ruud Lubbers to Helmut Kohl, May 31, 1985, file 505.MV 820 "Staatsvertrag," PA.

89. "Note à l'attention de Monsieur Jean-Paul Anglès."

90. "Ambassade van het Koninkrijk der Nederlanden, Paris," June 3, 1985, folder "Accord de Schengen à Cinq: Ratification par les Pays-Bas et publication (1985–86)," box 2 "Coordination," MEAE.

91. "Conversation entre l'ambassadeur du Luxembourg à Paris le 28 mai 1985," May 28, 1985, folder "Accord de Schengen à Cinq: Ratification par les Pays-Bas et publication (1985–86)," box 2 "Coordination," MEAE.

92. "Unterzeichnung des Abkommens," June 10, 1985.

93. "Unterzeichnung des Abkommens," June 10, 1985.

94. Discours Goebbels.

95. Lalumière Oral History

96. Goebbels Oral History.

97. Schengen Agreement, preamble.

98. Schengen Agreement, art. 32, preamble, art. 10.

99. Schengen Agreement, arts. 17, 13, 2, 4–5, 30.

100. Schengen Agreement, art. 2, 3.

101. Schengen Agreement, art. 11, 13, 15, 26, 22, 11.

102. Schengen Agreement, art. 24.

103. Schengen Agreement, art. 21(b).

104. Schengen Agreement, art. 25, 9.

105. Schengen Agreement, preamble, art. 2, 4, 6, 9, 17, 19, 21.

106. Rome Treaty, art. 48.

107. UDHR, art. 13.

108. Protocol no. 4, art. 2.

109. Schengen Agreement, preamble.

110. Lalumière Oral History.

111. Schengen Agreement, arts. 2, 17, 19.

112. Not just the 1985 treaty but also the 1990 convention implementing its terms remained largely silent on the issue of residence, a right of EU citizenship later enshrined by the 1992 Maastricht Treaty; see Maastricht Treaty, art. 8a.

113. Schengen Agreement, preamble.

114. Schengen Agreement, preamble.

115. Schengen Agreement, preamble.

116. Schengen Agreement, arts 20, 3, 20.

117. Schengen Agreement, art. 7.

118. Schengen Agreement, art. 29.

119. Schengen Agreement, art. 17, 18.

120. Anglès, "Réunion à Paris le 12 mars 1985."

121. "Projet d'accord à caractère confidentiel complémentaire à l'accord entre les gouvernements des États de l'Union Économique Benelux, de la République fédéral d'Allemagne et de la République française relative à la suppression graduelle des contrôles aux frontières communes," June 4, 1985, binder 1b BNL, Council Archives.

122. E. Cazimajou, "Accord de Schengen," note à l'attention du Cabinet du Ministre des affaires européennes, November 4, 1988, 4, folder "Lettre de M. Joxe (3 nov. 88)," box 5 "Coordination," MEAE.

123. "Projet d'accord à caractère confidentiel."

124. "Liste commune des pays, soumis à l'obligation du visa," note du Secrétariat général, August 28, 1990, folder "Schengen: Deuxième Semestre 1990," box 22 "Mouvement," MEAE. See Lebovics, *Bringing the Empire Back Home*, 59, 139, 273.

125. "Contrôles groupés aux postes juxtaposés: État de la situation, Annexe, Conclusions de la réunion du 12 décembre 1985, Avant-projet," November 29, 1985, box 17318, shelf 284 "Grenzkontrollen," PA.

126. "Fünf EG-Staaten unterzeichnen Grenzerleichterungs-Abkommen," *Süddeutsche Zeitung*, June 15–17, 1985; "Benelux-France-Allemagne: Frontières souriantes," *Le Soir*, June 14, 1985.

127. "Vandaag begin versoepeling grenscontrole," *Nieuwsblad van het Noorden*, June 15, 1985.

128. Gravier Oral History.

129. Eich Oral History.

130. Roger Deville, interview with the author, August 16, 2023 (hereafter Deville Oral History).

131. Van Hyfte Oral History.

132. Johann Wolfgang von Goethe, "The Experiment as Mediator of Object and Subject," *Nature Institute* (Fall 2010): 19–23. Victor Hugo, "The Schengen Castle" [1871], MNAHA, accessed October 25, 2021, https://collections.mnaha.lu/object /iiiilia24720/.

133. Maastricht Treaty, art. 8a.

134. Hreblay, *Libre circulation*, 31.

135. Waldemar Schreckenberger, "Von den Schengener Abkommen zu einer gemeinsamen Innen- und Justizpolitik (Die Dritte Säule)," *Verwaltungs-Archiv* 88, no. 3 (1997): 401.

136. "Rede des Bundeskanzlers, Dr. Helmut Kohl, vor dem Deutschen Bundestag am 27. Juni 1985 über die Zielsetzungen der Europapolitik der Bundesregierung," *Bulletin der Bundesregierung* 28, no. 75 (June 1985): 658, 662.

Chapter 3. A Return to the Moselle River

1. Convention implementing the Schengen Agreement of 14 June 1985 between the government of the States of the Benelux Economic Union, the Federal Republic of Germany and the French Republic on the gradual abolition of checks at their common borders, June 19, 1990, art. 29, OJ (L. 239), 22.09.2000, 19–62 (hereafter Schengen Convention).

2. See Renée Dedecker, "L'Asile et la libre circulation des personnes dans l'accord de Schengen," *Courrier hebdomadaire du CRISP* 8, no. 1393–94 (1993): 1–58.

3. Piet Dankert, "Discours de Piet Dankert sur la convention d'application de l'accord de Schengen," *Bulletin de documentation du Service Information et Presse, Ministère d'État*, no. 3 (June 19, 1990). On Schengen as laboratory, see Marie-Claire

Caloz-Tschopp, Micheline Fontolliet-Honoré, and Lode Van Outrive, *Europe: Montrez Patte Blanche!: Les Nouvelles Frontières du "Laboratoire Schengen"* (Geneva, 1993). Only the Belgian Paul de Keersmaeker had also signed the 1985 accord. The other signatories—government ministers and state secretaries for foreign affairs—were Edith Cresson of France; Lutz Stavenhagen of West Germany; Georges Wohlfart of Luxembourg; and Aad Kosto of the Netherlands. Because the Netherlands oversaw the central negotiating group in June 1990, Dankert also signed the convention. An Italian ambassador represented his country's bid for accession.

4. Dankert, "Discours de Piet Dankert"; "Moselortschaft Schengen geht in die EG-Geschichte ein," *Luxemburger Wort*, June 20, 1990; and see "Grenzen open? Niet voor 1992," *Nieuwsblad van het Noorden*, June 19, 1990; "L'Europe sans frontières en pointillé," *Le Monde*, June 20, 1990. On divisions concerning intergovernmental method and asylum policy, see "Asielakkoord EG tegen wens Kamer getekend," *Leeuwarder Courant*, June 16, 1990.

5. On the Single European Act and the path to Maastricht, see Jarausch, *Out of Ashes*, 784.

6. "Accord de Schengen: Satisfaction du Vice-président Bangemann," Commission des Communautés Européennes, November 14, 1989, 2, François Lamoureux Fonds 595, HAEU.

7. It is still the case, as Didier Bigo wrote of Schengen in 2005, that little attention has been directed to "the debate of the eighties and how all these norms were set up." Didier Bigo, "Frontier Controls in the European Union: Who Is in Control?," in *Controlling Frontiers: Free Movement into and within Europe*, ed. Didier Bigo and Elspeth Guild (Aldershot, UK, 2005), 66.

8. "Asielakkoord EG tegen wens Kamer getekend"; "Grenzen open? Niet voor 1992."

9. "Moselortschaft Schengen geht in die EG-Geschichte ein."

10. Hreblay, *Libre circulation*, 11.

11. "L'Europe sans frontières en pointillé," *Le Monde*, June 20, 1990.

12. Joseph Lorent, "Moselortschaft Schengen geht in die EG-Geschichte ein," *Luxemburger Wort*, June 20, 1990.

13. "5 Western European Countries to Establish a Common Border," *New York Times*, June 20, 1990; "5 EC Nations Agree on Common-Border Rules," *Washington Post*, June 20, 1990.

14. "L'Europe sans frontières en pointillé."

15. "L'Europe sans frontières est née . . . sur le papier," *Le Soir*, June 20, 1990.

16. Goebbels Oral History.

17. In West Germany, the Christian Democratic Union; in Belgium, the Christian People's Party; in Luxembourg, the Christian Social People's Party; in the Netherlands, the Christian Democratic Appeal.

18. Samy Cohen, "La Diplomatie française dans la cohabitation," *Esprit*, June 2000, 45–60; Michelle Hale Williams, *The Impact of Radical Right-Wing Parties in West European Democracies* (New York, 2006), 84; Paoli, "France and the Origins of Schengen," 263, 266–71; Alistair Cole, "The French Socialists," in *Political Parties and the European Union*, ed. John Gaffney (London, 2002), 731–85.

19. See Christopher A. Molnar, "'Greetings from the Apocalypse': Race, Migration, and Fear after German Reunification," *Central European History* 54, no. 3 (September 2021): 496–97; Rita Chin, *The Guest Worker Question in Postwar Germany* (New York, 2007), 144–57.

20. "Sommet occidental antiterroriste à Paris," *Le Figaro*, May 28, 1987; Franck Johannes, "Accord de cooperation antiterroriste: L'Espagne, après l'Italie et l'Allemagne," *Le Matin*, May 31, 1987.

21. François Lamoureux, "Accord de Schengen," note pour le Président, January 25, 1989, 3, François Lamoureux Fonds 194, HAEU.

22. L. Geysemans to Monsieur M. Beaux, December 22, 1986, Binder 2 "Schengen overleg correspondentie, 1984–1987," Council Archives; "Accord de Schengen: Groupe centrale de négociation des 2 et 3 mai 1989," May 2–3, 1989, folder "Schengen: Groupe Central de Négociation, Paris 2–3 mai 89," box 6 "Coordination," MEAE. See also Antonio Cruz, *An Insight into Schengen, Trevi and Other European Governmental Bodies*, briefing paper 1 (Brussels, 1990), 4.

23. *Completing the Internal Market: White Paper*, provisions 4, 1, 7, 18, 58.

24. "Rapport de la Commission sur la mise en œuvre d'une Union des passeports," *Bulletin des Communautés européennes* 7, no. 75 (Luxembourg: Office des publications officielles des Communautés européennes, July 3, 1975), 2.

25. *Completing the Internal Market: White Paper*, provisions 58, 94, 24.

26. *Completing the Internal Market: White Paper*, 25, 8, 25, 219, 220, 221, 25.

27. *Completing the Internal Market: White Paper*, 26, 27.

28. *Germany, France, Netherlands, Denmark and United Kingdom v. Commission*, Judgment of the Court, (1987) ECR., 3248 (hereafter *Germany v. Commission*).

29. *Germany v. Commission*, 3248.

30. *Germany v. Commission*, 3248.

31. *Germany v. Commission*, 3253.

32. Report for the hearing delivered in Joined Cases 281, 283 to 285 and 287 / 85 (1987) ECR 3212.

33. *Germany v. Commission*, 3252.

34. Alexander Mackenzie Stuart presided over the court in both cases.

35. *Germany v. Commission*, 3252.

36. *Germany v. Commission*, 3253.

37. Single European Act, art. 13, February 1986, 25 ILM. 503 (1986).

38. "Importance de l'accord de Schengen pour la Communauté," 1, annexed to "Accord de Schengen: Satisfaction du Vice-président Bangemann," Commission des Communautés Européennes, November 14, 1989, François Lamoureux Fonds 595, HAEU.

39. Single European Act, preamble, art. 13, 17, 30 (6a).

40. Single European Act, art. 18, "Political Declaration by the Governments of the Member States on the Free Movement of Persons." On the preference for intergovernmental institutions, such as the Council of Ministers, rather than supranational ones, see Andrew Moravcsik, "Negotiating the Single European Act: National Interests and

Conventional Statecraft in the European Community," *International Organization* 45, no. 1 (1991): 27.

41. Jean de Ruyt, *Le Leadership dans l'Union Européenne* (Louvain, 2015), 31; Gérard Bossuat, *Faire l'Europe sans Défaire la France: 60 Ans de Politique d'Unité Européenne des Gouvernements et des Présidents de la République Française, 1943–2003* (Brussels, 2005), 168.

42. François Lamoureux, "Accord de Schengen," Commission des Communautés Européennes, Le Cabinet du Président, January 22, 1990, 2, François Lamoureux Fonds 203, HAEU.

43. Pierre de Boissieu, "Interprétation de l'Acte Unique en ce qui concerne la circulation des étrangers," January 12, 1989, 1, folder "Schengen, Groupe Central de Négociation, 1 mars 1989," box 6 "Coordination," MEAE.

44. "Facilitation des contrôles et formalités applicables aux citoyens des États membres lors du franchissement des frontières intracommunautaires," Rapport de la Présidence du Comité des Représentants Permanents au Conseil, June 5, 1985, Marché Intérieur, box 349 "Lalumière Papers," MEAE.

45. De Boissieu, "Interprétation de l'Acte Unique," 1. On community border-crossing rules, see *Commission of the European Communities v. Kingdom of the Netherlands*, Case C-68 / 89, May 30, 1991; John Morijn, "Personal Conviction and Strategic Litigation in Wijsenbeek," in *EU Law Stories: Contextual and Critical Histories of European Jurisprudence*, ed. Fernanda Nicola and Bill Davies (Cambridge, UK, 2017), 178–200; Elspeth Guild, Steve Peers and Jonathan Tomkin, *The EU Citizenship Directive: A Commentary* (Oxford, 2014), 99.

46. "Un Pas vers l'Europe des citoyens," March 1989, 3–4, folder "Schengen: Oct. 86–déc. 1989," box 21 "Mouvement," MEAE.

47. Communiqué de presse, June 14, 1988, folder "Schengen: GCN Bonn, 26 oct. 1988," box 3 "Mouvement," MEAE.

48. Émile Cazimajou, "Intervention de M. l'Ambassadeur Cazimajou lors de la réunion du groupe des coordonnateurs," April 12, 1989, 2, 9, 14, François Lamoureux Fonds 595, HAEU.

49. F. Roelants to E. Cazimajou, "Exécution de l'accord de Schengen 1987–1990," December 3, 1987, 2, Binder 2 "Schengen overleg correspondentie, 1984–1987," Council Archives.

50. Émile Cazimajou, "Accord de Schengen," Note à l'attention du Cabinet du Ministre des affaires européennes, November 4, 1988, 3, folder "Lettre de M. Joxe (3 nov. 88)," box 5 "Coordination," MEAE.

51. *Refugee Appeal No.1 / 92 Re SA*, New Zealand, Refugee Status Appeals Authority, April 30, 1992.

52. "Exécution de l'Accord Benelux-France-Allemagne," June 26, 1985, 1–5, binder 1b BNL, Council Archives; "Rapport sur l'état des travaux du groupe de travail 'Police et sécurité,'" July 9, 1986, Binder 2 "Schengen overleg correspondentie, 1984–1987," Council Archives; "Conclusions de la réunion du 12 décembre 1985," November 29, 1985 [*sic*], 5, box 17318, shelf 284 "Grenzkontrollen," PA; "Programme de travail, groupe de travail IV," July 7, 1987, 1, Binder 2 "Schengen overleg correspondentie, 1984–1987," Council

Archives; "Conclusions de la réunion mixte du Sous-Groupe 3 'immigration clandestine' du groupe de travail I 'Police et sécurité' et du Comité de Rédaction I du groupe de travail II 'Circulation des Personnes,'" October 28, 1987, folder "GCN Bonn le 23 nov. 87," box 6 "Coordination," MEAE; Cruz, *Insight into Schengen*, 4.

53. "Conclusions de la réunion tenue à Bonn le 2 février 1987, groupe de travail IV," February 13, 1987, 2, Binder 2 "Schengen overleg correspondentie, 1984–1987," Council Archives; "Renforcement des contrôles à l'égard des ressortissants de pays sensibles en matière d'immigration irrégulière," Le Ministre de l'Intérieur et de la Décentralisation à Madame et Messieurs les Préfets, Commissaires de la République, November 12, 1985, 1, BNL-D-F, C-OJ-PV NOTES 1985, Council Archives.

54. "Renforcement des contrôles," 1. On continued reference to undesirables, including the "formulation of a common list of undesirable persons," see "Rapport au groupe de travail II 'Circulations des personnes,'" November 19, 1987, 2, folder "GCN Bonn le 23 nov. 87," box 6 "Coordination," MEAE. And see "Conclusions de la reunion tenue à Bruxelles le 20 avril 1988," April 25, 1988, 4, SCH / C 1985–1988 C-OJ-PV, Council Archives.

55. "Délivrance de visas à des ressortissants de pays tiers, qui posent des problèmes de sécurité pour les États du Benelux, la France et la République fédérale d'Allemagne," Concertation entre les pays du Benelux, la R.F.A et la République française, Groupe de Travail II: Circulation des personnes, November 28, 1985, BNL-D-F, C-OJ-PV NOTES 1985, Council Archives.

56. "Note de la délégation allemande," November 12, 1985, BNL-D-F, C-OJ-PV NOTES 1985, Council Archives.

57. Dr. Redies, "Abbau der Grenzkontrollen zwischen Frankreich, den Benelux Staaten und der Bundesrepublik Deutschland," April 1, 1986, box 17318, shelf 284, "Grenzkontrollen," PA.

58. "Note de la délégation du Benelux, Secret," November 4, 1985, box 40686, shelf 544 "Abbau Grenzformalitäten, Abkommen 'Schengen,'" PA.

59. Pierre Joxe, "Accord de Schengen: Préparation d'un avant projet de convention complémentaire," November 3, 1988, 2, folder "Lettre de M. Joxe (3 nov. 88)," box 5 "Coordination," MEAE.

60. E. Cazimajou, "Accord de Schengen: État des travaux de mise en œuvre de l'Accord", February 20, 1989, 4, 5, folder "Schengen: Oct. 86—déc. 1989," box 21 "Mouvement," MEAE.

61. "Accord de Schengen: Réunion du 6 octobre 1986 à Luxembourg," October 10, 1986, 2, 3, folder "Schengen: Oct. 86—déc. 1989," box 21 "Mouvement," MEAE.

62. Émile Cazimajou, "Accord de Schengen," November 24, 1987, 3, folder "GCN Bonn le 23 nov. 87," box 6 "Coordination," MEAE; "Droit de séjour des étrangers," Annexe, "Rapport au groupe de travail II 'Circulation des personnes,'" November 19, 1987, folder "GCN Bonn le 23 nov. 87," box 6 "Coordination," MEAE.

63. "Réunion des ministres et secrétaires d'état responsables de l'accord de Schengen," October 6, 1986, folder "Schengen: Oct. 86—déc. 1989," box 21 "Mouvement," MEAE; William Tuohy, "Asylum Seekers: W. Germany Swamped by Refugees," *Los Angeles Times*, August 2, 1986.

64. Cazimajou, "Accord de Schengen." On the German nation's return "with a vengeance," see Andreas Huyssen, "Nation, Race, and Immigration: German Identities after Unification," *Discourse* 16, no. 3 (Spring 1994): 8.

65. "Robert Goebbels à Son Excellence Monsieur l'Ambassadeur de l'Italie à Luxembourg," July 6, 1987, Binder 2 "Schengen overleg correspondentie, 1984–1987," Council Archives. Discussions with Italy began in July 1985. See "Allègement des contrôles aux frontières entre la France et l'Italie," July 25, 1985 and "Document de travail de la délégation française," July 25, 1985, folder "Allègement des contrôles aux frontières, Projet d'accord," box 6 "Mouvement," MEAE. See Ruben Zaiotti, "The Italo-French Row over Schengen, Critical Junctures, and the Future of Europe's Border Regime," *Journal of Borderlands Studies* 28, no. 3 (2013): 337–54; Simone Paoli, "The Schengen Agreements and their Impact on Euro-Mediterranean Relations: The Case of Italy and the Maghreb," *Journal of European Integration History* 21, no. 1 (2015): 139–40.

66. "Robert Goebbels à Son Excellence Monsieur l'Ambassadeur de l'Italie à Luxembourg."

67. "Allègement des contrôles aux frontières entre la France et l'Italie"; "Document de travail de la délégation française."

68. Zaiotti, "Italo-French Row," 344–45. See also Ruben Zaiotti, "Chronic Anxiety: Schengen and the Fear of Enlargement," in *The EU and the Eurozone Crisis: Policy Challenges and Strategic Choices*, ed. Finn Laursen (Farnham, UK, 2013), 162. On the rebuke of Italy, see Paoli, "Schengen Agreements," 132, 137.

69. L. Geysemans to Monsieur M. Beaux, December 22, 1986.

70. "Rapport au groupe de travail II 'Circulation des Personnes,'" Annexe, 2, November 19, 1987, folder "GCN Bonn le 23 nov. 87," box 6 "Coordination," MEAE.

71. "Renforcement des contrôles à l'égard des ressortissants de pays sensibles en matière d'immigration irrégulière."

72. "Procès-verbal de la réunion du Groupe de Travail II 'Circulation des personnes,'" February 10, 1987, folder "Négociation à cinq: Groupe de Travail 2 (visas immigration), 1985–1987," box 1 "Coordination," MEAE.

73. "Inventaire des conditions indispensables pour l'abolition des contrôles aux frontières communes," October 20, 1988, folder "Lettre de M. Joxe (3 nov. 88)," box 5 "Coordination," MEAE.

74. Joxe, "Accord de Schengen: Préparation d'un avant projet de convention complémentaire," 2. See Paoli, "France and the Origins of Schengen," 270–71.

75. Émile Cazimajou, "Accord de Schengen: Différend avec le Ministre de l'Intérieur," 3, 4, 5, folder "Joxe," box 5 "Coordination," MEAE; "Intervention de M. Pierre Joxe," May 29, 1989, 1, 9, 10, folder "Schengen: Débat français, 1986–1989," box 5 "Coordination," MEAE.

76. Cazimajou, "Accord de Schengen," 7.

77. "Discours de M. Korthals Altes, minister néerlandais de la Justice," March 16, 1989, 7, folder "Schengen: Groupe Central de Négociation, Paris 2–3 mai 89," box 6 "Coordination," MEAE.

78. "Intervention de M. Pierre Joxe," 41–42.

79. "Libre circulation des personnes en Europe," April 17, 1989, folder "Réunion Interministérielle: Préparatoire au Conseil Restreint du 19 avril 1989," box 8 "Mouvement," MEAE.

80. "Négociation de Schengen: Les points à négocier au niveau ministérial," April 19, 1989, folder "Réunion Interministérielle: Préparatoire au Conseil Restreint du 19 avril 1989," box 8 "Mouvement," MEAE; Isabelle Renouard, "Projet de convention complémentaire à l'accord de Schengen relative à la circulation des personnes: Statut de Berlin," April 19, 1989, folder "Schengen: Groupe Central de Négociation, Paris 2–3 mai 89," box 6 "Coordination," MEAE.

81. European Consultation on Refugees and Exiles, ed., *Refugee Policy in a Unifying Europe: Seminar Held in Zeist* (London, 1989), 4, 6.

82. Cazimajou, "Intervention de M. l'Ambassadeur Cazimajou lors de la réunion du groupe des coordonnateurs," 6, 12.

83. "Relations franco-allemandes et questions relatives au droit d'asile," April 18, 1989, 1–3, folder "Réunion Interministérielle: Préparatoire au Conseil Restreint du 19 avril 1989," box 8 "Mouvement," MEAE. See Jean Rossetto, "Le Droit d'asile en Europe—Évolution contemporaine," *Annuaire Français de Droit International* 39 (1993): 923; Loescher, "European Community and Refugees."

84. "Relations franco-allemandes," 4.

85. "Relations franco-allemandes," 4.

86. "Relations franco-allemandes," 1.

87. Paul Betts, "1989 revolutions, 25 years on," *OUP Blog* (blog), November 6, 2014, https://blog.oup.com/2014/11/1989-velvet-revolutions-berlin-wall/.

88. See Robert English, *Russia and the Idea of the West: Gorbachev, Intellectuals, and the End of the Cold War* (New York, 2000); David Childs, *The Fall of the GDR: Germany's Road to Unity* (London, 2001); Eric Solsten, ed., *Germany: A Country Study*, 3rd ed. (Washington, DC, 1995), 116.

89. Schengen Agreement, art. 29.

90. See Basic Law for the Federal Republic of Germany (1949), art. 16a.

91. Hanspeter Hellbeck, "Asylantenfrage," July 28, 1986, 3–4, 10, box 12463, shelf 203 "Grenzkontrollen für Personen, Waren, Kapital," PA. See "Hannspeter Hellbeck," available at Munzinger, accessed March 28, 2024, https://www.munzinger.de/search/go/document.jsp?id=00000018516.

92. "Réunion des ministres et secrétaires d'état chargés de l'exécution de l'accord de Schengen du 17 Décembre 1987 à Berlin," December 17, 1987, folder "Schengen: Oct. 86—déc. 1989," box 21 "Mouvement," MEAE.

93. Renouard, "Projet de convention complémentaire à l'accord de Schengen relative à la circulation des personnes: Statut de Berlin"; "Droit de séjour des étrangers," Annexe, "Rapport au groupe de travail II 'Circulation des personnes,'" November 19, 1987, folder "GCN Bonn le 23 nov. 87," box 6 "Coordination," MEAE.

94. See Charles S. Maier, *Dissolution: The Crisis of Communism and the End of East Germany* (Princeton, NJ: 1999), 108–67; Childs, *Fall of the GDR*, 64–91; Solsten, ed., *Germany*, 113–33; Hans-Hermann Hertle, "The Fall of the Wall: The Unintended

Self-Dissolution of East Germany's Ruling Regime," *Cold War International History Project Bulletin* 12 / 13 (Fall / Winter 2001): 131–64.

95. Mary Elise Sarotte, *The Collapse: The Accidental Opening of the Berlin Wall* (New York, 2014), 167; Lewis J. Edinger, *From Bonn to Berlin: German Politics in Transition* (New York, 1998), 13.

96. "Accord de Schengen: 'Question de Berlin,'" December 4, 1989, folder "GCN Bruxelles 4–6 déc. 1989," box 4 "Mouvement," MEAE. On the Bonn Group, see Petri Hakkarainen, *A State of Pace in Europe: West Germany and the CSCE, 1966–1975* (New York, 2011), 5, 85–99, 124, 171–73, 226–30.

97. Adrian Fortescue, "Note à M. Lamy," December 7, 1989, François Lamoureux Fonds 595, HAEU. See "Profile: Adrian Fortescue," *Politico*, October 10, 2001.

98. "Note de la Présidence allemande," December 11, 1989, and E. Cazimajou, "A propos des déclarations de la RFA au sujet de la RDA . . . ," December 12, 1989, folder "Schengen: Groupe Central Négociation, 13 déc. 1989," box 4 "Mouvement," MEAE.

99. Alphonse Berns to Émile Cazimajou, December 12, 1989, 4–6, folder "Schengen: Groupe Central Négociation, 13 déc. 1989," box 4 "Mouvement," MEAE. On Léa Linster, see Ulf Meyer zu Kueingdorf, ed., *Mal was leichtes—Das Frauen-Kochbuch: 33 x eine Frau mit Genuss* (Niedernhausen, 2010), 96.

100. F. Braun, "Note à l'attention de M. Brunner et M. Lamy," Commission des Communautés Européennes, December 18, 1989, François Lamoureux Fonds 595, HAEU.

101. Jan de Ceuster, "Compte-rendu de Réunion," December 15, 1989, François Lamoureux Fonds 195, HAEU; E. Cazimajou, "Accord de Schengen: Report de la signature de la Convention d'application," December 19, 1989, folder "Schengen: Groupe Central Négociation, 13 déc. 1989," box 4 "Mouvement," MEAE.

102. E. Cazimajou, "Accord de Schengen: Échec de la négociation relative à la convention d'application de l'accord," December 18, 1989, folder "Schengen: Groupe Central Négociation, 13 déc. 1989," box 4 "Mouvement," MEAE; Cazimajou, "Accord de Schengen: Report de la signature de la Convention d'application." On free travel as a demand of GDR activists and the dilemmas created by the movement of East Germans into the West, see Jarausch, *Out of Ashes*, 679–81. And see Stephen R. Burant, ed., *East Germany: A Country Study* (Washington, DC, 1988), xxi–xxii.

103. Cazimajou, "Accord de Schengen: Échec de la négociation"; Cazimajou, "Accord de Schengen: Report de la signature de la Convention d'application." See "L'Europe sans frontières est née."

104. "Déclaration commune des ministres et secrétaires d'état réunis à Schengen le 15 décembre 1989," folder "Schengen: Groupe Central Négociation, 13 déc. 1989," box 4 "Mouvement," MEAE; Cruz, *Insight into Schengen*, 6.

105. Cazimajou, "Accord de Schengen: Échec de la négociation."

106. Cazimajou, "Accord de Schengen: Échec de la négociation."

107. Cazimajou, "Accord de Schengen: Report de la signature de la Convention d'application." See Jean Quatremer, "L'Europe sans frontières trébuche a Schengen," *Le Monde*, December 15, 1989.

108. Quatremer, "L'Europe sans frontières"; "Coup de tonnerre sur les frontières," *Le Monde*, December 15, 1989.

109. Peter Zudeick, "Im Eimer," *Deutsches Allgemeines Sonntagsblatt*, September 1989.

110. Émile Cazimajou, "La presse et l'accord de Schengen," May 16, 1989, 1, folder "Schengen: Presse (1988–89)," box 5 "Coordination," MEAE.

111. See *Der Spiegel* coverage: "DDR-Flüchtlinge: Umfassender Beistand," *Der Spiegel*, September 10, 1989; "Eine Zeit geht zu Ende," *Der Spiegel*, September 3, 1989; "Berlin: Mompers Landsuche in der DDR," *Der Spiegel*, September 24, 1989; "Berlin— gefährlich für die Sache des Friedens," *Der Spiegel*, October 1, 1989; "Berlin—Prüfstein für unseren Mut," *Der Spiegel*, October 8, 1989; "Dann wird die Mauer fallen," *Der Spiegel*, October 15, 1989; "Berlin: Leben auf Parkbänken," *Der Spiegel*, October 22, 1989; "Es ist eine Revolution," *Der Spiegel*, November 5, 1989.

112. "Big Brother ersetzt den Zöllner," *Der Spiegel*, July 9, 1989.

113. "Ostblock—Sieg der Vernunft," *Der Spiegel*, October 8, 1989; "Magisches Datum," *Der Spiegel*, October 8, 1989.

114. "L'Accord de Schengen n'est plus secret," *Avenir et Liberté*, September 1989, Folder "Schengen, Presse (1988–89)," box 5 "Coordination," MEAE.

115. "Des milliers d'étrangers abusent du droit d'asile," *Présent*, November 16, 1989; Jeanne Smits, "Dans le brouillard du 'territoire Schengen,'" *Présent*, November 16, 1989. See Patrick Weil, "Immigration and the Rise of Racism in France: The Contradictions in Mitterrand's Policies," *French Politics and Society* 9, no. 3 / 4 (Summer / Fall 1991): 82–100; Pierre-André Taguieff and Patrick Weil "'Immigration,' fait national et 'citoyenneté,'" *Esprit*, May 1990, 87–102. On *Présent*, see James Shields, *The Extreme Right in France: From Pétain to Le Pen* (London, 2007), 181, 221.

116. "Coup de tonnerre sur les frontières."

117. Quatremer, "L'Europe sans frontières."

118. Quatremer, "L'Europe sans frontières."

119. See Maier, *Dissolution*, 195–214; Konrad H. Jarausch, *The Rush to German Unity* (New York, 1994), 126–49.

120. "Note du Président de la délégation allemande aux concertations Schengen," March 13, 1990, 2, folder "Protection des données," box 23 "Mouvement," MEAE. See also "Lettre du président de la délégation de la République Fédérale d'Allemagne au secrétaire général de l'Union Économique Benelux," March 22, 1990, folder "Protection des données," box 23 "Mouvement," MEAE.

121. "Note du président de la délégation allemande aux concertations Schengen," 2, 3.

122. Mr. Powell to Mr. Wall, January 20, 1990, in *German Unification 1989–90: Documents on British Policy Overseas*, ed. Patrick Salmon, Keith Hamilton, and Stephen Robert Twigge, series 3, vol. 7 (London, 2011), 215–18. See also Konrad H. Jarausch, *After Hitler: Recivilizing Germans, 1945–1949*, trans. Brandon Hunziker (New York, 2006), 224.

123. "Note du président de la délégation allemande aux concertations Schengen," 2.

124. Cruz, *Insight into Schengen*, 6–8.

125. "Chronicle 13 June 1990," Chronik der Mauer, accessed February 12, 2019, http://www.chronik-der-mauer.de/en/chronicle/_year1990/_month6/?moc=1.

126. Schengen Convention, preamble. Only a chapter on "aliens," detailing border-crossing rules, used the phrase "may move freely," restricted by visa requirements. See art. 19, 20.

127. Schengen Convention, declaration on the scope of the convention.

128. Schengen Agreement, preamble.

129. Schengen Convention, art. 1.

130. Schengen Convention, chapter 1, art. 2.

131. Schengen Convention, art. 10, 20, 29, 41, 5, 23, 109, 114.

132. Schengen Convention, title VII, art. 6. On the supremacy of Community law, see Adrian Fortescue, "Schengen Ministerial Meeting: Bonn, 13 November 1989," note to Mr. Bangemann, November 10, 1989, 3, François Lamoureux Fonds 595, HAEU.

133. Schengen Convention, art. 6, 41, 95.

134. Schengen Convention, art. 5, 9, 10. See Bigo and Guild, *Mise à l'Écart des Étrangers*.

135. Schengen Convention, art. 120, 121, joint declaration on art. 121, art. 71, 79, 80, 124, 120.

136. Schengen Convention, art. 139, joint declaration on art. 139, art. 140.

137. Schengen Convention, art. 22, 3, 4, 27, 41, 117. On the Dutch objection, see "Note du président de la délégation allemande aux concertations Schengen"; "Lettre du président de la délégation de la République Fédérale d'Allemagne au secrétaire général de l'Union Économique Benelux." On advancing accession, see "Accord de Schengen: Satisfaction du Vice-président Bangemann."

138. Schengen Convention, joint declaration on national asylum policies; "Conclusions, Session du Conseil Européen, Strasbourg, 8 et 9 décembre 1989," *Conclusions des Sessions Du Conseil Européen (1975–1990)*, 1989, 346, 348–49, available at European Council, accessed November 19, 2023, https://www.consilium.europa.eu/media/20577/1989_d_cembre_-_strasbourg__fr_.pdf.

139. On Schengen and the rule of first entry, see "Présentation du projet de convention determinant l'état responsable de l'examen d'une demande d'asile presentée dans un état membre des Communautées Européennes," n.d., folder "Schengen: Oct. 86—déc. 1989," box 21 "Mouvement," MEAE.

140. Schengen Convention, art., 30, 34, 28. See Rossetto, "Le Droit d'asile en Europe," 923–24. A French legislative report deemed the first entry rule the "fundamental aspect" of Schengen's asylum provisions. Paul Masson, "Rapport sur le projet de loi constitutionnelle relatif aux accords internationaux en matière de droit d'asile," Sénat, 1993, 14, François-Mitterrand Library, Bibliothèque nationale de France, Paris (hereafter BNF).

141. Convention Determining the State Responsible for Examining Applications for Asylum Lodged in One of the Member-States of the European Communities, preamble, 15 June 1990, 1997 OJ (C 254) 1 (hereafter Dublin Convention). On the Dublin Convention, see José J. Bolten, "From Schengen to Dublin: The New Frontiers of Refugee Law," in *Schengen: Internationalisation of Central Chapters*

of the Law on Aliens, Refugees, Privacy, Security and the Police, ed. H. Meijers and J.D.M. Steenbergen (Deventer, The Netherlands, 1991), 8–36; Agnès Hurwitz, "The 1990 Dublin Convention: A Comprehensive Assessment," *International Journal of Refugee Law* 11, no. 4 (1999): 646–77.

142. Schengen Convention, art. 29.

143. Committee of Experts for the Promotion of Education and Information in the Field of Human Rights, *Colloquy: "Human Rights without Frontiers"; Strasbourg, 30 November–1 December 1989; Proceedings* (Strasbourg, 1989). On unofficial access to convention draft, see *Colloquy*, 33 n. 14. On the colloquy, see "Appendix II: Conclusions and Recommendations of the Colloquy 'Human Rights without Frontiers,'" *Netherlands Quarterly of Human Rights* 8, no. 1 (March 1990): 85–87. Unlike the European Council and the Council of Ministers, the Council of Europe—the continent's main international institution overseeing human rights—is not part of the European Union.

144. *Colloquy*, 8.

145. *Colloquy*, 26–28.

146. *Colloquy*, 210–13, 49.

147. *Colloquy*, 6.

148. Schengen Convention, "Final Act: Joint Declaration on art. 121, Declaration on Scope of the Convention, Joint Declaration, Declaration by Ministers and State Secretaries."

149. "Convention d'application de l'accord de Schengen," Dossier d'information, Le Ministre délégué chargé des affaires européennes, May 1991, 5, 1, 7, folder "Liste des conventions," box 2b "Mouvement," MEAE.

150. "Convention d'application de l'accord de Schengen," 2. Italy signed an accession agreement on November 27, 1990. On Austria, see "Conclusions de la réunion tenue à Bruxelles le 20 avril 1988," 2.

151. "Aperçu des categories d'étrangers qui présentent un risque du point de vue de l'immigration illégale et de la sécurité nationale," November 4, 1985, box 40686, shelf 544, "Abbau Grenzformalitäten, Abkommen 'Schengen,'" PA.

152. Dankert, "Discours de Piet Dankert."

153. Lorent, "Moselortschaft Schengen."

154. See Didier Bigo, "Europe Passoire et Europe Forteresse: La Sécurisation / Humanitarisation de L'immigration," in *Immigration et Racisme en Europe*, ed. Andrea Rea (Brussels, 1998), 203–41.

Chapter 4. A Problem of Sovereignty

1. "Discussion de deux Projets de Loi devant l'Assemblée nationale, 2e séance du 3 juin 1991," in Tristan Mage, "Schengen: Un Modèle pour la construction européenne," vol. 2, May 1992, 170, BNF (hereafter National Assembly).

2. Henri de Bresson, "Les Contrôles aux frontières disaparaissent dans l'espace Schengen," *Le Monde*, March 25, 1995.

3. On the short twentieth century, see Hobsbawm, *Age of Extremes*. The ratification process has received limited attention in comparative studies of treatymaking; see Alexis Pauly, *Les Accords de Schengen: Abolition des frontières intérieures ou menace pour les libertés publiques?* (Maastricht, 1993); Christoph Hönnige, Sascha Kneip, and Astrid Lorenz, eds., *Verfassungswandel im Mehrebenensystem* (Wiesbadenm 2011); Pierre Michel Eisemann, ed., *L'Intégration du droit international et communautaire dans l'ordre juridique national* (The Hague, 1996).

4. Case no. 91–294 DC figures in existing studies as a straightforward endorsement of Schengen; see Boccardi, *Europe and Refugees*. On later cases testing the convention's specific provisions, see Elspeth Guild, "Adjudicating Schengen: National Judicial Control in France," *European Journal of Migration and Law* 1, no. 4 (1999): 419–39. See also Patrick Gaïa, "Commentaire de la décision du Conseil Constitutionnel no. 91–294 du 25 juillet 1991: Loi autorisant l'approbation de la convention d'application de l'accord de Schengen, du 14 juin 1985," *Revue de la Recherche Juridique* 17, no. 1 (1992): 25–54.

5. "Le Secret de Schengen," *Le Figaro*, May 14, 1989.

6. "Schengen Agreement: Opinion of the Dutch Council of State," *Statewatch*, January 1, 1991, accessed October 21, 2021, https://www.statewatch.org/statewatch-database/schengen-agreement-opinion-of-the-dutch-council-of-state/. See Francesco Cherubini, *Asylum Law in the European Union* (Abingdon, UK, 2015), 172; Zaiotti, *Cultures of Border Control*, 94.

7. Goebbels Oral History.

8. Hubert Blanc, "Schengen: Le Chemin de la libre circulation en Europe," *Revue du Marché Commun et de l' Union européene*, no. 351 (October 1991): 726.

9. "Résolution sur la signature du protocole additionnel à l'accord de Schengen," November 23, 1989, *Journal officiel des Communautés européennes*, in "Rapport fait au nom de la commission de contrôle chargée d'examiner la mise en place et le fonctionnement de la convention d'application de l'accord de Schengen du 14 juin 1985, créée en vertu d'une resolution adoptee par le Sénat le 26 juin 1991," Sénat, December 12, 1991, BNF.

10. "Résolution sur la signature du protocole additionnel à l'accord de Schengen."

11. "Résolution du Parlement européen du 14 mars 1990 sur la libre circulation des personnes dans le marché intérieur," *Journal officiel des Communautés européennes*, in "Rapport fait au nom de la commission de contrôle."

12. "Résolution du Parlement européen du 14 mars 1990 sur la libre circulation des personnes dans le marché intérieur."

13. See "Racism and xenophobia," *Statewatch*, 1991, accessed October 21, 2021, https://www.statewatch.org/statewatch-database/racism-and-xenophobia/.

14. Glynn Ford, *Report Drawn Up on Behalf of the Committee of Inquiry into Racism and Xenophobia on the Findings of the Committee of Inquiry* (Luxembourg, 1991), 129–30, accessed February 1, 2023, https://op.europa.eu/en/publication-detail/-/publication/d8734ae4-921b-487c-9086-2941571e1cf1.

15. Quoted in Antonio Cruz, *Schengen, Ad Hoc Immigration Group and other European Intergovernmental Bodies in View of a Europe without Internal Borders*, prepared for the Churches' Committee for Migrants in Europe, 1993, 5–6.

16. "Intervention de M. Antoine Noël, délégué pour la France du Haut Commissaire des Nations Unies pour les Réfugiés, devant la commission, le 5 juin 1991," Annex no. 1, 447, 494, BNF.

17. *Amnesty International Report 1991* (London, 1991), 18–19.

18. "Convention d'application de l'accord de Schengen: Préoccupations d'Amnesty International," June 1991, Annex no. 2, 497, BNF.

19. Goebbels Oral History.

20. Eric Branca, "Le Secret sur les accords de Schengen," *Valeurs Actuelles*, May 16, 1989.

21. "Le Problème de l'application des 'Accords de Schengen' de 1985 soulevé par le Senateur R.P.R. Paul Masson," *Bulletin Quotidien*, May 16, 1989, 22, François Lamoureux Fonds 595, HAEU.

22. Branca, "Secret sur les accords de Schengen."

23. Yves Daoudal, "Immigrés, terroristes, produits extra-européenns: La France livrée à toutes les invasions," *Présent*, May 18, 1989.

24. Branca, "Secret sur les accords de Schengen."

25. "Intervention de M. Pierre Joxe," 41.

26. "Des Associations s'inquiètent du sort future des demandeurs d'asile," *Le Monde*, April 26, 1989.

27. National Assembly, 170, 341–53. Gilles Paris, "La Construction europénne: Les Sénateurs approuvent les accords de Schengen malgré des inquiétudes sur leurs conséquences," *Le Monde*, June 29, 1991.

28. Blanc, "Schengen," 726.

29. National Assembly, 311, 197, 170.

30. National Assembly, 288, 231.

31. National Assembly, 197, 259, 189, 195, 249.

32. National Assembly, 320, 309, 307, 283, 282.

33. National Assembly, 268, 271.

34. National Assembly, 307–8, 242, 240.

35. On Gaullism and nationalism as "supreme sociological myth," see Sudhir Hazareesingh, *In the Shadow of the General: Modern France and the Myth of De Gaulle* (Oxford, 2012), 10.

36. National Assembly, 241.

37. National Assembly, 287, 274.

38. National Assembly, 327.

39. National Assembly, 267, 309, 158–59.

40. National Assembly, 337, 327.

41. National Assembly, 206, 232.

42. National Assembly, 170, 341; Gilles Paris, "La Construction européenne: Les Sénateurs approuvent les accords de Schengen malgré des inquiétudes sur leurs conséquences," *Le Monde*, June 29, 1991.

43. National Assembly, 341.

44. Xavier de Villepin, "Les Explications," October 22, 1991, 41, in "Rapport fait au nom de la commission de contrôle."

45. De Villepin, "Les Explications," 41.

46. Saisine par 60 députés, June 29, 1991, CC decision No.91-294 DC, 25 July 1991, I.1.

47. Saisine, I.1. See Carl-Ulrik Schierup, Peo Hansen, and Stephen Castles, *Migration, Citizenship, and the European Welfare State: A European Dilemma* (Oxford, 2006).

48. Saisine, I.1, I.2. On the difference between an unconstitutional transfer and a mere limitation of sovereignty, see CC Decision No.76-71 DC, December 29-30, 1976, 31, *Journal Officiel de la République Française* (December 31 1976): 7651.

49. Saisine, II; Schengen Convention, art. 40.2, 41.1.

50. Saisine, II.

51. Saisine, II; Convention for the Protection of Human Rights and Fundamental Freedoms, art. 8, November 4, 1950, E.T.S. no. 5, 213 UNTS 221, at 11, which entered into force September 3, 1953.

52. Saisine, II.

53. On Debré's contributions to wartime plans for French political institutions, which favored consolidating executive power, see Philip Nord, *France's New Deal: From the Thirties to the Postwar Era* (Princeton, NJ, 2010), 106-8.

54. See Hazareesingh, *In the Shadow of the General*, 45; Alan Riding, "Michel Debré, 84, Dies; De Gaulle Protégé and Ex-Premier," *New York Times*, August 3, 1996.

55. Michel Debré, *Entretiens avec le Général De Gaulle, 1961-1969* (Paris, 1993), 57-58.

56. Michel Debré, *La mort de l'État républicain* (Paris, 1947), 9.

57. Michel Debré, *La République et son pouvoir* (Paris, 1950), 98.

58. Constitution du 4 octobre 1958, Sénat, preamble, art. 3, accessed March 13, 2024, https://www.senat.fr/connaitre-le-senat/evenements-et-manifestations -culturelles/les-revisions-de-la-constitution/constitution-du-4-octobre-1958-texte -originel.html.

59. Michel Debré, *Français choisissons l'espoir* (Paris, 1979), 11, 15, 9 10; Saisine, II. See Brown, *Seventh Member State*, 95; Marker, *Black France, White Europe*, 2-4.

60. Michel Debré to Affaires Etrangères, Cabinet du Ministre, July 11, 1986, and Marie-Reine d'Haussy, "Accords sur les contrôles frontaliers: Projet de réponse à M. Michel Debré," August 1, 1986, folder "Schengen, Débat français 1986-1989," box 5 "Coordination," MEAE.

61. "Synthèse de la réunion du mardi 12 août sur les questions de visa et de circulation dans le cadre européen," August 27, 1986, folder "Négociation à Cinq: Group de travail 2 (visas immigration), 1985-87," box 1 "Coordination," MEAE.

62. "L'Europe contre la France," *Le Monde*, July 12, 1986.

63. Décision no. 91-294 DC du juillet 1991, Conseil Constitutionnel, July 25, 1991, "Loi autorisant l'approbation de la convention d'application de l'accord de

Schengen du 14 juin 1985 entre les gouvernements des États de l'Union économique Benelux, de la République fédérale d'Allemagne et de la République française relatif à la suppression graduelle des contrôles aux frontières communes," accessed October 31, 2023, after Compte rendu de la séance, https://www.conseil-constitutionnel .fr/sites/default/files/as/root/bank_mm/decisions/PV/pv1991-07-25.pdf (hereafter Décision no. 91–294 DC).

64. "Compte rendu de la séance du 25 juillet 1991," Conseil Constitutionnel [[CC]], July 25, 1991, 1 (Jacques Robert, rapporteur, conference resulted in decision No. 91–294 DC, accessed October 31, 2023, http://www.conseil-constitutionnel.fr /conseil-constitutionnel/root/bank_mm/decisions/PV/pv1991-07-25.pdf), (hereafter "Compte rendu de la séance"). See "Jacques Robert," available at Conseil Constitutionnel, accessed March 30, 2024, https://www.conseil-constitutionnel.fr/membres /jacques-robert.

65. "Compte rendu de la séance," 2.

66. "Compte rendu de la séance," 2.

67. "Compte rendu de la séance," 4–11.

68. "Compte rendu de la séance," 8–9.

69. "Compte rendu de la séance," 34, 25, 37.

70. Luc Cédelle, "Mort de l'ancien ministre Maurice Faure, à 92 ans," *Le Monde*, March 6, 2014.

71. "Compte rendu de la séance," 21, 22, 27.

72. "Compte rendu de la séance," 10, 24, 12–13.

73. Décision no. 91–294 DC, 26.

74. Décision no. 91–294 DC, 7–8, 15, 6–7, 19, 11, 10, 7–8, 10.

75. Décision no. 91–294 DC, 8, 5.

76. "Compte rendu de la séance," 26.

77. Décision no. 91–294 DC, 12–13.

78. Décision no. 91–294 DC, 22–23.

79. Décision no. 91–294 DC, 20.

80. "Compte rendu de la séance," 40.

81. "Compte rendu de la séance," 20.

82. Thierry Brehier, "Les Accords de Schengen n'impliquent pas de transfert de souveraineté," *Le Monde*, July 27, 1991.

83. Conseil Constitutionnel décision No. 93–325 DC du 13 août 1993, August 13, 1993, Rec. (Fr.), para. 2, 4, accessed November 17, 2023, https://www.conseil -constitutionnel.fr/decision/1993/93325DC.htm.

84. Décision No. 93–325 DC, para. 3. See Susan Soltesz, "Implications of the Conseil Constitutionnel's Immigration and Asylum Decision of August 1993," *Boston College International and Comparative Law Review* 8, no. 1 (December 1995): 279.

85. Texte intégral de la Constitution du 4 octobre 1958 en vigueur, art. 53–1, available at Conseil Constitutionnel, accessed March 13, 2024, https://www.conseil -constitutionnel.fr/le-bloc-de-constitutionnalite/texte-integral-de-la-constitution-du -4-octobre-1958-en-vigueur.

86. Quoted in Francesco Cherubini, *Asylum Law in the European Union* (Abingdon, UK, 2015), 172.

87. "European Parliament Opposes Schengen Agreement," *Statewatch*, May / June 1991, accessed October 21, 2021, https://www.statewatch.org/statewatch-database/european-parliament-opposes-schengen-agreement-1/.

88. "Dutch Social Democrats Suggest Alternative for Schengen Agreement," *Statewatch*, July / August 1991, accessed October 21, 2021, https://www.statewatch.org/statewatch-database/dutch-social-democrats-suggest-alternative-for-schengen-agreement/.

89. John Benyon, Lynne Turnbull, Andrew Willis, Rachel Woodward, and Adrian Beck, *Police Co-operation in Europe: An Investigation* (Leicester, 1993), 140.

90. "European Commission Dodges Immigration Issues—Again," *Statewatch*, July / August 1991, accessed October 21, 2021, https://www.statewatch.org/statewatch-database/european-commission-dodges-immigration-issues-again/.

91. Cruz, *Schengen*, 11.

92. Claude Gueydan, "Cooperation between Member States of the European Community in the Fight against Terrorism," in *Terrorism and International Law*, ed. Rosalyn Higgins and Maurice Flory (London, 1997), 116.

93. When joining Schengen to the EU, the 1997 Amsterdam Treaty stipulated that Europe's high court would have broad jurisdiction over EU rules but not over internal security. Protocol integrating the Schengen acquis into the framework of the European Union, art. 2, in Treaty of Amsterdam Amending the Treaty on European Union, the Treaties Establishing the European Communities and Certain Related Acts, 1997 (hereafter Treaty of Amsterdam), https://eur-lex.europa.eu/legal-content/EN/TXT/?uri=CELEX:11997D/TXT.

94. Peter Reichel, *Vergangenheitsbewältigung in Deutschland: Die Auseinandersetzung mit der NS-Diktatur von 1945 bis heute* (Munich, 2001).

95. Deutscher Bundestag, Plenarprotokoll 12 / 89 (April 30, 1992), 7296–7297 (hereafter Plenarprotokoll).

96. Plenarprotokoll, 7300.

97. Grundgesetz für die Bundesrepublik Deutschland, art. 16, 1949 available at Document Archiv, accessed March 13, 2024, http://www.documentarchiv.de/brd/1949/grundgesetz.html. See Kay Hailbronner, "Asylum Law Reform in the German Constitution," *American University International Law Review* 9, no. 4 (1994): 159.

98. Hailbronner, "Asylum Law Reform," 160.

99. Human Rights Watch, *"Germany for Germans": Xenophobia and Racist Violence in Germany* (London, 1995), 3, 5.

100. Plenarprotokoll, 7298, 7317, 7338.

101. Plenarprotokoll, 7325.

102. Plenarprotokoll, 7310–11, 7317, 7310.

103. Plenarprotokoll, 7310–11, 7307, 7306, 7340.

104. Plenarprotokoll, 7311, 7325, 7305, 7330, 7313.

105. Human Rights Watch, *Germany for Germans*, 3.

106. Plenarprotokoll, 7317. See Hailbronner, "Asylum Law Reform," 160.

107. Matthew J. Gibney, *The Ethics and Politics of Asylum: Liberal Democracy and the Response to Refugees* (Cambridge, UK, 2004), 102.

108. Basic Law for the Federal Republic of Germany, art. 16a.

109. Plenarprotokol, 7296–97.

110. Cruz, *Schengen*, 3.

111. National Assembly, 272.

112. Plenarprotokoll, 7341.

Chapter 5. A Place of Risk

1. "How M&S Expanded Internationally and Engaged with Customers around the World," Marks and Spencer Company Archive, accessed February 2, 2019, https://marksintime.marksandspencer.com/download?id=2842. See also Jean-Claude Fauveau, *Le Monde de la distribution: Les 100 plus grands groupes et leurs implantations européennes* (Paris, 1994).

2. "Quinze blessés dont deux grièvement," *Le Monde*, February 25, 1985.

3. "Habib Maamar devant la cour d'assises spéciale de Paris un terrorisme 'utilitaire,'" *Le Monde*, December 15, 1989.

4. On escalating political violence in the 1970s and 1980s, see Florence Gaub, "Trends in Terrorism," *European Union Institute for Security Studies* (March 2017): 1. Coinciding with the signing of the Schengen treaty, in June 1985, an airport bombing left three dead in Frankfurt; see "Arab Group Asserts It Planted Bomb in Frankfurt," *New York Times*, June 22, 1985. The violence highlighted regional security concerns and cross-border networks; see Dennis A. Pluchinsky, "Middle Eastern Terrorism in Europe: Trends and Prospects," *Terrorism* 14, no. 2 (1991): 67–76; John D. Occhipinti, *The Politics of EU Police Cooperation: Toward a European FBI?* (Boulder, CO, 2003), 44.

5. See Schengen Convention, art 6; "Declaration by the Ministers and State Secretaries," in Schengen Convention (hereafter Schengen Declaration). See also Schwache Glieder, "Terrorismus," *Der Spiegel*, April 27, 1987.

6. Schengen Declaration.

7. Europol commenced full operations in 1999, at the Strasbourg site of the SIS, expanding after the September 11, 2001 attacks. "Schengen Information System," European Commission, Migration and Home Affairs, accessed March 9, 2023, https://home-affairs.ec.europa.eu/policies/schengen-borders-and-visa/schengen-information-system_en. See also Rachel Woodward, "Establishing Europol," *European Journal on Criminal Policy and Research* 1, no. 4 (1993): 7–33. See Isaac Stanley-Becker, "As Attacks Continue, Brexit Could Hamper European Counterterrorism Efforts," *Washington Post*, March 24, 2017.

8. See Michel Foucault, *Discipline and Punish: The Birth of the Prison*, trans. Alan Sheridan (New York, 1979); Ayse Ceyhan, "Policing by Dossier: Identification and Surveillance in an Era of Uncertainty and Fear," in *Controlling Frontiers: Free Movement into and within Europe*, ed. Didier Bigo and Elspeth Guild (Aldershot, UK,

2005), 218; Tony Bunyan, "Just over the Horizon—the Surveillance Society and the State in the EU," *Race & Class* 51, no. 3 (January 2010): 1–12. On informational self-determination, see Thilo Weichert, "Das geplante Schengen-Informationssystem," *Computer und Recht* no. 1 (1990): 62–66.

9. Max Weber, "Politics as a Vocation," in *From Max Weber: Essays in Sociology*, ed. and trans. H. H. Gerth and C. Wright Mills (London, 1991): 77–128.

10. Michael Walzer, *Spheres of Justice: A Defense of Pluralism and Equality* (Oxford, 1983), 44, 61.

11. Weber, "Technical Advantages of Bureaucratic Organization," in *From Max Weber: Essays in Sociology*, ed. and trans. H. H. Gerth and C. Wright Mills (London, 1991), 214. See also Giorgio Agamben, "The Sovereign Police," in *The Politics of Everyday Fear*, ed. Brian Massumi (Minneapolis, 1993), 61–64.

12. Wouter van de Rijt, "Le Fonctionnement des institutions Schengen: 'Pragmatisme, toujours,'" in *Schengen's Final Days? The Incorporation of Schengen into the New TEU, External Borders and Information Systems*, ed. Monica Den Boer (Maastricht, 1998), 59.

13. Marcel Scotto, "Au Coeur du système d'information commun aux sept pays," *Le Monde*, March 30, 1995.

14. Scotto, "Au Coeur du système d'information commun."

15. Scotto, "Au Coeur du système d'information commun."

16. Schengen Convention, art. 92.

17. Foucault, *Discipline and Punish*, 206, 196, and more generally, 195–228.

18. Foucault, *Discipline and Punish*, 199–200.

19. Scotto, "Au coeur du système d'information commun."

20. Schengen Convention, art. 93, 92, 99.

21. Schengen Agreement, art. 9, 7.

22. "Télex du Ministère de l'Intérieur de la R.F.A. aux Ministères compétents dese pays du Benelux et de la France," April 9, 1985, 2, Binder 2 "Schengen overleg, correspondentie, 1984–1987," Council Archives.

23. "Télex du Ministère de l'Intérieur de la R.F.A.," 2.

24. "Exécution de l'Accord," Comité de coordination Benelux, November 13, 1985, 7, binder 1b BNL, Council Archives.

25. See Jürgen Simon and Jürgen Taeger, *Rasterfahndung: Entwicklung, Inhalt und Grenzen einer kriminalpolizeilichen Fahndungsmethode* (Baden-Baden, 1981); Peter Becker, *Dem Täter auf der Spur: Eine Geschichte der Kriminalistik* (Darmstadt, 2005).

26. The system's basic features still characterize INPOL-neu, introduced in 2003. K.-F. Koch and H. Risch, "The Bundeskriminalamt: The German Federal Criminal Police Office," in *Police Research in the Federal Republic of Germany: 15 Years Research Within the "Bundeskriminalamt"*, ed. R. V. Clarke (Berlin, 1991), 5; "European data network," *New Scientist*, January 5, 1984, 13.

27. "Réponse des delegations au questionnaire sur les besoins du système informatisé," August 27, 1990, folder "Réunion du groupe des coordonnateurs, Bruxelles—23 juillet 1990 et 13 sept 1990," box 13 "Mouvement," MEAE; "Conclusions de la réunion

tenue à Bonn le 2 février 1987," folder "SIS [système d'information Schengen], 1988–1989," box 5 "Coordination," MEAE.

28. "Rapport au Groupe central de négociation sur l'état des travaux du Groupe de Travail I 'Police et Sécurité' et des sous-groupes 'Stupéfiants,' 'Armes et munitions,' 'Immigration clandestine' et 'Echange de renseignements,' institués dans le cadre de l'accord de Schengen," December 4, 1986, 7, Binder 2 "Schengen overleg, correspondentie, 1984–1987," Council Archives. See also Hreblay, *Libre circulation*, 95–96.

29. "Note relative au projet de traité conventionnel dans le domaine de la protection des données concernant le Système d'Information Schengen (S.I.S.), CNIL," November 18, 1988, 1, folder "SIS—CNIL (1988–89)," box 5 "Coordination," MEAE.

30. "Note relative au projet de traité conventionnel"; Hreblay, *Libre circulation*, 98–101.

31. Brouwer, *Digital Borders*, 49, 50.

32. François Lamoureux, "Suppression des Frontières Physiques Intérieures," January 22, 1990, 2, François Lamoureux Fonds 203, HAEU.

33. "Vers une 'Europe des polices,'" *Le Républicain Lorrain*, April 29, 1987.

34. "Das Rätsel vom Frankfurter Flughafen," *Frankfurter Allgemeine Zeitung*, June 11, 2015.

35. Franck Johannes, "Accord de coopération antiterroriste: L'Espagne, après l'Italie et l'Allemagne," *Le Matin*, May 31, 1987. See "Red Brigades," Mapping Militant Organizations, Stanford University, last modified June 2018, accessed April 25, 2023, https://cisac.fsi.stanford.edu/mappingmilitants/profiles/red-brigades.

36. "Sommet occidental antiterroriste à Paris," *Le Figaro*, May 28, 1987.

37. Michael Evans, "Waverers Against Terrorism," *The Times*, May 29, 1987.

38. Bernard Purcell, "EEC Talks on Passport Racket," *Irish Independent*, April 28, 1987.

39. Peter Zudeick, "Im Eimer," *Deutsches Allgemeines Sonntagsblatt*, September 1989.

40. E. Cazimajou, "Accord de Schengen: État des travaux de mise en œuvre de l'Accord," February 20, 1989, 7, folder "Schengen Groupe central de négociation, 1 mars 1989," box 6 "Coordination," MEAE.

41. François Scheer to Renaud Denoix de Saint Marc, April 18, 1989, 2, folder "Réunion interministérielle préparatoire au Conseil restreint du 19 avril 1989," box 8 "Mouvement," MEAE.

42. E. Cazimajou, "Quelques réflexions à propos de l'accord de Schengen," December 2, 1989, 4, folder "Schengen Groupe central de négociation, 1 mars 1989," box 6 "Coordination," MEAE.

43. "Déclaration en matière de protection des données nominatives en relation avec le projet d'un système d'information commun des états signataires de l'accord de Schengen," March 16, 1989, 1, folder "Protection des données," box 23 "Mouvement," MEAE.

44. "Accords de Schengen, Groupe de Travail I (police et sécurité), compte-rendu de la réunion du sous-groupe 4 (échange de renseignements)," March 31, 1989,

folder "SIS [système d'information Schengen], 1988–1989," box 5 "Coordination," MEAE.

45. Schengen Convention, art. 92.

46. "S.I.S.: Réunion des 22–23 Mars 1989," 1–2, folder "Schengen: Oct. 86—déc. 1989," box 21 "Mouvement," MEAE.

47. Schengen Convention, art. 96, 99.

48. "S.I.S.: Réunion des 22–23 Mars 1989," 6.

49. "S.I.S.: Réunion des 22–23 Mars 1989," 4.

50. Cazimajou, "Accord de Schengen," 8.

51. "S.I.S.: Réunion des 22–23 Mars 1989," 4; Schengen Convention, art. 61.

52. Élisabeth Guigou, "Note pour Hubert Blanc," September 18, 1989, folder "Schengen: Oct. 86—déc. 1989," box 21 "Mouvement," MEAE.

53. Brouwer, *Digital Borders*, 51.

54. Cazimajou, "Accord de Schengen," 9.

55. "Accord de Schengen: Satisfaction du Vice-président Bangemann," Commission des Communautés Européennes, November 14, 1989, François Lamoureux Fonds 595, HAEU.

56. Cazimajou, "Accord de Schengen," 9.

57. Schengen Convention, art. 93.

58. "Legal Documents," Interpol, accessed March 13, 2024, https://www.interpol.int/en/Who-we-are/Legal-framework/Legal-documents.

59. "Anti-Anarchist Conference; It Was Opened at Rome with Many Nations Represented," *New York Times*, November 25, 1898. See Richard Bach Jensen, "The International Anti-Anarchist Conference of 1898 and the Origins of Interpol," *Journal of Contemporary History* 16, no. 2 (April 1981): 323–47; Mathieu Deflem, *Policing World Society: Historical Foundations of International Police Cooperation* (Oxford, 2004), 45–77.

60. Alain Guyomarch, "Problems and Prospects for European Police Cooperation after Maastricht," *Policing and Society: An International Journal* 5, no. 3 (1995), 249–61.

61. "1923—How Our History Started," Interpol, 16, accessed April 23, 2023, https://www.interpol.int/en/Who-we-are/INTERPOL-100/1923-how-our-history-started.

62. "Key dates," Interpol, accessed April 23, 2023, https://www.interpol.int/Who-we-are/INTERPOL-100/Key-dates#:~:text=each%20in%20prison.-,1989,Fran%C3%A7ois%20Mitterrand%2C%20on%2027%20November.

63. Constitution of the ICPO-INTERPOL, art. 2, I / CONS / GA / 1956 (2017).

64. See Malcolm Anderson, "The Agenda for Police Cooperation," in *Policing across National Boundaries*, ed. Malcolm Anderson and Monica den Boer (London, 1994), 11.

65. John Benyon et al., "Understanding Police Cooperation in Europe: Setting a Framework for Analysis", in *Policing across National Boundaries*, ed. Malcolm Anderson and Monica den Boer (London, 1994), 56.

66. Michael Fooner, *Interpol: Issues in World Crime and International Justice* (New York, 1989), 149, 150.

67. Jürgen Storbeck, interview with author, February 18, 2019 (hereafter Storbeck Oral History). See also Jürgen Storbeck, "Zwischenstaatliche Zusammenarbeit im Polizeialltag aus der Sicht einter Zentralstelle," in *Verbrechensbekämpfung in europäischer Dimension* (Wiesbaden, 1992), 155.

68. Cyrille Fijnaut, "Police Co-operation within Western Europe," in *The Containment of Organised Crime and Terrorism: Thirty-Five Years of Research on Police, Judicial and Administrative Cooperation*, ed. Cyrille J.C.F. Fijnaut (Leiden, 2016), 48, 49.

69. Paul Norman, "The European Dimension," in *Law, Power, and Justice in England and Wales*, ed. Ian K. McKenzie (Westport, CT, 1998), 96; Saarbrücken Accord, preamble, art. 2, 3, 5.

70. Storbeck Oral History.

71. Storbeck Oral History; Peter Andreas and Ethan Nadelmann, *Policing the Globe: Criminalization and Crime Control in International Relations* (Oxford, 2006), 99; James Sheptycki, *Transnational Crime and Policing: Selected Essays* (Abingdon, UK, 2011), 52.

72. Hreblay, *Libre circulation*.

73. *Statewatch*, May–June 1994, accessed October 21, 2021, https://www.statewatch.org/media/documents/docbin/bulletin/bul-4-3.pdf. See Eddie Bruce-Jones, *Race in the Shadow of Law: State Violence in Contemporary Europe* (Abingdon, UK, 2017); Sophie Body-Gendrot and Catherine Wihtol de Wenden, *Policing the Inner City in France, Britain, and the US* (Basingstoke, UK, 2014), especially 43–73.

74. Norman, "European Dimension"; Storbeck Oral History.

75. "Télex du Ministère de l'Intérieur de la R.F.A. aux Ministères compétents dese pays du Benelux et de la France," 1.

76. "Project d'Accord," annexed to Gilbert Guillaume, "Note à l'attention de Monsieur Jean-Paul Angles," May 7, 1985, art. 9, folder "Marché Intérieur—Session du 10 juin 1985," box 349 "Lalumière Papers," MEAE; Gilbert Guillaume, "Terrorism and International Law," *International & Comparative Law Quarterly* 53, no. 3 (July 2004): 548.

77. Jean-Marc Ancian, "Paris et Bonn renforcent antiterroriste," *Le Matin*, April 9, 1987, Coupures de Presse de Parlement européen CPPE-2019 01 / 04 / 198704 / 1987–28 / 04 / 1987 Juridique et des droits des citoyens (hereafter CPPE), HAEU.

78. Jan de Ceuster, "Rapport de mission, réunion des ministres et secrétaires d'état du groupe de Schengen à Bonn les 12 et 13 novembre 1989," Commission, November 21, 1989, 1, François Lamoureux Fonds 595, HAEU.

79. See Tony Bunyan, ed., *Statewatching the New Europe: A Handbook on the European State* (London, 1993); Eva Oberloskamp, *Codename TREVI: Terrorismusbekämpfung und die Anfänge einer europäischen Innenpolitik in den 1970er Jahren* (Berlin, 2016).

80. François Julien-Laferrière, "Entry, Residence and Employment of Foreigners in the Community," in *What Kind of Criminal Policy for Europe?*, ed. Mireille Delmas-Marty, Mark A. Summers, and Ginette Mongin (The Hague, 1996), 53.

81. "Première étape pour une police européenne," *Libération*, April 29, 1987; "Le Groupe 'Trevi' en réunion à Bruxelles," *La Libre Belgique*, April 27, 1987, CPPE, HAEU; Storbeck Oral History.

82. Trevi is widely understood as a precursor to Europol; less well-documented is Schengen's influence on Trevi. See Richard Clutterbuck, *Terrorism, Drugs and Crime in Europe after 1992* (London, 1990).

83. Alain Hevrendt, "Drogue, terrorisme et . . . immigration: Les Ministres européens voudraient harmoniser les procedures; Simple?," *La Libre Belgique*, April 9, 1987, CPPE, HAEU.

84. "Réunion des ministres et secrétaires d'état chargés de l'exécution de l'accord de Schengen du 17 décembre 1987 à Berlin," December 17, 1987, folder "Schengen: Oct. 86—déc. 1989," box 21 "Mouvement," MEAE.

85. Régis de Gouttes, "Compte rendu de la réunion du groupe coopération dans la lutte contre le terrorisme international," June 1, 1989, 5, folder "Terrorisme, 1989–90," box 23 "Mouvement," MEAE.

86. Pierre Joxe to Edith Cresson, March 16, 1989, 1, folder "Réunions informelles des ministres de l'intérieur organisés par Pierre Joxe," box 5 "Coordination," MEAE.

87. Joanna Apap, *The Rights of Immigrant Workers in the European Union: An Evaluation of the EU Public Policy Process and the Legal Status of Labour Immigrants from the Maghreb Countries in the New Receiving States* (The Hague, 2002), 21.

88. Blanc, "Schengen," 723.

89. Holly Wyatt-Walter, *The European Community and the Security Dilemma, 1979–92* (New York, 1997), 153; Martin Elvins, *Anti-Drugs Policies of the European Union: Transnational Decision-Making and the Politics of Expertise* (Basingstoke, UK, 2003), 88; "'The Palma Document' Free Movement of Persons. A Report to the European Council by the Coordinators' Group," Madrid, June 1989, 12–16, *Statewatch*, accessed December 30, 2023, http://www.statewatch.org/semdoc/assets/files/keytexts/ktch1.pdf.

90. "L'Accord de Schengen, II," *Bulletin Quotidien*, November 30, 1989, 22, François Lamoureux Fonds 595, HAEU.

91. "Libre circulation des personnes en Europe," April 17, 1989, folder "Réunion interministérielle préparatoire au conseil restreint du 19 avril 1989," box 8 "Mouvement," MEAE.

92. Jan de Ceuster, "Réunion du Groupe Central de Négociation de 'Schengen' à Bruxelles le 13 décembre 1989," Commission, December 15, 1989, 2, François Lamoureux Fonds 595, HAEU. See "A Europe to Be Steeped in Racism," *Guardian*, January 28, 1991.

93. Schengen Convention.

94. Schengen Declaration.

95. Schengen Convention, preamble, art. 2, titles III, VII, IV. Also see van de Rijt, "Le Fonctionnement des institutions Schengen: 'Pragmatisme, toujours.'"

96. Lalumière Oral History; Schengen Convention, art. 4, 6, 40, 44; and Schengen Declaration.

97. Schengen Convention, art. 29; and see art. 33.

98. Schengen Convention, art. 37, 38.

99. Schengen Convention, art. 59, 63, 40, 64. Schengen Declaration also provided for "improving and simplifying extradition practices."

100. Schengen Convention, art. 39, 40, 41.

101. Schengen Convention, art. 39, 40, 41.

102. Schengen Convention, art. 44, 47, 45.

103. Schengen Convention, art. 92, 94, 93.

104. Schengen Convention, art. 92, 95, 96, 99.

105. Schengen Convention, art. 99; Foucault, *Discipline and Punish*, 177.

106. Schengen Convention, art. 94, 92, 94, 104, 112, 113, 118.

107. Schengen Convention, art. 105, 106, 108, 114.

108. Council of Europe, Convention for the Protection of Individuals with regard to Automatic Processing of Personal Data, ETS no. 108, January 28, 1981; Council of Europe, Recommendation No. R (87) 15 of the Committee of Ministers to Member States regulating the use of personal data in the police sector, REC (87) 15, September 17, 1987. Data collection and personal privacy remained key in European policy-making. The General Data Protection Regulation, adopted in 2016 and enforceable as of 2018, superseded a 1995 European directive providing that "personal data should be able to flow freely" and that data systems must respect "fundamental rights and freedoms." See Directive 95 / 46 / EC of the European Parliament and of the Council of 24 October 1995 on the protection of individuals with regard to the processing of personal data and on the free movement of such data, OJ (L 281) (1995), 31–350, preamble, arts. 2–3

109. Schengen Convention, art. 117, 110, 111, 114, 109.

110. Schengen Convention, art. 115, 106, 131, 8, 6.

111. Council Decision 2005 / 211 / JHA of 24 February 2005 concerning the introduction of some new functions for the Schengen Information System, including in the fight against terrorism, OJ (L 68 / 44) (2005), accessed February 2, 2019, https://publications.europa.eu/en/publication-detail/-/publication/d0258379-0f37-4aa8-a2d9-666467d18005/language-en. See also Occhipinti, *EU Police Cooperation*, 57.

112. Patrick le Jeune, "Europol" (paper presented to the Joint Sessions of Workshops, European Consortium for Political Research, Limerick, March 30–April 4, 1992), 3–4; Monica den Boer, "The Quest for European Policing: Rhetoric and Justification in a Disorderly Debate," *Policing across National Boundaries*, ed. Malcolm Anderson and Monica den Boer (London, 1994), 180.

113. "Libre circulation des personnes en Europe," 4.

114. "Future Common Action on Home Affairs and Judicial Policy," Annex 1, Presidency Conclusions, European Council, June 28 and 29, 1991, 20, accessed November 13, 2023, https://www.consilium.europa.eu/media/20528/1991_june_-_luxembourg__eng_.pdf. See Woodward, "Establishing Europol," 12; Rhodri Jeffreys-Jones, "The Idea of a European FBI," in *Strategic Intelligence: Counterintelligence and Counterterrorism, Defending the National against Hostile Forces, Intelligence and the Quest for Security*, vol. 4, ed. Loch K. Johnson (Westport, CT, 2007), 73.

115. Storbeck Oral History.

116. Maastricht Treaty, art. K.1, 9. See Tony Bunyan, *Key Texts on Justice and Home Affairs in the European Union*, vol. 1, *(1976–1993): From Trevi to Maastricht* (Nottingham, 1997), 19–16.

117. Europol Convention, art. 7 (1). Member states ratified the convention over the next three years.

118. Council Decision 2005 / 211 / JHA; "Europol's Amended Regulation Enters into Force," Europol, June 28, 2022, accessed May 2, 2023, https://www.europol .europa.eu/media-press/newsroom/news/europols-amended-regulation-enters-force.

119. Proposal for a regulation of the European Parliament and of the council amending regulation (EU) 2018 / 1862 on the establishment, operation and use of the Schengen Information System (SIS) in the field of police cooperation and judicial cooperation in criminal matters as regards the entry of alerts by Europol, 2020 / 0350 (COD).

120. "Schengen Information System," European Commission, Migration and Home Affairs, accessed March 9, 2023, https://home-affairs.ec.europa.eu/policies /schengen-borders-and-visa/schengen-information-system_en.

121. Jean Boissonnat, "Au-delà de Schengen," *La Tribune*, June 4, 1991.

122. Jean-Michel Cordier, "Un Nouveau mur en Europe," *L'Humanité*, June 4, 1991.

123. "Europe to Be Steeped in Racism."

124. Michel Giot-Mikkelsen, "Polizeilicher Informationsaustausch im EG-Binnenmarkt," in *Verbrechensbekämpfung in europäischer Dimension*, ed. Deutschland Bundeskriminalamt (Wiesbaden, 1992), 151.

125. Yves Jouffa, Roland Kessous, and Gérard Soulier, "Contrôler la Police," *Le Monde*, May 4, 1989.

126. Jouffa, Kessous, and Soulier, "Contrôler la Police."

127. Jouffa, Kessous, and Soulier, "Contrôler la Police."

128. "Déclaration en matière de protection des données nominatives," 1.

129. "Déclaration en matière de protection des données nominatives."

130. "Déclaration en matière de protection des données nominatives." See also Els J. Kindt, *Privacy and Data Protection Issues of Biometric Applications: A Comparative Legal Analysis* (Leuven, 2013), 91.

131. Jacques Fauvet to Émile Cazimajou, February 14, 1989, folder "SIS—CNIL (1988–89)," box 5 "Coordination," MEAE.

132. Convention for the Protection of Individuals with regard to Automatic Processing of Personal Data, preamble.

133. Convention for the Protection of Individuals with regard to Automatic Processing of Personal Data, art. 4, 2, 6, 9, 18, 12, 8.

134. Bundesverfassungsgericht, 1 BvR 209 / 83, December 15, 1983, Guideline 1. On self-determination as an anti-colonial project, see Moyn, *Last Utopia*, 67. On privacy as a fundamental right, see Samuel Warren and Louis Brandeis, "The Right to Privacy," *Harvard Law Review* 4, no. 5 (December 1890): 193–220.

135. "État des signatures et des ratifications de la convention de 1981 sur la protection des personnes à l'égard du traitement automatisé des données," October 13, 1989, folder "Protection des données," box 23 "Mouvement," MEAE.

136. "Note relative au projet de traité conventionnel," 1–2.

137. Cazimajou, "Accord de Schengen: État des travaux de mise en œuvre de l'Accord," 7.

138. Cazimajou, "Accord de Schengen: État des travaux de mise en œuvre de l'Accord." See also "Accords de Schengen, Groupe de Travail I (police et sécurité), compte-rendu de la réunion du sous-groupe 4 (échange de renseignements)."

139. Scheer to Denoix de Saint Marc, April 18, 1989.

140. "Note relative au projet de traité conventionnel," 1–4.

141. Fauvet to Cazimajou, February 14, 1989, 1.

142. Jean-Pierre Puissoche, "Accords de Schengen: Réponse du ministre d'état au président de la CNIL," March 28, 1989, 1, folder "SIS—CNIL (1988–89)," box 5 "Coordination," MEAE.

143. "Négociation de Schengen: Les Points à négocier au niveau ministériel," April 19, 1989, folder "Réunion interministérielle: Préparatoire au Conseil Restreint du 19 avril 1989," box 8 "Mouvement," MEAE.

144. Scheer to Denoix de Saint Marc, April 18, 1989, 3.

145. "Négociation de Schengen: Les Points à négocier au niveau ministériel"; Scheer to Denoix de Saint Marc, April 18, 1989.

146. Cazimajou, "Accords de Schengen: Réunion du groupe central de négociation des 2 et 3 mai 1989," May 5, 1989, 3, folder "Schengen Groupe Central de Négociation, Paris 2–3 Mai 89," box 6 "Coordination," MEAE.

147. "Accords de Schengen, groupe de travail I (police et sécurité), compte-rendu de la réunion du sous-groupe 4 (échange de renseignements)."

148. Scheer to Denoix de Saint Marc, April 18, 1989.

149. "Négociation de Schengen: Les Points à négocier au niveau ministériel."

150. "'The Palma Document,'" 114, 115.

151. "Common Principles for the Protection of Individuals with Regard to the Use of Personalized Data Banks," Ministry of Foreign Affairs, Co-ordinating Committee Freedom of Movement for Persons, August 29, 1989, 2, folder "Protection des données," box 23 "Mouvement," MEAE.

152. "Berlin Resolution of the International Conference of Data Protection Commissioners of 30 August 1989," 1–2, available at Global Privacy Assembly, accessed March 14, 2024, http://globalprivacyassembly.org/wp-content/uploads/2015/02/11th-ICDPPC -Berlin-1989-Berlin-Resolution.pdf. On the Conference, see "History of the Assembly," Global Privacy Assembly, accessed May 5, 2023, https://globalprivacyassembly.org/the -assembly-and-executive-committee/history-of-the-assembly/.

153. "Additional Statement by the Data Protection Commissioners of the European Community (EC) Nations, Berlin Resolution of the International Conference of Data Protection Commissioners of 30 August 1989," in "Berlin Resolution of the International Conference of Data Protection Commissioners of 30 August 1989," 4–5.

154. "Communication de Monsieur le Sénateur Jacques Thyraud relative au Rapport sur l'Accord des Schengen, Commission Nationale de l'Informatique et des Libertés," n.d., folder "Protection des données," box 23 "Mouvement," MEAE.

155. "Accord de Schengen: Satisfaction du Vice-président Bangemann."

156. Lamoureux, "Suppression des Frontières," 3.

157. "Lettre du président de la délégation de la République Fédérale d'Allemagne au secrétaire général de l'Union Économique Benelux," March 22, 1990, 1–2, folder "Protection des données," box 23 "Mouvement," MEAE.

158. "Procès-verbal de la réunion des experts en matière de protection de la vie privée," May 28, 1990, folder "Protection des données," box 23 "Mouvement," MEAE.

159. Annie Bonnot, "Suite de Schengen," August 29, 1990, 3, folder "Schengen ratification," box 22 "Mouvement," MEAE.

160. Weichert, "Das geplante Schengen-Informationssystem," 62, 66.

161. "Peut-on envisage un Schengen réduit?," Ministère des Affaires Étrangères, Mission de Coordination Libre Circulation des Personnes, April 11, 1990, folder "Janvier—mai 1990," box 21 "Mouvement," MEAE.

162. Karen J. Alter, "'Who are the "Masters of the Treaty?': European Governments and the European Court of Justice," *International Organization 52*, no. 1 (Winter 1998): 141.

163. *Sans-papiers: Chroniques d'un mouvement*, IM'média / Reflex (Paris, 1997), 108–10.

164. Christophe Deschamps, "L'Europe en un visa," *Jeune Afrique Économie*, September 1990, folder "Convention application—Accord Schengen," box 22 "Mouvement," MEAE.

Chapter 6. *A* Sans-papiers *Claim to Free Movement as a Human Right*

1. Philippe Bernard, "Des 'Sans-papiers' investissent une église parisienne," *Le Monde*, June 30, 1996; Madjiguène Cissé, *Parole de sans-papiers* (Paris, 1999), 208.

2. Cissé, *Parole*, 9. See Kieran Oberman, "Immigration as a Human Right," in *Migration in Political Theory: The Ethics of Movement and Membership*, ed. Sarah Fine and Lea Ypi (Oxford, 2016), 32–56; "La Lutte pour la reconnaissance—Axel Honneth Paris, Cerf, Coll. 'Passages,' traduit de l'allemand par Pierre Rusch," *Recherches familiales*, no. 1 (2004): 149–55, accessed March 5, 2022, https://www.cairn.info /revue-recherches-familiales-2004-1-page-149.html.

3. Stefan Le Courant, "La Ville des sans-papiers: Frontières mouvantes et gouvernements des marges," *L'Homme*, no. 219–20 (July / December 2016): 209–32. On "right to the city," see David Harvey, *Rebel Cities: From the Right to the City to the Urban Revolution* (London, 2012); Henri Lefebvre, *The Production of Space*, trans. Donald Nicholson-Smith (Oxford, 1991).

4. Arendt, *Origins of Totalitarianism*, 296; and see Seyla Benhabib, *The Rights of Others: Aliens, Residents and Citizens* (Cambridge, UK, 2004).

5. Thomas Nail, "Sanctuary, Solidarity, Status!," in *Open Borders: In Defense of Free Movement*, ed. Reece Jones (Athens, GA, 2019), 28.

6. Arte Útil, "Kein Mensch ist Illegal," Archive, accessed March 3, 2022, https:// www.arte-util.org/projects/kein-mensch-ist-illegal/.

7. On the persistence of sans-papiers protest, see Bernard Schmid, "L'Allemagne aussi régularise," *Plein Droit* 73, no. 2 (2007): 31–34; Ute Lindemann, *"Faut-il ouvrir les frontières?* Bilanz und Perspetkiven der Sans-papiers-Bewegung," in *Sans-Papiers-Proteste und Einwanderungspolitik in Frankreich* (Wiesbaden, 2001): 145–60; Susi Meret and Waldemar Diener, "We Are Still Here and Staying! Refugee-Led Mobilizations and Their Struggles for Rights in Germany," in *Citizens' Activism and Solidarity Movements: Contending with Populism*, ed. Birte Siim et al. (Cham, 2019), 137–66; Thomas Swerts, "Marching beyond Borders: Noncitizen Citizenship and Transnational Undocumented Activism in Europe," in *Within and Beyond Citizenship: Borders, Membership and Belonging*, ed. Roberto G. Gonzales and Nando Sigona (Abingdon, UK, 2017): 126–42. On the sans-papiers and globalization, see McNevin, "Political Belonging." On people and capital, see Robert E. Goodin, "If People Were Money . . . ," in *Free Movement: Ethical Issues in the Transnational Migration of People and Money*, ed. Brian Barry and Robert E. Goodin (University Park, PA, 1992), 6–22; Cordelli and Levy, "The Ethics of Global Capital Mobility."

8. On colonialism and European integration, see "Aperçu des catégories d'étrangers"; R. N. Coudenhove-Kalergi, "Afrika," 1929, PAN / EU-28 1920–1934, HAEU. See also Hansen and Jonsson, *Eurafrica*; Gérard Bossuat and Marie-Thérèse Bitsch, eds., *L'Europe unie et l'Afrique: De l'Idée d'Eurafrique à la Convention de Lomé I; Actes du colloque international de Paris, 1er et 2 avril 2004* (Brussels, 2005); Yves Montarsolo, *L'Eurafrique contrepoint de l'idée d'Europe* (Aix-en-Provence, 2010); Brown, *The Seventh Member State*; Thomas Moser, *Europäische Integration, Dekolonisation, Eurafrika: Eine historische Analyse über Entstehungsbedingungen der Eurafrikanischen Gemeinschaft von der Weltwirtschaftskrise bis zum Jaunde-Vertrag, 1929–1963* (Baden-Baden, 2000).

9. Arjun Appadurai, *Fear of Small Numbers: An Essay on the Geography of Anger* (Durham, NC, 2006), xi.

10. Edward W. Said, *Culture and Imperialism* (New York, 1993), xxi.

11. "Trois cents Africains sans papiers occupent une église à Paris," *Le Monde*, March 20, 1996.

12. Emmanuel Terray, "Quelques réflexions à propos de la lutte des Sans-papiers," *Journal des Anthropologues*, no. 66–67 (1996): 249; Ababacar Diop, *Dans la peau d'un sans-papiers* (Paris, 1997), 78.

13. "Trois cents Africains sans papiers occupent une église à Paris."

14. Philippe Bernard, "Les Trois Cents Africains qui occupaient une église à Paris ont été évacués par les CRS," *Le Monde*, March 23, 1996. On racial categorization by French police, see Simon Behrman, *Law and Asylum: Space, Subject, Resistance* (Abingdon, UK, 2018), 206.

15. Bernard, "Les Trois Cents Africains."

16. Débats parlementaires, Assemblée nationale, 1 session of June 15, 1993, *Journal officiel de la République française* (1993): 1617, accessed November 27, 2022, http://archives.assemblee-nationale.fr/10/cri/1992-1993-ordinaire2/052.pdf (hereafter Débats parlementaires).

17. See Rosemarie Scullion, "Vicious Circles: Immigration and National Identity in Twentieth-Century France," *SubStance* 24, no. 1 / 2, issue 76 / 77 (1995): 30–48.

18. James F. Hollifield, *Immigrants, Markets, and States: The Political Economy of Postwar Europe* (Cambridge, MA, 1992), 57–58. See also Taguieff and Weil, "'Immigration.'"

19. See Alain Girard, "Opinion publique, immigration et immigrés," *Ethnologie française* T. 7, no. 3 (1977): 219–28; Véronique De Rudder, "La Tolérance s'arrête au seuil," *Pluriel*, no. 21 (1980): 3–13. On conservative retrenchment under d'Estaing, see Chin, *Crisis of Multiculturalism*, 113–14.

20. See Michèle Tribalat, "Chronique de l'immigration," *Population* 51, no. 1 (January–February 1996): 141–93; Gary P. Freeman, "Immigrant Labour and Racial Conflict: The Role of the State," in *Migrants in Modern France: Population Mobility in the Later 19th and 20th Centuries*, ed. Philip E. Ogden and Paul E. White (London, 1989), 166–67; Hollifield, *Immigrants, Markets, and States*, 74–83. On parallels in Germany, see Lauren Stokes, *Fear of the Family: Guest Workers and Family Migration in the Federal Republic of Germany* (New York, 2022).

21. "Les Conséquences de la loi du 9 septembre 1986 sur l'entrée et le séjour des étrangers," *Hommes & Migrations* 1118 (1989): 22–28. John E. Roemer et al., *Racism, Xenophobia, and Distribution: Multi-Issue Politics in Advanced Democracies* (Cambridge, MA, 2007), 250.

22. Edwige Rude-Antoine, "Statut juridique et devenir des jeunes étrangers non européens," *Hommes & Migrations* 1178, no. 1 (1994): 35–40; Gregory Mann, "Immigrants and Arguments in France and West Africa." *Comparative Studies in Society and History* 45, no. 2 (April 2003): 362–85; Emmanuelle Néraudau-d'Unienville, *Ordre public et droit des étrangers en Europe: La Notion d'ordre public en droit des étrangers à l'aune de la construction européenne* (Brussels, 2006), 31; Alec G. Hargreaves, *Multi-Ethnic France: Immigration, Politics, Culture and Society*, 2nd ed. (London, 2007), 180.

23. Roemer et al., *Racism, Xenophobia, and Distribution*, 255; Patrick Weil, *How to Be French: Nationality in the Making since 1789*, trans. Catherine Porter (Durham, NC, 2008), 163.

24. "LOI no. 97–396 du 24 avril 1997 portant diverses dispositions relatives à l'immigration," available at Légifrance, accessed November 27, 2022, https://www .legifrance.gouv.fr/jorf/id/JORFTEXT000000564968. On Debré's opposition to Schengen, see Sandra Lavenex, *The Europeanisation of Refugee Policies: Between Human Rights and Internal Security* (Aldershot, UK, 2001), 186; Thierry Blin, "Une Approche de la construction des cadres de l'action de 'Saint Bernard' au mouvement contre le projet de loi Debré," *L'Année sociologique* 50, no. 1 (2000): 119. On the Debré measure as a response to sans-papiers mobilization, see Behrman, *Law and Asylum*, 207.

25. "Projet de loi Debré," *Bok*, accessed March 17, 2024, https://www.bok.net/pajol /projloi.html.

26. "Un entretien avec Charles Pasqua," *Le Monde*, June 2, 1993.

27. Shelese Emmons, "The Debre Bill: Immigration Legislation or a National 'Front,'" *Indiana Journal of Global Legal Studies* 5, no. 1 (Fall 1997): 357.

28. See Christopher Rudolph, *National Security and Immigration: Policy Development in the United States and Western Europe since 1945* (Stanford, 2006), 156; Eleonore Kofman, Madalina Rogoz, and Florence Lévy, "Family Migration Policies in France," *NODE Policy Report*, BMWF / ICMPD (Vienna, 2010), 5.

29. Philippe Bernard, "En 1995, le nombre d'étrangers 'sans papiers' reconduits à la frontière a chuté de 10%," *Le Monde*, March 5, 1996; James A. Winders, *Paris Africain: Rhythms of the African Diaspora* (New York, 2006), 108; "Le Pen Convicted of Inciting Racial Hatred," *Irish Examiner*, May 11, 2006; "Le Pen Convicted of Inciting Racial Hatred for Anti-Muslim Remarks," *Associated Press*, April 2, 2004.

30. Débats parlementaires, 1613, 1609.

31. Débats parlementaires, 1613.

32. Débats parlementaires, 1615. On race and the tightening of asylum rules, see Steve Garner, "The European Union and the Racialization of Immigration, 1985–2006," *Race / Ethnicity: Multidisciplinary Global Contexts* 1, no. 1 (Autumn 2007): 61–87.

33. "France: Policing, Public Order," *Statewatch*, January 1, 1991, accessed October 21, 2021, https://www.statewatch.org/statewatch-database/france-policing-public-order/.

34. Décision No. 93-325 DC; Texte intégral de la Constitution du 4 octobre 1958 en vigueur, art. 53-1; Soltesz, "Implications," 303–5.

35. Claude-Valentin Marie, "The EC Member States and Immigration in 1993: Closed Borders, Stringent Attitudes" (Working Document, European Commission, 1995), 11, 60, 52, accessed October 21, 2021, http://aei.pitt.edu/8693/1/8693.pdf.

36. Reproduced in *Der Spiegel*, June 1993; and see "Edouard Balladur," *Der Spiegel*, June 6, 1993.

37. Marie, "The EC Member States and Immigration," 9.

38. Gary Younge, "Ambalavaner Sivanandan Obituary," *Guardian*, February 7, 2018.

39. Ambalavaner Sivanandan, editorial, in "Europe: Variations on a Theme of Racism," *Race and Class* 32, no. 3 (January / March 1991): v.

40. Maurice Glélé-Ahanhanzo, *Implementation of the Programme of Action for the Second Decade to Combat Racism and Racial Discrimination*, Commission on Human Rights, February 15, 1996, E / CN.4 / 1996 / 72, available at Human Rights Library, University of Minnesota, accessed November 27, 2022, http://hrlibrary.umn .edu/commission/thematic52/72-racis.htm. See also Isabelle Vichniac, "Un Rapport des nations unies critique les 'lois-cadenas' sur l'immigration," *Le Monde*, April 16, 1996. On postwar rights discourse and anti-colonialism, see Samuel Moyn, "The Universal Declaration of Human Rights of 1948 in the History of Cosmopolitanism," *Critical Inquiry* 40, no. 4 (Summer 2014): 365–84.

41. Philippe Bernard, "Des Africains qui occupaient un gymnase parisien sont menacés d'expulsion," *Le Monde*, March 26, 1996.

42. Bernard, "Des Africains"; "Saint-Ambroise: Expulsion confirmée pour 39 Africains," *L'Humanité*, March 26, 1996.

43. The minister was Michel Barnier, who would become the EU's chief Brexit negotiator. Henri de Bresson, "La Bonne Volonté européenne du gouvernement s'arrête à la frontière belge," *Le Monde*, March 27, 1996.

44. Bernard, "Des Africains."

45. Bresson, "La Bonne Volonté."

46. "La Ballade des sans-papiers," in *Sans-papiers: Chroniques d'un mouvement*, IM'média / Reflex (Paris, 1997), 15–18 (hereafter *Chroniques*). Alain Morice, "1996–1997: L'Épopée des Saint-Bernard," *Plein droit*, no. 101 (2014): 40–44.

47. Bernard, "Des Africains."

48. *Chroniques*, 15–23.

49. *Chroniques*, 15.

50. *Chroniques*, 17; Didier Fassin, "Les 'Clandestins' et l'État," *Le Monde*, April 3, 1996.

51. Diop, *Peau*, 95, 115.

52. *Chroniques*, 17.

53. "Les Médiateurs dénoncent la 'brutalité' du pouvoir à l'égard des sans-papiers," *Le Monde*, September 1, 1996; Marc Chemillier, email, August 20, 1996, *Bok*, accessed March 12, 2023, https://www.bok.net/pajol/zpajol/z8-20-00.html; Behrman, *Law and Asylum*, 206; Diop, *Peau*, 98, 105, 107, 108–9, 117, 158. On the sans-papiers and organized labor, see Marcus Kahmann, "When the Strike Encounters the Sans Papiers Movement: The Discovery of a Workers' Repertoire of Actions for Irregular Migrant Protest in France," *Transfer: European Review of Labour and Research* 21, no. 4 (November 2015): 413–28; Alain Morice, "Sans-papiers: Une Difficile Reconnaissance," *Plein droit*, no. 89 (June 2011): 5–8.

54. Diop, *Peau*, 102–3; Cissé, *Parole*, 59. See also Morice, "Saint-Bernard."

55. Diop, *Peau*, 75; "Réfugiées à la Cartoucherie de Vincennes, les familles maliennes demandent un médiateur," *Le Monde*, April 2, 1996; Cissé, *Parole*, 58.

56. Diop, *Peau*, 109, 125; Cissé, *Parole*, 60–61.

57. Diop, *Peau*, 134; Cissé, *Parole*, 53–54; Madjiguène Cissé, "Sans-papiers: Les Premiers Enseignements," *Politique, la revue*, no. 2 (Autumn 1996): 9–14.

58. "Mort de Stéphane Hessel à l'âge de 95 ans," *Le Monde*, February 27, 2013; "UN officials mourn 'one of the great champions of human rights,' Stéphane Hessel," *UN News*, February 27, 2013, accessed March 15, 2023, https://news.un.org/en/story/2013/02/432982.

59. Diop, *Peau*, 109–10; Henri Tincq, "Noël Copin, journaliste," *Le Monde*, March 5, 2007; Joseph Cunneen, "Noël Copin: Shining Example of a Catholic Journalist," *National Catholic Reporter*, March 30, 2007, 8; "Antoine Sanguinetti: 'Nous avons des devoirs absolus envers les Africains de Saint-Bernard,'" *L'Humanité*, August 14, 1996. On Sanguinetti, see, "Fédération internationale des ligues des droits de l'homme—Comments," Observatoire De L'Action Humanitaire, accessed October 28, 2022, http://www.observatoire-humanitaire.org/en/index.php?page=fiche-ong.php&part=commentaires&chapitre=326&id=32; Jean Weydert, "André Costes avec les immigrés," *Migrations Société* 1, no. 17 (January–August 2005): 3–14.

60. *Chroniques*, 17–18.

61. *Chroniques*, 18–20. See Ismaël Halissat, "Henri Coindé, le 'curé des sans-papiers,' est mort," *Libération*, February 21, 2018.

62. *Chroniques*, 19.

63. Dominique Simonnot, "Le Conseil d'état est saisi du dossier des sans-papiers," *Libération*, August 22, 1996; François Bonnet, "Plusieurs dispositions des lois Pasqua apparaissent désormais inapplicables," *Le Monde*, August 23, 1996.

64. François Bonnet, "Le Conseil d'état rappelle que l'administration peut régulariser les sans-papiers," *Le Monde*, August 24, 1996.

65. David Dufresne, "Une Centaine d'Africains pourraient être régularisés," *Libération*, August 23, 1996; David Dufresne and Dominique Simonnot, "Manif contre les expulsions de sans-papiers," *Libération*, August 28, 1996.

66. *Chroniques*, 22.

67. *Chroniques*, 22; Aude Dassonville and Erich Inciyan, "7h30, les cloches de Saint-Bernard sonnent à la volée," *Le Monde*, August 24, 1996; Cécile Prieur, "Un Charter à destination du Mali serait prévu pour samedi matin," *Le Monde*, August 24, 1996.

68. *Chroniques*, 22; Winders, *Paris Africain*, 105; Dufresne and Simonnot, "Manif contre les expulsions."

69. "France: Curbs Unlawful," *Statewatch*, accessed March 30, 2023, https://www.statewatch.org/statewatch-database/france-curbs-unlawful/; "Anger in French suburbs," *Statewatch*, accessed March 30, 2023, https://www.statewatch.org/statewatch-database/anger-in-french-suburbs/.

70. *Chroniques*, 5, 6, 29–30, 83, 98–99, 88.

71. Étienne Balibar, "What We Owe to the "Sans-papiers," trans. Jason Francis McGimsey and Erika Doucette (speech given at a French Filmmakers' Union event in Paris, March 1997), available at Transversal Texts, accessed March 6, 2019, https://transversal.at/transversal/0313/balibar/en. And see *Chroniques*, 22; Winders, *Paris Africain*, 105.

72. Sanguinetti, "Des Devoirs absolus."

73. See Chin, *Crisis of Multiculturalism*, 120; Hargreaves, *Multi-Ethnic France*, 177; Gatrell, *Unsettling of Europe*, 331.

74. Martin Schain, *The Politics of Immigration in France, Britain, and the United States: A Comparative Study* (New York, 2012), 55.

75. Roland Cayrol, "La Société française reste taraudée par le racisme," *Le Monde*, July 2, 1998.

76. "Faible mobilisation pour les sans-papiers," *Le Monde*, August 24, 1999; Miriam Iris Ticktin, *Casualties of Care: Immigration and the Politics of Humanitarianism in France* (Berkeley, CA, 2011), 31–37.

77. Cissé, *Parole*, 185–87; "Le 'Pont de l'Europe' sera inauguré le 23 septembre," *Le Monde*, September 14, 1960.

78. On the African diaspora and transnational anti-racist activism, see Manning Marable and Vanessa Agard-Jones, eds., *Transnational Blackness: Navigating the Global Color Line* (Basingstoke, UK, 2008), especially 205–44.

79. Cissé, *Parole*, 186, 185.

80. Cissé, *Parole*, 185–90.

81. "Struggle for 'Sans Papiers' and 'Illegalised' People Netherlands," *A-Infos News Service*, March 2, 1999, accessed March 10, 2019, https://www.ainfos.ca/99/mar/ainfos00006.html.

82. Cissé, *Parole*, 192–94; Hélène le Bail, "Les Sans-papiers au Japon: Renforcement des contrôles et émergence d'une mobilisation en faveur des régularisations," *Ebisu— Études Japonaises* 46, no. 1 (2011): 13–37. See also Madjiguène Cissé, "The Sans-Papiers: A Woman Draws the First Lessons," in *We Are Everywhere: The Irresistible*

Rise of Global Anticapitalism (London, 2003), 41, accessed March 6, 2019, http://artactivism.members.gn.apc.org/allpdfs/038-The%20Sans%20Papiers.pdf.

83. See "Herr im Haus," *Der Spiegel*, August 19, 1996; Diop, *Peau*, 161. On the Internet and globalization from below, see Zeynep Tufekci, *Twitter and Tear Gas: The Power and Fragility of Networked Protest* (New Haven, CT, 2017); Appadurai, *Fear of Small Numbers*. On cross-border "proletarian internationalism" at a different moment, see Peter Linebaugh, "All the Atlantic Mountains Shook," *Labour / Le Travailleur* 10 (Autumn 1982): 88; and on networks of dissent at a different moment, see Nathan Perl-Rosenthal, "Corresponding Republics: Letter Writing and Patriot Organizing in the Atlantic Revolutions, ca. 1760–1792" (PhD diss., Columbia University, 2011); William Beatty Warner, *Protocols of Liberty: Communication Innovation and the American Revolution* (Chicago, 2013).

84. Florian Schneider, interview, July 4, 1997, *Bok*, accessed March 8, 2019, http://www.bok.net/pajol/international/kassel/florian.en.html.

85. Quoted in Marie Friedmann Marquardt, Susanna J. Snyder, and Manuel A. Vasquez, "Challenging Laws: Faith-Based Engagement with Unauthorized Immigration," in *Constructing Immigrant "Illegality": Critiques, Experiences, and Responses*, ed. Cecilia Menjívar and Daniel Kanstroom (Cambridge, UK, 2014), 277.

86. John Zarobell, *Art and the Global Economy* (Oakland, CA, 2017), 108; Adrian Searle, "Documenta 13: Mysteries in the Mountain of Mud," *Guardian*, June 11, 2012.

87. Catherine David, "Introduction," *Documenta X* (1997), accessed November 27, 2022, https://www.scribd.com/document/460929476/DAVID-Introduction-What-can-be-the-meaning-and-purpose-of-a-documenta-today.

88. Svenja Gertheiss, "Migration under Control: Sovereignty, Freedom of Movement, and the Stability of Order," in *Resistance and Change in World Politics: International Dissidence*, ed. Svenja Gertheiss, Stefanie Herr, Klaus Dieter Wolf, and Carmen Wunderlich (Cham: 2017), 254.

89. Schneider interview; Gertheiss, "Migration under Control," 254; Florian Schneider and Hagen Kopp, "A Brief History of the Noborder Network," Tactical Media Files, March 31, 2010, accessed March 11, 2019, http://www.tacticalmediafiles.net/articles/3332/A-Brief-History-of-the-Noborder-Network.

90. Nicolas Boilloux, "Le Cri des sans-papiers de Saint-Bernard," *Autres Temps: Cahiers d'éthique sociale et politique*, no. 52 (1996): 89–91.

91. Schneider interview; Mogniss H. Abdallah, "Papiere für alle: Vers un mouvement européen des sans-papiers," *Agence IM'média* via *Bok*, December 19, 1998, accessed March 10, 2019, http://www.bok.net/pajol/international/allemagne/liga/mog-liga.html.

92. Martin Bright, "Europewide Arrest Power Planned," *Guardian*, October 10, 1999; "EU-Gipfel ringt um Asylfrage," *Der Spiegel*, October 15, 1999.

93. Schneider and Kopp, "Brief History."

94. Bright, "Europewide Arrest Power Planned"; "EU-Gipfel ringt um Asylfrage."

95. Schneider and Kopp, "Brief History."

96. Quoted in Gertheiss, "Migration under Control," 255; Pam Alldred, "No Borders, No Nations, No Deportations," *Feminist Review*, no. 73 (2003): 154.

97. Cissé, *Parole*, 184.

98. Diop, *Peau*, 9.

99. Cissé, "Premiers enseignements."

100. Diop, *Peau;* Cissé, "Premiers enseignements"; Cissé, *Parole.*

101. Diop, *Peau*, 9–10. See Frantz Fanon, *Black Skin, White Masks*, trans. Charles Lam Markmann (New York, 1967).

102. Diop, *Peau*, 11, 33, 38, 44, 46, 53–54.

103. Diop, *Peau*, 69–70.

104. Diop, *Peau*, 71, 95, 171.

105. Diop, *Peau*, 183, 171.

106. Diop, *Peau*, 182, 9, 10.

107. Diop, *Peau*, 9, 184.

108. Diop, *Peau*, 184, 183, 76.

109. Cissé, *Parole*, 7, 9.

110. Salem Gérard, *La Santé dans la ville: Géographie d'un petit espace dense; Pikine (Sénégal)* (Paris, 1998), 86, 89, 271.

111. Cissé, *Parole*, 27–34. Philippe Bernard, "La Mort de Madjiguène Cissé, pasionaria du mouvement des sans-papiers," *Le Monde*, May 18, 2023.

112. Cissé, *Parole*, 34, 46, 40, 78, 81.

113. Cissé, *Parole*, 51–52, 234–35, 180, 38.

114. Cissé, *Parole*, 180–82, 205, 204.

115. Cissé, *Parole*, 9, 21, 205, 20, 181.

116. Cissé, *Parole*, 156, 195, 148, 195.

117. Cissé, *Parole*, 196, 235, 185, 196.

118. Cissé, *Parole*, 113–25, 118.

119. Cissé, *Parole*, 125–27.

120. *Cissé v. France*, European Court of Human Rights, Application no. 51346 / 99, (April 9, 2002).

121. Protocol no. 4. Likewise, the free movement guarantee of the International Covenant on Civil and Political Rights applied only to movement inside a state; see UN General Assembly, Resolution 2200A, International Covenant on Civil and Political Rights, A / RES / 2022A (XXI) (December 16, 1966).

122. European Convention for the Protection of Human Rights and Fundamental Freedoms, November 4, 1950, 213 UNTS 221 (hereafter ECHR), art. 8, which entered into force September 3, 1953.

123. *Nasri v. France*, 18 / 1994 / 465 / 546, Council of Europe, European Court of Human Rights, June 21, 1995, para. 13.

124. *Nasri v. France*, para. 6–20.

125. *Nasri v. France*, para. 33, 41, 42, 46.

126. *Berrehab v. The Netherlands*, 3 / 1987 / 126 / 177, European Court of Human Rights, May 28, 1988.

127. *Moustaquim v. Belgium*, European Court of Human Rights, February 18, 1991, para. 13.

128. *Beldjoudi v. France*, Application no. 12083 / 86, European Court of Human Rights, March 26, 1992.

129. ECHR, art. 11.

130. *Cissé v. France*, para. 42, 45.

131. Cissé, *Parole*, 7.

132. *Cissé v. France*, para. 35, 41, 44.

133. *Cissé v. France*, para. 47.

134. *Cissé v. France*, para. 48, 50, 53.

135. *Cissé v. France*, para. 8, 10, 12, 13, 14, 52.

136. *Cissé v. France*, para. 50, 40, 50.

137. *Cissé v. France*, para. 46, 52.

138. *Cissé v. France*, para. 53.

139. Abdallah, "Papiere für alle." Sara Callaway and Benoit Martin, "Papers for All Sans-Papiers in Europe," December 1998, *Bok*, accessed April 4, 2019, https://www.bok.net/pajol/sanspap/blackwomen/blackwomen3.en.html. "Madjiguène Cissé quitte la France," *Libération*, July 26, 2000; Jean-Luc Martin-Lagardette, "Madjiguène Cissé: L'Ex-sans-papière aide les femmes à créer des richesses," *Ouvertures*, January 4, 2010.

140. See Benhabib, *Dignity in Adversity*. On subaltern political practice, see Getachew, "Universalism," especially 823.

141. Paul Ricœur, "Le Retour de l'Événement," *Mélanges de l'Ecole française de Rome: Italie et Méditerranée* 104, no. 1 (1992): 29.

142. On sans-papiers theory, see Isabelle Sommier, "Le Renouveau de la critique sociale depuis les Années 1990: Entre mythe et réalité," *Modern and Contemporary France* 20, no. 2 (May 2012): 153–68. On human rights, see Moyn, "Universal Declaration." See also on Euripides' *Medea*—"as a barbarian she has no rights, but as a human being she has"—in Bruno Snell, *The Discovery of the Mind* (New York, 1982), 250.

143. Jacques Derrida, "Derelictions of the Right to Justice (But What Are the 'Sans-papiers' Lacking?)," in *Negotiations: Interventions and Interviews, 1971–2001*, ed. Elizabeth Rottenberg (Stanford, 2002), 135.

144. Fassin, "'Clandestins.'"

145. Derrida, "Derelictions," 136.

146. Derrida, "Derelictions," 136, 134, 138, 139.

147. Derrida, "Derelictions," 140, 144, 143.

148. Balibar, "What We Owe to the 'Sans-papiers.'"

149. Étienne Balibar, "*Droit de cité* or Apartheid?," in Balibar, *We, the People of Europe? Reflections on Transnational Citizenship*, trans. James Swenson (Princeton, NJ, 2004), 45, 39, 44. See also Étienne Balibar and Immanuel Wallerstein, *Race, Nation, Class: Ambiguous Identities*, trans. Chris Turner (London, 1991); Carl-Ulrik Schierup, Peo Hansen, and Stephen Castles, *Migration, Citizenship, and the European Welfare State: A European Dilemma* (Oxford, 2006), especially 4–5; Krishnan Kumar, "The Idea of Europe: Cultural Legacies, Transnational Imaginings, and the Nation-State," in *Europe without Borders: Remapping Territory, Citizenship, and Identity in a Transnational Age*, ed. Mabel Berezin and Martin Schain (Baltimore, 2003), especially 48.

150. Balibar, "*Droit de cité*", 48, 49.

151. Étienne Balibar, "Outline of a Topography of Cruelty: Citizenship and Civility in the Era of Global Violence," in *We, the People of Europe? Reflections on Transnational Citizenship*, trans. James Swenson (Princeton, NJ, 2004), 123.

152. Miri Davidson, "Two Roads for Europe: An Interview with Étienne Balibar," Verso, August 10, 2015, accessed April 11, 2019, https://www.versobooks.com/blogs /2169-two-roads-for-europe-an-interview-with-etienne-balibar.

153. Cissé, *Parole*, 238.

154. Bernard, "Des Africains"; Derrida, "Derelictions," 139.

Epilogue

1. "Luxembourg and the EU," Grand Duchy of Luxembourg, last updated June 18, 2015, accessed December 11, 2023, https://www.eu2015lu.eu/en/la -presidence/luxembourg-et-ue/index.html.

2. "European Museum Schengen," Grand Duchy of Luxembourg, accessed December 11, 2023, https://www.eu2015lu.eu/en/la-presidence/luxembourg-et-ue/musee -schengen/index.html.

3. Martina Kneip, interview with the author, October 11, 2021 (hereafter Kneip Oral History).

4. "Europe a fêté le 25e anniversaire de la signature des Accords de Schengen," Europa Forum, accessed December 11, 2023, https://europaforum.public.lu/fr /actualites/2010/06/schengen-1306/index.html.

5. Ibid.

6. *Report of the High Level Panel on the Free Movement of Persons*, chaired by Mrs. Simone Veil, presented to the European Commission on 18 March 1997 (Brussels, 1997). See Sewell Chan, "Simone Veil, Ex-Minister Who Wrote France's Abortion Law, Dies at 89," *New York Times*, June 30, 2017.

7. "Simone Veil ou la mémoire de la Shoa," *AFP*, June 30, 2017.

8. *Report of the High Level Panel*, 6. See also "Timeline—The Schengen Area," European Council, accessed December 11, 2023, https://www.consilium.europa.eu/en /policies/schengen-area/timeline-schengen-area/.

9. *Report of the High Level Panel*, 15, 5, 6.

10. *Report of the High Level Panel*, 21, 28, 21.

11. "Report on the Veil Report," Committee on Civil Liberties and Internal Affairs Rapporteur: Mrs Anne-Marie Schaffner (1998), 7.

12. "Commission Communication to the European Parliament and the Council on the Follow-up to the Recommendations of the High-Level Panel on the Free Movement of Persons," Brussels, July 1, 1998, 2, 01.07.1998, COM (1998) 403 final.

13. "Du marché commun à l'Europe des citoyens," Europa, accessed December 11, 2023, https://europa.eu/50/news/article/080102_fr.htm.

14. Bernard-Henri Levy, "Imagining Europe," Europa, December 14, 2007, accessed December 12, 2023, https://europa.eu/50/news/views/071214_en.htm.

15. Robert Raymond, "Avant-Propos," in "50 ans après le Traité de Rome," special issue, *Revue d'économie financière* 88, no. 50 (April 2007): 7.

16. Catherine Lalumière, "Construction européenne au-delà de l'économie," in "50 ans après le Traité de Rome," special issue, *Revue d'économie financière* 88, no. 50 (April 2007): 195.

17. Lalumière, "Construction européenne au-delà de l'economie," 196, 197, 195, 198.

18. Lalumière, "Construction européenne au-delà de l'economie," 200, 199, 200, 199.

19. Pierre Lepidi and Amadou Ndiaye, "Les sans-papiers de Saint-Bernard, vingt ans après," *Le Monde*, August 22, 2016.

20. Nathaniel Herzberg, "Ababacar Diop, au nom de tous les sans-papiers," *Le Monde*, January 11, 1997.

21. Béatrice Bantman, "Sans-papiers: Leur chemin mène à Rome. Après les églises, ils occupent l'ambassade du Vatican à Paris," *Libération*, August 3, 1998.

22. Lepidi and Ndiaye, "Les sans-papiers de Saint-Bernard."

23. "Diop met vis-à-vis aux enchères," *Le Nouvel Obs*, January 2, 2001; Sylvia Zappi, "L'ex-sans-papiers Ababacar Diop, nouveau millionnaire et toujours communiste," *Le Monde*, July 23, 2000.

24. Joëlle Frasnetti, "Ababacar Diop, sans-papiers devenu millionnaire," *Le Parisien*, January 7, 2001.

25. Lepidi and Ndiaye, "Les sans-papiers de Saint-Bernard"; "Diop met vis-à-vis aux enchères."

26. Marie-Christine Tabet, "Ababacar Diop, porte-voix des sans-papiers de Saint Bernard," *Le Figaro*, August 22, 2007; Lepidi and Ndiaye, "Les sans-papiers de Saint-Bernard."

27. "Let's March for Our Freedom!" *Freedom not Frontex*, February 3, 2014, accessed December 12, 2023, https://freedomnotfrontex.noblogs.org/post/2014/02/03/lets-march-for-our-freedom-may-june-2014/; "Daily Reports," *Freedom not Frontex*, accessed December 12, 2023, https://freedomnotfrontex.noblogs.org/daily-reports-journaux/; Heinz Nigg, "Sans-papiers on Their March for Freedom 2014: How Refugees and Undocumented Migrants Challenge Fortress Europe," *Interface* 7, no. 1 (May 2015): 263–88. See also Elias Steinhilper and Ilker Ataç, "Escaping from Asylum to Act as Citizens: Political Mobilization of Refugees in Europe," *OpenDemocracy*, September 19, 2016; Marco Perolini, "We Don't Remember the O-Platz Protest Camp for the Sake of It: Collective Memories and Visibility of Migrant Activism in Berlin," *Sociology Compass* 16, no. 12 (December 2022): e13009.

28. Including the Collectif des Sans-Papiers in France, the Internazionale dei Sans-Papiers e Migranti in Italy, and the Refugee Movement Oranienplatz Berlin in Germany.

29. Nigg, "March for Freedom," 264; Steinhilper and Ataç, "Escaping from Asylum"; Fran Ilich and Luis Humberto Rosales, "Borderhack 2000," accessed December 12, 2023, http://subsol.c3.hu/subsol_2/contributors/ilichtext.html.

30. Pam Alldred, "No Borders, No Nations, No Deportations," *Feminist Review*, no. 73 (2003): 153; Napuli Langa, "About the Refugee Movement in Kreuzberg / Berlin," *Movements—Journal für kritische Migrations- und Grenzregimeforschung* 1, no. 2 (2015): 2; Steinhilper and Ataç, "Escaping from Asylum"; "We Need Change Now!," *Krytyka Polityczna & European Alternatives*, December 14, 2015, accessed

December 12, 2023, https://politicalcritique.org/world/eu/2014/we-need-change
-now/. For a literary account of the plight of African refugees in Europe, see Jenny
Erpenbeck, *Go, Went, Gone*, trans. Susan Bernofsky (New York, 2017).

31. Nigg, "March for Freedom," 272.

32. Langa, "About the Refugee Movement," 6, 1.

33. Nigg, "March for Freedom," 282.

34. "Daily Reports."

35. Nigg, "March for Freedom," 275–76.

36. Carine Eff and Patrick Mony, "Émigration choisie: Entretien avec Madjiguène
Cissé," *Vacarme* 1 no. 31 (Winter 2007); *Cissé v. France*; *Shmorgunov and Others v.
Ukraine*, nos. 15367 / 14 and 13 others, January 21, 2021.

37. *Shmorgunov v. Ukraine*, para. 16; Timothy Snyder and Tatiana Zhurzhenko,
"Diaries and Memoirs of the Maidan," *Eurozine*, June 27, 2014.

38. *Shmorgunov v. Ukraine*, para. 17; "Background on Schengen Enlargement,"
European Commission, MEMO / 07 / 619, March 31, 2008; "Projet d'accord à caractère confidentiel complémentaire à l'accord entre les gouvernements des états de
l'union économique Benelux, de la République fédéral d'Allemagne et de la république
française relative à la suppression graduelle des contrôles aux frontières communes,"
June 4, 1985, binder 1b BNL, Council Archives. On Maidan's significance, see Timothy
Snyder, *The Road to Unfreedom: Russia, Europe, America* (New York, 2018), 124–31,
137, 153. By December 2023, amid Russia's ongoing war, EU leaders had agreed to start
accession talks with Ukraine; see Peter Dickinson, "Historic Breakthrough for Ukraine
as EU Agrees to Begin Membership Talks," *Atlantic Council*, December 14, 2023,
accessed December 16, 2023, https://www.atlanticcouncil.org/blogs/ukrainealert
/historic-breakthrough-for-ukraine-as-eu-agrees-to-begin-membership-talks/.

39. Ukraine ratified the ECHR in 1997; see Ukraine, press country profile,
European Court of Human Rights.

40. *Shmorgunov v. Ukraine*, para. 163; ECHR, art. 3, 5, 11.

41. *Cissé v. France*, para 50.

42. *Navalnyy and Yashin v. Russia*, no. 76204 / 11, December 4, 2014; *Navalnyy
v. Russia* [GC], nos. 29580 / 12 and 4 others, November 15, 2018; *Laurijsen and
Others v. the Netherlands*, nos. 56896 / 17 and 4 others, November 21, 2023; *Éva Molnár v. Hungary*, no. 10346 / 05, October 7, 2008.

43. *Shmorgunov v. Ukraine*, para. 150, 521, 520.

44. *Hirsi Jamaa and Others v. Italy* [GC], no. 27765 / 09, February 23, 2012.

45. *Tarakhel v. Switzerland* [GC], no. 29217 / 12, November 4, 2014.

46. *Khlaifia and Others v. Italy* [GC], no. 16483 / 12, December 15, 2016.

47. *Khlaifia v. Italy*, para. 52.

48. Regulation (EC) No. 562 / 2006 of the European Parliament and of the Council
of March 15, 2006, establishing a Community Code on the rules governing the movement of persons across borders (Schengen Borders Code), art. 23; art. 12, para. 14;
preamble; para. 20. Subsequent revisions of the Code have enhanced member-state
authority to impose temporary checks and control all persons crossing external borders. See "Revision of the Schengen Borders Code," Briefing, EU Legislation in Progress, European Parliament, April 2022, 2, accessed December 16, 2023, https://www

.europarl.europa.eu/RegData/etudes/BRIE/2022/729390/EPRS_BRI(2022)729390 _EN.pdf. See Violeta Moreno-Lax, *Accessing Asylum in Europe: Extraterritorial Border Controls and Refugee Rights under EU Law* (Oxford, 2017), 47–80.

49. "Background on Schengen Enlargement." Poland and the other countries that underwent Schengen inspection in 2006 joined at the end of 2007.

50. See Christopher Chope, "Mass Arrival of Irregular Migrants on Europe's Southern Shores," doc. 11053, Committee on Migration, Refugees and Population, Parliamentary Assembly, Council of Europe, October 3, 2006.

51. William Spindler, "Between the Devil and the Deep Blue Sea: Mixed Migration to Europe," UNHCR, October 5, 2007, accessed December 18, 2023, https://www.unhcr .org/us/news/stories/between-devil-and-deep-blue-sea-mixed-migration-europe.

52. "UNHCR Urges Focus on Saving Lives as 2014 Boat People Numbers Near 350,000," UNHCR, December 10, 2014, accessed December 18, 2023, https://www .unhcr.org/news/stories/unhcr-urges-focus-saving-lives-2014-boat-people-numbers -near-350000.

53. Missing Migrants Project, accessed December 13, 2023, https:// missingmigrants.iom.int/.

54. Gabriele Del Grande, "Fortress Europe," accessed December 13, 2023, https:// fortresseurope.blogspot.com/p/la-strage.html.

55. Nannette Abrahams, *Biopolitics and Geopolitics of a European Border Regime in Senegal: Postcolonial Hip-Hop-Narratives on the Externalization and Securitization of Migration in Africa* (Zürich, 2022), 262.

56. See Stefano degli Uberti, "Victims of Their Fantasies or Heroes for a Day? Media Representations, Local History and Daily Narratives on Boat Migrations from Senegal," *Cahiers d'Études Africaines*, [Cahier] 213 / 214, no. 54 (2014): 81–113; Miranda Poeze, "High-Risk Migration: From Senegal to the Canary Islands by Sea," in *Long Journeys: African Migrants on the Road*, ed. Alessandro Triulzi and Robert Lawrence McKenzie (Leiden, 2013), 45–66; Catherine M. Appert, *In Hip Hop Time: Music, Memory, and Social Change in Urban Senegal* (New York, 2018), 99; Christian Vium, "Icons of Becoming: Documenting Undocumented Migration from West Africa to Europe," *Cahiers d'Études Africaines*, [Cahier] 213 / 214, no. 54 (2014): 228.

57. Poeze, "High-Risk Migration," 46.

58. For example, in 2005, there were 14,500 arrivals on Lampedusa and almost 5,000 on the Canary Islands. See Chope, "Mass Arrival of Irregular Migrants," 8, 3, 10; European Parliament resolution on Lampedusa, P6_TA(2005)0138, 1, 2, accessed December 16, 2023, https://www.europarl.europa.eu/doceo/document/TA-6-2005-0138 _EN.pdf; *Tarakhel v. Switzerland*, para 50; Philippe Fargues, "Four Decades of Cross-Mediterranean Undocumented Migration to Europe: A Review of the Evidence," International Organization for Migration, 2017, 10–11, accessed December 16, 2023, https:// publications.iom.int/system/files/pdf/four_decades_of_cross_mediterranean.pdf.

59. Matteo de Bellis, "Ten Years since the Lampedusa Shipwreck, What Lessons Have Been Learned?," Amnesty International, October 3, 2023, accessed December 18, 2023, https://www.amnesty.org/en/latest/news/2023/10/ten-years-since-the -lampedusa-shipwreck-what-lessons-have-been-learned/; Sarah Stillman, "Lampedusa's Migrant Tragedy, and Ours," *New Yorker*, October 10, 2013; "At Least 366

People Dead in Wreck 1 km from Lampedusa," *Watch the Med*, October 10, 2013, accessed December 18, 2023, https://watchthemed.net/reports/view/31.

60. Lizzy Davies, "Lampedusa Victims Include Mother and Baby Attached by Umbilical Cord," *Guardian*, October 10, 2013.

61. "Homily of Holy Father Francis," Vatican, July 8, 2013, accessed December 18, 2023, https://www.vatican.va/content/francesco/en/homilies/2013/documents/papa -francesco_20130708_omelia-lampedusa.html.

62. Langa, "About the Refugee Movement," 4.

63. William Spindler, "2015: The Year of Europe's Refugee Crisis," UNHCR, December 8, 2015, accessed December 18, 2023, https://www.unhcr.org/us/news /stories/2015-year-europes-refugee-crisis; Phillip Connor, "Number of Refugees to Europe Surges to Record 1.3 Million in 2015," *Pew Research Center*, August 2, 2016; Ameer Ayaz and Abdul Wadood, "An Analysis of European Union Policy towards Syrian Refugees," *Journal of Political Studies* 27, no. 2 (Summer 2020): 1–19; Fargues, "Four Decades," 11.

64. Georg Blume et al., "Was geschah wirklich?," *Zeit Online*, August 30, 2016; Thomas Meaney, "In the Centre of the Centre," *London Review of Books*, September 21, 2017. On migration and historical memory, see Isaac Stanley-Becker and Alexandra Rojkov, "At a Site of Nazi Terror, Muslim Refugees Reckon with Germany's Past," *Washington Post*, August 10, 2017. And see Isaac Stanley-Becker, "Rewriting History or Attending to the Past? Monuments Still Confound Europe, Too," *Washington Post*, August 19, 2017.

65. "Temporary Reintroduction of Border Control," European Commission, Migration and Home Affairs, accessed December 13, 2023, https://home-affairs.ec.europa .eu/policies/schengen-borders-and-visa/schengen-area/temporary-reintroduction -border-control_en. See also Raphael Bossong and Tobias Etzold, "The Future of Schengen: Internal Border Controls as a Growing Challenge to the EU and the Nordics," SWP Comment, No. 44, German Institute for International and Security Affairs (October 2018); Elspeth Guild et al., "What Is Happening to the Schengen Borders?" (CEPS Paper in Liberty and Security, No. 86, December 2015), 8.

66. "European Refugee Crisis: Dutch to Bring in More Border Spot Checks," *DutchNews*, September 14, 2015; "France Won't Open Arms to Refugees Like Germany," *The Local / AFP*, September 7, 2015; Ayaz and Wadood, "Analysis of European Union Policy towards Syrian Refugees," 1–2.

67. "Temporary Reintroduction of Border Control." See also Anne Weyembergh et al., "The Paris Terrorist Attacks: Failure of the EU's Area of Freedom, Security and Justice?," *EU Immigration and Asylum Law and Policy*, January 6, 2016.

68. Andrew Higgins and James Kanter, "More Border Controls as Europe Stalls on Migrant Quotas," *New York Times*, September 14, 2015. On asylum in Germany, and the plight of Syrian exile Amira Suleiman, see Isaac Stanley-Becker, "In Germany, Merkel Welcomed Hundreds of Thousands of Refugees: Now Many are Suing Her Government," *Washington Post*, July 26, 2017.

69. Spindler, "2015."

70. See William Outhwaite, "Migration Crisis and 'Brexit,'" in *The Oxford Handbook of Migration Crises*, ed. Cecilia Menjivar et al., 93–110 (Oxford, 2019); Wiener,

"Forging Flexibility—the British 'No' to Schengen"; Stanley-Becker, "Brexit Could Hamper European Counterterrorism Efforts."

71. Matthias Luecke and Tim Breemersch, *Schengen Border Controls: Challenges and Policy Options*, European Parliament (2016), 6, 5, 4; Bossong and Etzold, "Future of Schengen," 1.

72. Kneip Oral History; "Temporary Reintroduction of Border Control."

73. *Coronavirus and the Cost of Non-Europe: An Analysis of the Economic Benefits of Common European Action*, European Parliamentary Research Service (May 2020), 4.

74. "Temporary Reintroduction of Border Control." See updated Schengen Borders Code, Regulation (EU) 2016 / 399 of the European Parliament and of the Council of 9 March 2016 on a Union Code on the rules governing the movement of persons across borders, chapter 2, art. 25, para. 4. See Isaac Stanley-Becker, "Immigrant from UAE Held in Fatal Knife Attack at German Supermarket, Authorities Say," *Washington Post*, July 28, 2017; Isaac Stanley-Becker, "Finnish Police Investigating Fatal Stabbing an Act of Terrorism," *Washington Post*, August 19, 2017.

75. "Temporary Reintroduction of Border Control." On the ongoing refugee crisis, see James McAuley, "The Calais 'Jungle' Is Gone, but France's Migrant Crisis is far from Over," *Washington Post*, June 10, 2017. Borders also opened in response to crises; see Isaac Stanley-Becker, "Purim in Berlin: Ukrainian Jews Find Refuge in What Was Once Europe's 'Center of Darkness,'" *Washington Post*, March 19, 2022.

76. *NW v. Landespolizeidirektion Steiermark and Bezirkshauptmannschaft Leibnitz*, C-368 / 20 and C-369 / 20, 2022 ECR, para. 74.

77. *NW v. Landespolizeidirektion Steiermark and Bezirkshauptmannschaft Leibnitz*, para. 65, 3, 31, 44.

78. "Temporary Reintroduction of Border Control"; Kira Schacht, "Schengen States Extend Border Checks, Ignoring EU Court," *DW*, November 17, 2022; "Italy Suspends Open Border with Slovenia, Citing Increased Terror Threat as Mideast Violence Spikes," *Associated Press*, October 18, 2023; Lorne Cook, "Shooter Attack in Belgium Drives an EU Push to Toughen Border and Deportation Laws," *Associated Press*, October 19, 2023; Andreas Meyer-Feist, "'Schengen ist Kaputt,'" *Tagesschau*, October 19, 2023.

79. Robert Goebbels, letter to the author, November 15, 2023.

80. See Stanley-Becker, "Border Camps Show the Schengen Zone Only Ever Promised Europeans Free Movement"; *Khlaifia v. Italy*; Steve Scherer, "Italy Builds New Detention Centres to Speed Up Migrant Deportations," *Reuters*, May 9, 2017; Kevin Sieff and Isaac Stanley-Becker, "Europe Is Trying to Cut the Flow of Migrants from Africa. It Won't Be Easy," *Washington Post*, August 31, 2017.

81. Jean-Christophe Dupuis-Rémond, "Régionales 2015: Florian Philippot dépose une gerbe à Schengen," *France 3 Régions*, September 19, 2015.

82. Assma Maad, "'Je ne connais pas cette théorie du 'grand remplacement': L'Amnésie de Marine Le Pen," *Le Monde*, March 18, 2019. See also James McAuley, "How Gay Icon Renaud Camus Became the Ideologue of White Supremacy," *The Nation*, June 17, 2019.

83. "Schengen European Museum Ceiling Collapse, an EU Omen?," *Luxembourg Times*, May 12, 2016.

LIST OF ARCHIVES

Archives Diplomatiques: Affaires Etrangères, Commerce Extérieur et Coopération au Développement. Brussels, Belgium.
Affaires intérieures 18.778 / XXIX / I / 5 1978–1982
Coopération au Développement
Cooperation politique européenne 18779 / 16 1984–1985
Défense 18.778 / XXIX / II / 6 1981–1987
Central Archives of the Council of the European Union. Brussels, Belgium.
BNL-D-F, C-OJ-PV NOTES, 1985
BNL-D-F + gc red cc BNL, 1984–1985
Schengen overleg correspondentie, 1984–1987
François-Mitterrand Library. Bibliothèque Nationale de France. Paris, France.
Historical Archives. Court of Justice of the European Union. Luxembourg.
Affaire 293 / 83 F. Gravier contre Ville de Liège
Historical Archives. European Commission. Brussels, Belgium.
Conseil Européen de Fontainebleau 25–26 juin 1984
Historical Archives of the European Union. Florence, Italy.
Coupures de Presse de Parlement européen CPPE-2019 01 / 04 / 198704 / 1987–
28 / 04 / 1987 Juridique et des droits des citoyens
Femmes d'Europe
François Lamoureux Fonds
International Paneuropean Union
Parlement européen—Troisième legislature
Ministère de l'Europe et des Affaires Étrangères. La Courneuve, Seine-Saint-Denis, France.
Coordination interministérielle pour l'allègement des contrôles aux frontières, 1984–1991
Mouvement des Coordonnateurs libre circulation, 1985–1989
Secrétaire d'État auprès du Mre Charge des Affaires Européennes: Mme Catherine Lalumière, 7 décembre 1984–17 mars 1986
Politisches Archiv des Auswärtigen Amts. Berlin, Germany.
Abbau der Grenzkontrollen; Deutschland-Frankreich-Benelux—von Schengen-Abkommen, 1984–1986
Abbau Grenzformalitäten, Abkommen "Schengen," 1985, 190351
Europäischer Rat in Fontainebleau vom 25.6.1984–26.6.1984 421.26 (29), 1984
Grenzkontrollen für Personen, Waren, Kapital, 1983–1986
Staatsvertrag über die Verlegung der Personenkontrollen an die Außengrenzen
Übereinkommen vom 14.06.1985 zwischen den Regierungen der Staaten der

Benelux-Wirtschaftsunion, der Bundesrepublik Deutschland und der Französischen Republik betreffend den schrittweisen Abbau der Kontrollen an
den gemeinsamen Grenzen, 1985–1987, 463233
Übereinkommen vom 19.06.1990 zur Durchführung des Übereinkommens
von Schengen vom 14.06.85 zwischen den Regierungen der BENELUX-
Wirtschaftsunion, der Bundesrepublik Deutschland und der Französischen
Republik betreffend den schrittweisen Abbau der Kontrollen an den
gemeinsamen Grenzen (Schengener Durchführungsabkommen—SDÜ) ein-
schließlich: Erklärungen zur Nacheile gem. § 41 (9) Bilaterale Drogenverein-
barung Deutschland / Frankreich, 1985–1988, 463246

BIBLIOGRAPHY

Primary Sources

GOVERNMENT DOCUMENTS

International Treaties

Accord d'adhésion de la république italienne à la convention d'application de l'accord de Schengen du 14 juin 1985 entre les gouvernements des états de l'union économique Benelux, de la république fédérale d'Allemagne et de la république française relatif à la suppression graduelle des contrôles aux frontières communes, signée à Schengen le 19 juin 1990, *Journal officiel des Communautés européennes* 43, no. L239 [s.l.] (September 22, 2000).

Accord relatif à la suppression graduelle des contrôles aux frontières communes du Benelux, de la République fédérale d'Allemagne et de la France, 14 juin 1985, (Schengen Agreement), OJ (L239) (2000) [s.l.].

Consolidated Version of the Treaty on the Functioning of the European Union, June 7, 2016, 2016 OJ (C 202) 47.

Convention Determining the State Responsible for Examining Applications for Asylum Lodged in One of the Member-States of the European Communities, June 15, 1990, 1997 OJ (C 254) 1.

Convention Implementing the Schengen Agreement of 14 June 1985 between the government of the States of the Benelux Economic Union, the Federal Republic of Germany and the French Republic on the gradual abolition of checks at their common borders, June 19, 1990, art. 29, OJ (L. 239), 22.09.2000, 19–62.

European Convention for the Protection of Human Rights and Fundamental Freedoms, November 4, 1950, 213 UNTS 221 (entered into force September 3, 1953).

Protocol No. 4 to the Convention for the Protection of Human Rights and Fundamental Freedoms, Securing Certain Rights and Freedoms Other than Those Already Included in the Convention and in the First Protocol Thereto, opened for signature September 16, 1963, E.T.S. No. 46.

Protocol on the Privileges and Immunities of the European Communities, Brussels, April 8, 1965, 1348 UNTS 3.

Saarbrücken Accord, July 13, 1984, 1401 UNTS. 167.

Single European Act, February 17, 1986, 25 ILM 503 (1986).

Treaty Establishing the European Economic Community, March 25, 1957, 298 UNTS 11 (1958).

Treaty Instituting the Benelux Economic Union, February 3, 1958, 381 UNTS 165.

Treaty of Amsterdam Amending the Treaty on European Union, the Treaties Establishing the European Communities and Certain Related Acts, October 2, 1997, OJ (C340) 1 (1997).

Treaty of Lisbon Amending the Treaty on European Union and the Treaty Establishing the European Community, December 13, 2007, 2007 OJ (C 306) 1.

Treaty on European Union, February 7, 1992, 31 ILM. 247.

United Nations Documents

Annex I, List of Intergovernmental Organizations Seeking Accreditation to the Follow-up International Conference on Financing for Development to Review the Implementation of the Monterrey Consensus, Doha, Qatar, November 29–December 2, 2008. New York, General Assembly of the United Nations, 2008.

Convention Relating to the Status of Refugees, adopted July 28, 1951, 1954, 189 UNTS 137, entered into force April 22.

Implementation of the Programme of Action for the Second Decade to Combat Racism and Racial Discrimination, report by Mr. Maurice Glélé-Ahanhanzo, Special Rapporteur on Contemporary Forms of Racism, Racial Discrimination, Xenophobia and Related Intolerance, Submitted Pursuant to Commission on Human Rights Resolutions 1993 / 20 and 1995 / 12. Commission on Human Rights, E / CN.4 / 1996 / 72. February 15, 1996.

Recueil des Traités: Traités et accords internationaux enregistrés ou classes et inscrits au repertoire au secrétariat de l'organisation des Nations Unies, vol. 2386. New York, 1996.

UN General Assembly, Resolution 2200A, International Covenant on Civil and Political Rights, A / RES / 2022A (XXI) (December 16, 1966).

"UN Officials Mourn `One of the Great Champions of Human Rights,' Stéphane Hessel." *UN News*, February 27, 2013. Accessed March 15, 2023. https://news.un .org/en/story/2013/02/432982.

"UNHCR Urges Focus on Saving Lives as 2014 Boat People Numbers Near 350,000." UNHCR, December 10, 2014. Accessed December 18, 2023. https://www.unhcr .org/news/stories/unhcr-urges-focus-saving-lives-2014-boat-people-numbers -near-350000.

Universal Declaration of Human Rights, G.A. Res. 217A (III), U.N. Doc. A / 810 (1948).

European Communities/European Union Documents

Council of the European Union

Council Act of 26 July 1995 drawing up the Convention based on Article K.3 of the Treaty on European Union, on the establishment of a European Police Office (Europol Convention), art. 3 (1, 4), OJ (C 316 / 01) (1995).

Council Decision 2005 / 211 / JHA of 24 February 2005 concerning the introduction of some new functions for the Schengen Information System, including in the fight against terrorism, OJ (L 68 / 44) (2005), https:// publications.europa.eu/en/publication-detail/-/publication/d0258379-0f37 -4aa8-a2d9-666467d18005/language-en.

Council Decision 63 / 266 / EEC of 2 April 1963 Laying Down General Principles for Implementing a Common Vocational Training Policy, OJ (1963).

Council Decision of 22 December 2000 establishing a European Police College (CEPOL), art. 6, OJ (L 336 / 2) (2000).

"General Guidelines for Drawing Up a Community Programme on Vocational Training" (Adopted at the 162nd session of the Council held on July 26, 1971), (1971), OJ (C 81 / 5) (1971), https://eur-lex.europa.eu/legal-content/EN/TXT /PDF/?uri=CELEX:31971Y0812&from=EN.

Regulation (EEC) No. 1612 / 68 of the Council of 15 October 1968 on freedom of movement for workers within the Community (1968), OJ (L 257 / 2).

European Coal and Steel Community

Resolution adopted by the Foreign Ministers of the ECSC Member States at Messina. June 1–3, 1955. Accessed November 18, 2023. https://www.cvce.eu /obj/resolution_adopted_by_the_foreign_ministers_of_the_ecsc_member _states_messina_1_to_3_june_1955-en-d1086bae-0c13-4a00-8608 -73c75ce54fad.html.

Spaak, Paul-Henri. *The Brussels Report on the General Common Market*. Luxembourg, June 1956.

European Commission

"Commission Communication to the European Parliament and the Council on the Follow-up to the Recommendations of the High-Level Panel on the Free Movement of Persons," Brussels, July 1, 1998, COM (1998) 403 final.

"Commission Report on the Implementation of a Passport Union." *Bulletin of the European Communities*, supplement 7 (July 3, 1975).

"Communication from the Commission to the Council and the European Parliament on the Follow-Up to the Recommendations of the High-Level Panel on the Free Movement of Persons," COM (98) 403 final, July 1, 1998.

Completing the Internal Market: White Paper from the Commission to the European Council (Milan, 28–29 June 1985), COM (85) 310 final (June 14, 1985). Accessed June 17, 2022. http://europa.eu/documents/comm/white _papers/pdf/com1985_0310_f_en.pdf.

Consolidating the Internal Market. Communication from the Commission to the European Council, Fontainebleau. June 25–26, 1984, COM (84) / 350 final (July 9, 1984.

Directory of the Commission of the European Communities. June 1985. Accessed October 14, 2023. http://aei.pitt.edu/75545/.

Marie, Claude-Valentin. "The EC Member States and Immigration in 1993: Closed Borders, Stringent Attitudes." Working Document, European Commission, 1995. Accessed October 21, 2021. http://aei.pitt.edu/8693/1/8693.pdf.

Proposal for a Council Directive on a Right of Residence for Nationals of Member States in the Territory of Another Member State, COM (1979) 215 Final, OJ (C207) (July 31, 1979).

Proposal for a regulation of the European Parliament and of the council amending Regulation (EU) 2018 / 1862 on the establishment, operation and use of the Schengen Information System (SIS) in the field of police cooperation and judicial cooperation in criminal matters as regards the entry of alerts by Europol, 2020 / 0350 (COD), https://home-affairs.ec.europa.eu/system /files/2020-12/09122020_proposal_regulation_ep_council_amending _regulation_2018-1862_establishment_operation_use_sis_field_police _cooperation_judicial_cooperation_criminal_matters_com-2020_791_pe -2020-8991_en.pdf.

"Rapport de la Commission sur la mise en œuvre d'une Union des passeports," 7, no. 75 (Luxembourg: Office des publications officielles des Communautés européennes, July 3, 1975).

Report of the High Level Panel on the Free Movement of Persons, chaired by Mrs. Simone Veil, presented to the European Commission on March 18, 1997. Brussels, 1997.

"Report on the Establishment of a Working Party Instructed to Review the Possibility of the Establishment of a Passport Union at Community Level." *Bulletin of the European Communities*, supplement 7 (July 3, 1975).

"Schengen Area." EU Immigration Portal. Accessed October 23, 2023, https:// home-affairs.ec.europa.eu/policies/schengen-borders-and-visa/schengen -area_en.

"Schengen Information System." European Commission, Migration and Home Affairs. Accessed March 9, 2023. https://home-affairs.ec.europa.eu/policies /schengen-borders-and-visa/schengen-information-system_en.

"Temporary Reintroduction of Border Control." European Commission, Migration and Home Affairs. Accessed December 13, 2023. https://home-affairs.ec .europa.eu/policies/schengen-borders-and-visa/schengen-area/temporary -reintroduction-border-control_en.

European Council

Adonnino, Pietro. "A People's Europe: Reports from the Ad Hoc Committee." *Bulletin of the European Communities*, supplement 7 (March 29 and 30, 1985).

Adonnino, Pietro. Introductory letter from the Chairman to the President of the European Council, in "A People's Europe: Reports from the Ad Hoc Committee." *Bulletin of the European Communities*, supplement 7 / 85.

Annex 1, Presidency Conclusions, European Council, June 28 and 29, 1991, Luxembourg.

Conclusions de la réunion tenue à Bonn le 23 novembre 1987, Groupe central de négociation, 15 décembre 1987, SCH / C, 1985–1988, V-OJ-PV, European Council.

Conclusions du conseil européen de Fontainebleau. June 25 and 26, 1984. *Bulletin des Communautés européennes*, no. 6. Luxembourg: Office des publications officielles des Communautés européennes.

Conclusions, June 28 and 29, 1985. *Bulletin of the European Communities*, supplement 7.

Conclusions of the Fontainebleau European Council. June 25 and 26, 1984. *Bulletin of the European Communities*, no. 6 (Luxembourg, June 1984).

Conclusions of the Milan European Council, extract on the completion of the internal market. June 28 and 29, 1985. *Bulletin of the European Communities*, no. 6.

Conclusions, Session du Conseil européen, Strasbourg. December 8 and 9, 1989. *Conclusions des Sessions Du Conseil Européen (1975–1990)*. Accessed

November 19, 2023. https://www.consilium.europa.eu/media/20577/1989
_d_cembre_-_strasbourg__fr_.pdf.

"The Palma Document," Free Movement of Persons, A Report to the European
Council by the Coordinators' Group (Madrid, June 1989). Accessed December 30, 2023. http://www.statewatch.org/semdoc/assets/files/keytexts/ktch1
.pdf.

"Paris Summit, Final Communiqué." *Bulletin of the European Communities* 12.
December 9–10, 1974.

"Rapport du Comité ad hoc 'Europe des citoyens.' Rapport adressé au Conseil
européen de Bruxelles." March 29 and 30, 1985. *Bulletin des Communautés
européennes*, no. 3.

"Rapport du comité pour l'Europe des citoyens remis au Conseil européen de
Milan." June 28–29, 1985. *Bulletin des Communautés européennes*, supplement 7 / 85.

"Timeline—The Schengen Area." European Council. Accessed December 11,
2023. https://www.consilium.europa.eu/en/policies/schengen-area/timeline
-schengen-area/.

Tindemans, Leo. *Report on European Union, Presented to the European Council,
December 29, 1975. Bulletin of the European Communities*, supplement 1 (1976).

European Parliament

*Coronavirus and the Cost of Non-Europe: An Analysis of the Economic Benefits
of Common European Action*. European Parliamentary Research Service.
May 2020.

Directive 95 / 46 / EC of the European Parliament and of the Council of 24
October 1995 on the protection of individuals with regard to the processing
of personal data and on the free movement of such data, arts. 7, 25, OJ
(L 281) (1995), 31–350.

Draft Treaty Establishing the European Union. Bulletin of the European Communities 2. February 1984.

European Parliament resolution on Lampedusa, P6_TA (2005) 0138, 1, 2.
Accessed December 16, 2023. https://www.europarl.europa.eu/doceo
/document/TA-6-2005-0138_EN.pdf.

"Fact Sheets on the European Union." European Parliament. Accessed October 3, 2018. http://www.europarl.europa.eu/factsheets/en/home.

Ford, Glyn. *Report Drawn Up on Behalf of the Committee of Inquiry into Racism and Xenophobia on the Findings of the Committee of Inquiry*. European
Parliament. Luxembourg, 1991.

Luecke, Matthias, and Tim Breemersch, *Schengen Border Controls: Challenges
and Policy Options* (2016).

Mitterrand, François. Speech to the European Parliament. May 24, 1984. *Official
Journal of the European Communities*, no. 1–314.

Papahatzi, Elpida. *Free Movement of Persons in the European Union: Specific
Issues*. European Parliament Directorate General for Research, Civil Liberties Series, Working Document PE167.028. Brussels, May 1999.

"Pietro Adonnino." European Parliament. Accessed October 12, 2023. http://www.europarl.europa.eu/meps/en/957/PIETRO_ADONNINO_home.html.

Regulation (EC) No. 56 / 2006 of the European Parliament and of the Council of March 15, 2006, establishing a Community Code on the rules governing the movement of persons across borders (Schengen Borders Code).

Regulation (EU) 2016 / 399 of the European Parliament and of the Council of 9 March 2016 on a Union Code on the rules governing the movement of persons across borders.

"Revision of the Schengen Borders Code." Briefing, EU Legislation in Progress, European Parliament. April 2022. Accessed December 16, 2023. https://www.europarl.europa.eu/RegData/etudes/BRIE/2022/729390/EPRS_BRI(2022)729390_EN.pdf.

Statement by Jacques Delors, President of the Commission, to the European Parliament and his reply to the ensuing debate. March 12, 1985. *Bulletin of the European Communities*, supplement 4 / 85.

Other International Documents

Council of Europe

Chope, Christopher. "Mass Arrival of Irregular Migrants on Europe's Southern Shores." Committee on Migration, Refugees and Population, Parliamentary Assembly, Council of Europe. Doc. 11053. October 3, 2006.

Council of Europe. Convention for the Protection of Individuals with regard to Automatic Processing of Personal Data. ETS No. 108, January 28, 1981.

Council of Europe. Recommendation No. R (87) 15 of the Committee of Ministers to Member States regulating the use of personal data in the police sector. REC (87) 15. September 17, 1987.

European Court of Human Rights

Ukraine, press country profile, European Court of Human Rights.

Interpol

"1923—How Our History Started." Interpol. Accessed April 23, 2023. https://www.interpol.int/en/Who-we-are/INTERPOL-100/1923-how-our-history-started.

ICPO-INTERPOL I / CONS / GA / 1956 (2017).

"Key Dates." Interpol. Accessed April 23, 2023. https://www.interpol.int/Who-we-are/INTERPOL-100/Key-dates#:~:text=each%20in%20prison.-,1989,Fran%C3%A7ois%20Mitterrand%2C%20on%2027%20November.

"Legal Documents." Interpol. Accessed March 14, 2024. https://www.interpol.int/en/Who-we-are/Legal-framework/Legal-documents.

National Government Documents

Assemblée nationale, Débats parlementaires, 1 séance du 15 juin 1993. *Journal officiel de la République française* 30, no. 1 (1993). Accessed, November 27, 2022. http://archives.assemblee-nationale.fr/10/cri/1992-1993-ordinaire2/052.pdf.

Basic Law for the Federal Republic of Germany of 1949.

"The Benelux." Luxembourg Government. Accessed October 21, 2023. https://gouvernement.lu/en/dossiers/2018/benelux.html.

"Bericht der Bundesregierung zur Lage der Nation im geteilten Deutschland." *Bulletin des Presse- und Informationsamtes der Bundesregierung*, no. 30 (March 1984).

Constitution du 4 octobre 1958, Sénat. Accessed March 13, 2024. https://www.senat.fr /connaitre-le-senat/evenements-et-manifestations-culturelles/les-revisions-de-la -constitution/constitution-du-4-octobre-1958-texte-originel.html.

Deutscher Bundestag, Plenarprotokoll 12 / 89 (April 30, 1992).

"European Museum Schengen." Le Gouvernement du Grand-Duché Luxembourg. Accessed December 11, 2023. http://www.eu2015lu.eu/en/la-presidence /luxembourg-et-ue/musee-schengen/index.

LOI no 97–396 du 24 avril 1997 portant diverses dispositions relatives à l'immigration. Accessed November 27, 2022. https://www.legifrance.gouv.fr/jorf/id/JORFTEX T000000564968.

"Luxembourg and the EU." Grand Duchy of Luxembourg. Updated June 18, 2015. Accessed December 11, 2023. https://www.eu2015lu.eu/en/la-presidence/luxem bourg-et-ue/index.html.

"Rede des Bundeskanzlers, Dr. Helmut Kohl, vor dem Deutschen Bundestag am 27. Juni 1985 über die Zielsetzungen der Europapolitik der Bundesregierung." *Bulletin der Bundesregierung* 28, no. 75 (June 1985).

"Schengen Agreement: Opinion of the Dutch Council of State." *Statewatch*, January 1, 1991. https://www.statewatch.org/statewatch-database/schengen-agreement -opinion-of-the-dutch-council-of-state/.

Texte intégral de la Constitution du 4 octobre 1958 en vigueur. Accessed March 13, 2024. https://www.conseil-constitutionnel.fr/le-bloc-de-constitutionnalite/texte -integral-de-la-constitution-du-4-octobre-1958-en-vigueur.

Judicial Decisions

Beldjoudi v. France, Application no. 12083 / 86, European Court of Human Rights, March 26, 1992.

Belgian State v. Humbel, Case 263 / 86, 1988, ECR.

Berrehab v. The Netherlands, 3 / 1987 / 126 / 177; 10730 / 84, European Court of Human Rights, May 28, 1988.

Blaizot v. University of Liège, Case 24 / 86, 1988 ECR.

Bundesverfassungsgericht, 1 BvR 209 / 83, December 15, 1983.

CC Decision No. 76–71 DC, December 29–30, 1976, 31, *Journal Officiel de la République Française*, December 31, 1976.

CC Decision No. 93–325 DC, August 13, 1993, 2, http://www.conseil-constitutionnel.fr /conseil-constitutionnel/root/bank/download/93325Dca93325dc.pdf.

Cissé v. France, European Court of Human Rights, Application no. 51346 / 99, April 9, 2002.

Commission of the European Communities v. Kingdom of the Netherlands, Case C-68 / 89, 1991 ECR.

Conseil Constitutionnel [Constitutional Court], Compte rendu de la séance du jeudi 25 juillet 1991, 34 (Jacques Robert, Rapporteur, Conference resulted in decision No. 91–294 DC), http://www.conseil-constitutionnel.fr/conseil-constitutionnel /root/bank_mm/decisions/PV/pv1991-07-25.pdf.

Decision No. 91–294 DC, July 25, 1991, appended to Conseil Constitutionnel [Constitutional Court], Compte rendu de la séance du jeudi 25 juillet 1991.

Forcheri v. Belgium, Case 152 / 82, 1983 ECR.

French Republic v. Cisse, No. 97081307, Court of Cassation, Criminal Division, June 4, 1998.

Gravier v. City of Liège, Case 293 / 83, 1985 ECR.

———. Advocate General Sir Gordon Slynn, Opinion 596 (1985).

Germany, France, Netherlands, Denmark and United Kingdom v. Commission, Joined Cases 281, 283 to 285 and 287 / 85, 1987 ECR.

———. Report for the hearing delivered in Joined Cases 281, 283 to 285 and 287 / 85, 1987 ECR.

Gül v. Switzerland, Application no. 23218 / 94, European Court of Human Rights, February 19, 1996.

Hirsi Jamaa and Others v. Italy [GC], no. 27765 / 09, February 23, 2012.

Khlaifia and Others v. Italy [GC], no. 16483 / 12, December 15, 2016.

Laurijsen and Others v. the Netherlands, nos. 56896 / 17 and 4 others, November 21, 2023.

Molnár v. Hungary, no. 10346 / 05, October 7, 2008.

Moustaquim v. Belgium, Application no. 12313 / 86, European Court of Human Rights, February 18, 1991.

Navalnyy and Yashin v. Russia, no. 76204 / 11, December 4, 2014.

Nasri v. France, 18 / 1994 / 465 / 546, European Court of Human Rights, June 21, 1995.

Navalnyy v. Russia [GC], nos. 29580 / 12 and 4 others, November 15, 2018.

NV Algemene Transporten Expeditie Onderneming van Gend en Loos v. Netherlands Inland Revenue Administration, Case 26 / 62, 1963 ECR.

NW v. Landespolizeidirektion Steiermark and Bezirkshauptmannschaft Leibnitz, C-368 / 20 and C-369 / 20, 2022 ECR.

Refugee Appeal No. 1 / 92 Re SA, New Zealand, Refugee Status Appeals Authority, April 30, 1992.

Saisine par 60 députés, June 29, 1991, CC decision No. 91–294 DC, July 25, 1991.

Shmorgunov and Others v. Ukraine, nos. 15367 / 14 and 13 others. January 21, 2021.

Tarakhel v. Switzerland [GC], no. 29217 / 12, November 4, 2014.

Wijsenbeek, Case C-378 / 97, 1999 ECR I-6207.

ARTICLES, BOOKS, REPORTS, AND WEBSITES

Abdallah, Mogniss H. "Papiere für alle: Vers un mouvement européen des sans-papiers." *Agence IM'média*. December 19, 1998. Accessed March 10, 2019. http://www.bok.net/pajol/international/allemagne/liga/mog-liga.html.

Agamben, Giorgio. "The Sovereign Police." In *The Politics of Everyday Fear*, edited by Brian Massumi, 61–64. Minneapolis, 1993.

Amnesty International Report 1991. London, 1991.

"Appendix II Conclusions and Recommendations of the Colloquy 'Human Rights without Frontiers.'" *Netherlands Quarterly of Human Rights* 8, no. 1 (March 1990): 85–87.

Arendt, Hannah. *The Origins of Totalitarianism*. New York, 1951.

"At Least 366 People Dead in Wreck 1 km from Lampedusa." *Watch the Med.* October 10, 2013. Accessed December 18, 2023. https://watchthemed.net/reports/view/31.

"Background on Schengen Enlargement." European Commission. MEMO / 07 / 619. March 31, 2008.

Balibar, Étienne. "Le droit de cité ou l'apartheid?" In *Sans-papiers: L'Archaïsme fatal,* edited by Étienne Balibar, Monique Chemillier-Gendreau, Jacqueline Costa-Lascoux, and Emmanuel Terray, 89–110. Paris, 1999.

———. *We, the People of Europe? Reflections on Transnational Citizenship.* Translated by James Swenson. Princeton, NJ, 2004.

———. "What We Owe to the 'Sans-papiers.'" Translated by Jason Francis Mc Gimsey and Erika Doucette. Speech given at a French Filmmakers' Union event in Paris, March 1997. Accessed March 6, 2019. http://eipcp.net/transversal/0313/balibar/en.

Balibar, Étienne, and Immanuel Wallerstein. *Race, Nation, Class: Ambiguous Identities.* Translated by Chris Turner. London, 1991.

"La Ballade des sans-papiers." In *Sans-papiers: Chroniques d'un mouvement,* 15–22. IM'média / Reflex. Paris, 1997.

"Bericht der Bundesregierung zur Lage der Nation im geteilten Deutschland." *Bulletin des Presse- und Informationsamtes der Bundesregierung,* no. 30 (March 1984).

"Berlin Resolution of the International Conference of Data Protection Commissioners of 30 August 1989." Global Privacy Assembly. Accessed March 14, 2024. http:// globalprivacyassembly.org/wp-content/uploads/2015/02/11th-ICDPPC-Berlin -1989-Berlin-Resolution.pdf.

Blackstone, William. *Commentaries on the Laws of England in Four Books with Notes Selected from the Editions of Archbold, Christian, Coleridge, Chitty, Stewart, Kerr, and Others, Barron Field's Analysis, and Additional Notes, and a Life of the Author by George Sharswood.* Vol. 1, book. 1. Philadelphia, 1893.

Blanc, Hubert. "Schengen: Le Chemin de la libre circulation en Europe." *Revue du Marché Commun et de l' Union européene,* no. 351 (October 1991): 722–26.

Boilloux, Nicolas. "Le Cri des sans-papiers de Saint-Bernard." *Autres Temps: Cahiers d'éthique sociale et politique,* no. 52 (1996): 89–91.

Boggs, Carl, and David Plotke, eds. *The Politics of Eurocommunism: Socialism in Transition.* Montreal, 1980.

Bunyan, Tony. *Key Texts on Justice and Home Affairs in the European Union.* Vol. 1, *(1976–1993): From Trevi to Maastricht.* Nottingham, 1997.

Bunyan, Tony, ed. *Statewatching the New Europe: A Handbook on the European State.* London, 1993.

Burant, Stephen R., ed. *East Germany: A Country Study.* Washington, DC, 1988.

Busch, Heiner. "Europa—ein 'Mekka der Kriminalität?' EG-Grenzöffnung und international Polizeikooperation." *Kritische Justiz* 23, no. 1 (1990): 1–13.

Buzan, Barry. "New Patterns of Global Security in the Twenty-First Century." *International Affairs* 67, no. 3 (July 1991): 431–51.

Callaway, Sara, and Benoit Martin. "Papers for All Sans-Papiers in Europe." *Bok.* December 1998. Accessed April 4, 2019. https://www.bok.net/pajol/sanspap /blackwomen/blackwomen3.en.html.

Caloz-Tschopp, Marie-Claire, Micheline Fontolliet-Honoré, and Lode Van Outrive. *Europe: Montrez patte blanche!; Les Nouvelles Frontières du 'laboratoire Schengen'.* Geneva, 1993.

"Chronicle 13 June 1990." *Chronik der Mauer, Zentrum für Zeithistorische Forschung Postdam e.V., Bundeszentrale für politische Bildung, and Deutschlandradio.* Accessed February 12, 2019. http://www.chronik-der-mauer.de/en/chronicle/ _year1990/_month6/?moc=1.

"50 ans après le Traité de Rome." Special issue, *Revue d'économie financiére* 88, no. 50 (April 2007).

Cissé, Madjiguène. *Parole de Sans-papiers.* Paris, 1999.

———. "The Sans-Papiers: A Woman Draws the First Lessons." In *We Are Everywhere: The Irresistible Rise of Global Anticapitalism,* 38–45. London, 2003. http:// artactivism.members.gn.apc.org/allpdfs/038-The%20Sans%20Papiers.pdf.

———. "Sans-papiers: Les Premiers enseignements." *Politique, la revue,* no. 2 (Autumn 1996): 9–14.

Coles, G. "Speech." In *Colloquy: "Human Rights without Frontiers"; Strasbourg, 30 November—1 December 1989; Proceedings,* edited by Committee of Experts for the Promotion of Education and Information in the Field of Human Rights, 7–8. Strasbourg, 1989.

"Colloquy 'Human Rights without Frontiers.'" *Netherlands Quarterly of Human Rights* 8, no. 1 (March 1990): 62–63.

Committee of Experts for the Promotion of Education and Information in the Field of Human Rights, ed. *Colloquy: "Human Rights without Frontiers"; Strasbourg, 30 November—1 December 1989; Proceedings.* Strasbourg, 1989.

Connor, Phillip. "Number of Refugees to Europe Surges to Record 1.3 Million in 2015." *Pew Research Center.* August 2, 2016.

"Les Conséquences de la loi du 9 septembre 1986 sur l'entrée et le séjour des étrangers." *Hommes & Migrations* 1118 (1989): 22–28.

Coudenhove-Kalergi, Richard. "Memorandum on the Organization of a Parliament for Europe." February 12, 1947. Accessed November 19, 2023. https://www.cvce .eu/content/publication/2003/10/8/4a3090c1-8247-4fd3-ad6b-2c9adb4b2203 /publishable_en.pdf.

———. *Crusade for Pan-Europe: Autobiography of a Man and a Movement.* New York, 1943.

———. "Das paneuropäische Manifest." In *Die Idee Europa, 1300–1946: Quellen zur Geschichte der politischen Einigung,* edited by Rolf Hellmut Foerster. Munich, 1963.

———. *Pan-Europe.* Anonymous translation. New York, 1926.

Council of Europe. *Yearbook of the European Convention on Human Rights.* The Hague, 1976.

Cruz, Antonio. *An Insight into Schengen, Trevi and Other European Governmental Bodies.* Briefing paper 1. Brussels, 1990.

———. *Schengen, Ad Hoc Immigration Group and Other European Intergovernmental Bodies in View of a Europe without Internal Borders.* Brussels, 1993.

"Daily Reports." *Freedom not Frontex.* Accessed December 12, 2023. https://noblogs .org/daily-reports-journaux/.

Dankert, Piet. "Discours de Piet Dankert sur la convention d'application de l'accord de Schengen (Schengen, 19 juin 1990)." *Bulletin de documentation du Service Information et Presse, Ministère d'État*, no. 3 (1990): 10–11.

——. "La Signature de la Convention d'application de l'accord de Schengen.'" *Bulletin de documentation du Service Information et Presse, Ministère d'État*, no. 3 (1990).

Daoudal, Yves. "Immigrés, terroristes, produits extra-européenns: La France livrée à toutes les invasions." *Présent*. May 18, 1989.

Das Heidelberger Programm. Heidelberg, Sozialdemokratischen Partei Deutchlands, 1925. Marxists Internet Archive. Accessed October 3, 2023. https://www.marxists .org/deutsch/geschichte/spd/1925/heidelberg.htm.

David, Catherine. "Introduction." *Documenta X*. 1997. Accessed November 27, 2022. https://www.scribd.com/document/460929476/DAVID-Introduction-What-can -be-the-meaning-and-purpose-of-a-documenta-today.

Davidson, Miri. "Two Roads for Europe: An Interview with Étienne Balibar." Verso. August 10, 2015. Accessed April 11, 2019. https://www.versobooks.com/blogs/2169 -two-roads-for-europe-an-interview-with-etienne-balibar.

De Bellis, Matteo. "Ten Years Since the Lampedusa Shipwreck, What Lessons Have Been Learned?" Amnesty International. October 3, 2023. Accessed December 18, 2023. https://www.amnesty.org/en/latest/news/2023/10/ten-years-since-the -lampedusa-shipwreck-what-lessons-have-been-learned/.

De Rougement, Denis. "Message to Europeans." Centre virtuel de la connaissance sur l'Europe. May 10, 1948. Accessed October 8, 2023. https://www.cvce.eu/content /publication/1997/10/13/b14649e7-c8b1-46a9-a9a1-cdad800bccc8/publishable _en.pdf.

De Rudder-Paurd, Véronique. "La Tolérance s'Arrête au Seuil." *Pluriel*, no. 21 (1980): 3–13.

Debré, Michel. *Entretiens avec le Général De Gaulle, 1961–1969*. Paris, 1993.

——. *Français choisissons l'espoir*. Paris, 1979.

——. *La mort de l'État républicain*. Paris, 1947.

——. *La République et son pouvoir*. Paris, 1950.

Del Grande, Gabriele. "Fortress Europe." *Fortress Europe* (blog). Accessed December 13, 2023. https://fortresseurope.blogspot.com/p/la-strage.html.

Derrida, Jacques. "Derelictions of the Right to Justice (But What Are the 'Sans-papiers' Lacking?)." In *Negotiations: Interventions and Interviews, 1971–2001*, edited by Elizabeth Rottenberg, 133–44. Stanford, 2002.

Diop, Ababacar. *Dans la peau d'un sans-papier*. Paris, 1997.

"'Discours de Monsieur Robert Goebbels, secrétaire d'état aux affaires étrangères sur l'accord relatif à la suppression graduelle des contrôles aux frontières communes du Benelux, de la République Fédérale d'Allemagne et de la France." *Bulletin de documentation*, no. 4 (June–August 1985).

"Erklärung von Bundeskanzler Helmut Kohl und Staatspräsident François Mitterrand zum Abbau der Grenzkontrollen anlässlich der deutsch-französischen Konsultationen am 29. Und 30. Oktober 1984 in Bad Kreuznach." *Bulletin des Presse- und Informationsamtes der Bundesregierung*, no. 131 (November 1984).

Ernst and Whinney. *Research on the 'Cost of Non-Europe': Basic Findings.* Luxembourg, 1988.

"Europe a fêté le 25e anniversaire de la signature des Accords de Schengen." Europa Forum, Grand-Duché de Luxembourg. June 13, 2010. Accessed December 11, 2023. http://www.europaforum.public.lu/fr/actualites/2010/06/schengen-1306/index .html.

Europe: Harmonization of Asylum Policy: Amnesty International's Concerns,' Summary. November 1990.

European Consultation on Refugees and Exiles, ed. *Refugee Policy in a Unifying Europe: Seminar Held in Zeist, Netherlands, 5–7 April 1989.* London, 1989.

"European Data Network," *New Scientist.* January 5, 1984.

"Europol's Amended Regulation Enters into Force." Europol. June 28, 2022. Accessed May 2, 2023. https://www.europol.europa.eu/media-press/newsroom/news /europols-amended-regulation-enters-force.

Everling, Ulrich. "The Court of Justice as a Decisionmaking Authority." *Michigan Law Review* 82, no. 5 / 6 (April–May 1984): 1294–1310.

Fanon, Frantz. *Black Skin, White Masks.* Translated by Charles Lam Markmann. New York, 1967.

Fargues, Philippe. "Four Decades of Cross-Mediterranean Undocumented Migration to Europe: A Review of the Evidence." International Organization for Migration. 2017. Accessed December 16, 2023. https://publications.iom.int/system/files/pdf /four_decades_of_cross_mediterranean.pdf.

Fauveau, Jean-Claude. *Le Monde de la distribution: Les 100 plus grands groupes et leurs implantations européennes.* Paris, 1994.

"Fédération internationale des ligues des droits de l'homme—Comments." Observatoire De L'Action Humanitaire. Accessed October 28, 2022. http://www .observatoire-humanitaire.org/en/index.php?page=fiche-ong.php&part =commentaires&chapitre=326&id=32.

Fooner, Michael. *Interpol: Issues in World Crime and International Justice.* New York, 1989.

"Foreign and Colonial." *The Spectator.* August 25, 1849.

Foucault, Michel. *Discipline and Punish: The Birth of the Prison.* Translated by Alan Sheridan. New York, 1979.

"Frontex, the European Border and Coast Guard Agency, after One Year." Frontex. October 6, 2017. Accessed April 4, 2019. https://frontex.europa.eu/media-centre /news/news-release/frontex-the-european-border-and-coast-guard-agency-after -one-year-BJMHvS.

Gaïa, Patrick. "Commentaire de la décision du Conseil Constitutionnel no. 91–294 du 25 juillet 1991: Loi autorisant l'approbation de la convention d'application de l'accord de Schengen, du 14 juin 1985." *Revue de la Recherche Juridique* 17, no. 1 (1992): 25–54.

"Germany for Germans": Xenophobia and Racist Violence in Germany. Human Rights Watch. London, 1995.

Giot-Mikkelsen, Michel. "Polizeilicher Informationsaustausch im EG-Binnenmarkt." In *Verbrechensbekämpfung in europäischer Dimension*, edited by Deutschland Bundeskriminalamt, 145–54. Wiesbaden, 1992.

Halff, Antoine. "When Mitterrand Cozied up to Marshal Petain: French in a Furor over a President's Secret Past." *Forward.* September 9, 1994.

"Hannspeter Hellbeck." Available at Munzinger. Accessed March 28, 2024. https://www.munzinger.de/search/go/document.jsp?id=00000018516.

Hayek, Friedrich A. "The Economic Conditions of Interstate Federalism." Originally printed in *New Commonwealth Quarterly.* Reprinted in *Individualism and Economic Order*, 255–72. Chicago, 1980.

"Homily of Holy Father Francis." Vatican. July 8, 2013. Accessed December 18, 2023. https://www.vatican.va/content/francesco/en/homilies/2013/documents/papa-francesco_20130708_omelia-lampedusa.html.

Hreblay, Vendelin. *La Libre circulation des personnes: Les Accords de Schengen.* Paris, 1994.

Hugo, Victor. *The Schengen Castle.* 1871. Watercolor on paper. Accessed October 25, 2021. https://collections.mnaha.lu/object/mnha24720/.

Huyssen, Andreas. "Nation, Race, and Immigration: German Identities after Unification." *Discourse* 16, no. 3 (Spring 1994): 6–28.

Ilich, Fran, and Luis Humberto Rosales. "Borderhack 2000." Accessed December 12, 2023. http://subsol.c3.hu/subsol_2/contributors/ilichtext.html.

"Jacques Robert." Available at Conseil Constitutionnel. Accessed March 30, 2024, https://www.conseil-constitutionnel.fr/membres/jacques-robert.

Julien-Laferriere, François. "The Treatment of Refugees and Asylum Seekers at Points of Entry." In *Colloquy: "Human Rights without Frontiers"; Strasbourg, 30 November—1 December 1989; Proceedings*, edited by Committee of Experts for the Promotion of Education and Information in the Field of Human Rights, 23–34. Strasbourg, 1989.

Kant, Immanuel. "Idea for a Universal History with a Cosmopolitan Purpose." *Political Writings*, edited by Hans Reiss, translated by H. B. Nisbet. 2nd ed. Cambridge, UK, 1991.

Kant, Immanuel. "Perpetual Peace." *Political Writings*, edited by Hans Reiss, translated by H. B. Nisbet. 2nd ed. Cambridge, UK, 1991.

Keohane, Robert O., and Stanley Hoffman, eds. *The New European Community: Decisionmaking and Institutional Change.* New York, 1991.

Kohl, Helmut. *Deutschlands Zukunft in Europa: Reden und Beiträge des Bundeskanzlers.* Herford, Germany, 1990.

Koopmans, Thijmen. "The Judicial System Envisaged in the Draft Treaty." EUI. Working Paper No. 85 / 145. European Policy Unit. January 1985.

Lalumière, Catherine. "Welcome Speech." In *Colloquy: "Human Rights without Frontiers"; Strasbourg, 30 November—1 December 1989; Proceedings*, edited by Committee of Experts for the Promotion of Education and Information in the Field of Human Rights, 5–6. Strasbourg, 1989.

Langa, Napuli. "About the Refugee Movement in Kreuzberg / Berlin." *Movements—Journal für kritische Migrations- und Grenzregimeforschung* 1, no. 2 (2015).

Le Jeune, Patrick. "Europol." Paper presented to the Joint Sessions of Workshops, European Consortium for Political Research, Limerick, March 30–4 April, 1992.

"Legal Documents." Interpol. Accessed March 14, 2024. https://www.interpol.int/en/Who-we-are/Legal-framework/Legal-documents.

"Let's March for Our Freedom!" *Freedom not Frontex*. March 2, 2014. Accessed December 12, 2023. https://freedomnotfrontex.noblogs.org/post/2014/02/03/lets-march-for-our-freedom-may-june-2014/.

Levy, Bernard-Henri. "Imagining Europe." Europa. December 14, 2007. Accessed December 12, 2023. https://europa.eu/50/news/views/071214_en.htm.

Lipgens, Walter. *A History of European Integration*. Oxford, 1982.

Loescher, Gil. "The European Community and Refugees." *International Affairs* 65, no. 4 (Autumn 1989): 617–36.

M&S International. "How M&S Expanded Internationally and Engaged with Customers Around the World." Marks and Spencer Company Archive. Accessed February 2, 2019. https://marksintime.marksandspencer.com/download?id=2842.

Martin-Lagardette, Jean-Luc. "Madjiguène Cissé: L'Ex-sans-papière aide les femmes à créer des richesses." *Ouvertures*. January 4, 2010.

McDonald, Marci. "The Truckers' Highway Revolt." *Maclean's*. March 5, 1984.

Murray, John L. "Fundamental Rights in the European Community Legal Order." *Fordham Int'l L.J.* 531 (2008): 531–50.

Nigg, Heinz. "Sans-papiers on Their March for Freedom 2014: How Refugees and Undocumented Migrants Challenge Fortress Europe." *Interface* 7, no. 1 (May 2015): 263–88.

Nobel, Peter. "Problems Relating to the Reception of Migrants at Entry Points: Rights and Education of New Arrivals." In *Colloquy: "Human Rights without Frontiers"; Strasbourg, 30 November–1 December 1989; Proceedings*, edited by Committee of Experts for the Promotion of Education and Information in the Field of Human Rights, 35–50. Strasbourg, 1989.

Pluchinsky, Dennis A. "Middle Eastern Terrorism in Europe: Trends and Prospects." *Terrorism* 14, no. 2 (1991): 67–76.

"Projet de loi Debré." *Bok*. Accessed March 17, 2024. https://www.bok.net/pajol/projloi.html.

Ricœur, Paul. "Le Retour de l'Evénement." *Meélanges de l'Ecole française de Rome: Italie et Meéditerraneée* 104, no. 1 (1992): 29–35.

Sans-papiers: Chroniques d'un mouvement. IM'média / Reflex. Paris, 1997.

Scherer, Steve. "Italy Builds New Detention Centres to Speed Up Migrant Deportations." *Reuters*. May 9, 2017. https://www.reuters.com/article/us-europe-migrants-italy-deportations/italy-builds-new-detention-centers-to-speed-up-migrant-deportations-idUSKBN1851T7.

Schneider, Florian. Interview. *Bok*. July 4, 1997. Accessed March 8, 2019. http://www.bok.net/pajol/international/kassel/florian.en.html.

Schneider, Florian, and Hagen Kopp. "A Brief History of the Noborder Network." Tactical Media Files. March 31, 2010. Accessed March 11, 2019. http://www.tacticalmediafiles.net/articles/3332/A-Brief-History-of-the-Noborder-Network.

Sivanandan, Ambalavaner. Editorial. "Europe: Variations on a Theme of Racism." *Race and Class* 32, no. 3 (January / March 1991): v–vi.

Smits, Jeanne. "Dans le brouillard du 'territoire Schengen.'" *Présent*. November 16, 1989.

Snyder, Timothy, and Tatiana Zhurzhenko. "Diaries and Memoirs of the Maidan." *Eurozine*. June 27, 2014.

Spaak, Paul-Henri. "Europe in a Western Community." *The Annals of the American Academy of Political and Social Science* 282, no. 1 (July 1952): 45–52.

——. "The Integration of Europe: Dreams and Realities." *Foreign Affairs*. October 1950.

——. Letter. September 9, 1944. Centre virtuel de la connaissance sur l'Europe. Accessed November 18, 2023. https://www.cvce.eu/en/obj/circular_letter_from _paul_henri_spaak_london_9_september_1944-en-7360a69f-943d-442f-98a5 -b0feeb017a91.html.

Spindler, William. "2015: The Year of Europe's Refugee Crisis." UNHCR. December 8, 2015. Accessed December 18, 2023. https://www.unhcr.org/us/news/stories/2015 -year-europes-refugee-crisis.

——. "Between the Devil and the Deep Blue Sea: Mixed Migration to Europe." UNHCR. October 5, 2007. Accessed December 18, 2023. https://www.unhcr.org /us/news/stories/between-devil-and-deep-blue-sea-mixed-migration-europe.

Spinelli, Altiero. "L'Union européenne des fédéralistes en 1952." *La voix fédéraliste*. Organe de l'Organisation Luxembourgeoise du Mouvement Européen, No. 1. Luxembourg: Organisation Luxembourgeoise du Mouvement Européen. 3. Accessed October 26, 2023. https://www.cvce.eu/en/obj/altiero_spinelli_the_union_of _european_federalists_in_1952-en-a3cbcc45-033e-4fb9-9cce-49ebf371d786 .html.

Spinelli, Altiero, and Ernesto Rossi. *The Ventotene Manifesto*. Centre virtuel de la connaissance sur l'Europe. June 1941. Accessed February 23, 2023. https://www .cvce.eu/obj/the_manifesto_of_ventotene_1941-en-316aa96c-e7ff-4b9e-b43a -958e96afbecc.html.

Statewatch (London, England), 1991–1999.

Storbeck, Jürgen. "Zwischenstaatliche Zusammenarbeit im Polizeialltag aus der Sicht einer Zentralstelle." In *Verbrechensbekämpfung in europäischer Dimension*, edited by Deutschland Bundeskriminalamt, 155–67. Wiesbaden, 1992.

"Struggle for 'Sans Papiers' and 'Illegalised' People Netherlands." *A-Infos News Service*. March 2, 1999. Accessed March 10, 2019. https://www.ainfos.ca/99/mar /ainfos00006.html.

Stuart, Alexander Mackenzie. "The European Communities and the Rule of Law." Delivered at the Institute of Advanced Legal Studies. London, 1977.

Útil, Arte. "Kein Mensch ist Illegal." Archive. Accessed March 3, 2022. https://www .arte-util.org/projects/kein-mensch-ist-illegal/.

Warren, Samuel, and Louis Brandeis. "The Right to Privacy." *Harvard Law Review* 4, no. 5 (December 1890): 193–220.

"We Need Change Now!" *Krytyka Polityczna & European Alternatives*. December 14, 2015. Accessed December 12, 2023. https://politicalcritique.org/world/eu/2014 /we-need-change-now/.

Weber, Max. "Politics as a Vocation." In *The Vocation Lectures*, edited by David Owen and Tracy B. Strong, translated by Rodney Livingstone. Indianapolis, 2004 [1919].

Weichert, Thilo. "Das geplante Schengen-Informationssystem." *Computer und Recht*, no. 1 (1990): 62–66.

"Wim van Eekelen." Indonesia-Nederland Society. Accessed October 8, 2021. https:// www.indonesia-nederland.org/about-us/board-of-trustees/wim-van-eekelen/.

NEWSPAPERS

Associated Press (New York), 2004–23.
BBC News (London, England), 2011.
Bild (Berlin, Germany), 1984.
La Croix (Paris, France), 2000.
Daily Telegraph (London, England), 1984.
Deutsches Allgemeines Sonntagsblatt (Hamburg, Germany), 1989.
Deutsche Welle (Bonn, Germany), 2022.
DutchNews (Netherlands), 2015.
Les Échos (Paris, France), 1996.
L'Express (Paris, France), 1997.
Le Figaro (Paris, France), 1989–96.
Financial Times (London, England), 2011.
Frankfurter Allgemeine Zeitung (Frankfurt, Germany), 2015.
Frankfurter Rundschau (Frankfurt, Germany), 1984.
Guardian (London, England), 1976–2012.
L'Humanité (Paris, France), 1954–96.
Independent (London, England), 2015.
Irish Examiner (Cork, Ireland), 2006.
Irish Independent (Dublin, Ireland), 1987.
Irish Times (Dublin, Ireland), 1974–85.
Leeuwarder Courant (Leeuwarden, The Netherlands), 1990.
Libération (Paris, France), 1987–2018.
La Libre Belgique (Brussels, Belgium), 1986, 2017.
The Local / AFP (Paris, France), 2015.
London Review of Books (London, England), 2017.
Los Angeles Times (Los Angeles, US), 1986.
Luxembourg Times, 2016.
Luxemburger Wort (Luxembourg City, Luxembourg), 1990.
Le Matin (Lausanne, Switzerland), 1984.
Le Monde (Paris, France), 1989–2019.
Le Monde DIplomatique (Paris, France), 2021.
New Statesman (London, England), 2018.
New York Times (New York City, US), 1974–2017.
New Yorker (New York, US), 2013.
Nieuwsblad van het Noorden (Groningen, The Netherlands), 1985–92.
Le Nouvel Obs (Paris, France), 2001.
Nu.nl (Hoofddorp, Netherlands), 2014.
Observer (London, England), 1985.
OpenDemocracy (London, England), 2016.
Le Parisien (Paris, France), 2001.
Le Point (Paris, France), 1984.
Politico (Arlington, US), 2001.

Présent (Paris, France), 1989.

Le Quotidien de Paris (Paris, France), 1984.

Le Républicain Lorrain (Metz, France), 1987.

Reuters (London, England), 2017.

Rhein-Neckar-Zeitung (Heidelberg, Germany), 2017.

Le Soir (Brussels, Belgium), 1985–92.

Der Spiegel (Hamburg, Germany), 1984–2005.

Süddeutsche Zeitung (Munich, Germany), 1985.

Tagesschau (Hamburg, Germany), 2023.

The Times (London), 1987.

Times of India (Mumbai, Maharashtra, India), 1984.

La Tribune (Paris, France), 1991.

Valeurs Actuelles (Paris, France), 1989.

Washington Post (Washington, DC, US), 1984–2021.

Die Zeit (Hamburg, Germany), 2016.

ORAL HISTORIES

Carl, Willi. Interview by the author. July 22, 2023.

Deville, Roger. Interview by the author. August 16, 2023.

Eich, Irene-Maria. Interview by the author. August 31, 2023.

Goebbels, Robert. Interview by the author. November 1, 2021.

Gravier. Françoise. Interview by the author. September 13, 2023.

Kneip, Martina. Interview by the author. October 11, 2021.

Kremlis, Georges. Interview by the author. February 19, 2018.

Lalumière, Catherine. Interview by the author. October 19, 2017.

Storbeck, Jürgen. Interview by the author. February 18, 2019.

Van Hyfte, Guy. Interview by the author. August 16, 2023.

Secondary Sources

BOOKS AND REPORTS

Abdelal, Rawi. *Capital Rules: The Construction of Global Finance.* Cambridge, MA, 2007.

Abrahams, Nannette. *Biopolitics and Geopolitics of a European Border Regime in Senegal: Postcolonial Hip-Hop-Narratives on the Externalization and Securitization of Migration in Africa.* Zurich, 2022.

Abrams, Richard K., Peter Cornelius, Per L. Hedfors, and Gunnar Tersman. *The Impact of the European Community's Internal Market on the EFTA.* Washington, DC, 1990.

Adams, Thomas McStay. *Europe's Welfare Traditions Since 1500: Reform without End.* Vol. 2, *1700–2000.* London, 2023.

Agier, Michel. *Gérer les indésirables: Des Camps de réfugiés au gouvernement humanitaire.* Paris, 2008.

Alexander, Robin. *Die Getriebenen: Merkel und die Flüchtlingspolitik; Report aus dem Inneren der Macht.* Munich, 2017.

Alter, Karen. *The European Court's Political Power: Selected Essays.* Oxford, 2009.

Anderson, Karen M. *Social Policy in the European Union.* London, 2015.

Anderson, Malcom, and Joanna Apap, eds. *Police and Justice Co-operation and the New European Borders.* The Hague, 2002.

Anderson, Malcolm, and Monica den Boer, eds. *Policing across National Boundaries.* London, 1994.

Anderson, Malcolm, Monica den Boer, Peter Cullen, William C. Gilmore, Charles Raab, and Neil Walker. *Policing the European Union.* Oxford, 1995.

Anderson, Malcolm, and Eberhard Bort, eds. *The Frontiers of Europe.* London, 1998.

Andreas, Peter, and Ethan Nadelmann. *Policing the Globe: Criminalization and Crime Control in International Relations.* Oxford, 2006.

Andry, Aurélie Dianara. *Social Europe, the Road Not Taken: The Left and European Integration in the Long 1970s.* Oxford, 2022.

Apap, Joanna. *The Rights of Immigrant Workers in the European Union: An Evaluation of the EU Public Policy Process and the Legal Status of Labour Immigrants from the Maghreb Countries in the New Receiving States.* The Hague, 2002.

Appadurai, Arjun. *Fear of Small Numbers: An Essay on the Geography of Anger.* Durham, NC, 2006.

Appert, Catherine M. *In Hip Hop Time: Music, Memory, and Social Change in Urban Senegal.* New York, 2018.

Baker, William F. *Jacques Prévert.* New York, 1967.

Barry, Brian, and Robert E. Goodin, eds. *Free Movement: Ethical Issues in the Transnational Migration of People and Money.* University Park, PA, 1992.

Bauman, Mechthild. *Der deutsche Fingerabdruck: Die Rolle der deutschen Bundesregierung bei der Europäisierung der Grenzpolitik.* Baden-Baden, 2006.

Becker, Peter. *Dem Täter auf der Spur: Eine Geschichte der Kriminalistik.* Darmstadt, 2005.

Behrman, Simon. *Law and Asylum: Space, Subject, Resistance.* Abingdon, UK, 2018.

Benhabib, Seyla. *The Claims of Culture: Equality and Diversity in the Global Era.* Princeton, NJ, 2002.

———. *Dignity in Adversity: Human Rights in Troubled Times.* Cambridge, UK, 2011.

———. *The Rights of Others: Aliens, Residents and Citizens.* Cambridge, UK, 2004.

Benyon, John, Lynne Turnbull, Andrew Willis, Rachel Woodward, and Adrian Beck. *Police Co-operation in Europe: An Investigation.* Leicester, 1993.

Berezin, Mabel, and Martin Schain, eds. *Europe without Borders: Remapping Territory, Citizenship, and Identity in a Transnational Age.* Baltimore, 2003.

Bergström, Maria, and Anna Jonsson Cornell, eds. *European Police and Criminal Law Co-operation.* Oxford, 2014.

Betts, Paul. *Ruin and Renewal: Civilizing Europe after World War II.* New York, 2020.

Bickerton, Christopher J., Dermot Hodson, and Uwe Puetter, eds. *The New Intergovernmentalism: States and Supranational Actors in the Post-Maastricht Era.* Oxford, 2015.

Bigo, Didier, ed. *The Field of the EU Internal Security Agencies*. Paris, 2007.

———. *Polices en Réseaux: L'Expérience européenne*. Paris, 1996.

Bigo, Didier, and Elspeth Guild, eds. *Controlling Frontiers: Free Movement into and within Europe*. Aldershot, UK. 2005.

Body-Gendrot, Sophie, and Catherine Wihtol de Wenden. *Policing the Inner City in France, Britain, and the US*. Basingstoke, UK, 2014.

Bond, Martyn. *Hitler's Cosmopolitan Bastard: Count Richard Coudenhove-Kalergi and His Vision of Europe*. Montreal, 2011.

Bossuat, Gérard. *Faire l'Europe sans défaire la France: 60 Ans de politique d'unité européenne des gouvernements et des présidents de la République Française, 1943–2003*. Brussels, 2005.

Bossuat, Gérard, and Marie-Thérèse Bitsch, eds. *L'Europe unie et l'Afrique: De l'idée d'Eurafrique à la Convention de Lomé I; Actes du colloque international de Paris, 1er et 2 avril 2004*. Brussels, 2005.

Boyce, Robert. *The Great Interwar Crisis and the Collapse of Globalization*. New York, 2009.

Broberg, Morten, and Niels Fenger. *Preliminary References to the European Court of Justice*. Oxford, 2010.

Broeders, Dennis. *Breaking Down Anonymity: Digital Surveillance of Irregular Migrants in Germany and the Netherlands*. Amsterdam, 2009.

Brouwer, Evelien. *Digital Borders and Real Rights: Effective Remedies for Third-Country Nationals in the Schengen Information System*. Leiden, 2008.

Brown, Megan. *The Seventh Member States: Algeria, France, and the European Community*. Cambridge, MA, 2022.

Bruce-Jones, Eddie. *Race in the Shadow of Law: State Violence in Contemporary Europe*. Abingdon, UK, 2017.

Burgess, Michael. *Federalism and European Union: Political Ideas, Influences, and Strategies in the European Community, 1972–1987*. London, 1991.

Burgin, Angus. *The Great Persuasion: Reinventing Free Markets since the Depression*. Cambridge, MA, 2012.

Buschak, Willy. *Die Vereinigten Staaten von Europa sind unser Ziel: Arbeiterbewegung und Europa im frühen 20. Jahrhundert*. Essen, 2014.

Caffier, Michel. *La Moselle: Une Rivière et ses hommes*. Nancy, 1985.

Carr, Matthew. *Fortress Europe: Dispatches from a Gated Continent*. New York, 2016.

Carrera, Serio, Marco Stefan, Ngo Chun Luk, and Lina Vosyliūtė. *Die Zukunft des Schengen-Raums: Aktuelle Entwicklungen und Herausforderungen des Schengen-Regelungsrahmens seit 2016*. Brussels, 2018.

Cherubini, Francesco. *Asylum Law in the European Union*. Abingdon, UK, 2015.

Childs, David. *The Fall of the GDR: Germany's Road to Unity*. London, 2001.

Chin, Rita. *The Crisis of Multiculturalism in Europe: A History*. Princeton, NJ, 2017.

———. *The Guest Worker Question in Postwar Germany*. New York, 2007.

Christiansen, Thomas, and Christine Reh. *Constitutionalizing the European Union*. New York, 2009.

Christofferson, Thomas R. *The French Socialists in Power, 1981–1986*. Newark, 1991.

Clavin, Patricia. *Securing the World Economy: The Reinvention of the League of Nations, 1920–1946*. Oxford, 2013.

Clutterbuck, Richard. *Terrorism, Drugs and Crime in Europe after 1992*. London, 1992.

Comte, Emmanuel. *The History of the European Migration Regime: Germany's Strategic Hegemony*. Abingdon, UK, 2018.

Consiglio dell'Ordine degli Avvocati di Roma. Minutes no. 14 of the meeting of March 28, 2013. Accessed March 25, 2024, https://www.ordineavvocatiroma.it/wp -content/uploads/2022/04/28%20marzo%202013%20n.%2014.pdf.

Conway, Martin. *Western Europe's Democratic Age, 1945–1968*. Princeton, NJ, 2020.

Conway, Martin, and Kiran Klaus Patel, eds. *Europeanization in the Twentieth Century: Historical Approaches*. Houndmills, UK, 2010.

Cunha, Alexandre M., and Carlos Eduardo Suprinyak, eds. *Political Economy and the International Order in Interwar Europe*. Cham, 2021.

Davies, Gareth. *Nationality Discrimination in the European Internal Market*. The Hague, 2003.

Davis, Muriam Haleh. *Markets of Civilization: Islam and Racial Capitalism in Algeria*. Durham, NC, 2022.

de Grazia, Victoria. *Irresistible Empire: America's Advance through Twentieth-Century Europe*. Cambridge, MA, 2005.

De l'Autre Côté du Périph. *Citoyen Spectateur*. Montreuil, 1999.

De Ruyt, Jean. *Le Leadership dans l'Union Européenne*. Louvain, 2015.

DeBardeleben, Joan, ed. *Soft or Hard Borders? Managing the Divide in an Enlarged Europe*. Aldershot, UK, 2005.

Debons, Claude, and Joël Le Coq. *Routiers, les raisons de la colère*. Paris, 1997.

Deflem, Mathieu. *Policing World Society: Historical Foundations of International Police Cooperations*. Oxford, 2004.

Defrance, Corine. *Entre Guerre froide et intégration Européenne: Reconstruction et intégration, 1945–1963*. Villeneuve-d'Ascq, 2012.

Dinan, Desmond. *Europe Recast: A History of European Union*. Basingstoke, UK, 2004.

Dinan, Desmond, ed. *Origins and Evolution of the European Union*. 2nd ed. Oxford, 2014.

Earl, Jennifer, and Katrina Kimport. *Digitally Enabled Social Change: Activism in the Internet Age*. Cambridge, MA, 2011.

Edinger, Lewis J. *From Bonn to Berlin: German Politics in Transition*. New York, 1998.

Eichengreen, Barry. *The European Economy since 1945 Coordinated Capitalism and Beyond*. Princeton, NJ, 2007.

Eisemann, Pierre Michel, ed. *L'Intégration du droit international et communautaire dans l'ordre juridique national*. The Hague, 1996.

Elvins, Martin. *Anti-Drugs Policies of the European Union, Transnational Decision-Making and the Politics of Expertise*. Basingstoke, UK, 2003.

English, Robert. *Russia and the Idea of the West: Gorbachev, Intellectuals, and the End of the Cold War*. New York, 2000.

Erpenbeck, Jenny. *Go, Went, Gone*. Translated by Susan Bernofsky. New York, 2017.

Fernández-Rojo, David. *EU Migration Agencies the Operation and Cooperation of FRONTEX, EASO and EUROPOL*. Cheltenham, UK, 2021.

Fisher, Marc. *After the Wall: Germany, the Germans and the Burdens of History*. New York, 1995.

Frieden, Jeffry A. *Global Capitalism: Its Fall and Rise in the Twentieth Century*. New York, 2006.

Garavini, Giuliano. *After Empires: European Integration, Decolonization and the Challenge from the Global South: 1957–1986*. Oxford, 2012.

Gaspard, Françoise. *Une Petite Ville en France*. Paris, 1990.

Gatrell, Peter. *The Unsettling of Europe: How Migration Reshaped a Continent*. New York, 2019.

Geddes, Andrew. *Immigration and European Integration: Towards Fortress Europe?* Manchester, 2000.

Gérard, Salem. *La Santé dans la ville: Géographie d'un petit espace dense; Pikine Sénégal*. Paris, 1998.

Gerstle, Gary. *The Rise and Fall of the Neoliberal Order: America and the World in the Free Market Era*. Oxford, 2022.

Giauque, Jeffrey Glen. *Grand Designs and Visions of Unity: The Atlantic Powers and the Reorganization of Western Europe, 1955–1963*. Chapel Hill, NC, 2002.

Gibney, Matthew J. *The Ethics and Politics of Asylum: Liberal Democracy and the Response to Refugees*. Cambridge, UK, 2004.

Gillingham, John. *European Integration, 1950–2003: Superstate or New Market Economy?* Cambridge, UK, 2003.

Goldberg, David Theo. *The Threat of Race: Reflections on Racial Neoliberalism*. Malden, MA, 2008.

Graglia, Piero. *Altiero Spinelli*. Bologna, 2008.

Groenendijk, Kees, Elspeth Guild, and Paul Minderhoud, eds. *In Search of Europe's Borders*. The Hague, 2003.

Guild, Elspeth. *Security and Migration in the 21st Century*. Cambridge, UK, 2009.

Guild, Elspeth, Steve Peers, and Jonathan Tomkin. *The EU Citizenship Directive: A Commentary*. Oxford, 2014.

Habermas, Jürgen. *The Crisis of the European Union: A Response*. Translated by Ciaran Cronin. Cambridge, UK, 2012.

Hansen, Peo, and Sandy Brian Hager. *The Politics of European Citizenship: Deepening Contradictions in Social Rights & Migration Policy*. New York, 2010.

Hansen, Peo, and Stefan Jonsson. *Eurafrica: The Untold History of European Integration and Colonialism*. London, 2014.

Hargreaves, Alec G. *Multi-Ethnic France: Immigration, Politics, Culture and Society*. 2nd ed. London, 2007.

Harvey, David. *A Brief History of Neoliberalism*. Oxford, 2005.

———. *Rebel Cities: From the Right to the City to the Urban Revolution*. London, 2012.

Hazareesingh, Sudhir. *In the Shadow of the General: Modern France and the Myth of De Gaulle*. Oxford, 2012.

Hobsbawm, Eric. *The Age of Extremes: The Short Twentieth Century, 1914–1991*. London, 1994.

Hollifield, James F. *Immigrants, Markets, and States: The Political Economy of Postwar Europe.* Cambridge, MA, 1992.

Holmes, Douglas R. *Integral Europe: Fast-Capitalism, Multiculturalism, Neofascism.* Princeton, NJ, 2000.

Hönnige, Christoph, Sascha Kneip, and Astrid Lorenz, eds. *Verfassungswandel im Mehrebenensystem.* Wiesbaden, 2011.

Isidori, Emanuele. *Pedagogia, Sport e Relazioni Internazionali: Dall'analisi del Contesto alla Metodologia di Sviluppo.* Rome, 2016.

Isiksel, Turkuler. *Europe's Functional Constitution: A Theory of Constitutionalism beyond the State.* Oxford, 2016.

Jachec, Nancy. *Europe's Intellectuals and the Cold War: The European Society of Culture, Post-war Politics, and International Relations.* London, 2015.

Jacobson, David. *Rights across Borders: Immigration and the Decline of Citizenship.* Baltimore, 1996.

James, Harold. *Europe Contested: From the Kaiser to Brexit.* London, 2019.

———. *Europe Reborn: A History, 1914–2000.* Harlow, 2003.

———. *Making the European Monetary Union.* Cambridge, MA, 2012.

Jansen, Nils. *Binnenmarkt, Privatrecht und Europäische Identität: Eine Historische und Methodische Bestandsaufnahme.* Tübingen, 2004.

Jarausch, Konrad H. *After Hitler: Recivilizing Germans, 1945–1949.* Translated by Brandon Hunziker. New York, 2006.

———. *Embattled Europe: A Progressive Alternative.* Princeton, NJ, 2021.

———. *Out of Ashes: A New History of Europe in the Twentieth Century.* Princeton, NJ, 2015.

———. *The Rush to German Unity.* New York, 1994.

Joppke, Christian, ed. *Challenge to the Nation-State: Immigration in Western Europe and the United States.* Oxford, 1998.

Joubert, Chantal, and Hans Bevers. *Schengen Investigated: A Comparative Interpretation of the Schengen Provisions on International Police Cooperation in the Light of the European Convention on Human Rights.* The Hague, 1996.

Jovanović, Miroslav N. *The Economics of European Integration: Limits and Prospects.* Cheltenham, UK, 2005.

Judt, Tony. *Postwar: A History of Europe since 1945.* London, 2005.

Kahanec, Martin, and Klaus F. Zimmerman, eds. *EU Labor Markets after Post-Enlargement Migration.* Berlin, 2010.

Karanja, Stephen Kabera. *Transparency and Proportionality in the Schengen Information System and Border Control Co-operation.* Leiden, 2008.

Keohane, Robert O., and Stanley Hoffman, eds. *The New European Community: Decisionmaking and Institutional Change.* New York, 1991.

Kindt, Els J. *Privacy and Data Protection Issues of Biometric Applications: A Comparative Legal Analysis.* Leuven, 2013.

King, Steven, and Anne Winter, eds. *Migration, Settlement and Belonging in Europe, 1500–1930s: Comparative Perspectives.* New York, 2013.

Kingsley, Patrick. *The New Odyssey: The Story of Europe's Refugee Crisis.* London, 2016.

Knapp, Andrew. *Government and Politics in Western Europe: Britain, France, Italy, Germany*. New York, 1998.

Krell, Christian. *Sozialdemokratie und Europa: Die Europapolitik von SPD, Labour Party und Parti Socialiste*. Wiesbaden, 2009.

Kühne, Hans Heiner. *Kriminalitätsbekämpfung durch innereuropäische Grenzkontrollen?* Berlin, 1991.

Kundnani, Hans. *Eurowhiteness: Culture, Empire and Race in the European Project*. New York, 2023.

Laacher, Smaïn. *Mythologie du Sans-papiers*. Paris, 2009.

Laudon, Kenneth C. *The Dossier Society: Value Choices in the Design of National Information Systems*. New York, 1986.

Laursen, Finn, ed. *Designing the European Union: From Paris to Lisbon*. Basingstoke, UK, 2012.

Lavenex, Sandra. *The Europeanisation of Refugee Policies: Between Human Rights and Internal Security*. Aldershot, UK, 2001.

Lebovics, Herman. *Bringing the Empire Back Home: France in the Global Age*. Durham, NC, 2004.

Lefebvre, Henri. *The Production of Space*. Translated by Donald Nicholson-Smith. Oxford, 1991.

Lindemann, Ute. *Sans-Papiers-Proteste und Einwanderungspolitik in Frankreich*. Wiesbaden, 2001.

Lindner, Johannes. *Conflict and Change in EU Budgetary Politics*. Abingdon, UK, 2006.

Longo, Michael. *Constitutionalising Europe: Process and Practices*. New York, 2006.

Loukaidēs, Loukēs G. *Essays on the Developing Law of Human Rights*. Dordrecht, 1995.

Lützeler, Paul Michael, and Michael Gehler, eds. *Die Europäische Union zwischen Konfusion und Vision*. Vienna, 2021.

Maas, Willem. *Creating European Citizens*. Lanham, MD, 2006.

Maas, Willem, ed. *Democratic Citizenship and the Free Movement of People*. Leiden, 2013.

Maier, Charles S. *Dissolution: The Crisis of Communism and the End of East Germany*. Princeton, NJ, 1999.

———. *Once within Borders: Territories of Power, Wealth, and Belonging Since 1500*. Cambridge, MA, 2016.

———. *The Project-State and Its Rivals: A New History of the Twentieth and Twenty-First Centuries*. Cambridge, MA, 2023.

Mandel, Ruth. *Cosmopolitan Anxieties: Turkish Challenges to Citizenship and Belonging in Germany*. Durham, NC, 2008.

Marable, Manning, and Vanessa Agard-Jones, eds. *Transnational Blackness: Navigating the Global Color Line*. Basingstoke, UK, 2008.

Marcowitz, Reiner, and Andreas Wilkens, eds. *Une "Europe des citoyens": Société civile et identité européenne de 1945 à Nos Jours*. Bern, 2014.

Marker, Emily. *Black France, White Europe: Youth, Race, and Belonging in the Postwar Era.* Ithaca, NY, 2022.

Martin, Jamie. *The Meddlers: Sovereignty, Empire, and the Birth of Global Economic Governance.* Cambridge, MA, 2022.

Mattelart, Armand. *The Globalization of Surveillance: The Origin of the Securitarian Order.* Translated by Susan Gruenheck Taponier and James A. Cohen. Cambridge, UK, 2010.

Mazower, Mark. *Dark Continent: Europe's Twentieth Century.* New York, 2000.

———. *Governing the World: The History of an Idea, 1815 to the Present.* New York, 2012.

———. *No Enchanted Palace: The End of Empire and the Ideological Origins of the United Nations.* Princeton, NJ, 2009.

Meyer zu Kueingdorf, Ulf, ed. *Mal was Leichtes - Das Frauen-Kochbuch: 33 x eine Frau mit Genuss.* Niedernhausen, 2010.

Mickolus, Edward F., Todd Sandler, and Jean M. Murdock. *International Terrorism in the 1980s: A Chronology of Events.* Vol. 2, *1984–1987.* Ames, Iowa, 1989.

Milward, Alan S. *The European Rescue of the Nation-State.* London, 1992.

Monforte, Pierre. *Europeanizing Contention: The Protest against "Fortress Europe" in France and Germany.* New York, 2014.

Montarsolo, Yves. *L'Eurafrique contrepoint de l'idée d'Europe.* Aix-en-Provence, 2010.

Moravcsik, Andrew. *The Choice for Europe: Social Purpose and State Power from Messina to Maastricht.* Ithaca, NY, 1999.

———, ed. *Europe Without Illusions: The Paul-Henri Spaak Lectures, 1994–1999.* Lanham, MD, 2005.

———. *European Union and World Politics.* London, 2006.

Moreno-Lax, Violeta. *Accessing Asylum in Europe: Extraterritorial Border Controls and Refugee Rights under EU Law.* Oxford, 2017.

Moser, Thomas. *Europäische Integration, Dekolonisation, Eurafrika: Eine historische Analyse über Entstehungsbedingungen der Eurafrikanischen Gemeinschaft von der Weltwirtschaftskrise bis zum Jaunde-Vertrag, 1929–1963.* Baden-Baden, 2000.

Moyn, Samuel. *Not Enough: Human Rights in an Unequal World.* Cambridge, MA, 2018.

———. *The Last Utopia.* Cambridge, MA, 2010.

Nadelmann, Ethan A. *Cops across Borders: The Internationalization of U.S. Criminal Law Enforcement.* University Park, PA, 1993.

Néraudau-d'Unienville, Emmanuelle. *Ordre Public et droit des etrangers en Europe: La Notion d'ordre public en droit des etrangers à l'aune de la construction européenne.* Brussels, 2006.

Nesser, Petter. *Islamic Terrorism in Europe.* London, 2015.

Nicolaïdis, Kalypso, and Robert Howse, eds. *The Federal Vision: Legitimacy and Levels of Governance in the United States and the European Union.* Oxford, 2001.

Nord, Philip. *France's New Deal: From the Thirties to the Postwar Era.* Princeton, NJ, 2010.

O'Brennan, John. *The Eastern Enlargement of the European Union.* Abingdon, UK, 2006.

O'Keeffe, David, and Patrick Twomey, eds. *Legal Issues of the Amsterdam Treaty.* Oxford, 1999.

Oberloskamp, Eva. *Codename TREVI: Terrorismusbekämpfung und die Anfänge einer europäischen Innenpolitik in den 1970er Jahren.* Berlin, 2016.

Occhipinti, John D. *The Politics of EU Police Cooperation: Toward a European FBI?* Boulder, CO, 2003.

Ofrath, Avner. *Colonial Algeria and the Politics of Citizenship.* London, 2023.

Pagden, Anthony, ed. *The Idea of Europe: From Antiquity to the European Union.* Cambridge, UK, 2002.

Palayret, Jean-Marie. *Une Université pour l'Europe: Préhistoire de l'Institute Universitaire Européen de Florence, 1948–1976.* Florence, 1996.

Paoli, Simone. *Frontiera Sud: L'Italia e la nascita dell'Europa di Schengen.* Florence, 2018.

Patel, Kiran Klaus. *Projekt Europa: Eine kritische Geschichte.* Munich, 2018.

Pauly, Alexis. *Les Accords de Schengen: Abolition des frontières intérieures ou menace pour les libertés publiques?* Maastricht, 1993.

Paxton, Robert O., and Julie Hessler. *Europe in the Twentieth Century.* 5th ed. Boston, 2012.

Perl-Rosenthal, Nathan. "Corresponding Republics: Letter Writing and Patriot Organizing in the Atlantic Revolutions, ca. 1760–1792." PhD diss., Columbia University, 2011.

Pistone, Sergio. *The Union of European Federalists: From the Foundation to the Decision on Direct Election of the European Parliament.* Milan, 2008.

Pudlat, Andreas. *Schengen: Zur Manifestation von Grenze und Grenzschutz in Europa.* Hildesheim, 2013.

Reichel, Peter. *Vergangenheitsbewältigung in Deutschland: Die Auseinandersetzung mit der NS-Diktatur von 1945 bis heute.* Munioch, 2001.

Rist, Gilbert. *The History of Development: From Western Origins to Global Faith.* London, 1997.

Roemer, John E., Woojin Lee, and Karine Van der Straeten. *Racism, Xenophobia, and Distribution: Multi-Issue Politics in Advanced Democracies.* Cambridge, MA, 2007.

Rooke, Octavius. *The Life of the Moselle.* London, 1858.

Rosenberg, Andrew S. *Undesirable Immigrants: Why Racism Persists in International Migration.* Princeton, NJ, 2022.

Rudolph, Christopher. *National Security and Immigration: Policy Development in the United States and Western Europe Since 1945.* Stanford, 2006.

Said, Edward W. *Culture and Imperialism.* New York, 1993.

Salmon, Patrick, Keith Hamilton, and Stephen Robert Twigge, eds. *German Unification 1989–90: Documents on British Policy Overseas.* Series 3. Vol. 7. London, 2011.

Sané, Madamy, and Jacques Gaillot. *Sorti l'ombre: Journal d'un Sans-papiers.* Montreuil, 1996.

Sarotte, Mary Elise. *The Collapse: The Accidental Opening of the Berlin Wall.* New York, 2014.

Sassen, Saskia. *Globalization and Its Discontents.* New York, 1998.

———. *Guests and Aliens.* New York, 1999.

———. *Transnational Economies and National Migration Policies.* Amsterdam, 1996.

Schain, Martin A. *The Border: Policy and Politics in Europe and the United States.* New York, 2019.

———. *The Politics of Immigration in France, Britain, and the United States: A Comparative Study.* New York, 2012.

Schierup, Carl-Ulrik, Peo Hansen, and Stephen Castles. *Migration, Citizenship, and the European Welfare State: A European Dilemma.* Oxford, 2006.

Schmitt-Kilian, Jörg. *Von Koblenz zu Rhein und Mosel: Orte an und über dem Wasser.* Messkirch, 2012.

Schreckenberger, Waldemar. "Von den Schengener Abkommen zu einer gemeinsamen Innen- und Justizpolitik (die dritte Säule)." *Verwaltungs-Archiv* 88, no. 3 (1997): 389–415.

Schütze, Robert. *European Union Law.* Cambridge, UK, 2015.

Shepard, Todd. *The Invention of Decolonization: The Algerian War and the Remaking of France.* Ithaca, NY, 2006.

Sheptycki, James. *Transnational Crime and Policing: Selected Essays.* Abingdon, UK, 2011.

Shields, James. *The Extreme Right in France: From Pétain to Le Pen.* London, 2007.

Shore, Cris. *Building Europe: The Cultural Politics of European Integration.* London, 2000.

Short, Philip. *Mitterrand: A Study in Ambiguity.* London, 2014.

Siebold, Angela. *Zwischen Grenzen: Die Geschichte des Schengen-Raums aus deutschen, französischen und polnischen Perspektiven.* Paderborn, 2013.

Siméant, Johanna. *La Cause des Sans-papiers.* Paris, 1998.

Simon, Jürgen, and Jürgen Taeger. *Rasterfahndung: Entwicklung, Inhalt und Grenzen einer kriminalpolizeilichen Fahndungsmethode.* Baden-Baden, 1981.

Slobodian, Quinn. *Globalists: The End of Empire and the Birth of Neoliberalism.* Cambridge, MA, 2018.

Sluga, Glenda. *Internationalism in the Age of Nationalism.* Philadelphia, 2015.

Snell, Bruno. *The Discovery of the Mind.* New York, 1982.

Snyder, Timothy. *The Road to Unfreedom: Russia, Europe, America.* London, 2018.

Solsten, Eric, ed. *Germany: A Country Study.* 3rd ed. Washington, DC, 1995.

Soysal, Yasemin Nuhoglu. *Limits of Citizenship: Migrants and Postnational Membership in Europe.* Chicago, 1994.

Stirk, Peter. *A History of European Integration since 1914.* London, 1996.

Stobbe, Holk. *Undokumentierte Migration in Deutschland und den Vereinigten Staaten: Interne Migrationskontrollen und die Handlungsspielräume von Sans Papiers.* Göttingen, 2004.

Stokes, Lauren. *Fear of the Family: Guest Workers and Family Migration in the Federal Republic of Germany.* New York, 2022.

Stone-Sweet, Alec. *Governing with Judges: Constitutional Politics in Europe.* Oxford, 2000.

———. *The Judicial Construction of Europe.* New York, 2004.

Stovall, Tyler. *White Freedom: The Racial History of an Idea.* Princeton, NJ, 2021.

Streeck, Wolfgang. *How Will Capitalism End?: Essays on a Failing System.* London, 2016.

Teasdale, Anthony, and Timothy Bainbridge. *The Penguin Companion to European Union.* New York, 1995.

Theiller, Béatrice, Roseline Sestacq, and Eva Lumanisha. *La République à l'ecole des Sans-papiers: Trajectoires et devenir de Sans-papiers régularisés.* Paris, 2008.

Ther, Philipp. *Europe since 1989: A History.* Princeton, NJ, 2016.

Ticktin, Miriam Iris. *Casualties of Care: Immigration and the Politics of Humanitarianism in France.* Berkeley, CA, 2011.

Tindemans, Leo. *De memoires: Gedreven door een overtuiging.* Tielt, 2002.

Tower, Charles. *Along Germany's River of Romance, the Moselle: The Little Traveled Country of Alsace and Lorraine; Its Personality, Its People, and Its Associations.* New York, 1913.

Trilling, Daniel. *Lights in the Distance: Exile and Refuge at the Borders of Europe.* London, 2018.

Tufekci, Zeynep. *Twitter and Tear Gas: The Power and Fragility of Networked Protest.* New Haven, CT, 2017.

Van Middelaar, Luuk. *The Passage to Europe: How a Continent Became a Union.* Translated by Liz Waters. New Haven, CT, 2013.

Van Middelaar, Luuk, and Philippe Van Parijs, eds. *After the Storm: How to Save Democracy in Europe.* Tielt, 2015.

Van Oudenaren, John. *Uniting Europe: European Integration and the Post-Cold War World.* Lanham, MD, 2000.

Vauchez, Antione. *Brokering Europe: Euro-Lawyers and the Making of a Transnational Polity.* New York, 2015.

Walker, Neil, ed. *Europe's Area of Freedom, Security, and Justice.* Oxford, 2012.

Wallerstein, Immanuel. *World-Systems Analysis: An Introduction.* Durham, NC, 2004.

Walzer, Michael. *Spheres of Justice: A Defense of Pluralism and Equality.* Oxford, 1983.

Warner, William Beatty. *Protocols of Liberty: Communication Innovation and the American Revolution.* Chicago, 2013.

Weatherill, Stephen. *The Internal Market as a Legal Concept.* Oxford, 2017.

Weber, Max. *From Max Weber, Essays in Sociology.* Edited and translated by H. H. Gerth and C. Wright Mills. London, 1991.

Weil, Patrick. *How to Be French: Nationality in the Making since 1789.* Translated by Catherine Porter. Durham, NC, 2008.

Weiler, J.H.H. *The Constitution of Europe: "Do the New Clothes Have an Emperor?" and Other Essays on European Integration.* Cambridge, UK, 1999.

Weller, Shane. *The Idea of Europe: A Critical History.* Cambridge, UK, 2021.

Williams, Michelle Hale. *The Impact of Radical Right-Wing Parties in West European Democracies.* New York, 2006.

Winders, James A. *Paris Africain: Rhythms of the African Diaspora.* New York, 2006.

Wyatt-Walter, Holly. *The European Community and the Security Dilemma, 1979–92.* New York, 1997.

Yergin, Daniel, and Joseph Stanislaw. *The Commanding Heights: The Battle between Government and the Marketplace That Is Remaking the Modern World.* New York, 1998.

Zahra, Tara. *Against the World: Anti-Globalism and Mass Politics Between the World Wars*. New York, 2023.

——. *The Great Departure: Mass Migration from Eastern Europe and the Making of the Free World*. New York, 2016.

Zaiotti, Ruben. *Cultures of Border Control: Schengen and the Evolution of European Frontiers*. Chicago, 2011.

Zarobell, John. *Art and the Global Economy*. Oakland, CA, 2017.

Zielonka, Jan. *Europe as Empire: The Nature of the Enlarged European Union*. Oxford, 2006.

ARTICLES AND CHAPTERS

Alldred, Pam. "No Borders, No Nations, No Deportations." *Feminist Review*, no. 73 (2003): 152–57.

Alter, Karen J. "Who are the 'Masters of the Treaty?': European Governments and the European Court of Justice." *International Organization* 52, no. 1 (Winter 1998): 121–47.

"Altiero Spinello: An Unrelenting Federalist." European Commission. Accessed February 23, 2023. https://european-union.europa.eu/system/files/2021-07/eu-pioneers -altiero-spinelli_en.pdf.

Anderson, Malcolm. "The Agenda for Police Cooperation." *Policing across National Boundaries*, edited by Malcolm Anderson and Monica den Boer, 3–21. London, 1994.

Anweoti, Anil. "The Myth of Eurooclcrooioi European Integration in the 1970c." *L'Europe en formation* 353–54, no. 3 (November 2009): 39–53.

Ayaz, Ameer, and Abdul Wadood. "An Analysis of European Union Policy towards Syrian Refugees." *Journal of Political Studies* 27, no. 2 (Summer 2020): 1–19.

Barron, Pierre, Anne Bory, and Sébastien Chauvin. "State Categories and Labour Protest: Migrant Workers and Fight for Legal Status in France." *Work, Employment and Society* 30, no. 4 (2016): 631–48.

Benyon, John, Lynne Turnbull, Andrew Willis, and Rachel Woodward. "Understanding Police Cooperation in Europe: Setting a Framework for Analysis." In *Policing across National Boundaries*, edited by Malcolm Anderson and Monica den Boer, 46–68. London, 1994.

Berthelet, Pierre. "La 'Gouvernance Schengen': Le Sentier périlleux de la féforme; Commentaires et analyses sur les travaux en cours." *Revue du Droit de l'Union Européenne*, no. 4 (2012): 655–78.

Betts, Paul. "1989 Revolutions, 25 Years On." *OUP Blog* (blog). November 6, 2014. https://blog.oup.com/2014/11/1989-velvet-revolutions-berlin-wall/.

Bigo, Didier. "Europe passoire et Europe forteresse: La Sécurisation / humanitarisation de l'immigration." In *Immigration et Racisme en Europe*, edited by Andrea Rea, 203–41. Brussels, 1998.

——. "Frontier Controls in the European Union: Who Is in Control?" In *Controlling Frontiers: Free Movement into and within Europe*, edited Didier Bigo and Elspeth Guild, 49–99. Aldershot, UK, 2005.

Bigo, Didier, and Elspeth Guild. "La Mise à l'écart des étrangers. La Logique du visa Schengen." *Politique étrangère* 70, no. 2 (2005): 445–47.

Blin, Thierry. "Une Approche de la construction des cadres de l'action de 'Saint Bernard' au mouvement contre le projet de loi Debré." *Anné Sociologique* 50, no. 1 (2000): 119–46.

Blume, Georg et al. "Was geschah wirklich?" *Zeit Online.* August 30, 2016. https://www .zeit.de/2016/35/grenzoeffnung-fluechtlinge-september-2015-wochenende-angela -merkel-ungarn-oesterreich.

Bolten, José J. "From Schengen to Dublin: The New Frontiers of Refugee Law." In *Schengen: Internationalisation of Central Chapters of the Law on Aliens, Refugees, Privacy, Security and the Police,* edited by H. Meijers and J.D.M. Steenbergen, 8–36. Deventer, The Netherlands, 1991.

Bossong, Raphael, and Tobias Etzold. "The Future of Schengen: Internal Border Controls as a Growing Challenge to the EU and the Nordics." SWP Comment, no. 44, German Institute for International and Security Affairs. October 2018.

Bréchon, Pierre, and Subrata Kumar Mitra. "The National Front in France: The Emergence of an Extreme Right Protest Movement." *Comparative Politics* 25, no. 1 (October 1992): 63–82.

Bunyan, Tony. "Just over the Horizon—the Surveillance Society and the State in the EU." *Race & Class* 51, no. 3 (January 2010): 1–12.

Buschak, Willy. "Enthusiasm for Europe and Europeanization in the Labor Movement of the 1920s." In *Reconsidering Europeanization: Ideas and Practices of (Dis-)Integrating Europe since the Nineteenth Century,* edited by Florian Greiner, Peter Pichler, and Jan Vermeiren. Berlin, 2022.

Calandri, Elena, Simone Paoli, and Antonio Varsori, eds. "Peoples and Borders: Seventy Years of Migration in Europe, from Europe, to Europe [1945–2015]." Special Issue, *Journal of European Integration History* (2017).

"Catherine Lalumière." Maison de l'Europe de Paris. Accessed October 21, 2021. https:// paris-europe.eu/catherine-lalumiere-presidente/.

Ceyhan, Ayse. "Policing by Dossier: Identification and Surveillance in an Era of Uncertainty and Fear." In *Controlling Frontiers: Free Movement into and within Europe,* edited by Didier Bigo and Elspeth Guild, 209–32. Aldershot, UK, 2005.

Cohen, Samy, "La Diplomatie française dans la cohabitation." *Esprit,* June 2000, 45–60.

Cole, Alistair. "The French Socialists." In *Political Parties and the European Union,* edited by John Gaffney, 71–85. London, 2002.

Coleman, Nils. "From Gulf War to Gulf War: Years of Security Concern in Immigration and Asylum Policies at European Level." In *Terrorism and the Foreigner: A Decade of Tension Around the Rule of Law in Europe,* edited by Elspeth Guild and Anneliese Baldaccini, 3–84. Leiden, 2007.

Conway, Martin. "Democracy in Postwar Western Europe: The Triumph of a Political Model." *European History Quarterly* 32, no. 1 (2002): 59–84.

Coppel, Jason, and Aidan O'Neill. "The European Court of Justice: Taking Rights Seriously?" *Common Market Law Review* 29 (1992): 669–92.

Cordelli, Chiara, and Jonathan Levy. "The Ethics of Global Capital Mobility." *American Political Science Review* 116, no. 2 (May 2022): 439–52.

"Council of Europe: European Political Community." *International Organization* 9, no. 2 (May 1955): 301–2.

"Court of Justice." Centre virtuel de la connaissance sur l'Europe. Accessed May 2, 2019. https://www.cvce.eu/en/education/unit-content/-/unit/d5906df5-4f83-4603-85f7-0cabc24b9fe1/c89b0195-280c-4fbb-bcb1-ac400d20852d.

Cunneen, Joseph. "Noël Copin: Shining Example of a Catholic Journalist." *National Catholic Reporter*, March 30, 2007, 8.

De Moor, Anne. "Article 7 of Treaty of Rome Bites." *Modern Law Review* 48, no. 4 (July 1985): 452–59.

Decroly, Vincent. "Le Devoir d'asile." In *A la lumière des Sans-papiers*, edited by Antoine Pickels, 231–38. Brussels, 2001.

Dedecker, Renée. "L'Asile et la libre circulation des personnes dans l'accord de Schengen." *Courrier hebdomadaire du CRISP* 8, no. 1393–94 (1993): 1–58.

Den Boer, Monica. "The Incorporation of Schengen into the TEU: A Bridge too Far?" In *The Treaty of Amsterdam: Challenges and Opportunities for the European Union*, edited by Jens Monar and Wolfgang Wessels, 206–320. London, 2001.

———. "The Quest for European Policing: Rhetoric and Justification in a Disorderly Debate." In *Policing across National Boundaries*, edited by Malcolm Anderson and Monica den Boer, 174–96. London, 1994.

———, ed. *Schengen's Final Days? The Incorporation of Schengen into the New TEU, External Borders and Information Systems.* Maastricht, 1998.

Den Boer, Monica, and Laura Corrado. "For the Record or off the Record: Comments about the Incorporation of Schengen into the EU." *European Journal of Migration and Law* 1, no. 4 (1999): 397–418.

Denord, François, and Antoine Schwartz. "L'Économie (très) politique du traité de Rome." *Politix*, no. 89 (April 2010): 35–56.

Denton, Geoffrey. "Re-structuring the EC Budget: Implications of the Fontainebleau Agreement." *Journal of Common Market Studies* 23, no. 2 (December 1984): 117–40.

"Du marché commun à l'Europe des citoyens." Europa. Accessed December 11, 2023. https://europa.eu/50/news/article/080102_fr.htm.

Dupuis-Rémond, Jean-Christophe. "Régionales 2015: Florian Philippot dépose une gerbe à Schengen." *France 3 Régions*. September 19, 2015. https://france3-regions.francetvinfo.fr/grand-est/regionales-2015-florian-philippot-depose-une-gerbe-schengen-811037.html.

Edward, David. "Lord Mackenzie-Stuart of Dean, LLB, LLD." Royal Society of Edinburgh. Accessed May 10, 2019. https://www.rse.org.uk/cms/files/fellows/obits_alpha/mackenzie-stuart_lord.pdf.

Eff, Carine, and Patrick Mony. "Émigration choisie: Entretien avec Madjiguène Cissé." *Vacarme* 1, no. 31 (Winter 2007).

Emmons, Shelese. "The Debre Bill: Immigration Legislation or a National 'Front.'" *Indiana Journal of Global Legal Studies* 5, no. 1 (Fall 1997): 357–66.

Erickson, Jon. "The Spectacle of the Anti-Spectacle: Happenings and the Situationist International." *Discourse* 14, no. 2 (Spring 1992): 36–58.

Ferguson, Niall. "Crisis, What Crisis? The 1970s and the Shock of the Global." In *The Shock of the Global: The 1970s in Perspective*, edited by Niall Ferguson, Charles S. Maier, Erez Manela, and Daniel J. Sargent, 1–21. Cambridge, MA, 2010.

Feyen, Benjamin, and Ewa Krzaklewska. "'Generation ERASMUS'—The New Europeans? A Reflection." In *The ERASMUS Phenomenon—Symbol of a New European Generation?*, edited by Benjamin Feyen and Ewa Krzaklewska, 229–42. Frankfurt am Main, 2013.

Fijnaut, Cyrille. "Police Co-operation within Western Europe." In *The Containment of Organised Crime and Terrorism: Thirty-Five Years of Research on Police, Judicial and Administrative Cooperation*, edited by Cyrille J.C.F. Fijnaut, 47–62. Leiden, 2016.

Fitoussi, J.-P., and E. S. Phelps. "Causes of the 1980s Slump in Europe." Brookings Papers on Economic Activity, no. 2 (1986), 487–520.

Freeman, Gary P. "Immigrant Labour and Racial Conflict: The Role of the State." In *Migrants in Modern France: Population Mobility in the Later 19th and 20th Centuries*, edited by Philip E. Ogden and Paul E. White, 160–76. London, 1989.

Garner, Steve. "The European Union and the Racialization of Immigration, 1985–2006." *Race / Ethnicity: Multidisciplinary Global Contexts* 1, no. 1 (Autumn 2007): 61–87.

Gaub, Florence. "Trends in Terrorism." European Union Institute for Security Studies. March 2017.

Gerlach, Alex. "Dubliner Asylrechtskonvention und Schengener Abkommen: Lohnt sich die Ratifikation?" *Zeitschrift für Rechtspolitik* 26, no. 5 (May 1993): 164–66.

Gertheiss, Svenja. "Migration under Control: Sovereignty, Freedom of Movement, and the Stability of Order." In *Resistance and Change in World Politics: International Dissidence*, edited by Svenja Gertheiss, Stefanie Herr, Klaus Dieter Wolf, and Carmen Wunderlich, 243–80. Cham, 2017.

Getachew, Adom. "Universalism after the Post-colonial Turn." *Political Theory* 44, no. 6 (December 2016): 821–45.

Girard, Alain. "Opinion publique, immigration et immigrés." *Ethnologie Française* 7, no. 3 (1977): 219–28.

Gori, Gisella. "Mademoiselle Gravier and Equal Access to Education: Success and Boundaries of European Integration." In *EU Law Stories: Contextual and Critical Histories of European Jurisprudence*, edited by Fernanda Nicola and Bill Davies, 446–70. Cambridge, UK, 2017.

Grabbe, Heather. "The Sharp Edges of Europe: Extending Schengen Eastwards." *International Affairs* 76, no. 3 (July 2000): 519–36.

Gueydan, Claude. "Cooperation between Member States of the European Community in the Fight against Terrorism." In *Terrorism and International Law*, edited by Rosalyn Higgins and Maurice Flory, 97–124. London, 1997.

Guild, Elspeth. "Adjudicating Schengen: National Judicial Control in France." *European Journal of Migration and Law* 1, no. 4 (1999): 419–39.

———. "Danger—Borders under Construction: Assessing the First Five Years of Border Policy in an Area of Freedom, Security and Justice." In *Freedom, Security and Justice in the European Union: Implementation of the Hague Programme*, edited by Jaap W. de Zwaan and Flora A.N.J. Goudappel, 62–67. The Hague, 2006.

———. "The Single Market, Movement of Persons and Borders." In *The Law of the Single European Market: Unpacking the Premises*, edited by Catherine Barnard and Joanne Scott, 295–310. Oxford, 2002.

Guild, Elspeth Evelien Brouwer, Kees Groenendijk, and Sergio Carrera. "What Is Happening to the Schengen Borders?" CEPS Paper in Liberty and Security, no. 86 (December 2015).

Guillaume, Gilbert. "Terrorism and International Law." *International & Comparative Law Quarterly* 53, no. 3 (July 2004): 537–48.

Guyomarch, Alain. "Problems and Prospects for European Police Cooperation after Maastricht." *Policing and Society: An International Journal* 5, no. 3 (1995): 249–61.

Hailbronner, Kay. "Asylum Law Reform in the German Constitution." *American University International Law Review* 9, no. 4 (1994): 159–79.

Handley, David H. "Public Opinion and European Integration: The Crisis of the 1970s." *European Journal of Political Research* 9, no. 4 (December 1981): 335–64.

Hansen, Peo. "Decolonization and the Spectre of the Nation-State." *The British Journal of Sociology* 73, no. 1 (January 2022): 35–49.

Hellman, Jacqueline, and María José Molina García. "La Erosión del proceso de integración europea como consecuencia de ciertas restricciones a la libre circulación de personas." *Revista Universitaria Europea*, no. 22 (June 2015): 23–54.

Hertle, Hans-Hermann. "The Fall of the Wall: The Unintended Self-Dissolution of East Germany's Ruling Regime." *Cold War International History Project Bulletin* 12 / 13 (Fall / Winter 2001): 131–64.

"Historique." Académie Royale des Beaux-Arts de Liège ESAHR. Accessed November 19, 2023. https://www.academieroyaledesbeauxartsliege.be/historique/.

"History of the Assembly." Global Privacy Assembly. Accessed May 5, 2023. https://globalprivacyassembly.org/the-assembly-and-executive-committee/history-of-the-assembly/.

Hollifield, James F. "Immigration and the Republican Tradition in France." In *Controlling Immigration: A Global Perspective*, edited by James Hollifield, Philip L. Martin, and Pia Orrenius, 157–87. 3rd ed. Stanford, 2014.

Hurwitz, Agnès. "The 1990 Dublin Convention: A Comprehensive Assessment." *International Journal of Refugee Law* 11, no. 4 (1999): 646–77.

Ireland, Patrick R. "Demander la lune: La Participation politique des immigrés dans la communauté européenne." *Revue européenne des migrations internationals* 10, no. 1 (1994): 457–80.

———. "Facing the True 'Fortress Europe': Immigrant and Politics in the EC." *Journal of Common Market Studies* 29, no. 5 (September 1991): 457–80.

Isiksel, Turkuler. "Cosmopolitanism and International Economic Institutions." *Journal of Politics* 82, no. 1 (January 2020): 211–24.

———. "The Dream of Commercial Peace." In *After the Storm: How to Save Democracy in Europe*, edited by Luuk van Middelaar and Philippe Van Parijs, 27–40. Tielt, 2015.

———. "The Rights of Man and the Rights of the Man-Made: Corporations and Human Rights." *Human Rights Quarterly* 38, no. 2 (May 2016): 294–349.

Jackson, Ben. "At the Origins of Neo-Liberalism: The Free Economy and the Strong State, 1930–1947." *The Historical Journal* 53, no. 1 (January 2010): 129–51.

Jeffreys-Jones, Rhodri. "The Idea of a European FBI." In *Strategic Intelligence: Counterintelligence and Counterterrorism, Defending the National against Hostile Forces, Intelligence and the Quest for Security.* Vol. 4, edited by Loch K. Johnson. Westport, CT, 2007.

Jensen, Richard Bach. "The International Anti-Anarchist Conference of 1898 and the Origins of Interpol." *Journal of Contemporary History* 16, no. 2 (April 1981): 323–47.

Johnson, Nigel. "From Vocational Training to Education: The Development of a No-Frontiers Education Policy for Europe?" *Education and the Law* 11, no. 3 (1999): 199–213.

Joppke, Christian. "The Evolution of Alien Rights in the United States, Germany, and the European Union." In *Citizenship Today: Global Perspectives and Practices*, edited by T. Alexander Aleinikoff and Douglas Klusmeyer, 36–62. Washington, DC, 2001.

Jørgensen, Stine. "The Right to Cross-Border Education in the European Union." *Common Market Law Review* 46, no. 5 (2009): 1567–90.

Julien-Laferrière, François. "Entry, Residence and Employment of Foreigners in the Community." In *What Kind of Criminal Policy for Europe?*, edited by Mireille Delmas-Marty, Mark A. Summers, and Ginette Mongin, 51–85. The Hague, 1996.

Kahmann, Marcus. "When the Strike Encounters the Sans Papiers Movement: The Discovery of a Workers' Repertoire of Actions for Irregular Migrant Protest in France." *Transfer: European Review of Labour and Research* 21, no. 4 (November 2015): 413–28.

Koch, K.-F., and H. Risch. "The Bundeskriminalamt: The German Federal Criminal Police Office." In *Police Research in the Federal Republic of Germany: 15 Years Research within the "Bundeskriminalamt"*, edited by R. V. Clarke, 3–22. Berlin, 1991.

Kofman, Eleonore, Madalina Rogoz, and Florence Lévy. "Family Migration Policies in France." *NODE Policy Report.* BMWF / ICMPD. Vienna, 2010.

Küsters, Hanns Jürgen. "Helmut Kohl und Frankreich: Einführung." *Historisch-Politische, Mitteilungen* 20, no. 1 (2013): 229–42.

Lappenküper, Ulrich. "Le Plus Germanophile des chefs d'état Français? François Mitterrand und Deutschland, 1916–1996." *Historische Zeitschrift* 297, no. 2 (2013): 390–416.

Laurent, Pierre-Henri. "Paul-Henri Spaak and the Diplomatic Origins of the Common Market, 1955–1956." *Political Science Quarterly* 85, no. 3 (September 1970): 373–96.

Laursen, Johnny N., and Thorten B. Olesen. "A Nordic Alternative to Europe? The Interdependence of Denmark's Nordic and European Policies, 1945–1998." *Contemporary European History* 9, no. 1 (2000): 59–92.

Le Bail, Hélène. "Les Sans-papiers au Japon: Renforcement des contrôles et émergence d'une mobilisation en faveur des régularisations." *Ebisu— Études Japonaises* 46, no. 1 (2011): 13–37.

Le Courant, Stefan. "La Ville des sans-papiers: Frontières mouvantes et gouvernements des marges." *L'Homme*, no. 219–20 (July / December 2016): 209–32.

Leprince, Chloé et Odile Dereuddre. "Simone Veil sur la Shoah: 'Nous n'avons pas parlé parce qu'on n'a pas voulu nouse écouter.'" *France Culture.* June 30, 2017.

Linebaugh, Peter. "All the Atlantic Mountains Shook." *Labour / Le Travailleur*, 10 (Autumn 1982): 87–121.

Longo, Matthew. "Right of Way? Defining Freedom of Movement within Democratic Societies." In *Democratic Citizenship and the Free Movement of People*, edited by Willem Maas, 31–56. Leiden, 2013.

Loukaidēs, Loukēs G. "Personality and Privacy under the European Convention on Human Rights." *British Yearbook of International Law* 61, no. 1 (January 1991): 175–97.

"La Lutte pour la reconnaissance—Axel Honneth Paris, Cerf, Coll. 'Passages,' traduit de l'allemand par Pierre Rusch." *Recherches familiales*, no. 1 (2004): 149–55. Accessed March 5, 2022. https://www.cairn.info/revue-recherches-familiales-2004-1-page -149.htm.

Lynch, Frances M. B. "De Gaulle's First Veto: France, the Rueff Plan and the Free Trade Area." *Contemporary European History* 9, no. 1 (March 2000): 111–35.

"Lyon: Le 'Tata' sénégalais, cimetière militaire des tirailleurs, a été tagué." *20 Minutes.* December 9, 2015.

Maas, Willem. "Free Movement and the Differences that Citizenship Makes." In "Peoples and Borders: Seventy Years of Migration in Europe, from Europe, to Europe [1945–2015]," edited by Elena Calandri, Simone Paoli, and Antonio Varsori. Special issue, *Journal of European Integration History* (2017): 91–108.

Mahmood, Shiraz. "The Schengen Information System: An Inequitable Data Protection Regime." *International Journal of Refugee Law* 7, no. 2 (January 1995): 179–200.

Maier, Charles S. "'Malaise': The Crisis of Capitalism in the 1970s." In *The Shock of the Global: The 1970s in Perspective*, edited by Niall Ferguson, Charles S. Maier, Erez Manela, and Daniel J. Sargent, 25–48. Cambridge, MA, 2010.

Mancini, Federico. "The Free Movement of Workers in the Case Law of the European Court of Justice." In *Democracy and Constitutionalism in the European Union: Collected Essays*, edited by Federico Mancini, 123–36. Oxford, 2000.

Mann, Gregory. "Immigrants and Arguments in France and West Africa." *Comparative Studies in Society and History* 45, no. 2 (April 2003): 362–85.

Marquardt, Marie Friedmann, Susanna J. Snyder, and Manuel A. Vasquez. "Challenging Laws: Faith-Based Engagement with Unauthorized Immigration." In *Constructing Immigrant "Illegality": Critiques, Experiences, and Responses*, edited by Cecilia Menjívar and Daniel Kanstroom, 272–97. Cambridge, UK, 2014.

McNevin, Anne. "Political Belonging in a Neoliberal Era: The Struggle of the Sans-Papiers." *Citizenship Studies* 10, no. 2 (May 2006): 135–51.

Menon, Anand, and Stephen Weatherill. "Democratic Politics in a Globalising World: Supranationalism and Legitimacy in the European Union." LSE Law, Society and Economy Working Papers 13 / 2007. Accessed March 4, 2023. https://www.lse.ac .uk/law/working-paper-series/2007-08/WPS13-2007MenonandWeatherill.pdf.

Meret, Susi and Waldemar Diener. "We Are Still Here and Staying! Refugee-Led Mobilizations and Their Struggles for Rights in Germany." In *Citizens' Activism and*

Solidarity Movements: Contending with Populism, edited by Birte Siim, Anna Krasteva, and Aino Saarinen, 137–66. Cham, 2019.

Molnar, Christopher A. "'Greetings from the Apocalypse': Race, Migration, and Fear after German Reunification." *Central European History* 54, no. 3 (September 2021): 496–97.

Moravcsik, Andrew. "Negotiating the Single European Act: National Interests and Conventional Statecraft in the European Community." *International Organization* 45, no. 1 (1991): 19–56.

Morice, Alain. "1996–1997: L'Epopée des Saint-Bernard." *Plein droit*, no. 101 (2014): 40–44.

———. "Sans-papiers: Une Difficile Reconnaissance." *Plein Droit*, no. 89 (June 2011): 5–8.

Morijn, John. "Personal Conviction and Strategic Litigation in Wijsenbeek." In *EU Law Stories: Contextual and Critical Histories of European Jurisprudence*, edited by Fernanda Nicola and Bill Davies, 178–200. Cambridge, UK, 2017.

Mouchard, Daniel. "Les Mobilisations des 'sans' dans la France contemporaine: L'Émergence d'un radicalisme autolimité." *Revue Française de Science Politique* 52, no. 4 (2002): 425–47.

Moyn, Samuel. "The Universal Declaration of Human Rights of 1948 in the History of Cosmopolitanism." *Critical Inquiry* 40, no. 4 (Summer 2014): 365–84.

Nail, Thomas. "Sanctuary, Solidarity, Status!" In *Open Borders: In Defense of Free Movement*, edited by Reece Jones, 23–33. Athens, GA, 2019.

Neal, Andrew W. "Securitization and Risk at the EU Border: The Origins of FRONTEX." *Journal of Common Market Studies* 47, no. 2 (March 2009): 333–56.

Norman, Paul. "The European Dimension." In *Law, Power, and Justice in England and Wales*, edited by Ian K. McKenzie, 91–108. Westport, CT, 1998.

Novotná, Markéta. "Schengen Cooperation: What Scholars Make of It." *Journal of Borderlands Studies* (April 2020).

Oberman, Kieran. "Immigration as a Human Right." In *Migration in Political Theory: The Ethics of Movement and Membership*, edited by Sarah Fine and Lea Ypi, 32–56. Oxford, 2016.

Orluc, Katiana. "Decline or Renaissance: The Transformation of European Consciousness after the First World War." In *Europe and the Other and Europe as the Other*, edited by Bo Stråth, 123–55. Brussels, 2000.

Outhwaite, William. "Migration Crisis and 'Brexit.'" In *The Oxford Handbook of Migration Crises*, edited by Cecilia Menjívar, Marie Ruiz, and Immanuel Ness, 93–110. Oxford, 2019.

Paoli, Simone. "France and the Origins of Schengen: An Interpretation." In "Peoples and Borders: Seventy Years of Migration in Europe, from Europe, to Europe, 1945–2015," edited by Elena Calandri, Simone Paoli, and Antonio Varsori. Special issue, *Journal of European Integration History* (2017): 255–80.

———. "The Schengen Agreements and Their Impact on Euro-Mediterranean Relations: The Case of Italy and the Maghreb." *Journal of European Integration History* 21, no. 1 (2015): 125–46.

Passerini, Luisa. "From the Ironies of Identity to the Identities of Irony." In *The Idea of Europe: From Antiquity to the European Union*, edited by Anthony Pagden, 191–208. Cambridge, UK, 2002.

Pastore, Ferruccio, Paola Monzini, and Giuseppe Sciortino, "Schengen's Soft Underbelly? Irregular Migration and Human Smuggling across Land and Sea Borders to Italy." *International Migration* 44, no. 4 (2006): 95–119.

Patel, Kiran Klaus. "Widening and Deepening? Recent Advances in European Integration History." *Neue Politische Literatur* 64, no. 2 (July 2019): 327–57.

Patel, Kiran Klaus, and Wolfram Kaiser. "Continuity and Change in European Cooperation during the Twentieth Century." *Contemporary European History* 27, no. 2 (2018): 165–82.

"Paul De Keersmaeker." Vlaams Parlement. Accessed December 30, 2023, https://www.vlaamsparlement.be/nl/vlaamse-volksvertegenwoordigers-het-vlaams-parlement/paul-de-keersmaeker.

Perolini, Marco. "We Don't Remember the O-Platz Protest Camp for the Sake of It: Collective Memories and Visibility of Migrant Activism in Berlin." *Sociology Compass* 16, no. 12 (December 2022): e13009.

Piser, Karina. "What a Foiled Plot to Execute Muslims Reveals about Islamophobia in France." *Nation*. July 10, 2018.

Poeze, Miranda. "High-Risk Migration: From Senegal to the Canary Islands by Sea." In *Long Journeys: African Migrants on the Road*, edited by Alessandro Triulzi and Robert Lawrence McKenzie, 45–66. Leiden, 2013.

"Prof. Tim Koopmans Passed Away on Christmas Eve." *European Public Law Organization*. January 2, 2016. Accessed May 12, 2019. https://www1.eplo.int/newsitem/764/prof.-tim-koopmans-passed-away-on-christmas-eve.

"Le Projet seneclic au Senegal (2005)." Afrique Nouvelles Technologies. July 20, 2012.

Pudlat, Andreas. "Der lange Weg zum Schengen-raum: Ein Prozess im vier-PhaseModell." *Journal of European Integration History* 17, no. 2 (2011): 303–26.

Rass, Christoph. "Temporary Labour Migration and State-Run Recruitment of Foreign Workers in Europe, 1919–1975: A New Migration Regime?" *International Review of Social History* 57, no. S20 (2012): 191–224.

Rayo, Andreu Olesti. "El Espacio Schengen y la reinstauración de los controles en las fronteras interiores de los Estados miembros de la Unión Europea." *Revista d'estudis autonòmics i federals*, no. 15 (2012): 44–84.

"Red Brigades." Mapping Militant Organizations, Stanford University. Last modified June 2018. Accessed April 25, 2023. https://cisac.fsi.stanford.edu/mappingmilitants/profiles/red-brigades.

"Robert Goebbels." Europa Nu. Accessed October 21, 2021. https://www.europa-nu.nl/id/vhzna0ij85u3/robert_goebbels.

Rossetto, Jean. "Le Droit d'asile en Europe—Évolution contemporaine." *Annuaire Français de Droit International* 39 (1993): 919–35.

Rothschild, Emma. "Global Commerce and the Question of Sovereignty in the Eighteenth-Century Provinces." *Modern Intellectual History* 1, no. 1 (April 2004): 3–25.

Rude-Antoine, Edwige. "Statut juridiique et devenir des jeunes étrangers non euro-péens." *Hommes & Migrations* 1178, no. 1 (1994): 35–40.

Rust, Val D. "The Right to Education for Employment and Mobility: Norway and Yugoslavia." In *Human Rights and Education*. Vol. 3, edited by N. Bernstein Tar-row, 121–38. Oxford, 1987.

Sassen, Saskia. "The Repositioning of Citizenship and Alienage: Emergent Subjects and Spaces for Politics." *Globalizations* 2, no. 1 (2005): 79–94.

Savino, Mario. "Global Administrative Law Meets 'Soft' Powers: The Uncomfortable Case of Interpol Red Notices." *New York University Journal of International Law and Politics* 43, no. 2 (2010): 263–336.

Scharpf, Fritz W. "The Asymmetry of European Integration, or Why the EU Cannot Be a 'Social Market Economy.'" *Socio-Economic Review* 8, no. 2 (2010).

Schmid, Bernard. "L'Allemagne aussi régularise." *Plein Droit* 73, no. 2 (2007): 31–34.

Schomburg, Wolfgang. "Criminal Matters: Transnational Ne Bis in Idem in Europe—Conflict of Jurisdictions—Transfer of Proceedings." *ERA Forum* 12, no. 3 (2012).

Schutte, Julian J. E. "Schengen: Its Meaning for the Free Movement of Persons in Europe." *Common Market Law Review* 28 (1991): 549–70.

Scullion, Rosemarie. "Vicious Circles: Immigration and National Identity in Twentieth-Century France." *SubStance* 24, no. 1 / 2, issue 76 / 77 (1995): 30–48.

Shapiro, Martin. "'Deliberative,' 'Independent' Technocracy vs. Democratic Politics: Will the Globe Echo the EU?" *Law and Contemporary Problems* 68, no. 3–4 (Summer–Autumn 2005): 341–56.

Sohler, Karin. "France." In *REGINE - Regularisations in Europe*, edited by Martin Baldwin-Edwards and Albert Kraler, 235–83. Amsterdam, 2009.

Soltesz, Susan. "Implications of the Conseil Constitutionnel's Immigration and Asylum Decision of August 1993." *Boston College International and Comparative Law Review* 18, no. 1 (1995): 265–315.

Sommier, Isabelle. "Le Renouveau de la critique sociale depuis les années 1990: Entre Mythe et réalité." *Modern and Contemporary France* 20, no. 2 (May 2012): 153–68.

Stanley-Becker, Isaac. "'An Inseparable Pair': Freedom and Security in the Schengen Space." In *Sites of Modernity—Places of Risk: Risk and Security in Germany since the 1970s*, edited by Martin Geyer, 150–70. New York, 2023.

Surkis, Judith. "Minor Threats and the Biopolitics of Youth." *Comparative Studies of South Asia, Africa and the Middle East* 41, no. 3 (December 2021): 413–21.

Swerts, Thomas. "Marching beyond Borders: Non-citizen Citizenship and Transna-tional Undocumented Activism in Europe." In *Within and Beyond Citizenship: Borders, Membership and Belonging*, edited by Roberto G. Gonzales and Nando Sigona, 126–42. Abingdon, UK, 2017.

Taguieff, Pierre-André, and Patrick Weil. "'Immigration,' fait national et 'citoyenneté.'" *Esprit* 161, no. 5 (May 1990): 87–102.

Terray, Emmanuel. "Quelques réflexions à propos de la lutte des Sans-papiers." *Journal des Anthropologues*, no. 66–67 (1996): 249–53.

Towle, Simon. "European Refugee Policy: Schengen v. European Convention of Human Rights." In *Colloquy: "Human Rights without Frontiers"; Strasbourg, 30 November— 1 December 1989; Proceedings*, edited by Committee of Experts for the Promotion of Education and Information in the Field of Human Rights, 207–15. Strasbourg, 1989.

Tribalat, Michèle. "Chronique de l'Immigration." *Population* 51, no. 1 (January–February 1996): 141–93.

Uberti, Stefano degli. "Victims of Their Fantasies or Heroes for a Day? Media Representations, Local History and Daily Narratives on Boat Migrations from Senegal." *Cahiers d'Études Africaines*, Cahier 213 / 214, 54 (2014): 81–113.

Van de Rijt, Wouter. "Le Fonctionnement des institutions Schengen: 'Pragmatisme, toujours.'" In *Schengen's Final Days? The Incorporation of Schengen into the New TEU, External Borders and Information Systems*, edited by Monica den Boer. Maastricht, 1998.

Van Outrive, Lode. "Historia del Acuerdo y del Convenio de Schengen." *Revista CIDOB d'Afers Internacionals*, no. 54 (May 2001): 43–61.

Velling, Johannes. "Schengen, Dublin und Maastricht—Etappen auf dem Weg zu einer europäischen Inlnligrationspolitik." ZEW Discussion Papers, no. 93–11 (1993).

Veron, Daniel. "Quand les sans-papiers prennent la parole: Espaces d'interlocution et énonciation du tort." *Variations*, no. 18 (April 2013).

Vium, Christian. "Icons of Becoming: Documenting Undocumented Migration from West Africa to Europe." *Cahiers d'Études Africaines* 54, Cahier 213 / 214 (2014).

Von Goethe, Johann Wolfgang. "The Experiment as Mediator of Object and Subject." *Nature Institute* (Fall 2010): 19–23.

Wagner, Eckart. "The Integration of Schengen into the Framework of the European Union." *Legal Issues of Economic Integration* 25, no. 2 (1998): 1–60.

Watson, Philippa. "Case 293 / 83, *Gravier v. City of Liège*." *Common Market Law Review* 24, no. 1, (1987): 89–97.

Weil, Patrick. "Immigration and the Rise of Racism in France: The Contradictions in Mitterrand's Policies." *French Politics and Society* 9, no. 3 / 4 (Summer / Fall 1991): 82–100.

Weiler, J.H.H. "A Quiet Revolution: The European Court of Justice and Its Interlocutors." *Comparative Political Studies* 26, no. 4 (January 1994): 510–34.

Wert, Bertrand. "Security Governance in the Largest Border-Metropolis of the Schengen Area: The Lille 'Eurodistrict' Case Study." *Journal of Borderlands Studies* 23, no. 3 (September 2008): 95–108.

Weydert, Jean. "André Costes avec les immigrés." *Migrations Société* 1, no. 17 (January–August 2005): 3–14.

Weyembergh, Anne, Chloé Brière, Henri Labayle, Philippe De Bruycker, and David Watt. "The Paris Terrorist Attacks: Failure of the EU's Area of Freedom, Security and Justice?" *EU Immigration and Asylum Law and Policy*. January 6, 2016.

Wiener, Antje. "Forging Flexibility—the British 'No' to Schengen." *European Journal of Migration and Law* 1, no. 4 (January 1999): 441–63.

Winter, Anne. "Caught between Law and Practice: Migrants and Settlement Legislation in the Southern Low Countries in a Comparative Perspective, c. 1700–1900." *Rural History* 19, no. 2 (October 2008): 137–62.

Woodward, Rachel. "Establishing Europol." *European Journal on Criminal Policy and Research* 1, no. 4 (1993).

Wytinck, Peter. "The Application of Community Law in Belgium." *Common Market Law Review* 30, no. 5 (1993): 981–1020.

Zaiotti, Ruben. "Chronic Anxiety: Schengen and the Fear of Enlargement." In *The EU and the Eurozone Crisis: Policy Challenges and Strategic Choices*, edited by Finn Laursen, 161–76. Farnham, UK, 2013.

———. "The Italo-French Row over Schengen, Critical Junctures, and the Future of Europe's Border Regime." *Journal of Borderlands Studies* 28, no. 3 (2013): 337–54.

INDEX